THE ART OF

FUTURAMA™

Matt Groening

ᐱᗐᐱ ᗐᐅᘘ ᗐᘘ ᘘᗐᐱᘘᗐᐱᗐᐱ

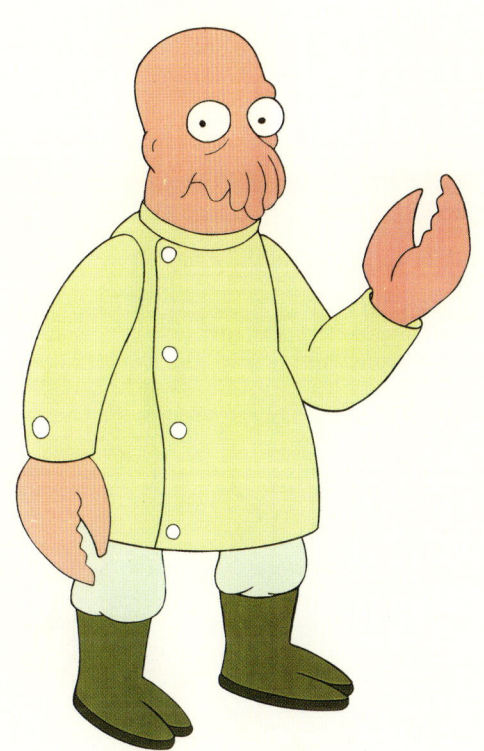

Abrams ComicArts • New York

For Bongo Entertainment, Inc.:
Editor in Chief: Christopher Ungar
Art Director: Jason Ho
Editor: Karen Bates

Legal Guardian: Melanie Tomanov

Book design and production by Serban Cristescu
Interviews conducted and edited by Jamie Angell
Additional Art by Mike Rote
Scanning by Serban Cristescu, Evan Jackson,
Tim Kumerrow, and Chris Ungar

For Abrams ComicArts:
Editor: Charles Kochman
Assistant Editor: Lydia Nguyen
Art Director: Shawn Dahl
Managing Editor: Megan Carlson
Production Manager: Alison Gervais

Library of Congress Cataloging Number 2024931540

ISBN 978-1-4197-7350-1

ABRAMS The Art of Books
195 Broadway, New York, NY 10007
abramsbooks.com

The ACV tags throughout the book refer to
episode numbers. For a list of titles and airdates,
see the Episode Guide on pages 172 and 173.

Cover art by Serban Cristescu and Mike Rote
Endpapers: Post-robot party panic sequence storyboard
with dialogue and acting notes (4ACV08) by Albert Calleros
Title page: Early Zoidberg pitch image by Bill Morrison and Christopher Ungar

ACKNOWLEDGMENTS

A very special thank you to all the folks at Rough Draft for their
help in researching the original materials for this book, especially
Peter Avanzino, Dwayne Carey-Hill, Crystal Chesney-Thompson,
Samantha Harrison, Claudia Katz, Rich Moore, Gregg Vanzo, Scott Vanzo,
and Eric Whited, for lending their time and insights
to make this book a success

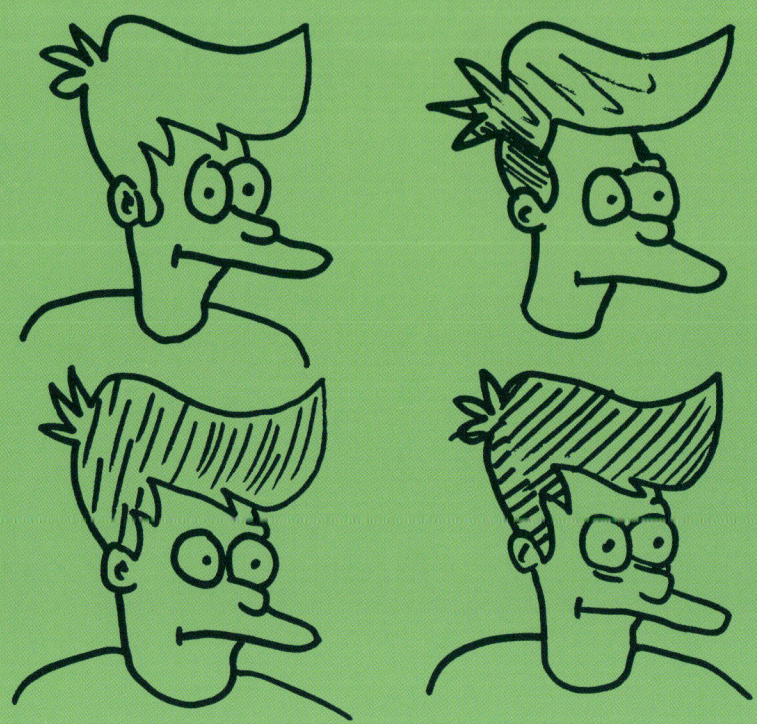

Fry head concepts
by Matt Groening

This book would not have been possible
without the invaluable contributions of
Matt Groening, David X. Cohen, Susan Grode,
Bill Morrison, and Mili Smythe

THE *FUTURAMA* JOURNEY

⅄ᒧ♢ ⊡ᒐᒲᒲᒐᒲ♅ᒲ♅ ⤬ᒲᒲᒷᒲ♢⅄ᒲ

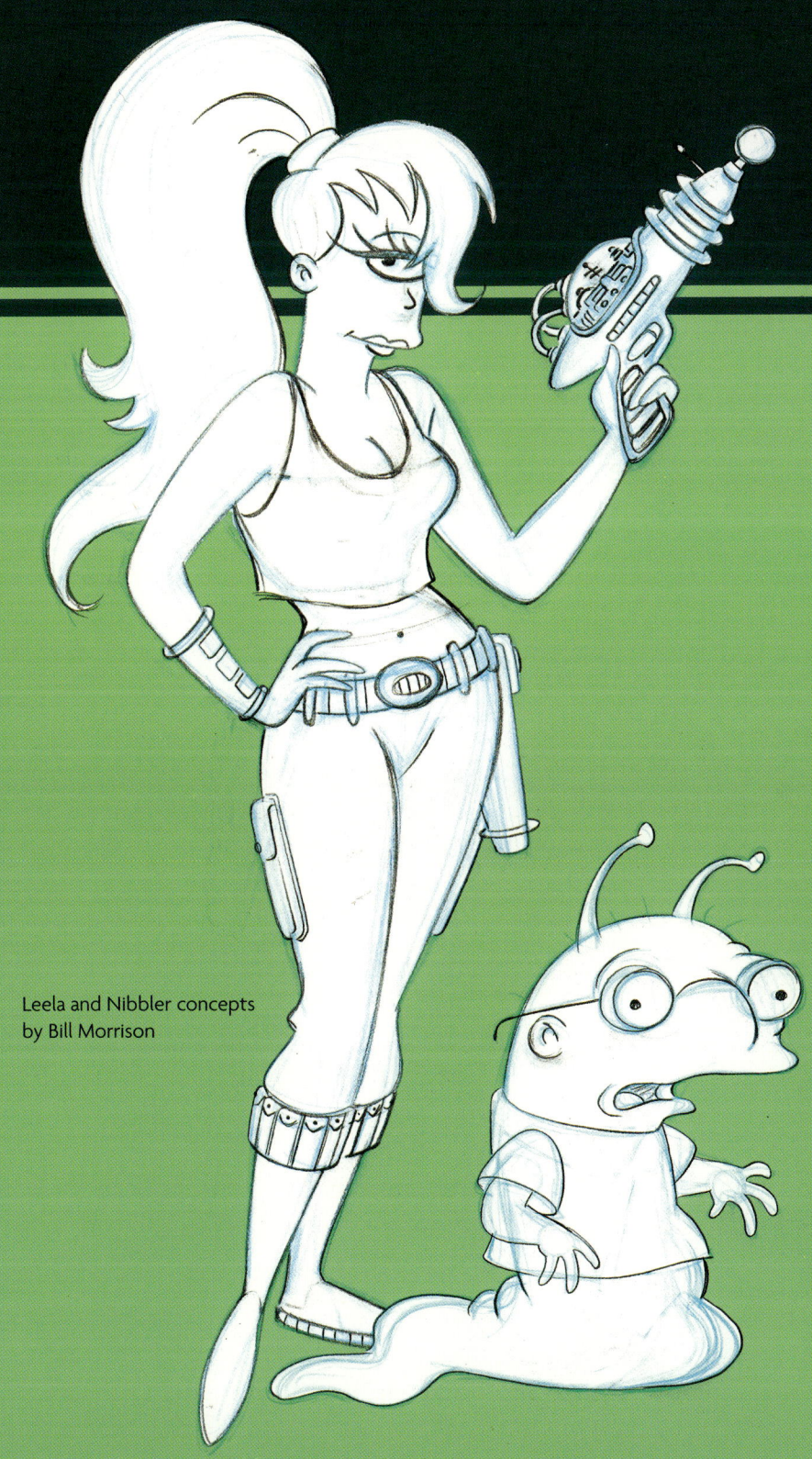

Leela and Nibbler concepts
by Bill Morrison

PREFACE

In the Future, We Were Promised Propeller Beanies!

In the not-really good old days, squirmy boys in Davy Crockett coonskin caps obsessed over big, bad, clunky robots. In movies and comic books and on TV, mechanical metal men lurched all over the place, bleeping and blooping and grabbing and strangling. On the rumpus room floor, battery-operated toy robots rolled along and shot out scary sparks. Knowing these unstoppable robots were coming to kill you made you both tingle and tinkle. Because all kids knew that's the deal with robots: You can't reason with them. If they've been programmed by a mad scientist to eradicate you, it's Goodbye, Junior. No matter how much you plead, when the robot's dial is set to Destroy All Humans, you're a goner. And even when an occasional robot would trundle along who seemed nice enough, like Robby the Robot in the 1956 film *Forbidden Planet*, more typical was that giant mechanical bastard in the 1939 Bela Lugosi movie serial *The Phantom Creeps*. First the hidden wall-panel would fly up, then the jumbo robot with a hideous gargoyle head would dart out, then he'd throttle you to death, and as a final insult your limp body would get thrown around.

And then there was your fiendish older brother Bart, I mean Mark, who enjoyed exploiting your fear of robots. Just as we sat down to watch *The Wizard of Oz* on TV for the very first time in 1961, he stared with bulging eyes and said: "I hate to tell ya this, but there's a heartless robot in this movie, and not only that, he carries a big axe." And after a terrifying two hours (flying monkeys, apple-throwing trees, the Lollipop Guild), you'd think the terror was over. But no. That's when Mark lured you down into the basement, where your photographer dad had a film-developing darkroom. Only you didn't know what a darkroom was. To you it was the Dark Room: pitch-black, chemical-smelling, with a scary door and a spooky coal chute from which a robot might slide out right at you. Normally you wouldn't venture into the Dark Room, but Mark said there was a bowl of custard down there, knowing you were hopelessly addicted to that deliciously smooth and creamy vanilla dessert treat. So you're down there poking around and salivating, when suddenly the lights went out and a huge robot lunged at you while you wet your pants and screamed your fool head off. Of course it turned out to be Mark wearing a couple of corrugated cardboard boxes and making robot noises. But in the gloom you were convinced you were about to be robo-murdered. And there was no custard either.

Eventually I grew up, and my fear of robots tapered off to occasional recurring nightmares about being trapped inside a futuristic amusement park after closing time and hiding from

Pitch image of Fry in commuter pod by Bill Morrison and Serban Cristescu

laser-beam-shooting killer security robots. I always wake up with a jolt just as they zap me. (Yes, I still have that dream.) My fear of robots gradually turned into a love of all things futuristic. After school I hung out at the Multnomah County Library, where I devoured Robert A. Heinlein's juvenile novels *Space Cadet, Red Planet, Farmer in the Sky, Between Planets, Starman Jones, The Star Beast, Tunnel in the Sky, Citizen of the Galaxy,* and *Have Spacesuit—Will Travel*. Then I started haunting downtown Portland's musty old used bookstores, where I bought and plowed through piles of cheap science-fiction paperbacks. My favorites were Frederik Pohl and C. M. Kornbluth's *The Space Merchants*; Robert Sheckley's *Immortality, Inc.*; Arthur C. Clarke's *Childhood's End* and *The City and the Stars*; Eando Binder's *I, Robot*; all the robot books by Isaac Asimov; Kurt Vonnegut Jr.'s *The Sirens of Titan, Canary in a Cat House,* and *Cat's Cradle*; and the annual *Best S-F* anthologies edited by Judith Merril.

Then came adulthood, followed by visions of Krusty, Poochie, Itchy and Scratchy, and all their wacky yellow cartoon pals. That's when brainiac writer David X. Cohen and I started concocting what eventually became *Futurama*. (Early rejected titles included *Doomsville* and *Aloha Mars*.) During lunch breaks over two years we talked about Stanislaw Lem and *The Prisoner* and Philip K. Dick and *The Twilight Zone* and Alfred Bester and *Star Trek* and Neal Stephenson and *The Three Stooges in Orbit*. We thought up Fry the unfrozen dope, Bender the robot cook with no sense of taste, Leela the cyclops with a secret, and Dr. Zoidberg, the medical doctor who has no understanding of human anatomy. We settled on a far-future dystopian workplace comedy with sci-fi hijinks. When we finally pitched the show to Fox, we were so overprepared the execs greenlit the show just to get us to stop talking.

Then we hooked up with upstart Glendale animation company Rough Draft Studios, and they blew our minds with piles of inspired designs. We loved Rough Draft because they loved cartoons and laughed at our stupid jokes. The suits at Fox were dubious at first because Rough Draft was founded by animators: "You can't let inmates run the asylum," they warned us. But we were as crazy as the animators, and we were stubborn, so Rough Draft got the job. (All over town, animators at more conventional studios cheered quietly.) Over the last twenty-odd years, hundreds of animators and designers and writers and actors and musicians have collaborated to make the show so wild and surprising. Many of the pioneering *Futurama* artists and producers with incipient carpal tunnel syndrome are featured in these pages: Peter Avanzino, Dwayne Carey-Hill, Crystal Chesney-Thompson, Dave Cooper, Bret Haaland, Samantha Harrison, Dale Hendrickson, Claudia Katz, Rich Moore, Bill Morrison, Mili Smythe, Gregg Vanzo, Scott Vanzo, and Eric Whited. One thing these inspired artists had in common was that they always delivered more than expected.

You can feel the shared exuberance and collaborative goofiness throughout this book. So please enjoy the curvy lines and crazy colors, and know that we loved what we were doing back then. And even better, after all these years, we are still having a blast.

Your pal,
Matt Groening
September 2024

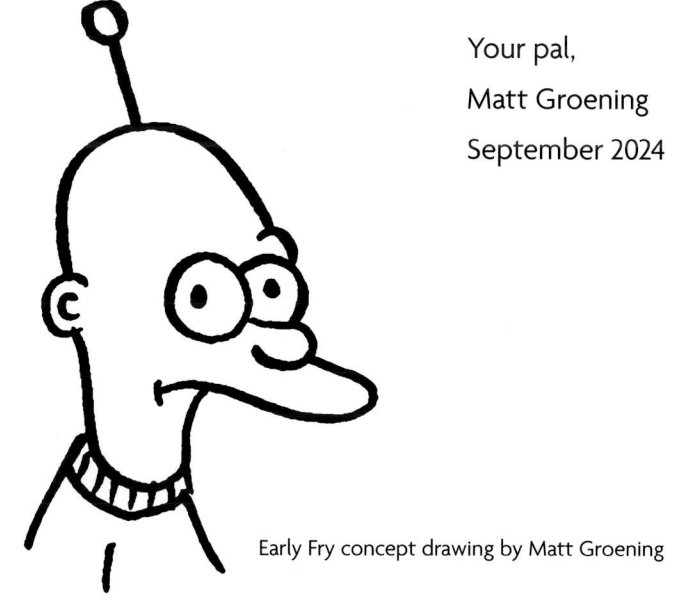

Early Fry concept drawing by Matt Groening

I was tremendously honored when Matt Groening asked me to write the introduction, foreword, or preface to this book. I didn't ask which because I don't know the difference anyway. I'll check the bold print above this paragraph when the book comes out and see if it provides any clues.

Speaking of me, I'm not much use when it comes to drawin' stuff. I mean, sure, I have my own inimitable style, but that's about it. When I attempt to draw something, I find myself conjuring up an abstract model of it in my mind, focused entirely on the function of each part and how the parts connect together, but not at all on what it actually looks like. If you ask me to draw a chihuahua, for example, I'll put down a body and the right number of legs, heads, and tails (4, 1, 1), connected in the appropriate ways, whereas if you ask me to draw a unicorn, I'll draw the same thing, plus a horn. I know exactly where the horn connects (the forehead, FY!). I just don't know how to make a unicorn forehead. If you get the degree of curvature of a unicorn's forehead even slightly wrong, it looks like it was drawn by a three-year-old. Or me.

My style works well when the object I'm trying to draw is some kind of abstract ideal. I'm great at squares and also cubes. The one and only character I ever designed for *Futurama* was a gear-based robot dancer at Bender's favorite robot strip club. This is right in my wheelhouse! The entire joke is based on a character embodying the pure, unadorned concept of a gyrating hip gear—from mathematical model to page with no stops in between.

Despite my utter lack of drawing skills, an awesome part of my job is that I get to give artistic notes to the highly trained, highly regarded professional artists who produced the stunning works that fill this volume. And they have to listen to me!

The arrangement works better than you might think. For lack of other options, I'm forced to communicate in terms of emotions and adjectives. Can that space boat be junkier? Can Zoidberg's pants be more depressing? Can Kif's planet be squishier? I don't give a lot of specifics on how to achieve these results, because... I... can't! This gives the artists a lot of freedom. And left to their own devices, they produce consistently spectacular results. I honestly don't know how they do it. It's like everything is a cube to them!

I have similar conversations when discussing voice acting with our all-star cast, or music with our extraordinary composer,

Stripper robot (2ACV06) by Eric Keyes

Chris Tyng. As Chris said to me just this week as I was attempting to discuss the musical score for an upcoming episode, "I can score any adjective you throw at me."

All this is to say there's a division of artistic labor on a show like *Futurama*. For the most part, writers write, animators draw, actors act, composers make music, and sound designers make funny noises. There's some overlap . . . writer Ken Keeler also composes songs, for example, and Matt Groening writes, draws, and occasionally makes funny noises. But that's the exception that muddies the rule. My responsibility as showrunner is to make sure all these different artists are working toward the same goal at every moment of an episode—to convey the intended emotion or joke or plot point with maximum firepower.

So, each time we finish a new script, I have a meeting with our supervising director at Rough Draft Studios, Peter Avanzino, to discuss the visuals. Invariably in a state of despair, he thumbs through the pages, reading out impossible-to-animate stage directions that he's marked with Post-it Notes. Things like, "The invisible ship swoops by in all its dazzling magnificence, unseen by Fry and Leela." He glowers at me. "How are we supposed to show that?!" I shrug and deliver my standard reply: "That's your problem." Immediately, I see the gears beginning to turn in his head . . . gears being the one thing I can visualize.

And somehow, he and the brilliant artists at Rough Draft invariably come through, conceiving and creating fantasticalities far beyond what a writer with limited visual vocabulary can imagine, let alone describe. Their clever, beautiful, and humorous achievements explode from the confines of this volume. I can't begin to understand how they work these miracles. But, luckily, I don't need to.

David X. Cohen
September 2024 / 3024

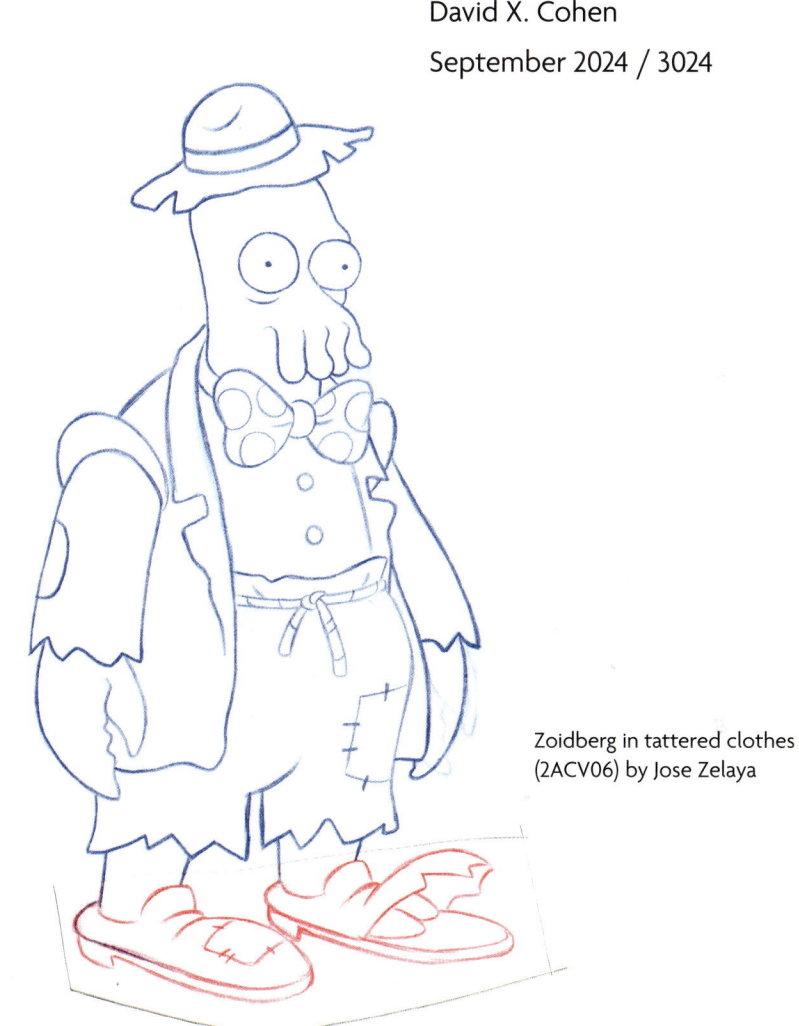

Zoidberg in tattered clothes (2ACV06) by Jose Zelaya

David X. Cohen is a longtime collaborator of Matt Groening and an animation mainstay, having written for *The Simpsons* in its late-middle-early days before becoming the head writer, showrunner, and executive producer of *Futurama*. Cohen has won four Primetime Emmy Awards, two of which are for *Futurama* as "Outstanding Animated Program."

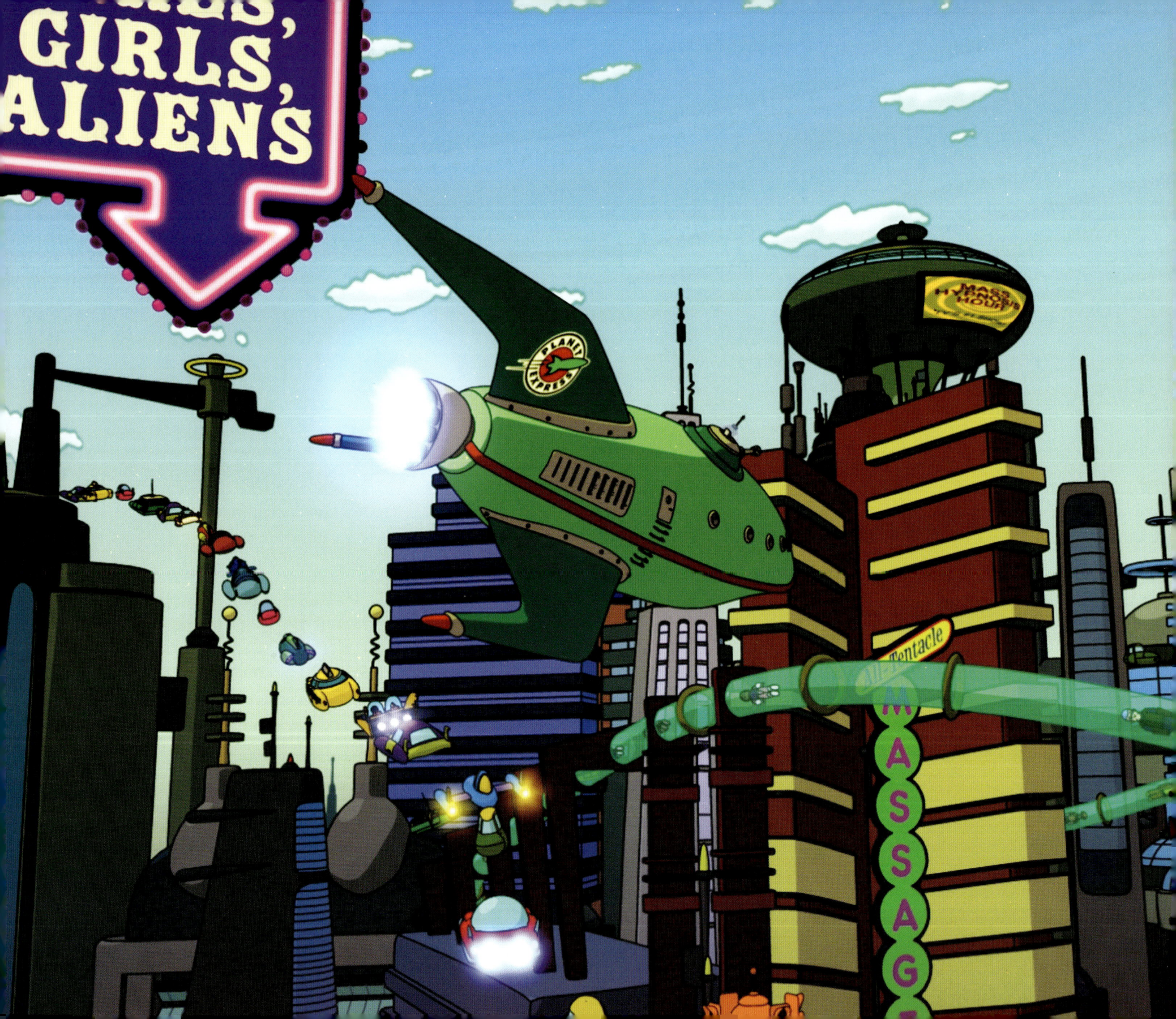

FOREWORD

In late 1997, Matt Groening came over to Rough Draft to meet with Rich Moore, Gregg Vanzo, and me to discuss *Futurama*, a new project he was developing for Fox. He pitched us the series, armed with character designs he had drawn in his quintessential Sharpie-style and some visual development he had commissioned. He wanted us onboard and we were thrilled!

It's worth noting we started production in 1998 in a world without the Internet and the instant access to visual reference we've all become so accustomed to. We were rolling old school. Since I have no drawing skills, I handled research and became an avid patron of bookstores, especially their architecture sections. We found inspiration in some obvious places—Norman Bel Geddes's designs from the 1939 World's Fair, the Streamline Design movement, and New York City as we know it—and some not so obvious—the silhouettes of water towers, silos, and other industrial architecture.

Under the guidance of Rich Moore, Mili Smythe, and Matt, the initial crew of character and background designers did an incredible job laying the foundations, figuring out the visual design rules, and building out this giant new storytelling universe. A universe that, to this day, continues to expand with each season.

Rich and I knew the visual success of the show depended on creating a whole new Groening-verse that was larger and more visually sophisticated than *The Simpsons*, and the ability to deliver fan-worthy sci-fi visuals—epic space battles, locales, FX, etc. The only way to produce this was to integrate 2D and 3D animation. Fortunately, Rough Draft was one of the first studios to set up a digital pipeline in 1994 with *The Maxx*. Our head of computer graphics, Scott Vanzo, and lead 3D artist, Eric Whited, worked tirelessly to figure out how to cel shade and light the 3D animation so it blended seamlessly with the 2D animation. At the time, this tight integration was pretty revolutionary.

The final component was the unique and sophisticated color palette created by Bari Kumar, Samantha Harrison, and the rest of the color key artists. This whole new color landscape helped set *Futurama* apart from any other animated series at the time.

When the show premiered on March 28, 1999, it was heralded as one of the best-looking shows on television!

This book is a tribute to all the talented artists who helped mold, shape, and build the beautiful, stunning, epic and (twenty-five years later) ever-expanding *Futurama* universe.

A galactic thank you does not seem big enough.

Claudia Katz
September 2024

Claudia Katz is an Emmy Award–winning producer who joined Rough Draft Studios in 1994 to produce *The Maxx*. Since then, she has helped build Rough Draft into a top-tier animation studio in film and television. In addition to overseeing production and Executive Producing duties, she also heads in-house development. Recent work includes serving as executive producer on the return of *Futurama* for Hulu, *Disenchantment* for Netflix, and *Clash-A-Rama* for Supercell. Other work includes *Tarantula*, *Futurama* (all seasons), *Napoleon Dynamite*, *Sit Down, Shut Up*, *The Simpsons Movie*, *Looney Tunes* theatrical shorts, *Drawn Together*, and *Star Wars: Clone Wars I & II*. She has received an Annecy Award for her work on *The Maxx*, Emmy, Annie, and Hugo Awards for *Futurama*, and Emmy Awards for *Star Wars: Clone Wars I & II*.

Opposite: Opening title sequence by Eric Whited

PRE-DEPARTURE: GLIMMERS AND GLEAMS

Matt Groening's pitch to Fox for *Futurama* was put together with David X. Cohen and the design assistance of Mili Smythe, Bill Morrison, Dave Cooper, and Dale Hendrickson, but the genesis of the show goes back to Matt's childhood.

Matt Groening: I remember as a kid thinking old science fiction books would be great in a visual medium. Humor is tough to pull off in genre fiction, but there were some really funny novels I thought could work. For instance, Jerome Beatty Jr.'s children's novels *Matthew Looney's Voyage to the Earth* and *Matthew Looney's Invasion of the Earth*; *Martians, Go Home* by Frederic Brown; and Harry Harrison's *The Stainless Steel Rat*, *The Stainless Steel Rat's Revenge*, and *The Stainless Steel Rat Saves the World*. In fact, a major original inspiration for *Futurama* was the 1992 novel *Snow Crash* by Neal Stephenson. But most of the onscreen science fiction I watched growing up was disappointing. The sophisticated ideas in literary science fiction were far more advanced than the space opera movies and TV shows of the late fifties and early sixties. I thought, wouldn't it be great to be able to make a show using some of the ambitious ideas of smart science fiction novels? And doubly great, what if we could do something funny while also going for real emotion? Most so-called funny science fiction isn't much of a laugh riot. So, the big quandary was whether we could make it work and whether people could get on board with jokes about aliens and robots.

Another thing about on-screen science fiction was that almost everything was built around a military premise. The future invariably featured a military fascist organization to which you either belonged or were opposed, and the characters were always looking out of portholes and following orders. I wanted to do something different. So, unlike *Star Trek*, *Star Wars*, or almost every other science fiction series, we made *Futurama* a commercial operation and a delivery service. And frankly, I don't know how Planet Express stays in business, since they only deliver one package every few episodes.

Another problem we wanted to avoid was the present catching up with the future. Having read, and then lived through 1984, and with 2001 on the horizon, we decided to set *Futurama* a thousand years in the future. While life expectancy has improved over the last fifty years, we figured we'd chance it. Though, to be fair, the fact we're still doing the show in 2024 is something I didn't anticipate.

Using the science-fiction trope of H. G. Wells's *The Sleeper Awakes* and Woody Allen's *Sleeper*, we made Fry the stand-in for our audience, allowing us to explain all the crazy stuff we planned to see in the future. A small art team was assembled to rough out what the future would look like and what aliens, humans, and robots would populate that world. In order to be slightly less cartoony, we made the *Futurama* characters a more realistic four heads high, rather than the three heads high of *The Simpsons*.

I mean, when you think about *The Simpsons*, man, those are some big heads. We briefly even considered having five fingers rather than four, but decided to go easy on the animators.

I always say our job was often to show Matt what he didn't want, because it sparked him to figure out what he did want, which was brilliant.

— Bill Morrison

At the beginning, Matt and David wrote short, descriptive paragraphs of each character. Leela's was very brief: *She's an alien cyclops delivery-ship pilot.* In one early Bill Morrison drawing, Leela had a head piece, fangs, and a tail, with tentacle-like arms and two long fingers. Mili Smythe and Dale Hendrickson also worked on the character designs, and they'd riff on each other's work, accumulating different versions of the characters with Matt as the quarterback adding his own designs. Having designers with different sensibilities collaborating on the look of *Futurama*'s characters and backgrounds added to the sense that this was a world that owed its existence to a multiplicity of forces, lending it more credibility.

Adding to that, New New York became a character in itself, being visibly built upon what was left of the original New York.

With old buildings mixed with newer structures on different levels, the story of the city is embedded in the strata of its design. With nothing too slick or clean, Dave Cooper's cityscapes possess a real sense of human scale, attempting to depict the history of the city over time.

What you see on the following pages are sketches leading up to the show's pitch in 1998.

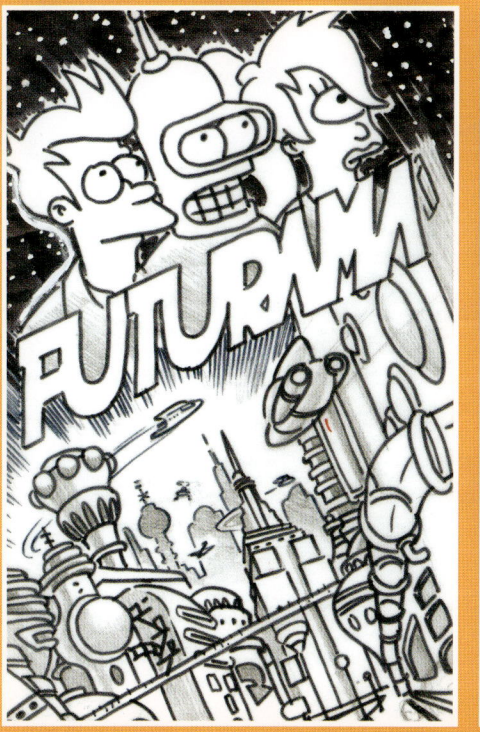
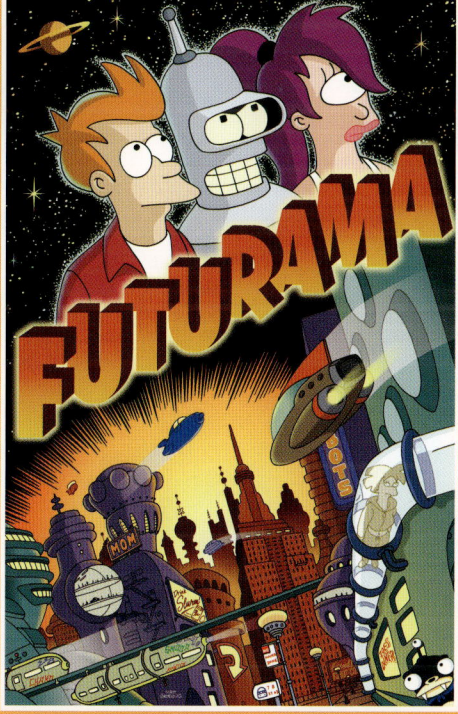

Early publicity image by Mili Smythe, Bill Morrison, and Serban Cristescu.

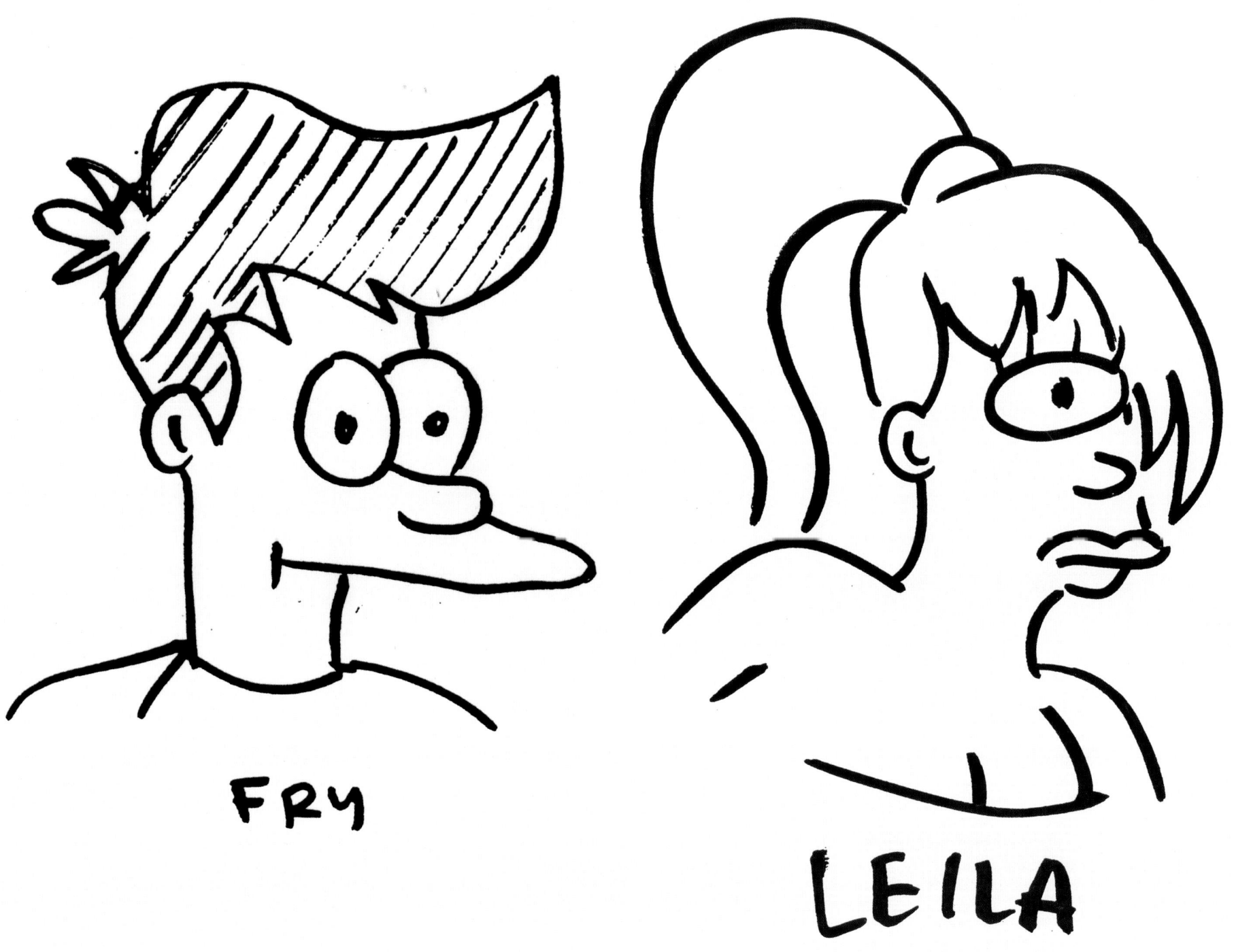

FRY

LEILA

Early concept art of Fry, Leela, Bender, and Amy
by Matt Groening

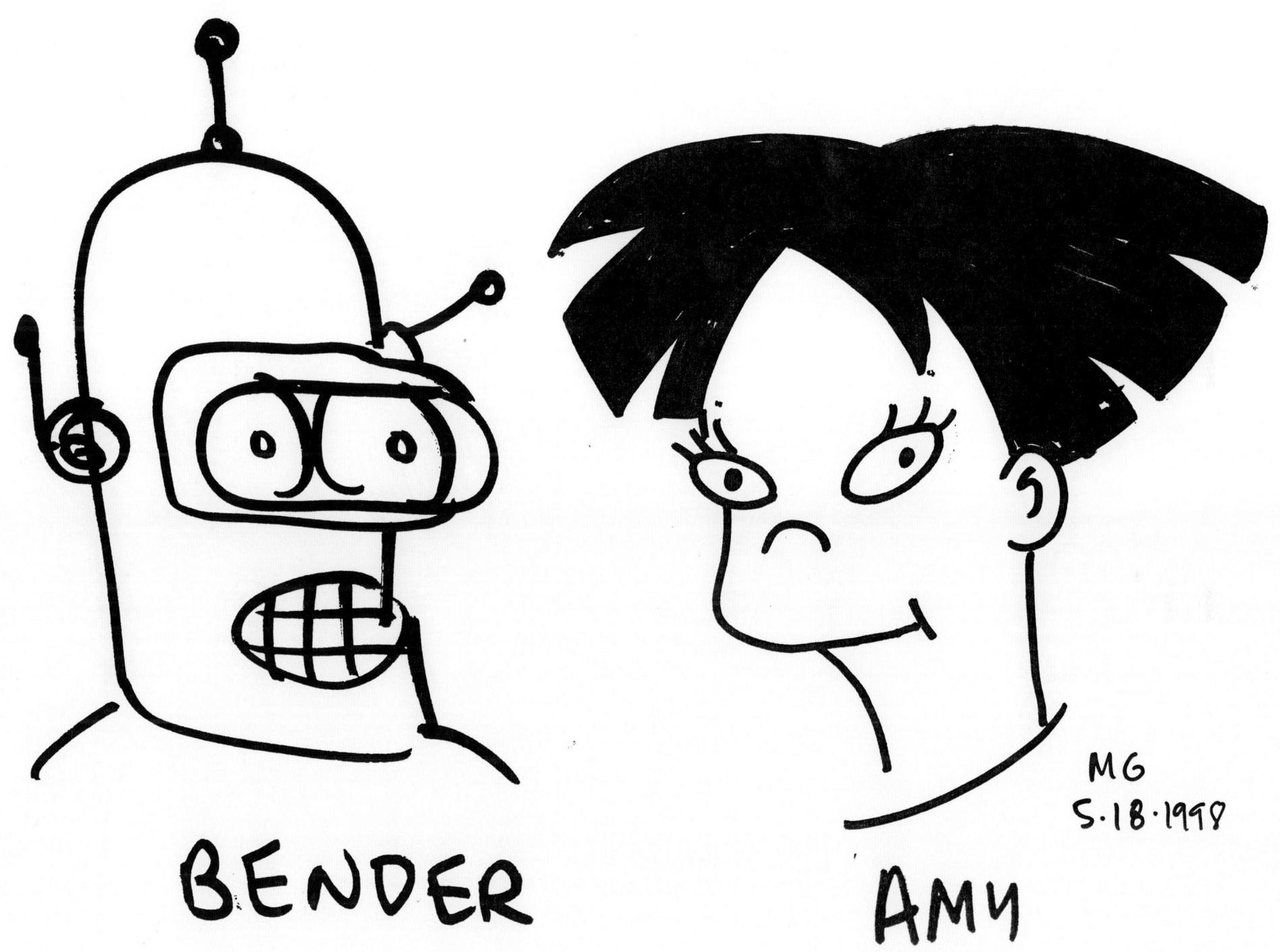

BENDER

AMY

MG
5·18·1998

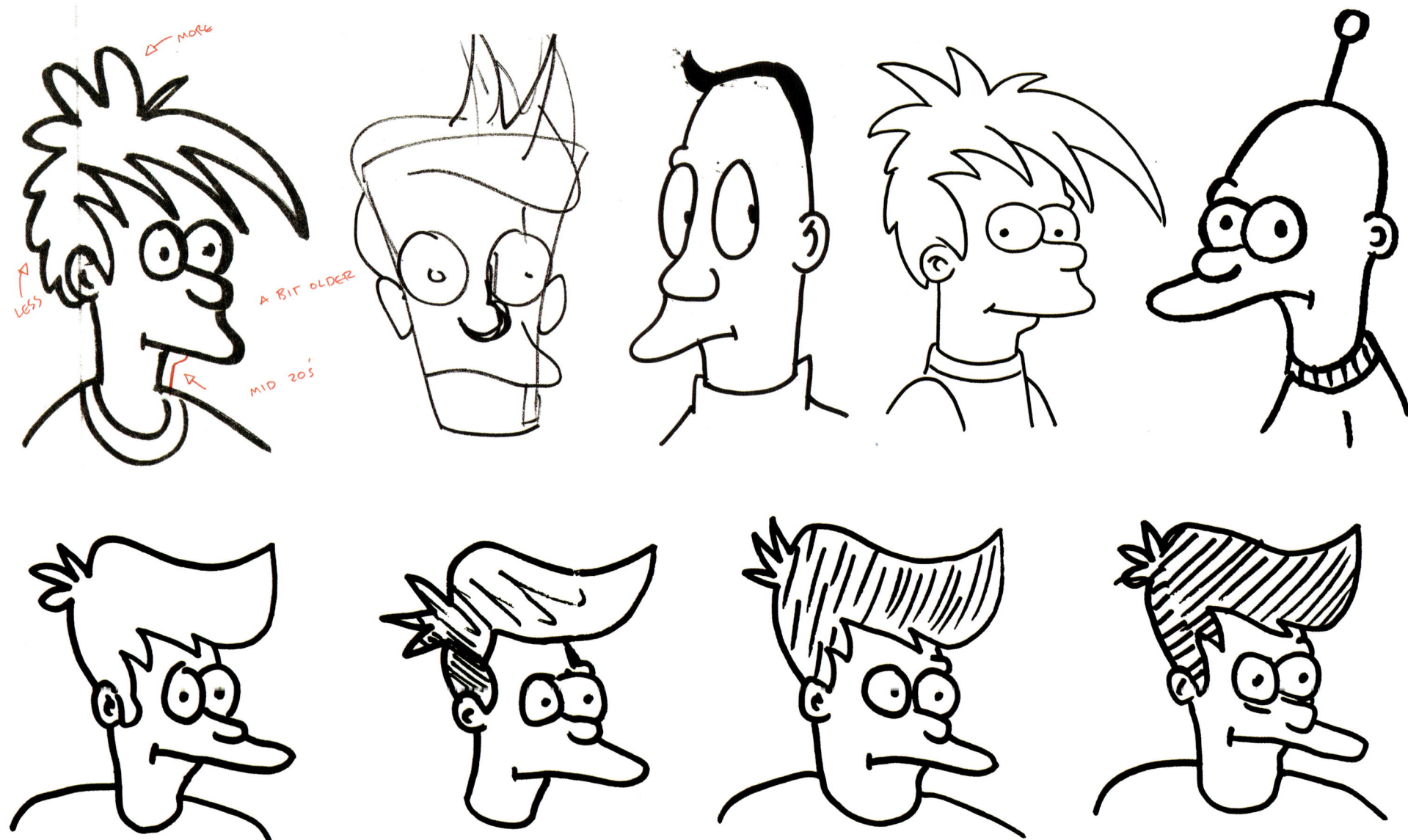

14

Above:
Early sketches of Fry by Matt Groening
and Bill Morrison

Opposite, top:
Early sketches of Fry by Dale Hendrickson

Opposite, bottom (from left to right):
Early sketches of Fry by Dale Hendrickson
and Bill Morrison
Color exploration of Fry by Chris Ungar

We had trouble designing Fry.
Matt pointed out the problem was he looks just like Bart with teenage hair.
So Matt gave him a second bump on his nose. Now it's original. Now it's Fry!
That's the thing about Matt, it can be one little change that tips it into being
original and makes everything work.

— Rich Moore

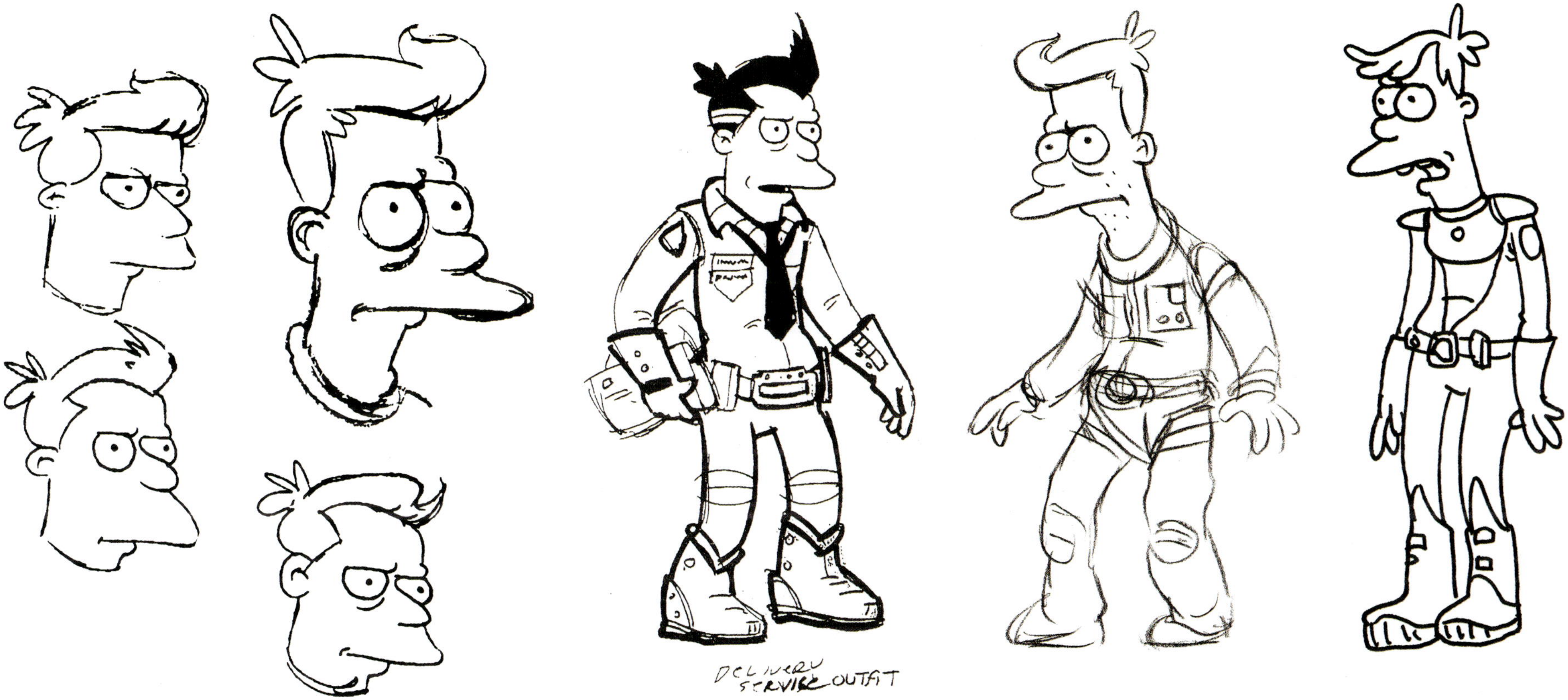

DELIVERY
SERVICE OUTFIT

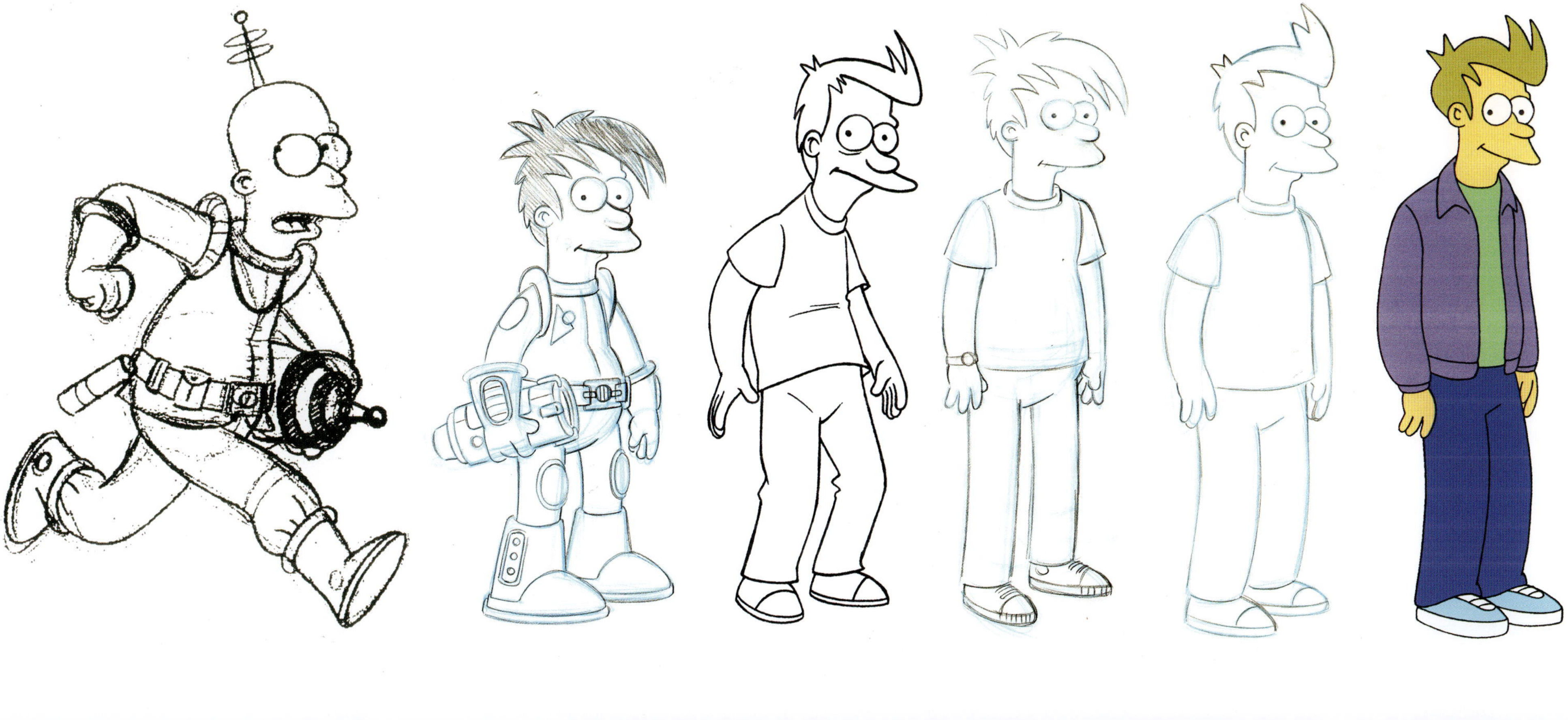

15

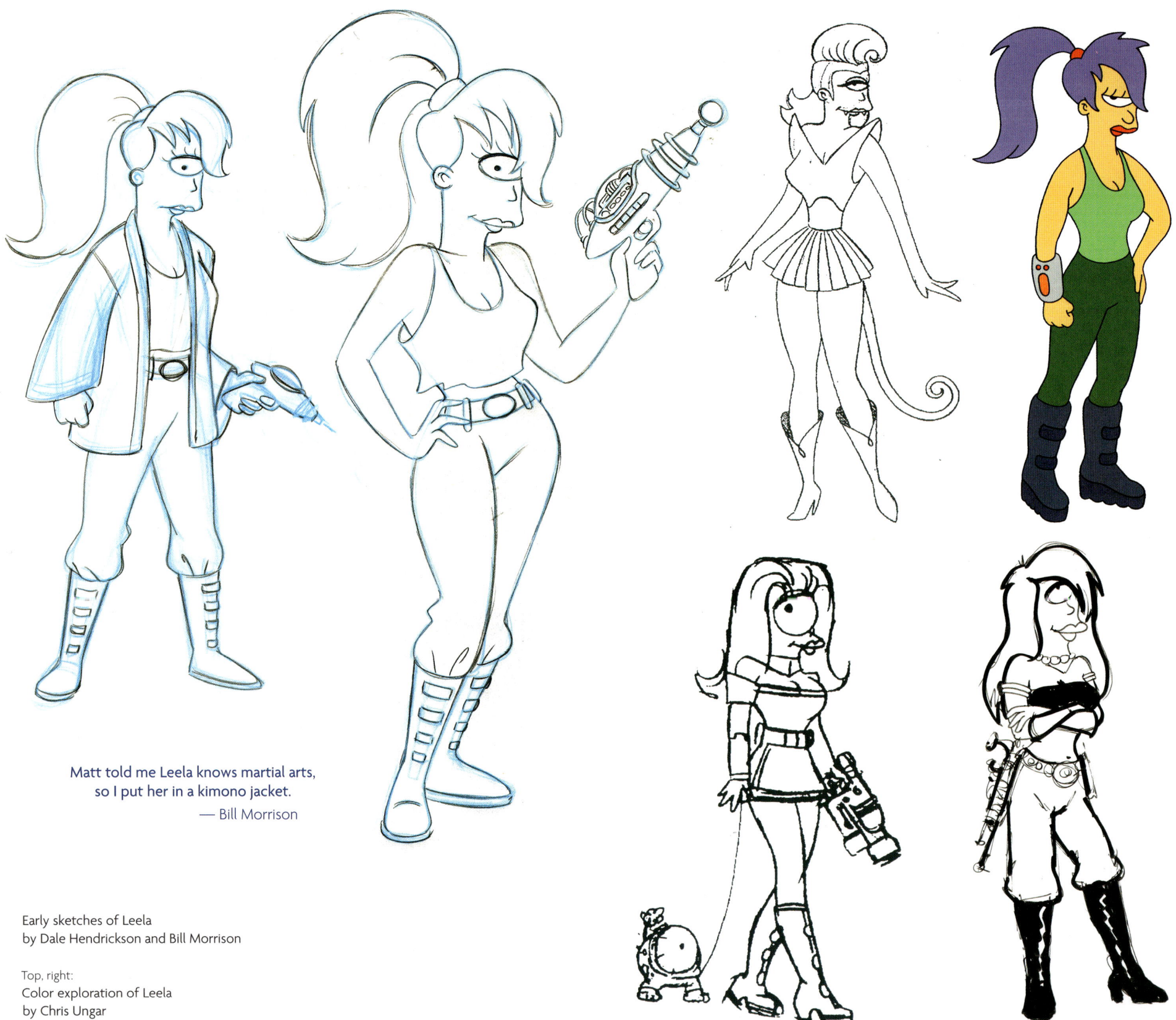

Matt told me Leela knows martial arts,
so I put her in a kimono jacket.

— Bill Morrison

Early sketches of Leela
by Dale Hendrickson and Bill Morrison

Top, right:
Color exploration of Leela
by Chris Ungar

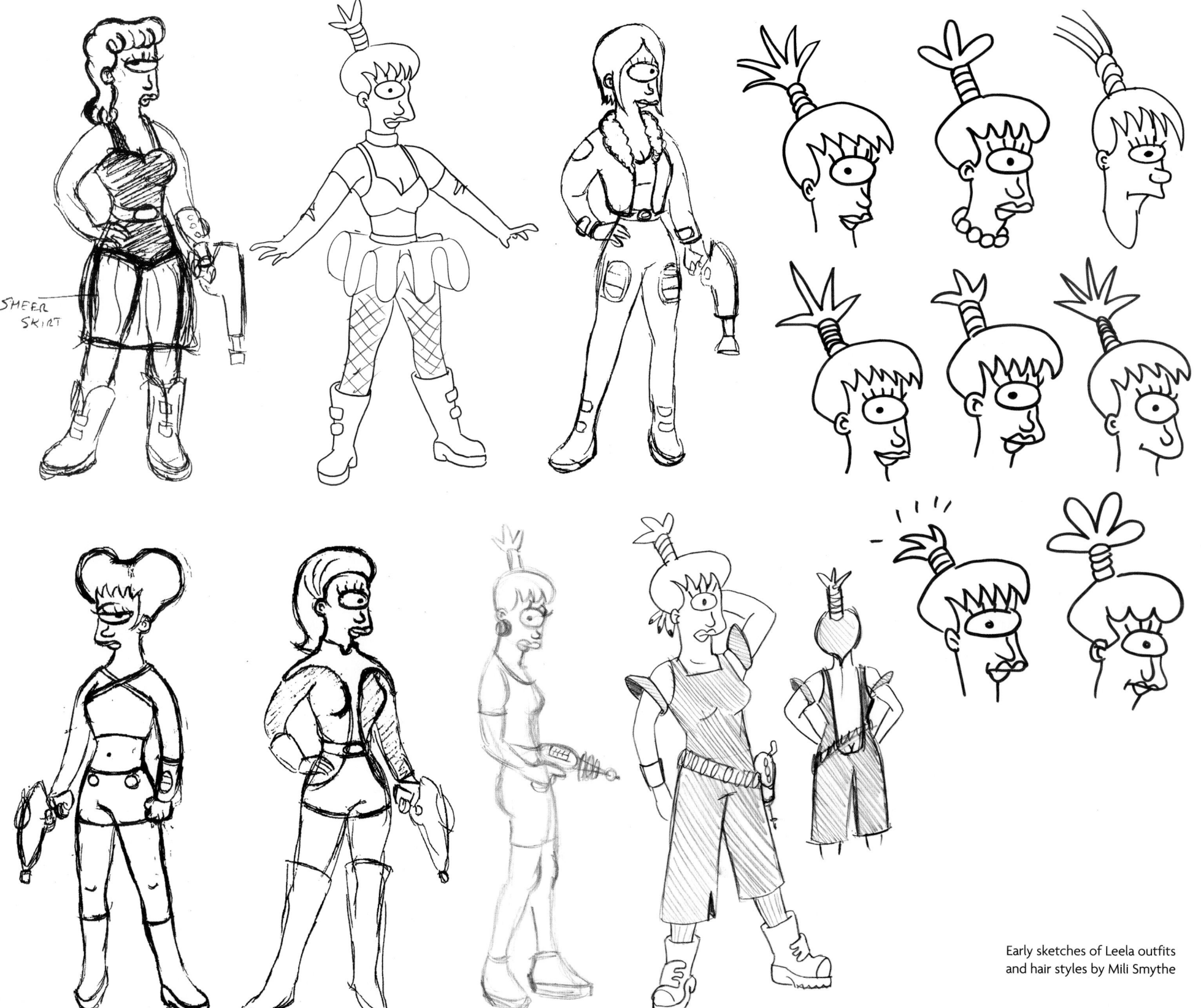

Early sketches of Leela outfits
and hair styles by Mili Smythe

SHEER
SKIRT

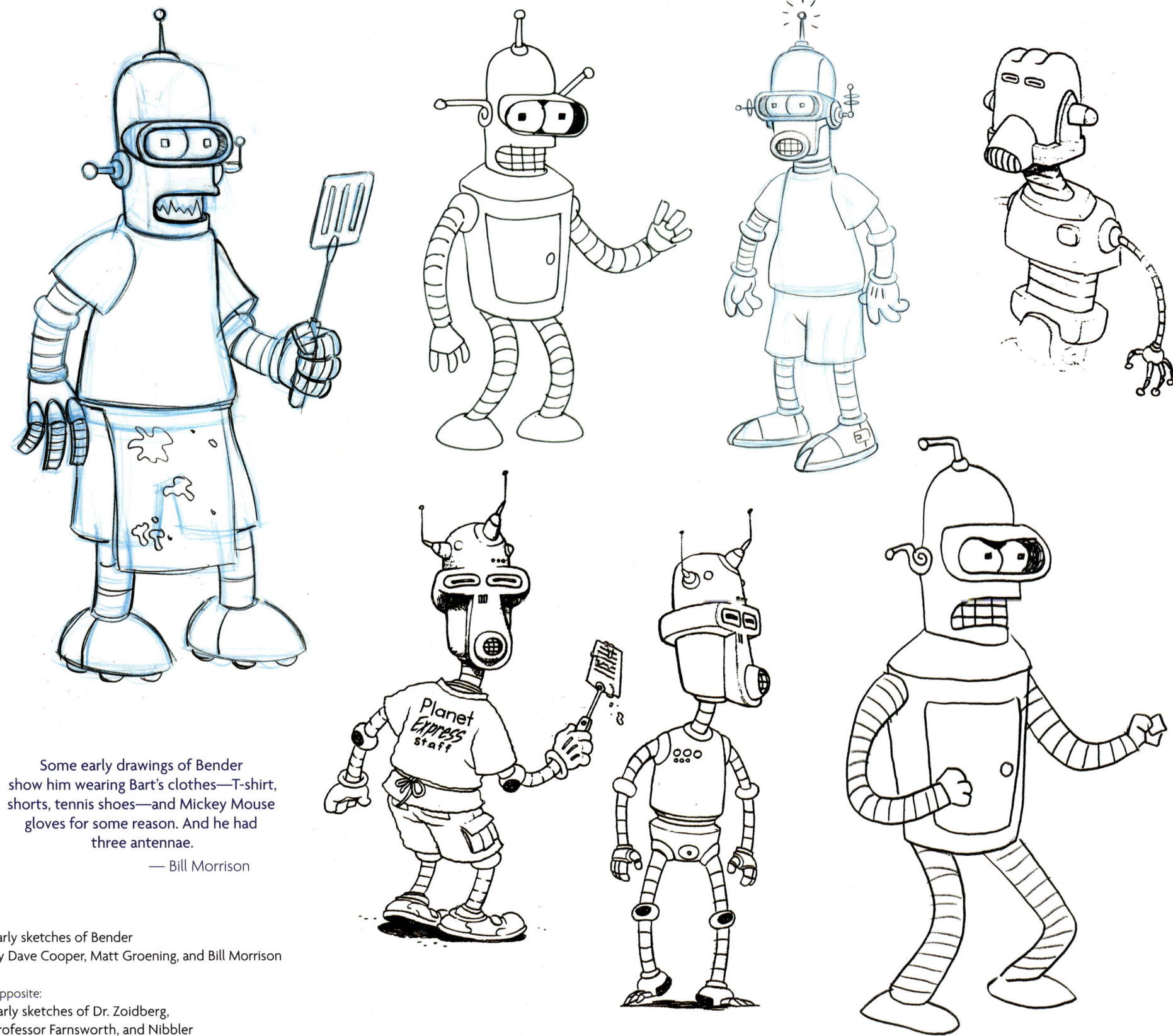

18

Some early drawings of Bender
show him wearing Bart's clothes—T-shirt,
shorts, tennis shoes—and Mickey Mouse
gloves for some reason. And he had
three antennae.

— Bill Morrison

Early sketches of Bender
by Dave Cooper, Matt Groening, and Bill Morrison

Opposite:
Early sketches of Dr. Zoidberg,
Professor Farnsworth, and Nibbler
by Matt Groening and Bill Morrison

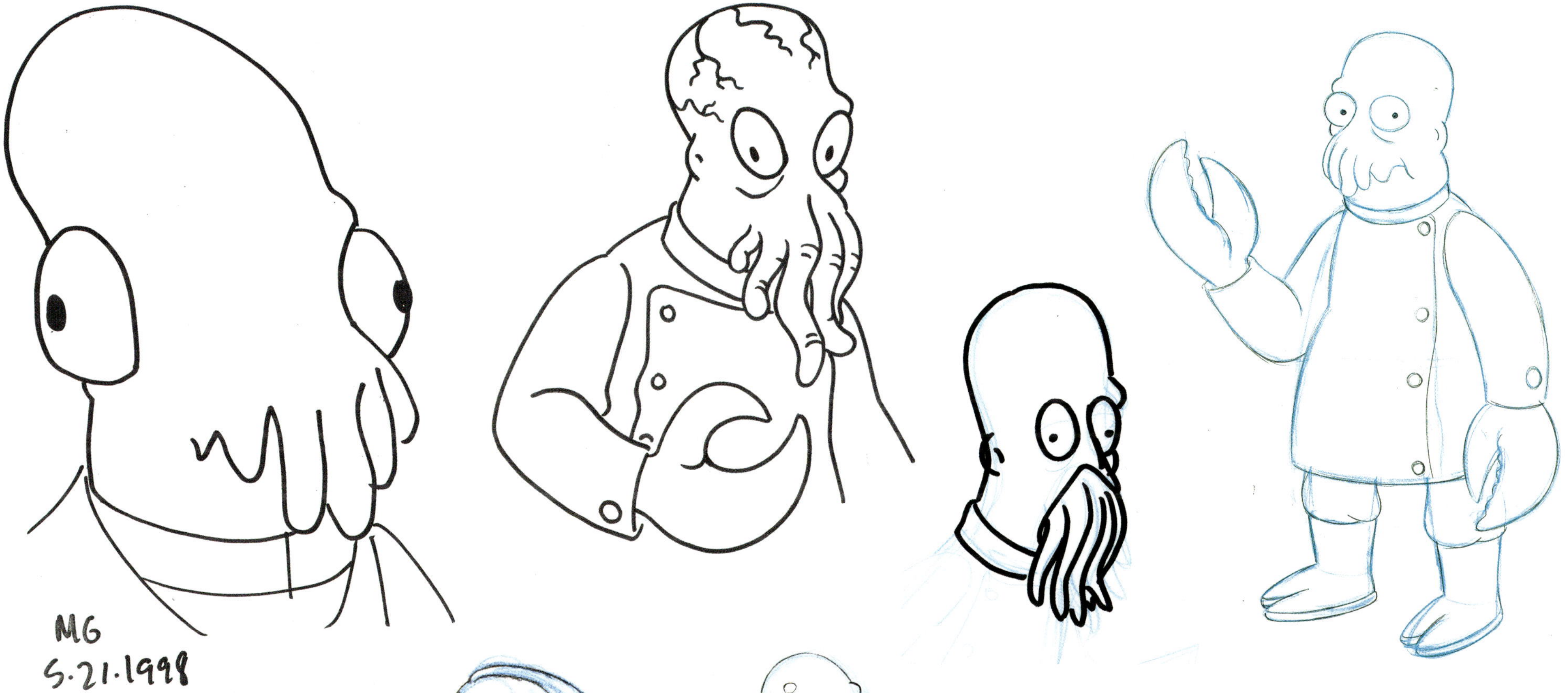

MG
5.21.1998

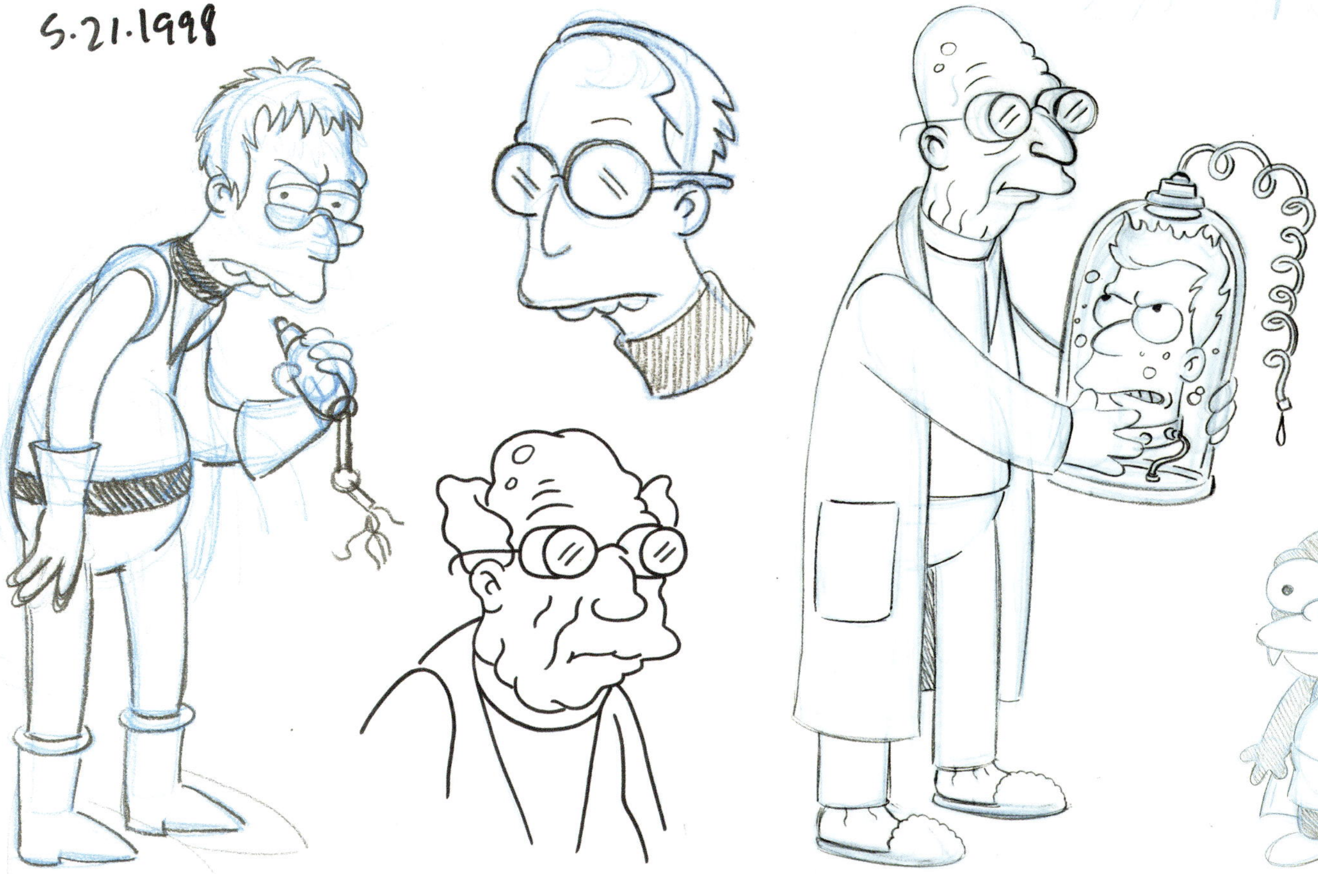

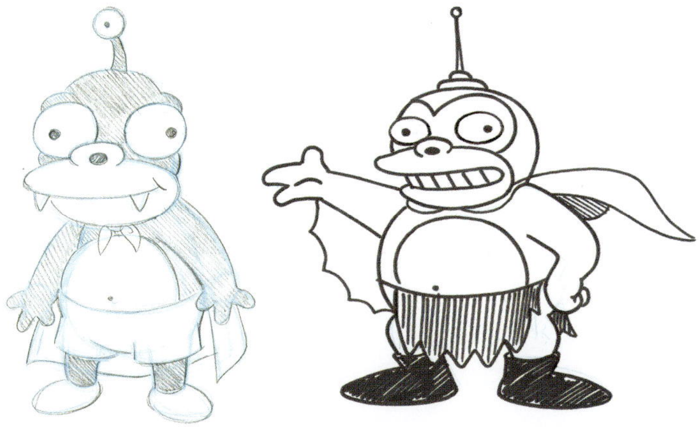

By combining Mili Smythe's
freewheeling style and Bill Morrison's
very slick, professional style with my crummy
drawing, we came up with the
charm of *Futurama*.

— Matt Groening

Top:
Early sketches of Amy Wong
by Bill Morrison

Early color exploration for Amy Wong
by Chris Ungar

Bottom:
Early sketches of Amy Wong
by Mili Smythe

Opposite:
Hair styles exploration for Amy Wong
by Mili Smythe

> When I designed, I would always try
> to think of what would make Matt laugh,
> even if I didn't think it would necessarily
> be the thing he picked.
> — Mili Smythe

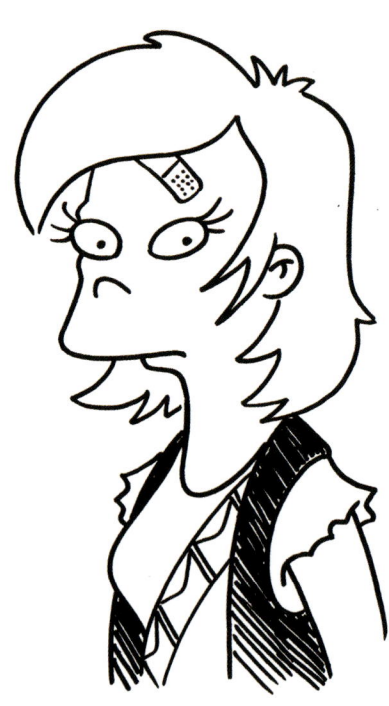
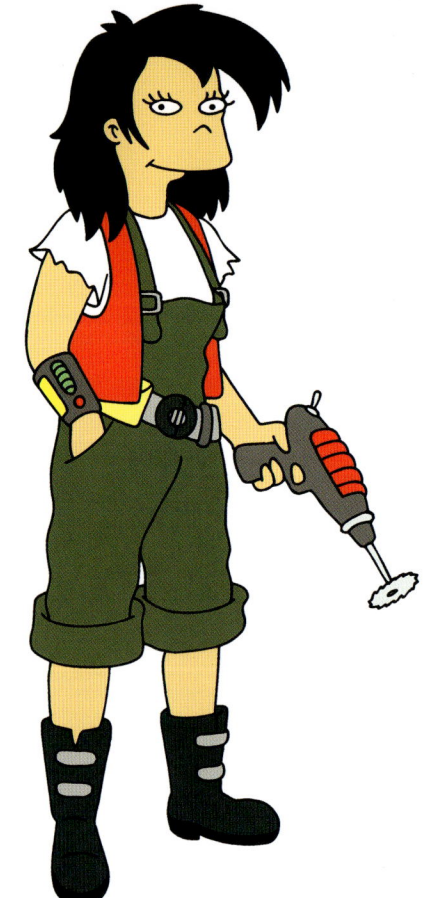
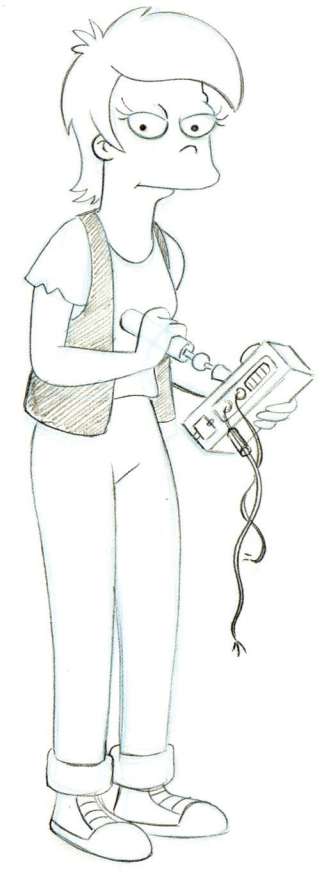

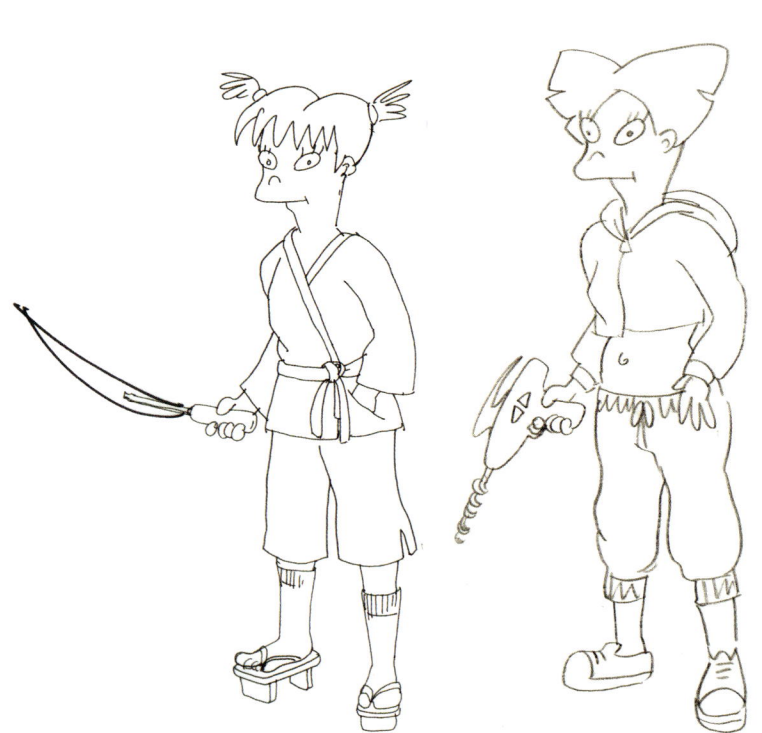
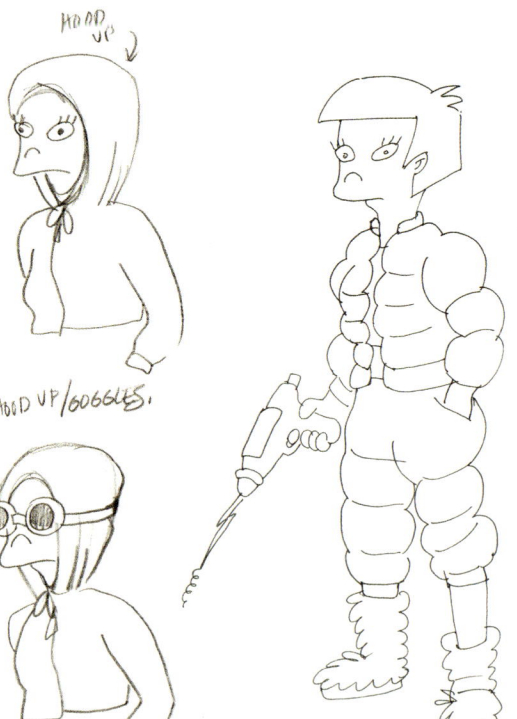
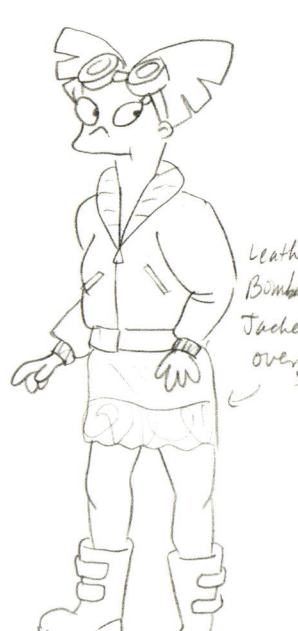
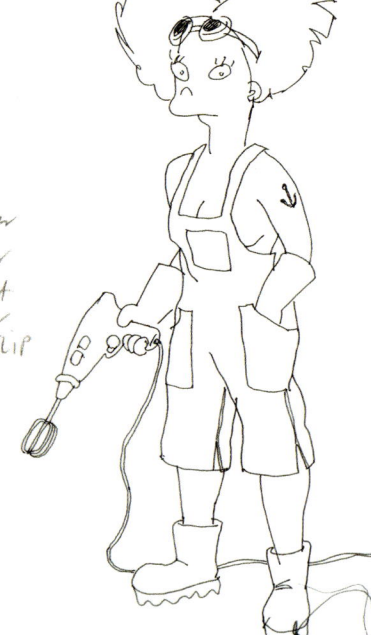

HOOD UP

HOOD UP/GOGGLES.

Leather Bomber Jacket over SLIP

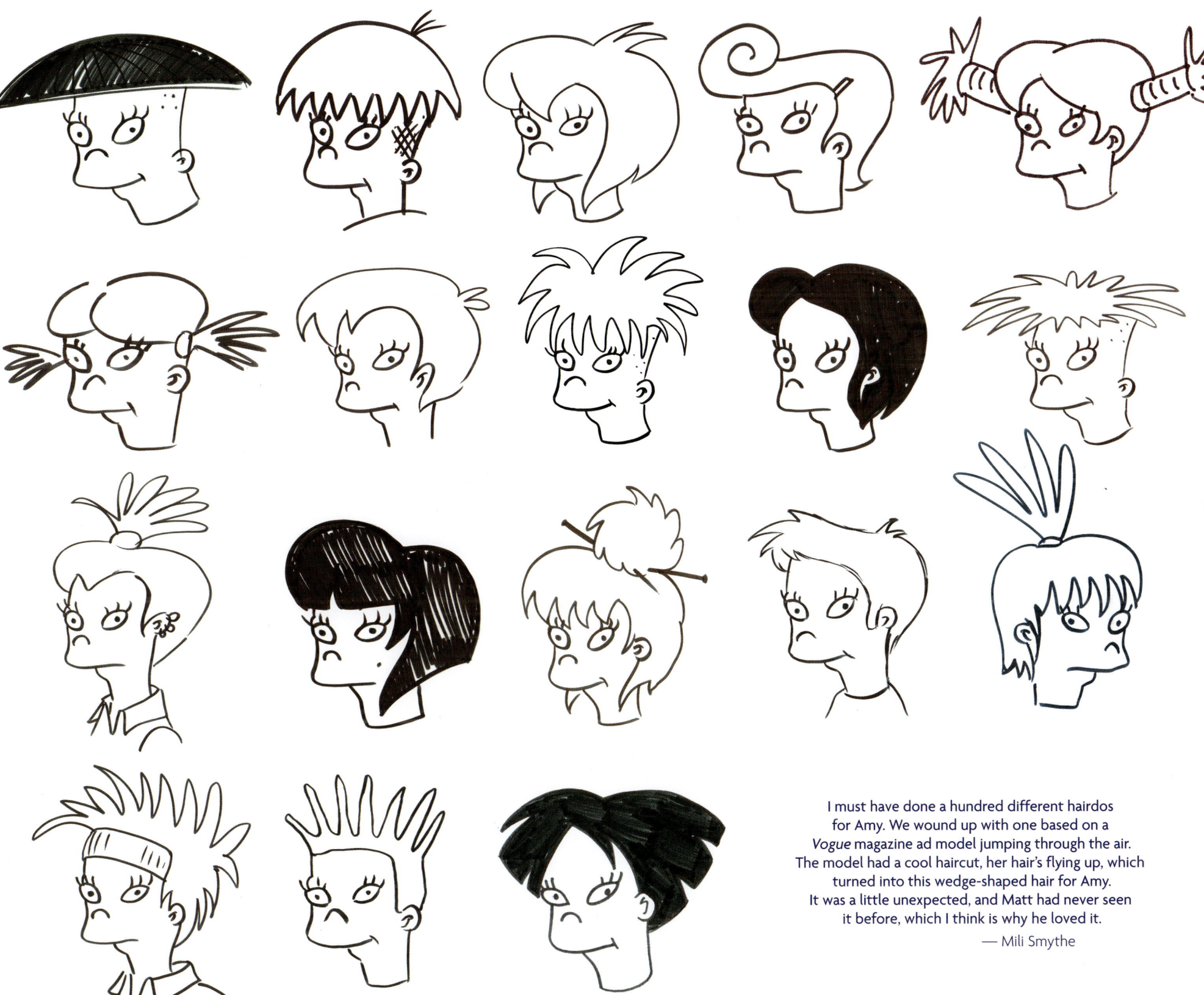

I must have done a hundred different hairdos
for Amy. We wound up with one based on a
Vogue magazine ad model jumping through the air.
The model had a cool haircut, her hair's flying up, which
turned into this wedge-shaped hair for Amy.
It was a little unexpected, and Matt had never seen
it before, which I think is why he loved it.

— Mili Smythe

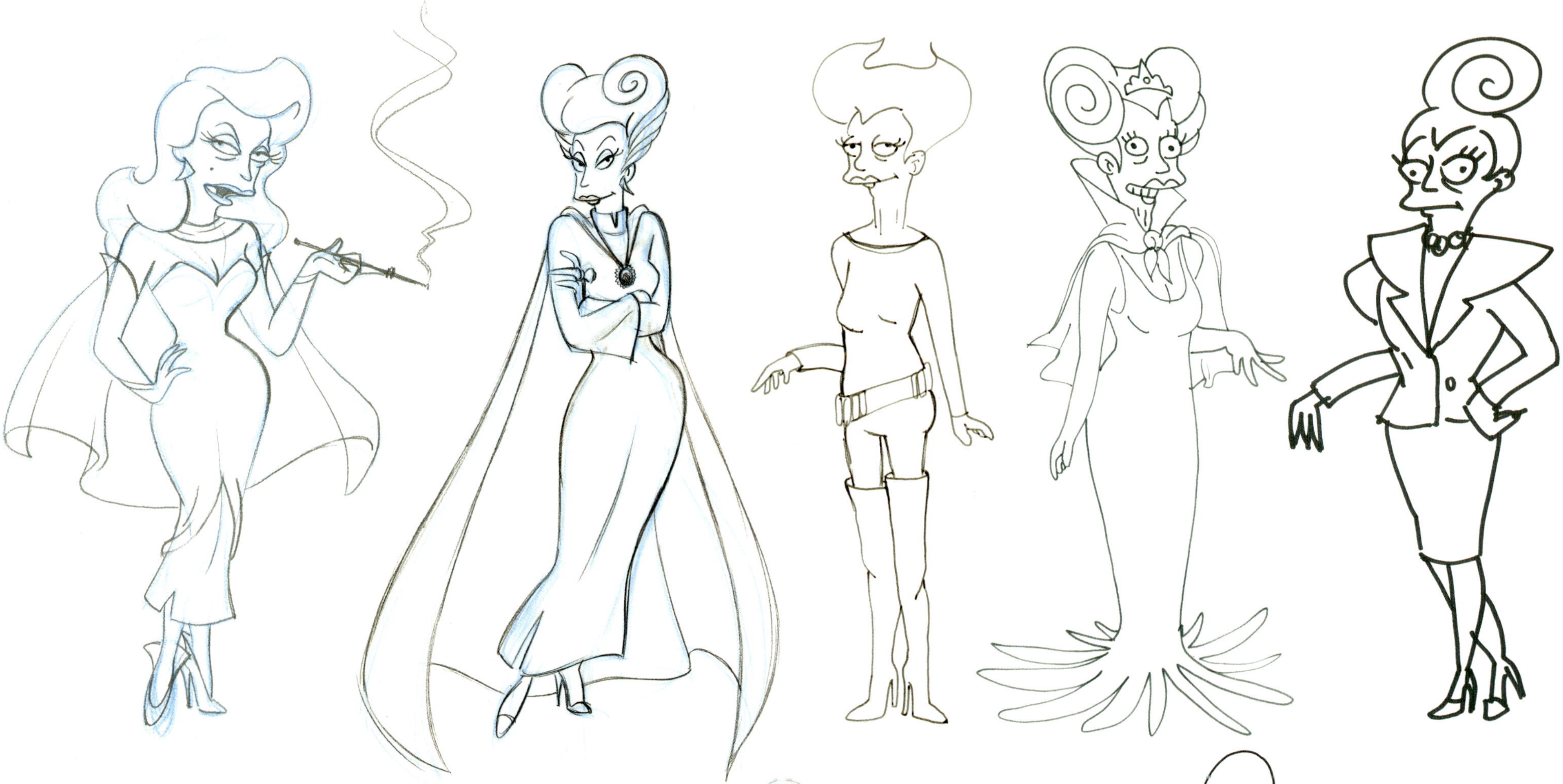

The writers had this idea of Mom being thin and sexy. I thought, okay, but how can we cut against all this Disney-style voluptuousness? So, I did a bunch of different Moms. When I did the skinny Mom with the droopy boobs and ass, all the writers laughed. Then I came up with this idea that she had a fat suit, so she could be both. And there's a little story right there in the design that the writers could use.

— Mili Smythe

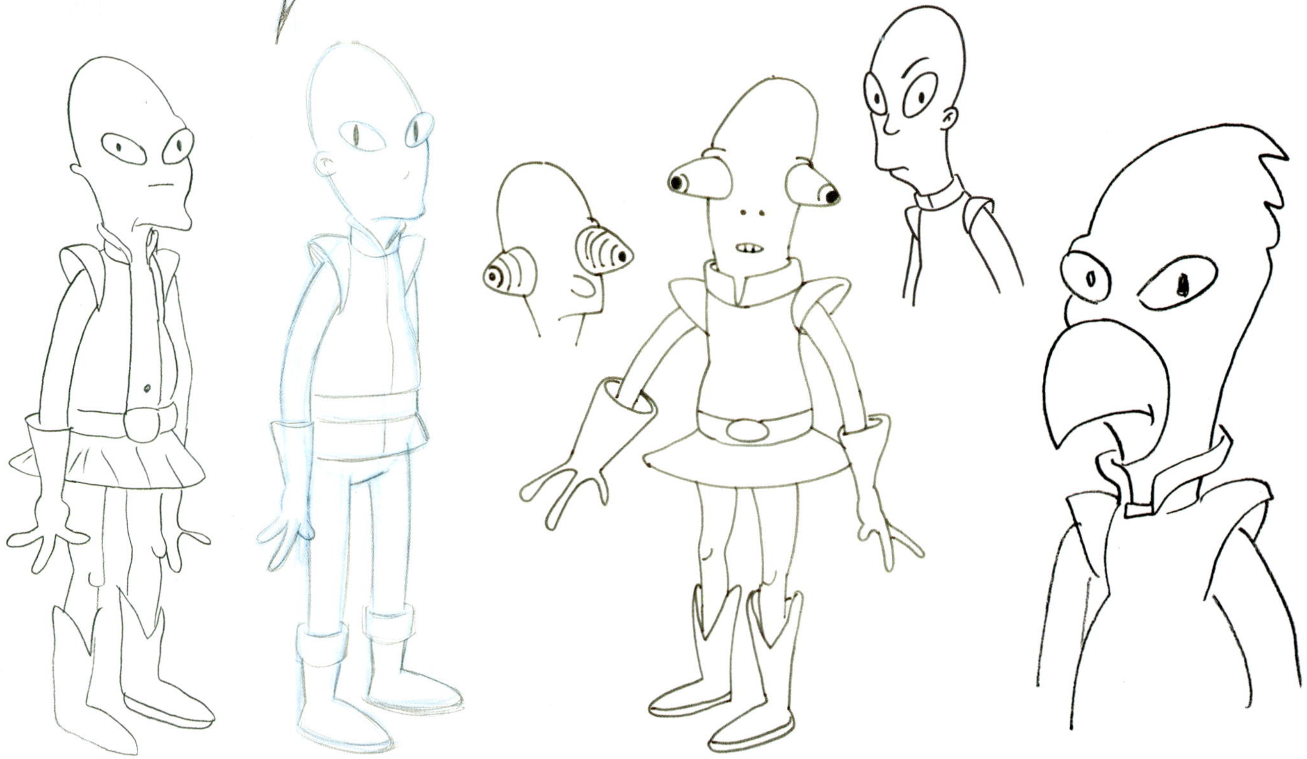

Early sketches of Mom and Kif Kroker by Matt Groening, Bill Morrison, and Mili Smythe

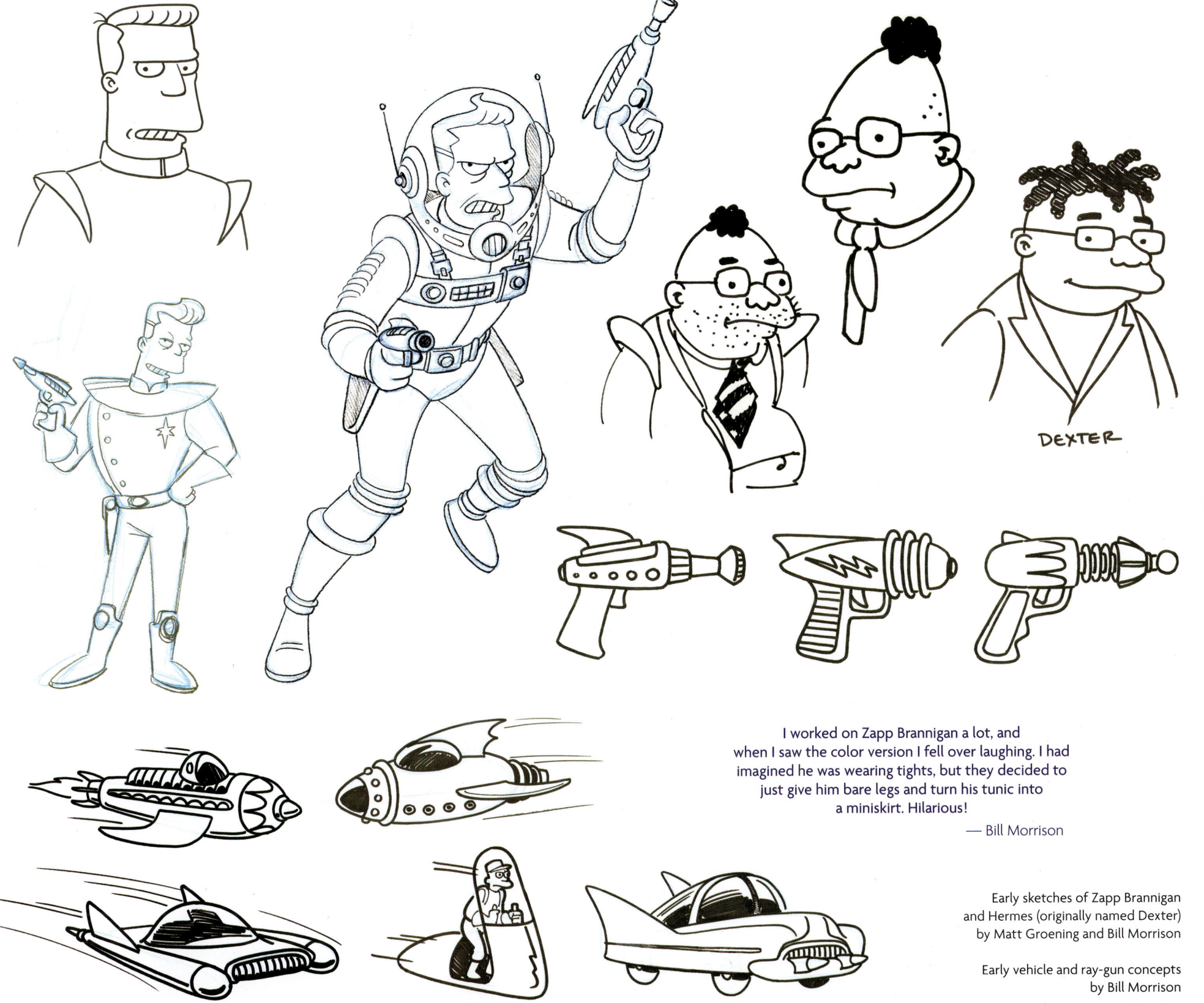

DEXTER

I worked on Zapp Brannigan a lot, and
when I saw the color version I fell over laughing. I had
imagined he was wearing tights, but they decided to
just give him bare legs and turn his tunic into
a miniskirt. Hilarious!

— Bill Morrison

Early sketches of Zapp Brannigan
and Hermes (originally named Dexter)
by Matt Groening and Bill Morrison

Early vehicle and ray-gun concepts
by Bill Morrison

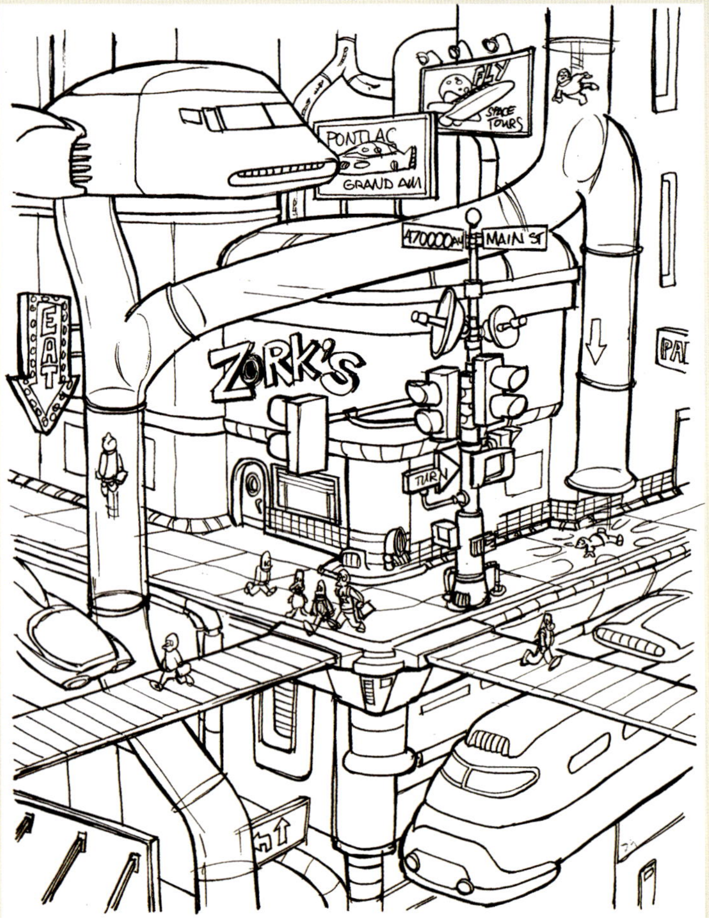

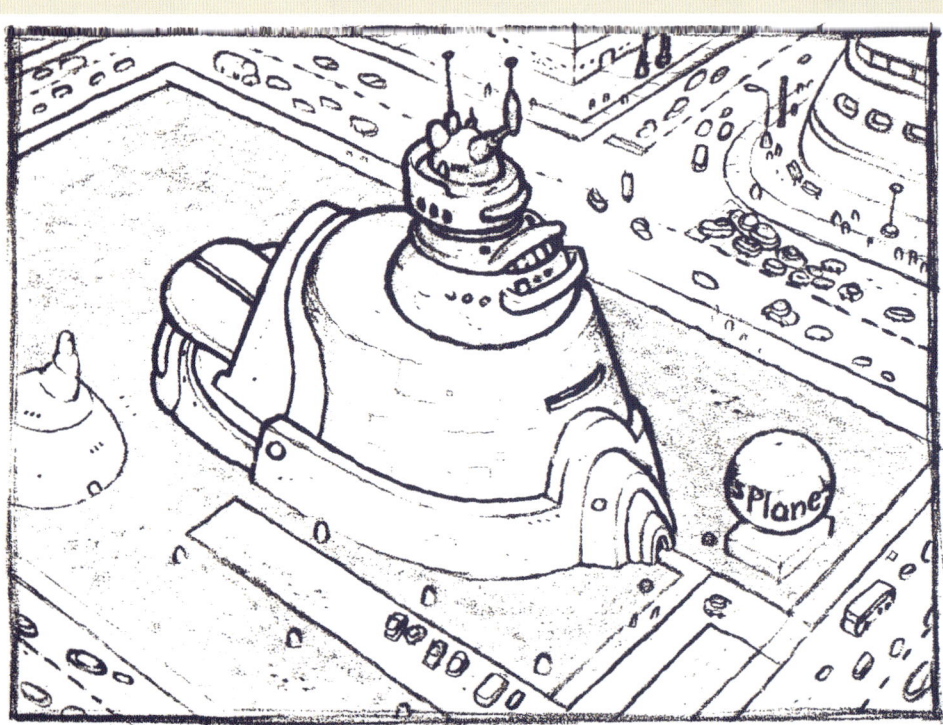

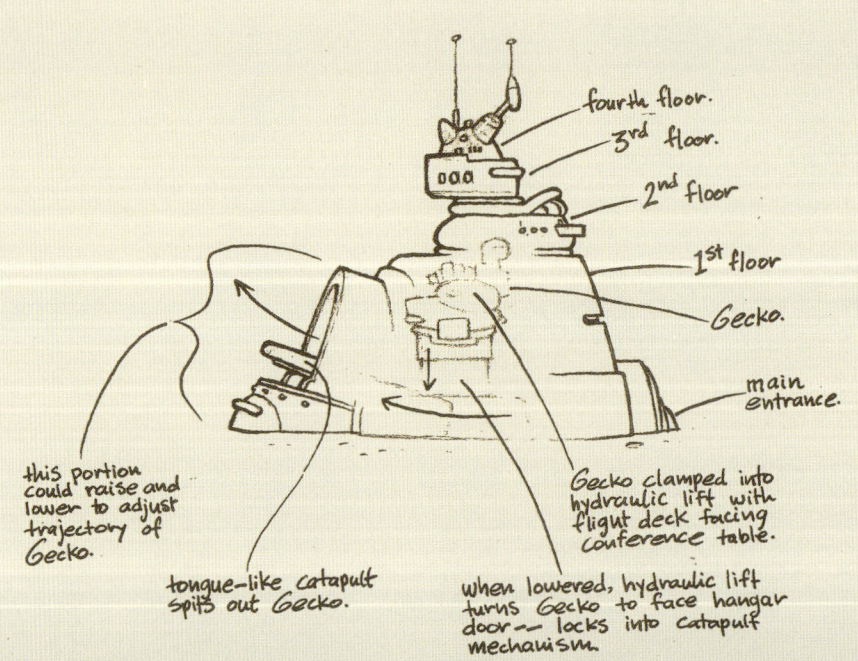

fourth floor.

3rd floor.

2nd floor

1st floor

Gecko.

main entrance.

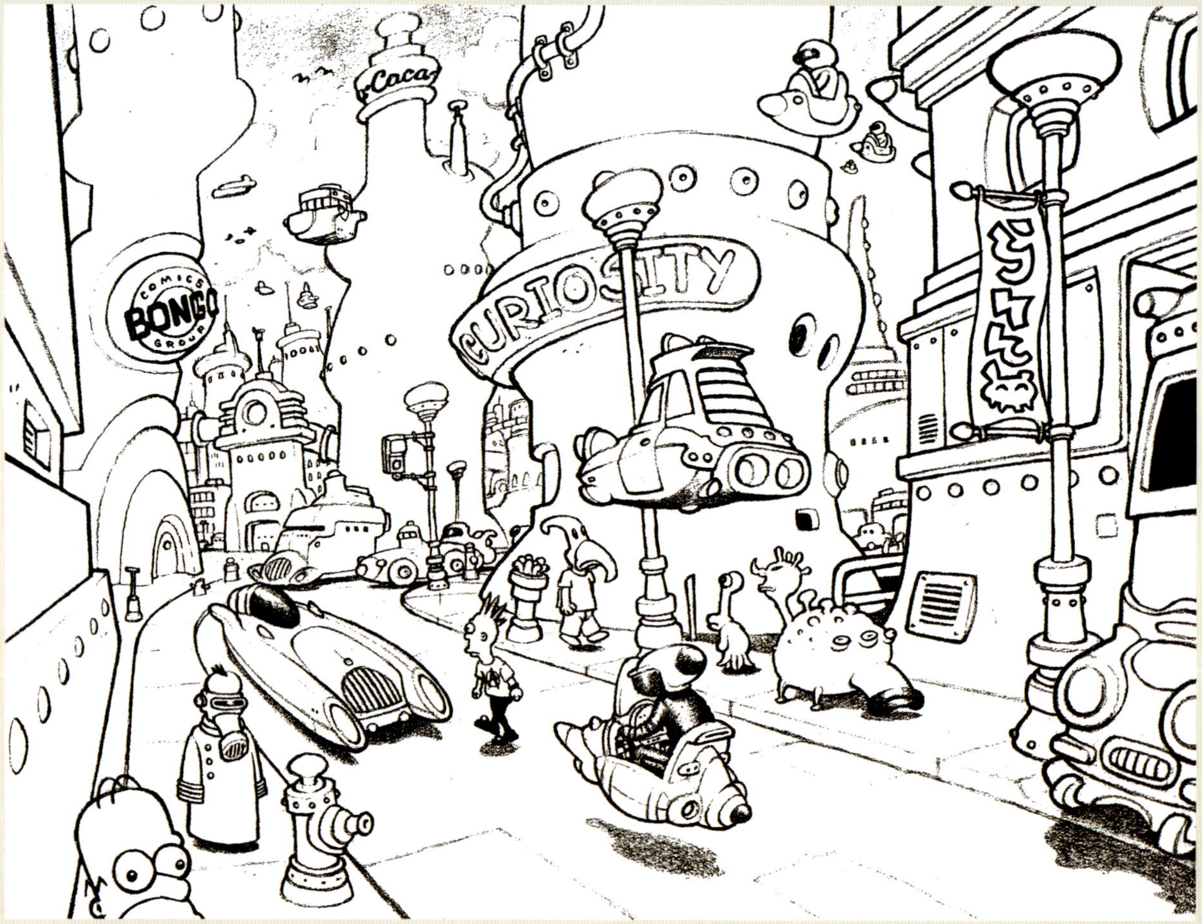

this portion could raise and lower to adjust trajectory of Gecko.

Gecko clamped into hydraulic lift with flight deck facing conference table.

tongue-like catapult spits out Gecko.

when lowered, hydraulic lift turns Gecko to face hangar door — locks into catapult mechanism.

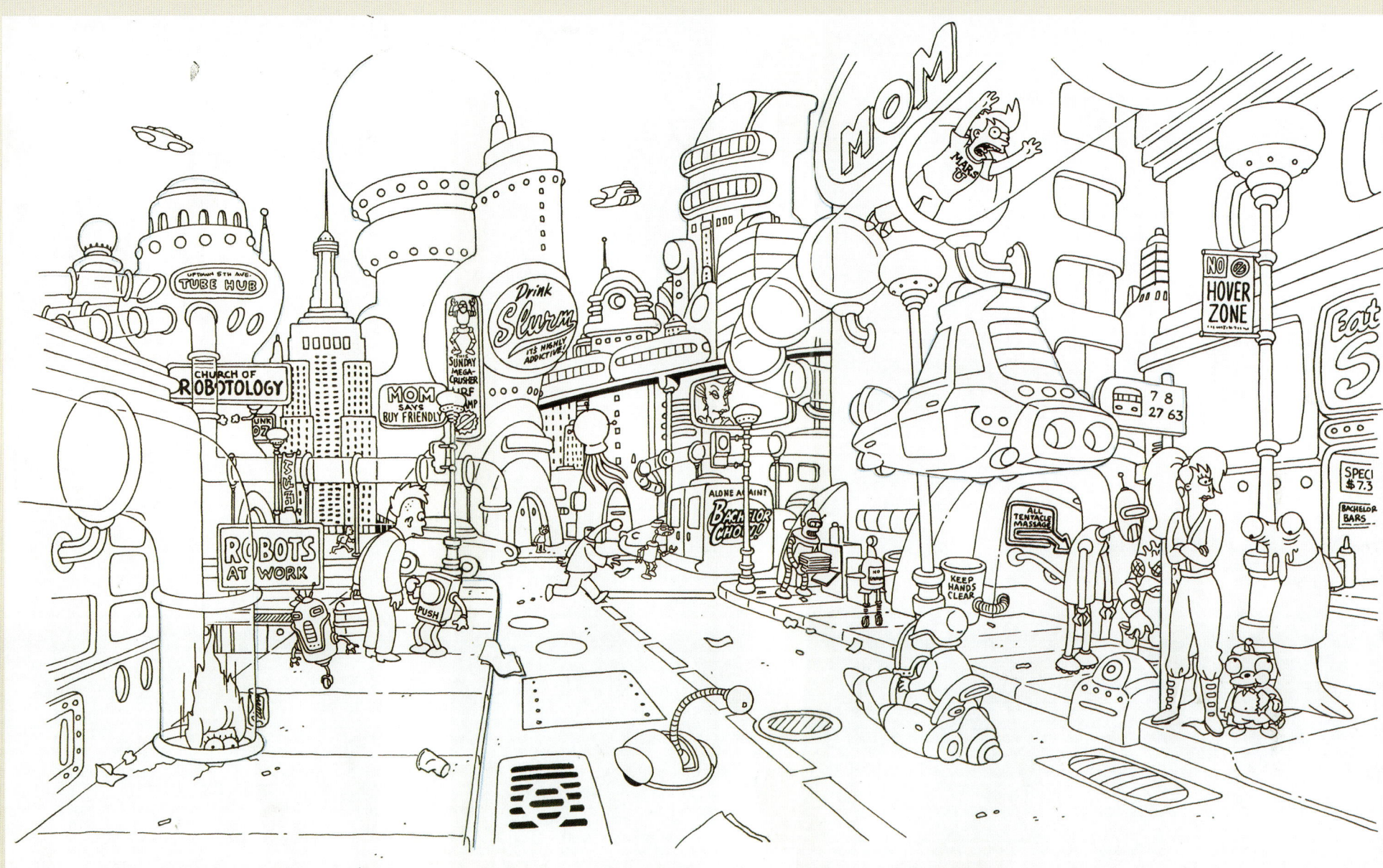

Early New New York street background design
by Dave Cooper and Bill Morrison

Opposite page, top:
New New York scenes
by Dave Cooper

Opposite page, bottom::
Early Planet Express building design
by Dave Cooper

At first I was adamant we not do time travel.
If we did it, I figured we'd begin to rely on it. It would
be a very easy way out. Then, sure enough, we start
doing time travel and it is the greatest
solution to telling stories.

— Matt Groening

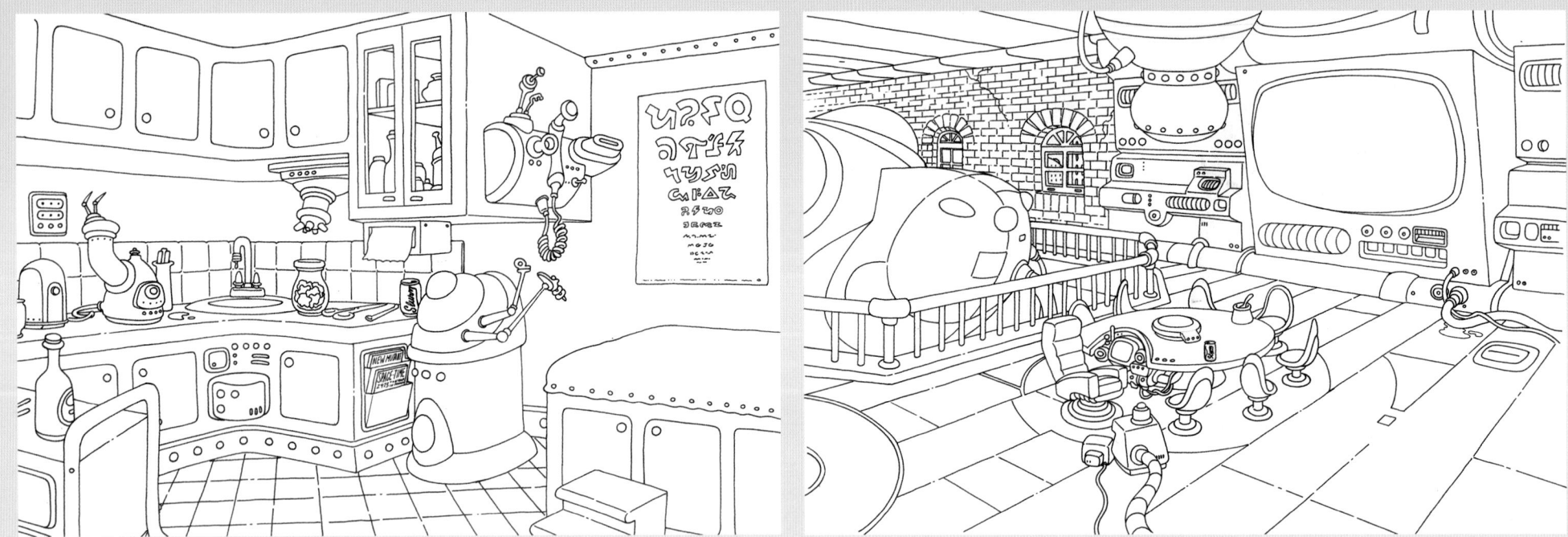

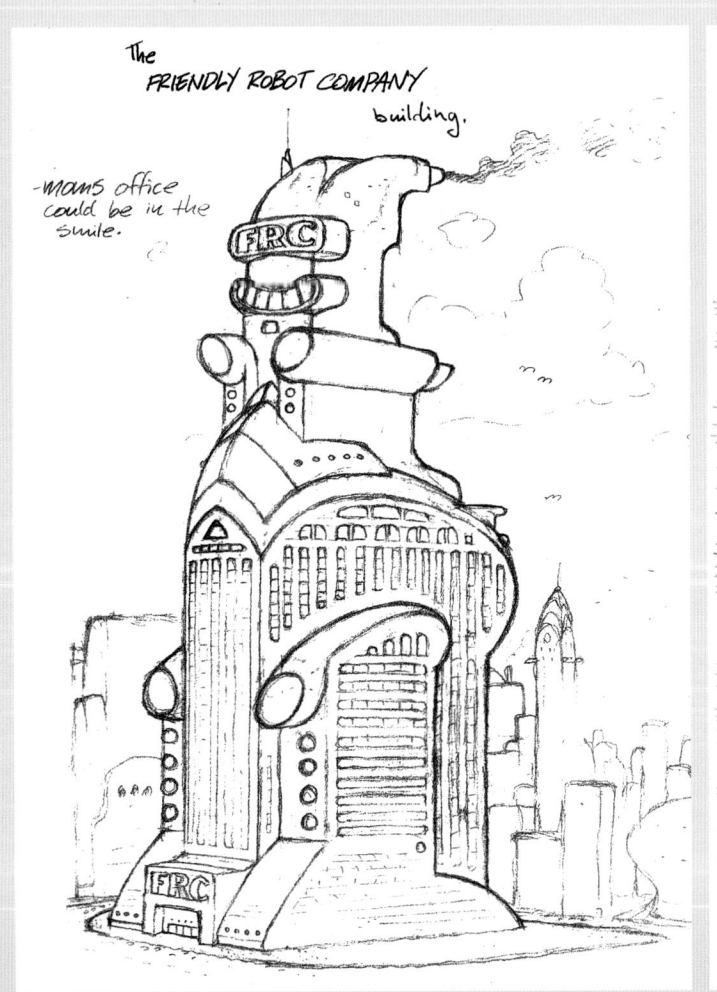

The
FRIENDLY ROBOT COMPANY
building.

-moms office
could be in the
smile.

FRC

FRC

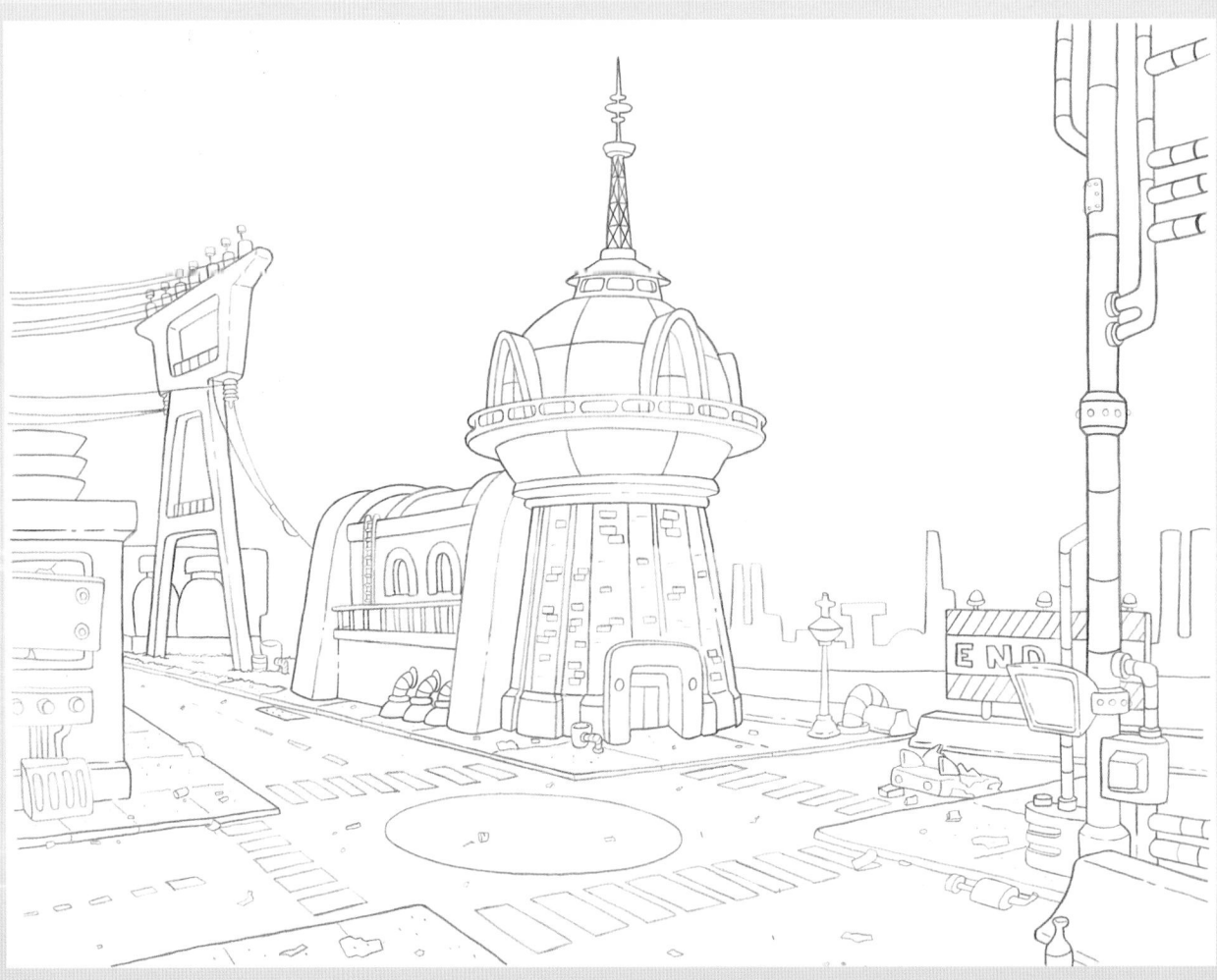

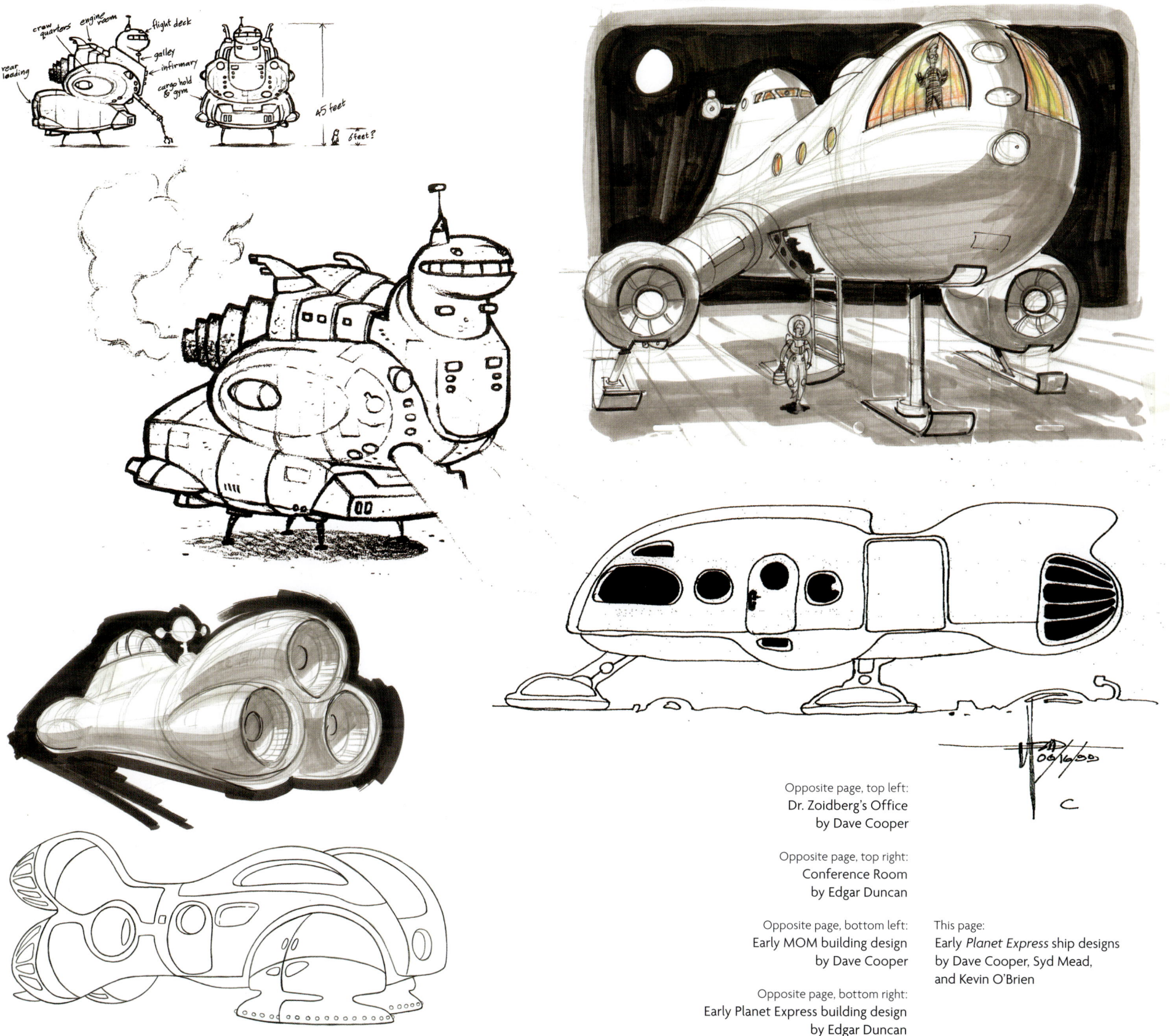

Opposite page, top left:
Dr. Zoidberg's Office
by Dave Cooper

Opposite page, top right:
Conference Room
by Edgar Duncan

Opposite page, bottom left:
Early MOM building design
by Dave Cooper

Opposite page, bottom right:
Early Planet Express building design
by Edgar Duncan

This page:
Early *Planet Express* ship designs
by Dave Cooper, Syd Mead,
and Kevin O'Brien

crew quarters   engine room   flight deck
rear loading   galley   infirmary   cargo hold & gym

45 feet
6 feet?

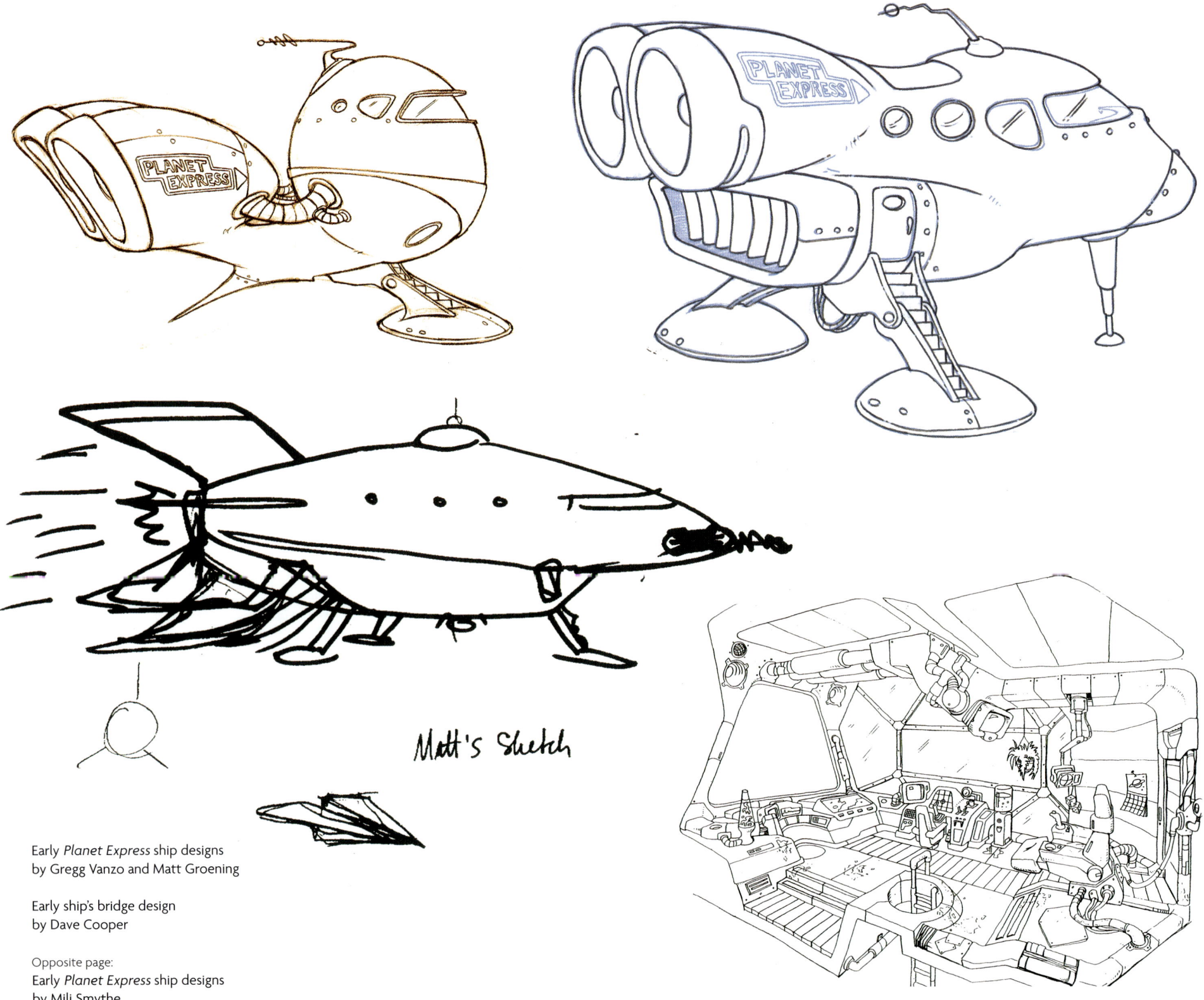

Matt's Sketch

28

Early *Planet Express* ship designs
by Gregg Vanzo and Matt Groening

Early ship's bridge design
by Dave Cooper

Opposite page:
Early *Planet Express* ship designs
by Mili Smythe

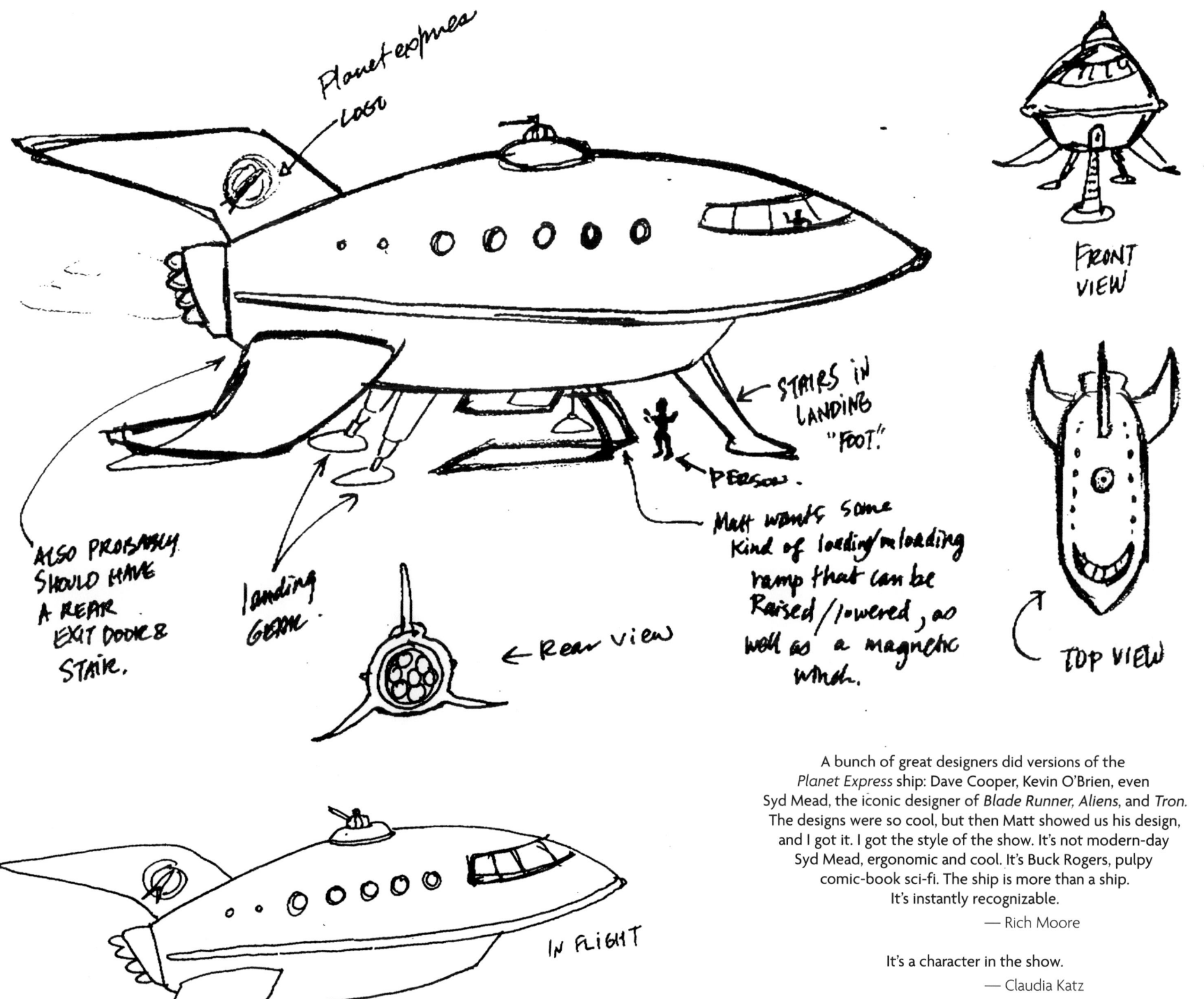

Planet express Logo

FRONT VIEW

STAIRS IN LANDING "FOOT"

PERSON.

Matt wants some Kind of loading/unloading ramp that can be Raised/lowered, as well as a magnetic winch.

TOP VIEW

ALSO PROBABLY SHOULD HAVE A REAR EXIT DOOR & STAIR.

landing GEAR.

← Rear view

IN FLIGHT

A bunch of great designers did versions of the *Planet Express* ship: Dave Cooper, Kevin O'Brien, even Syd Mead, the iconic designer of *Blade Runner*, *Aliens*, and *Tron*. The designs were so cool, but then Matt showed us his design, and I got it. I got the style of the show. It's not modern-day Syd Mead, ergonomic and cool. It's Buck Rogers, pulpy comic-book sci-fi. The ship is more than a ship. It's instantly recognizable.

— Rich Moore

It's a character in the show.

— Claudia Katz

Following pages:
Brooklyn Bridge (7ACV15) by Alex Lee

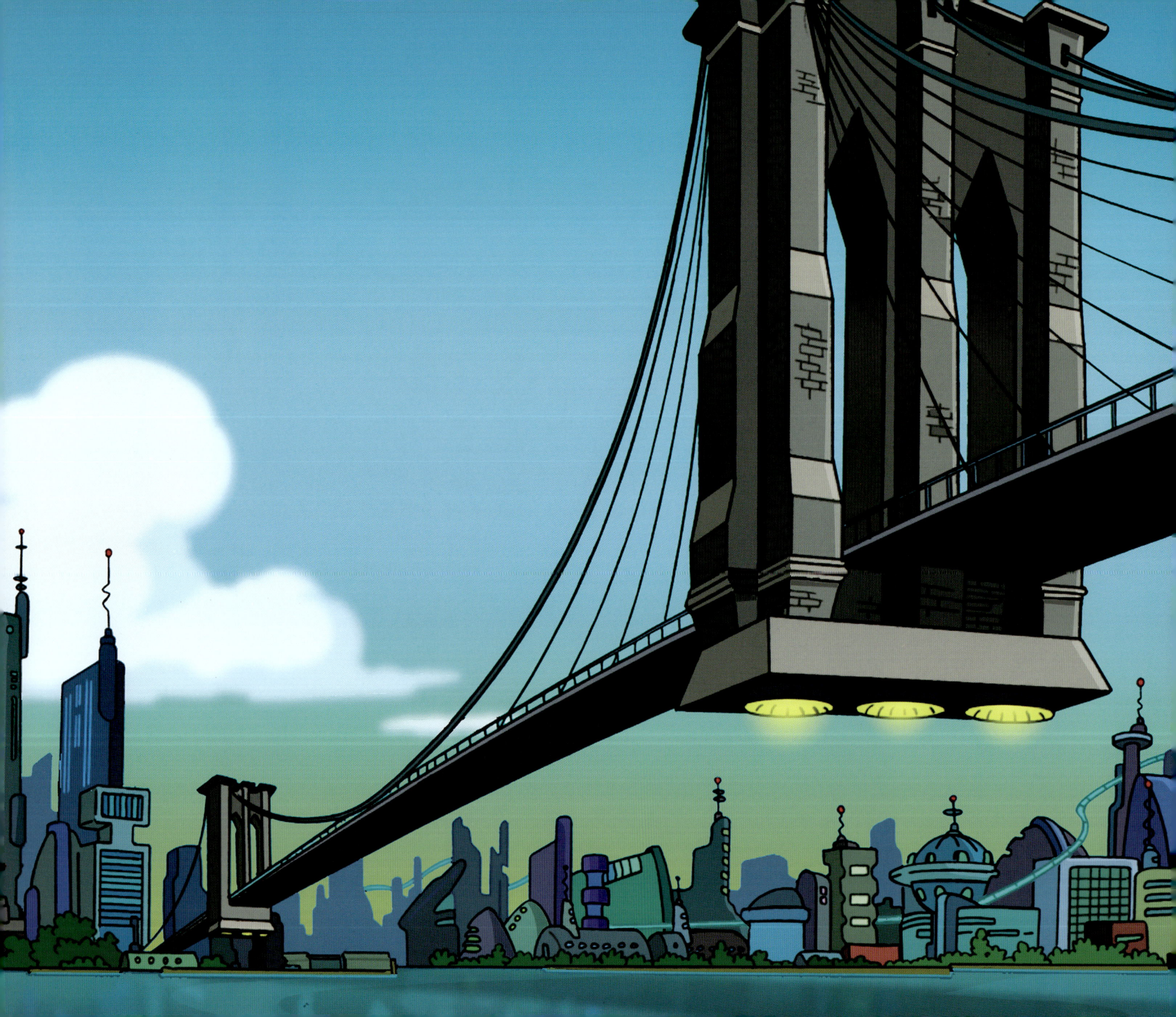

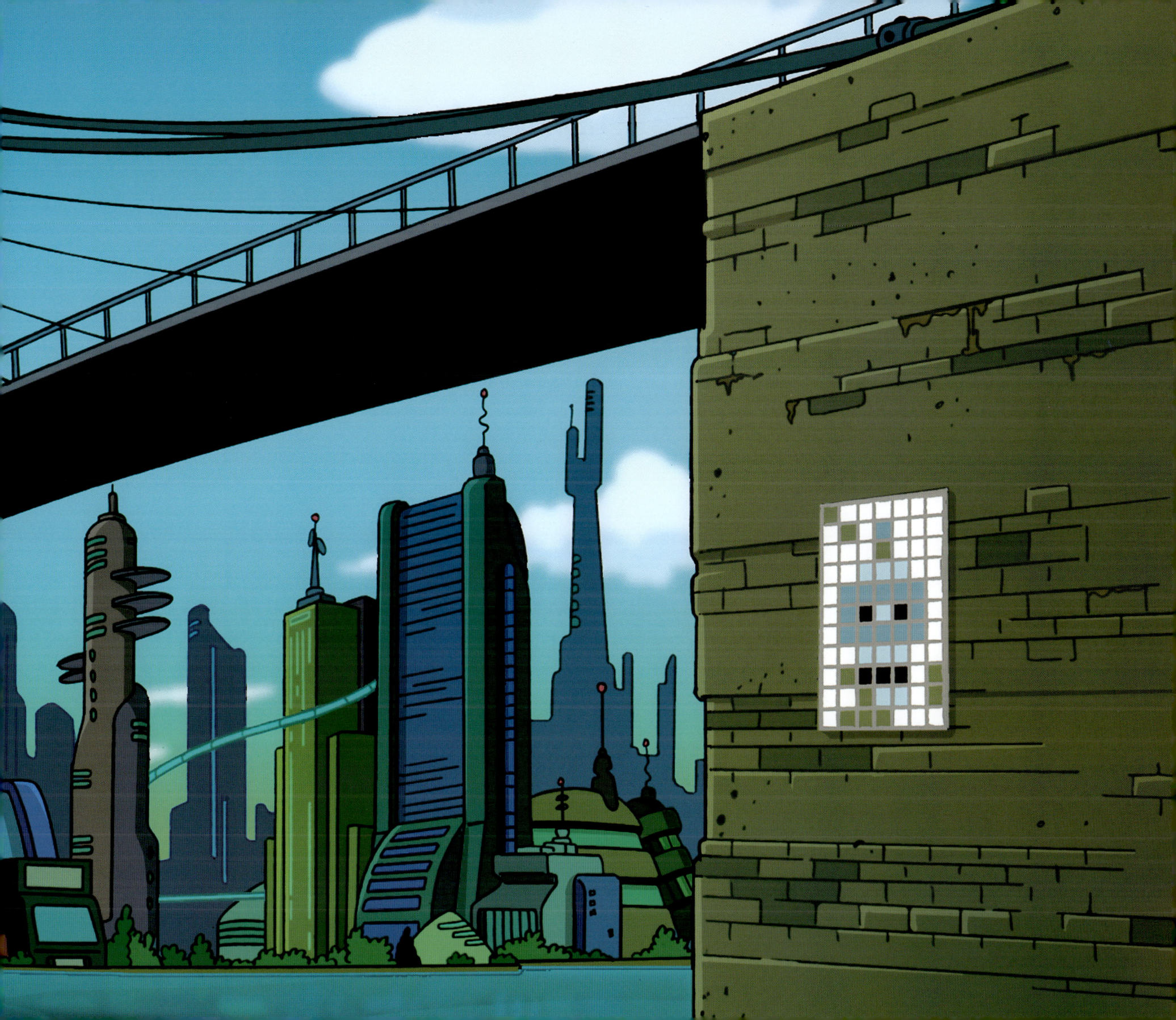

CLEARANCE TO TAXI: PERSONNEL PROFILES

Rich Moore: I first heard about *Futurama* in 1990, during season two of *The Simpsons*, before Rough Draft existed. Matt took the *Simpsons* directors to lunch and told us about his new idea for a sci-fi animated show. He said, "If you think of *The Simpsons* as kind of my *Flintstones*, this would be my *Jetsons*." And we're like, "Whoa, that sounds really cool, Matt. Are you working on it now?" He says, "Yeah. I don't have stuff to show you, but I'm developing this. And I look forward to sharing it with you guys at some point."

Much time passes. It's seven years later. I'm at Rough Draft now with Gregg Vanzo, Claudia Katz, and Bret Haaland. We have a small studio, doing interstitials, commercials, and things like that. Out of the blue, Matt calls us, saying, "I have this new show I'm going to do for Fox. I want you guys to work on it." All of us being from *The Simpsons*, we really wanted to land a prime time show. Speaking for myself, I just got this taste of blood in my mouth. "This is the one we're going to get. I know we can do this better than anyone in town." And Claudia agreed.

If you think of *The Simpsons* as kind of my *Flintstones*, this would be my *Jetsons*.
— Matt Groening

Claudia Katz: Only, Fox was hesitant: "Rough Draft? We don't know..." It was clearly easier for them to hand the show over to the studio they were already working with. So, Matt set up a meeting at Fox for Rich, Gregg, and myself to meet with one of the executives. He basically said, "Look, I understand you're all like super creative and talented and that's great. And your work is excellent and you guys are probably like an A-plus. And I get it. But you guys don't have a proven track record. And to be honest, I think there's a slight chance of you failing and I'd rather not take that chance."

We leave the meeting crestfallen. And I really stewed on that. I figured we needed to show Matt what we can do, because he's the only one who can fight for us. I called Rich the next morning and he agreed. We had the original artwork, so we told Matt's producer we were doing a demo. "Great, great," he said. Over the next two weeks, we used Matt's drawings to put together a ninety-second animation demo. During this time, I talked to the producer and started getting a very weird vibe. So, I asked Rich Moore to call Matt and just tell him we have this demo. Rich calls Matt: "Did you know we did a demo for *Futurama?*" Matt expressed surprise, then tells us to come over so we can watch it together. We drive to Santa Monica, and Matt loves it. Then this slight look of horror comes over his face. He gets up and says, "I'll be right back" and leaves the room. We don't know what to think. Turns out Fox was giving the show to the other studio that afternoon. Matt stopped it. If we'd got there an hour later, we'd have been sunk.

Fortunately, we get the show. Then, Fox says, "You can't hire anybody from *The Simpsons, Family Guy,* or *King of the Hill,* even if they want to work with you." A whole list of rules we needed to abide by.

Matt Groening: We had a lot of blockades putting the show together. I was called by producers for one of the other shows threatening that if we stole any of their animators there'd be hell to pay. And the sad part was that so many animators working on some of these other shows really wanted to work with Rough Draft. There was also hesitation about working with Rough Draft Studios from some executives at Fox, since Rough Draft was run by animators. They compared it to "letting the inmates run the asylum." All this was just baffling to me. Later, I'd even hear rumors of the show falling apart and the animators not knowing what they're doing. It was weird, 'cause everything seemed to be running very well. Turns out you don't have to believe the gossip about yourself, if you know it's not true.

Claudia Katz: Later, when one Fox executive saw our work, he said, "This is probably the best-looking animated show we've ever done." He was very gracious about it, but we got off to an inauspicious start. It was the show that almost wasn't. To me, it's always bonded us with Matt in an extra-special way because, if he hadn't gone to bat for us, who knows what would have happened.

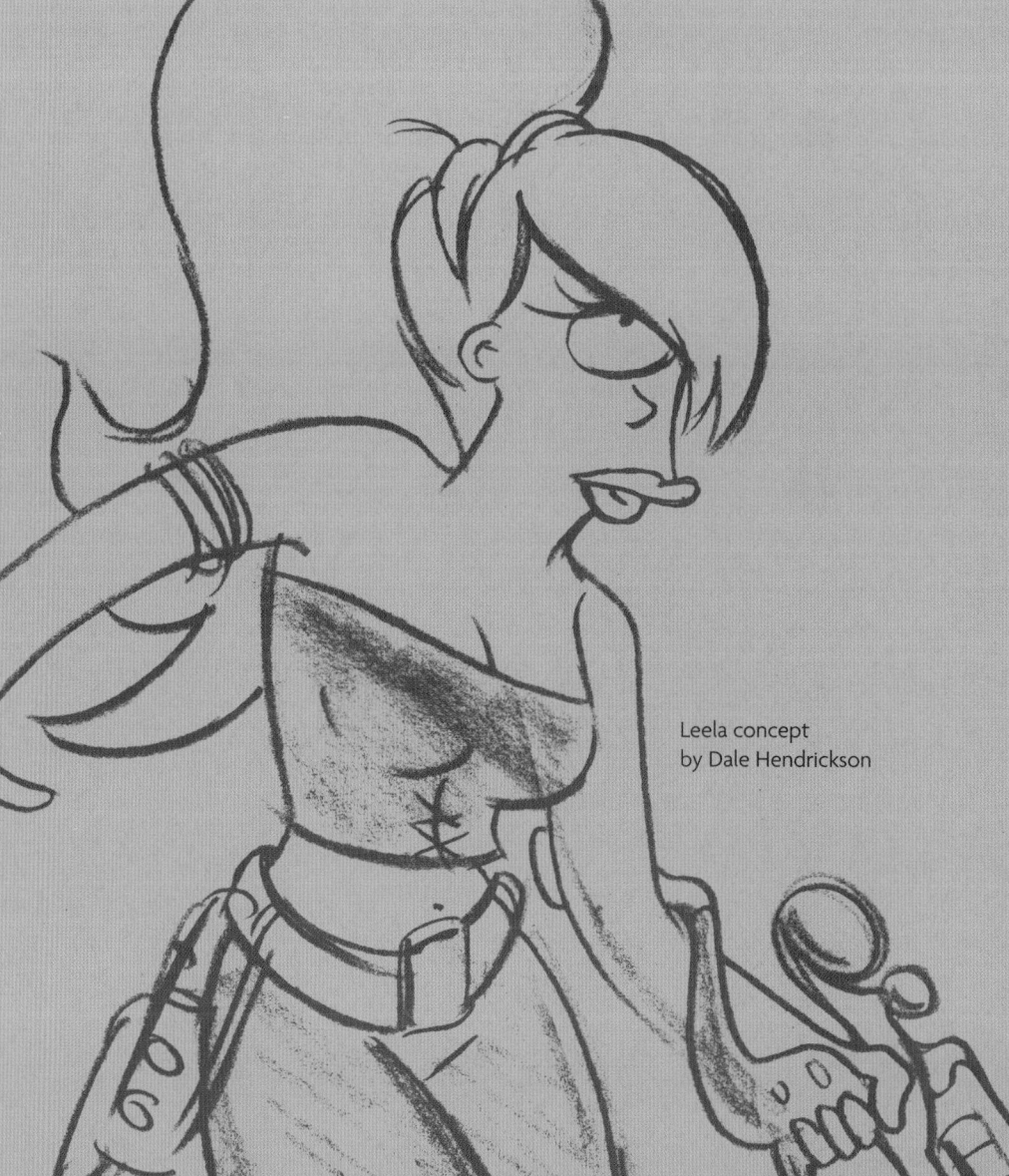

Leela concept
by Dale Hendrickson

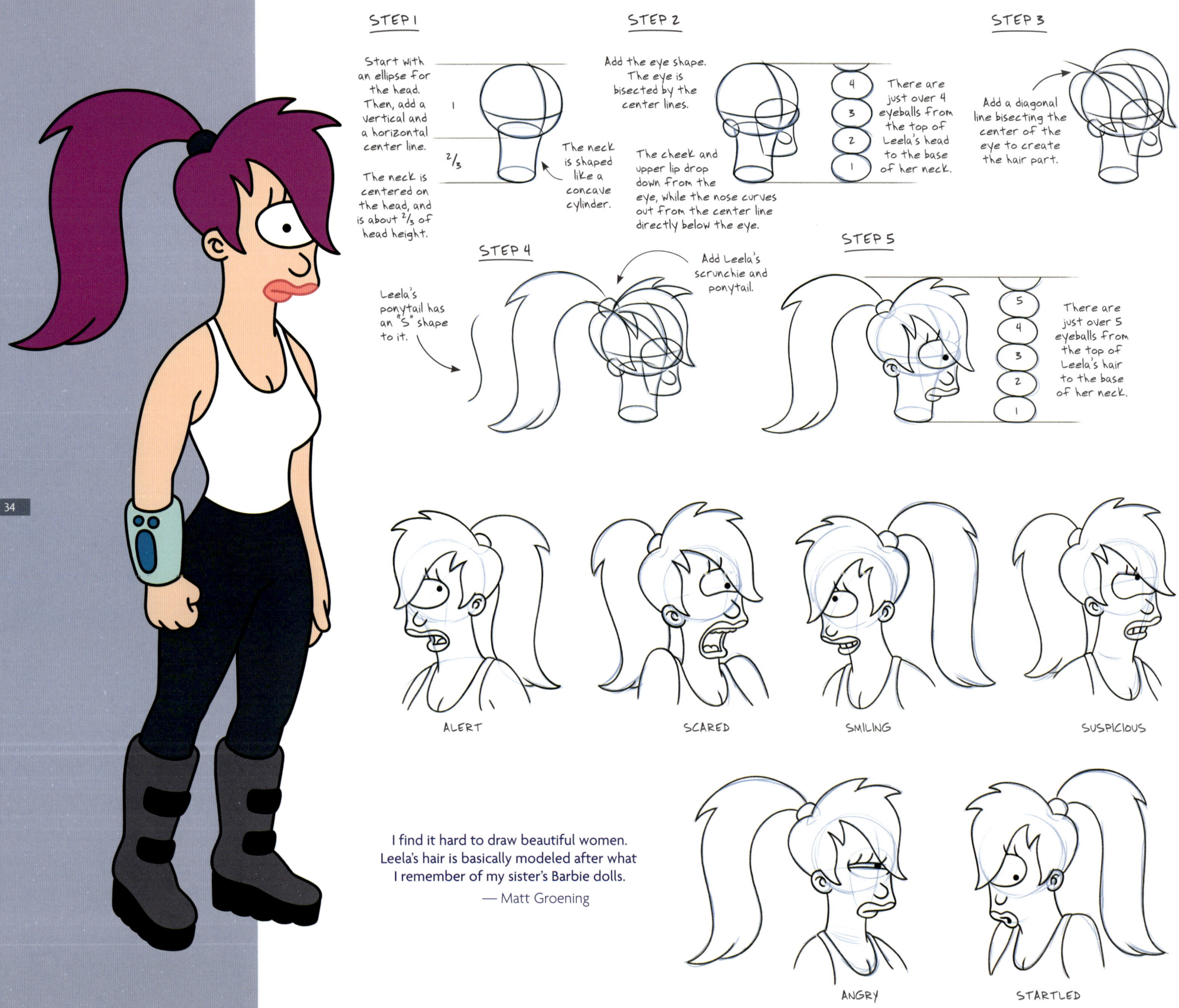

STEP 1

Start with an ellipse for the head. Then, add a vertical and a horizontal center line.

The neck is centered on the head, and is about ⅔ of head height.

1

⅔

The neck is shaped like a concave cylinder.

STEP 2

Add the eye shape. The eye is bisected by the center lines.

The cheek and upper lip drop down from the eye, while the nose curves out from the center line directly below the eye.

4
3
2
1

There are just over 4 eyeballs from the top of Leela's head to the base of her neck.

STEP 3

Add a diagonal line bisecting the center of the eye to create the hair part.

STEP 4

Leela's ponytail has an "S" shape to it.

Add Leela's scrunchie and ponytail.

STEP 5

5
4
3
2
1

There are just over 5 eyeballs from the top of Leela's hair to the base of her neck.

ALERT

SCARED

SMILING

SUSPICIOUS

I find it hard to draw beautiful women. Leela's hair is basically modeled after what I remember of my sister's Barbie dolls.

— Matt Groening

ANGRY

STARTLED

34

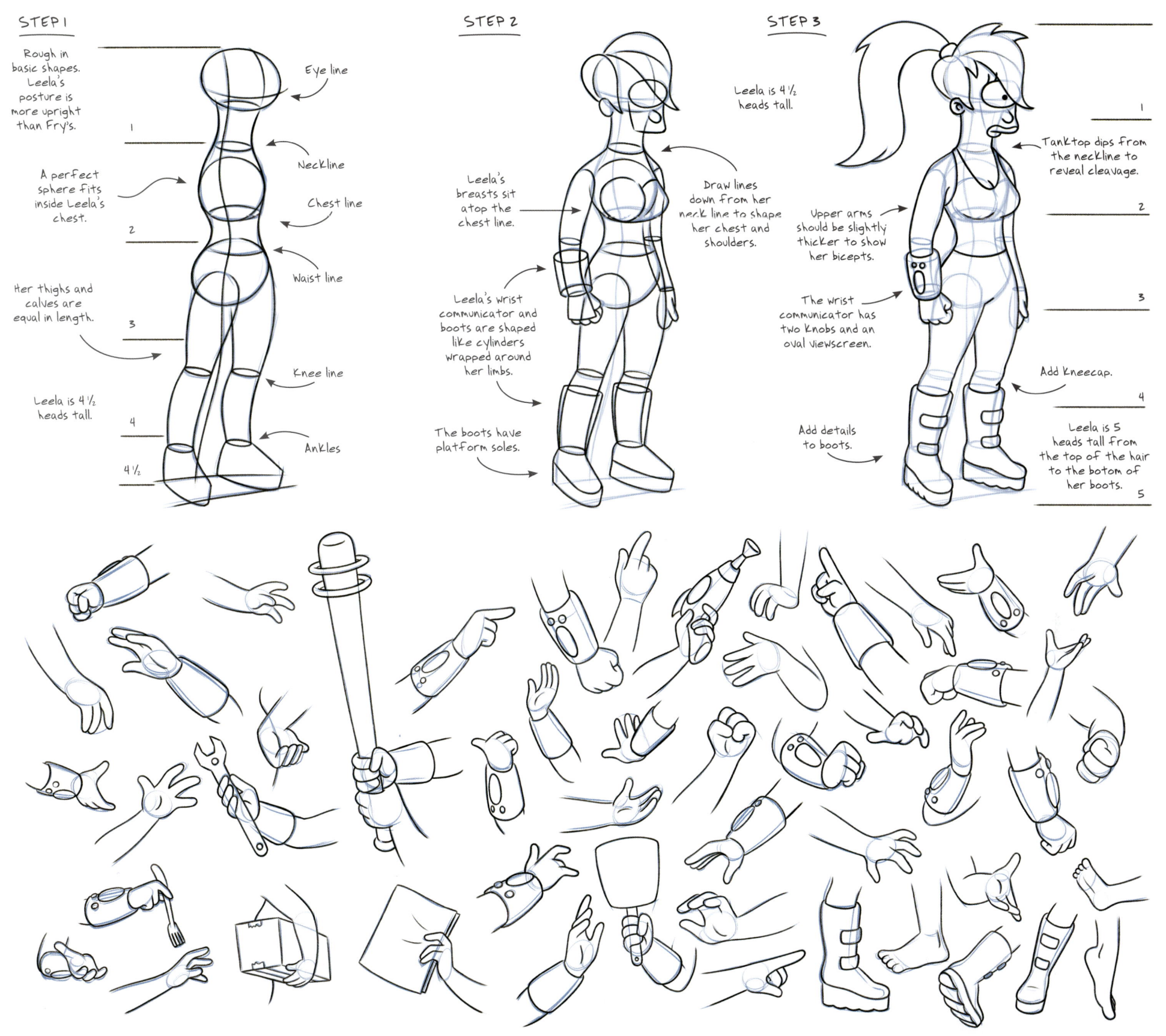

STEP 1

Rough in basic shapes. Leela's posture is more upright than Fry's.

A perfect sphere fits inside Leela's chest.

Her thighs and calves are equal in length.

Leela is 4 ½ heads tall.

Eye line

Neckline

Chest line

Waist line

Knee line

Ankles

1
2
3
4
4 ½

STEP 2

Leela is 4 ½ heads tall.

Leela's breasts sit atop the chest line.

Draw lines down from her neck line to shape her chest and shoulders.

Leela's wrist communicator and boots are shaped like cylinders wrapped around her limbs.

The boots have platform soles.

STEP 3

Tanktop dips from the neckline to reveal cleavage.

Upper arms should be slightly thicker to show her bicepts.

The wrist communicator has two knobs and an oval viewscreen.

Add details to boots.

Add Kneecap.

Leela is 5 heads tall from the top of the hair to the botom of her boots.

1
2
3
4
5

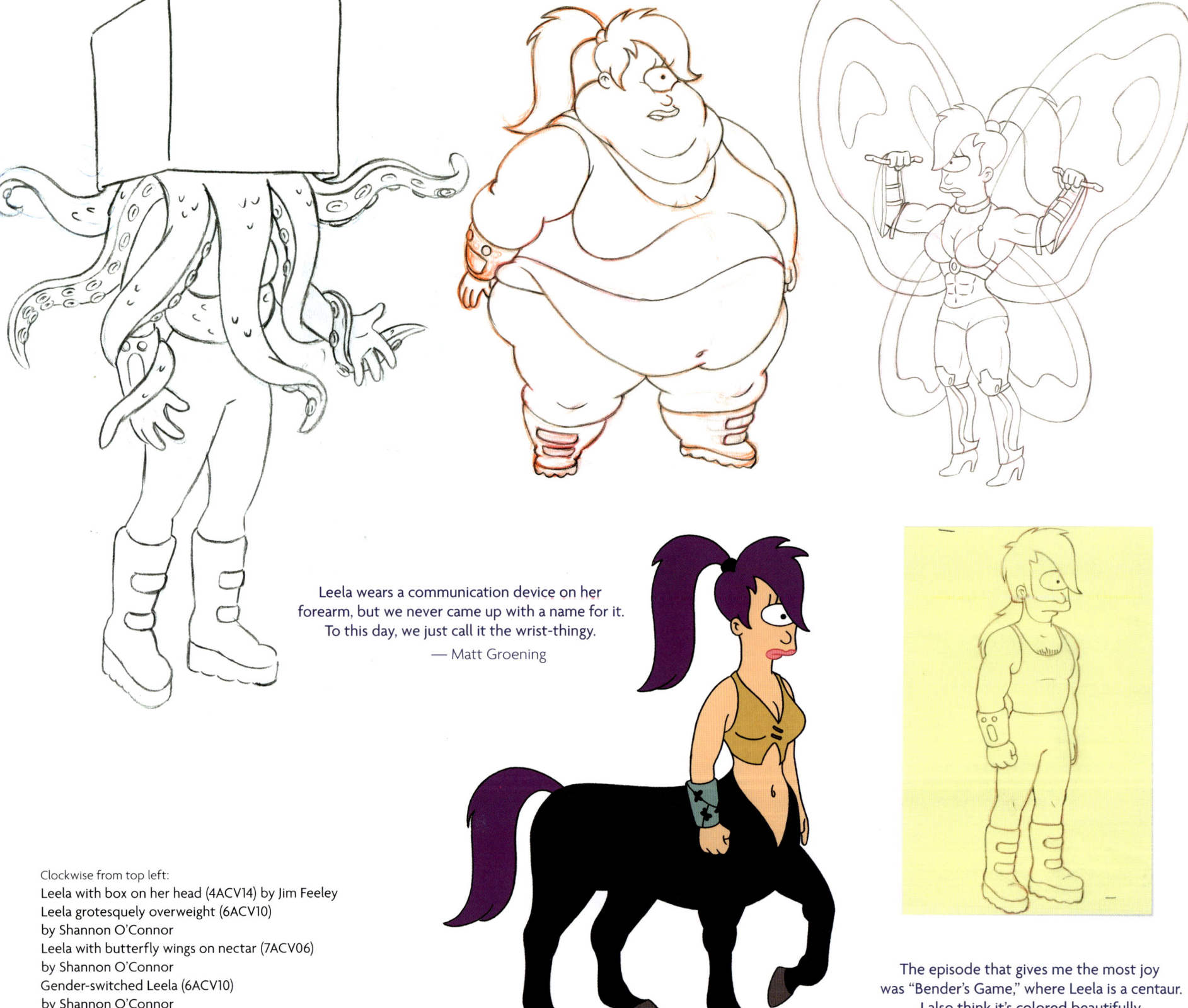

Leela wears a communication device on her forearm, but we never came up with a name for it. To this day, we just call it the wrist-thingy.

— Matt Groening

Clockwise from top left:
Leela with box on her head (4ACV14) by Jim Feeley
Leela grotesquely overweight (6ACV10)
by Shannon O'Connor
Leela with butterfly wings on nectar (7ACV06)
by Shannon O'Connor
Gender-switched Leela (6ACV10)
by Shannon O'Connor
Centaur Leela (5ACV11) by Jim Feeley

The episode that gives me the most joy was "Bender's Game," where Leela is a centaur. I also think it's colored beautifully.

— Samantha Harrison

36

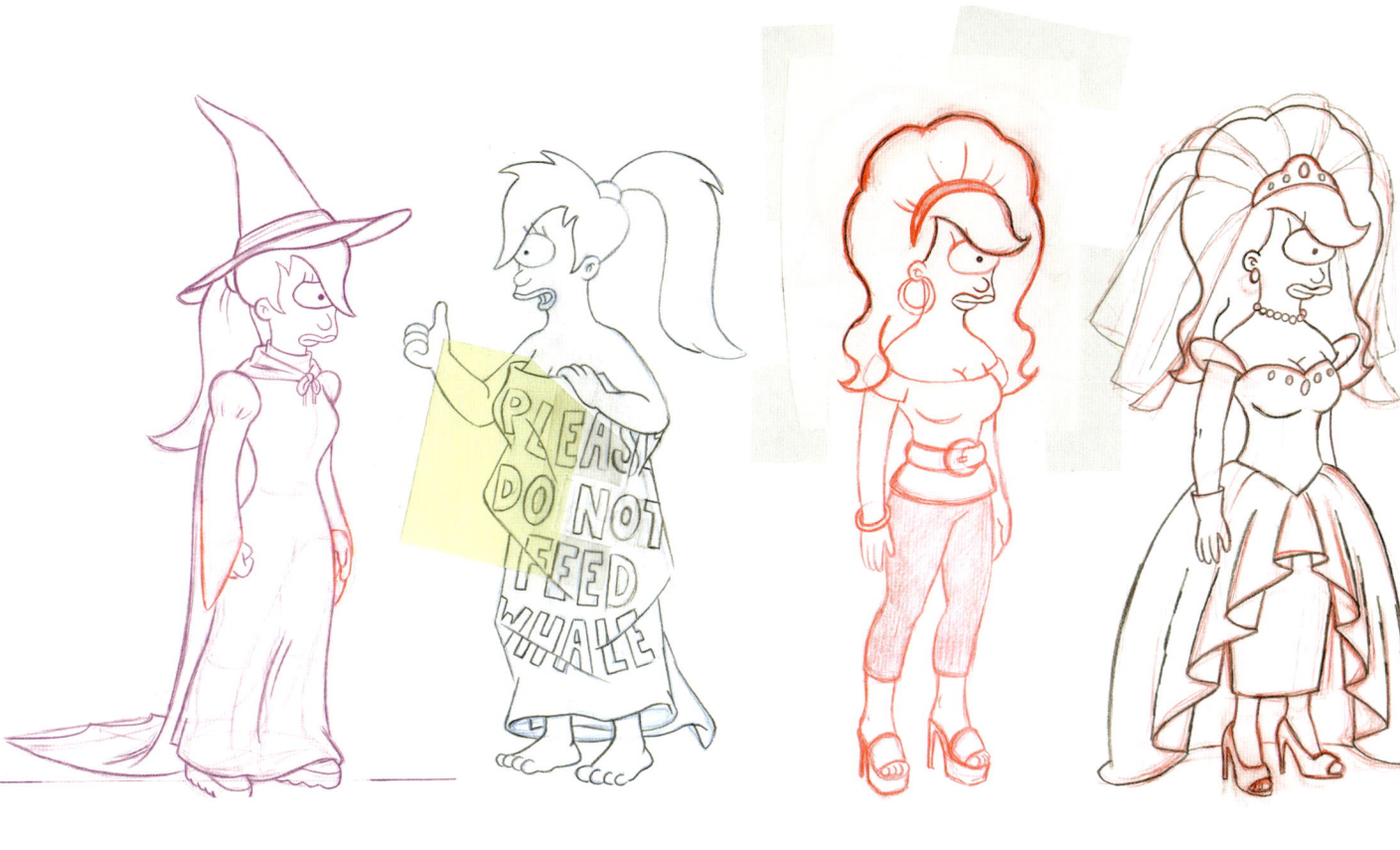

37

Top (from left to right):
Leela in witch's robe (3ACV08)
by Kevin M. Newman
Leela wrapped in banner (4ACV16)
by Jim Feeley
Leela as Peg Bundy (2ACV09)
by Anna Chambers
Leela in tacky wedding dress (2ACV09)
by Anna Chambers

Bottom (from left to right):
Building blocks Leela (6ACV01)
by Chad E. Cooper
Bobblehead Leela (4ACV15)
by Jim Feeley
Crude Leela robot (6ACV01)
by Shannon O'Connor
Leela as otter (3ACV02)
by Kevin M. Newman
Baby Leela (4ACV02)
by Jim Feeley
Leela as salmon (7ACV13)
by Shannon O'Connor

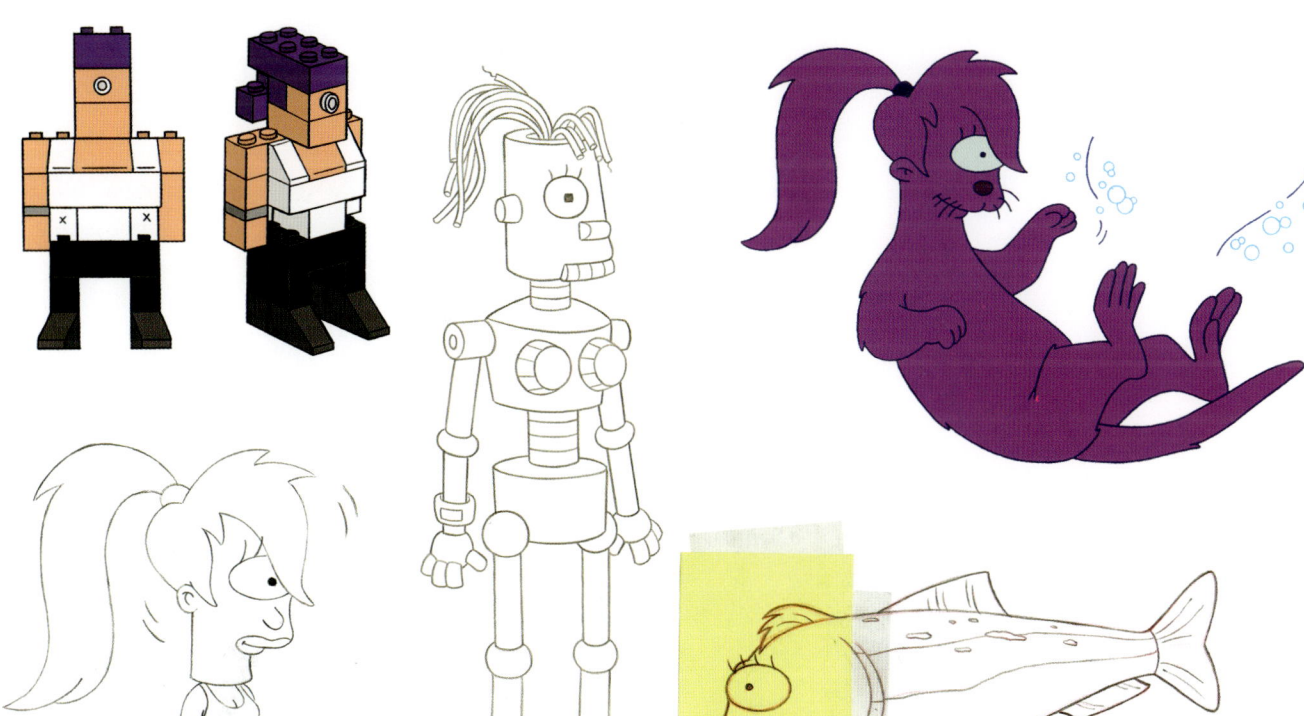

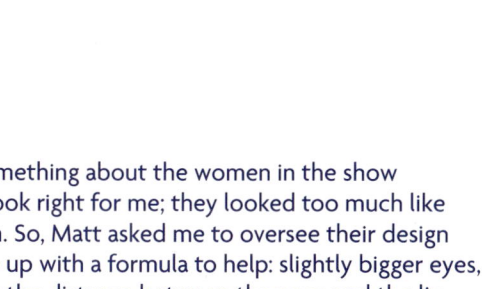

Something about the women in the show
didn't look right for me; they looked too much like
the men. So, Matt asked me to oversee their design
and I came up with a formula to help: slightly bigger eyes,
shorten the distance between the nose and the lip,
and give them cheekbones. Don't let the
contour of the face be a square.

— Mili Smythe

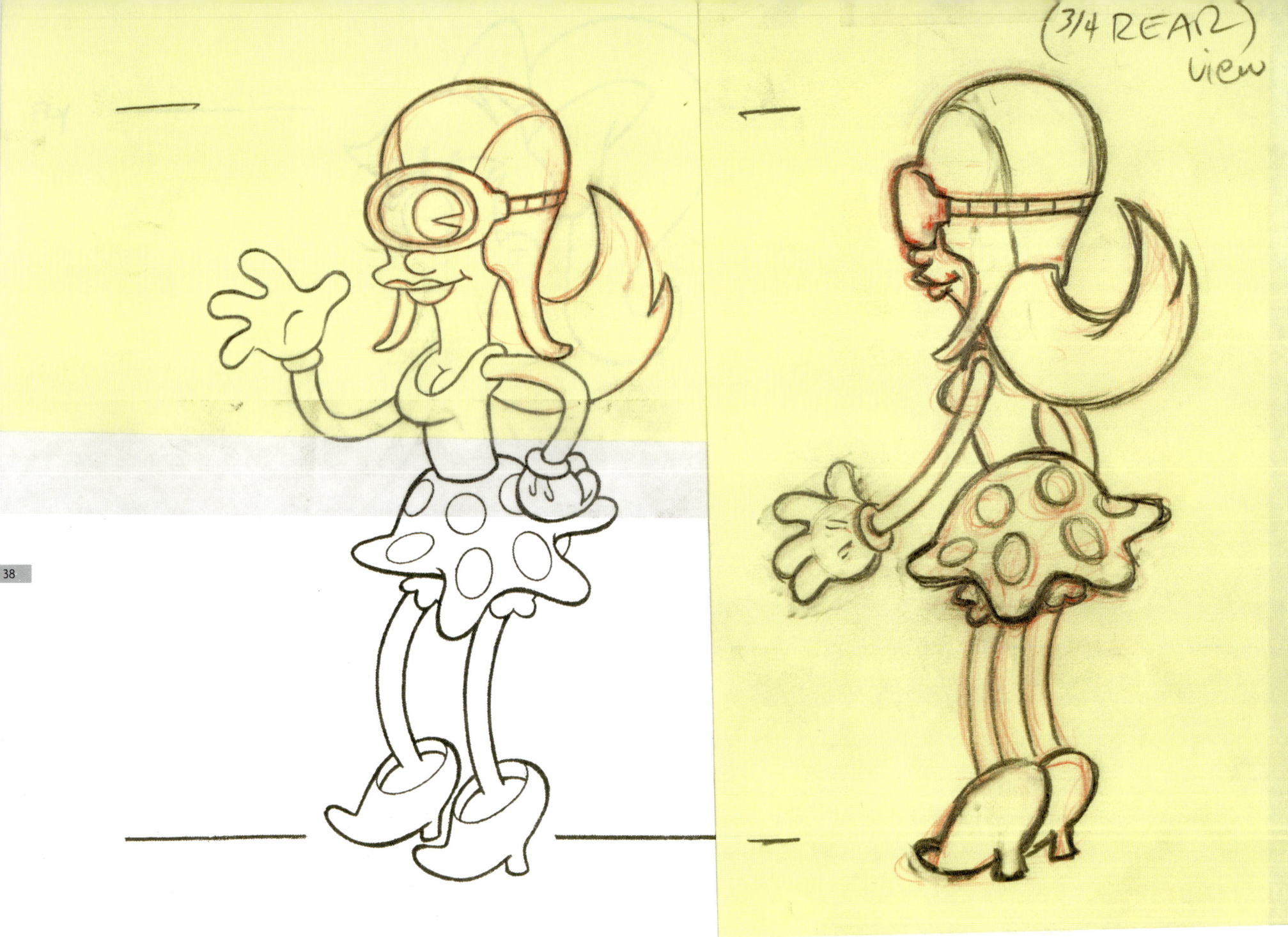

Futurama's characters live in a soft,
kind-of-lazy-posture world.
Except Leela—she's like an action hero in it.

— Peter Avanzino

Fleischer-style Leela (6ACV26) by Shannon O'Connor

Opposite:
Leela variations
by Yacine Elghorri, Jim Feeley, Eric Keyes,
Kevin M. Newman, Shannon O'Connor,
David Swift, and Gregg Vanzo

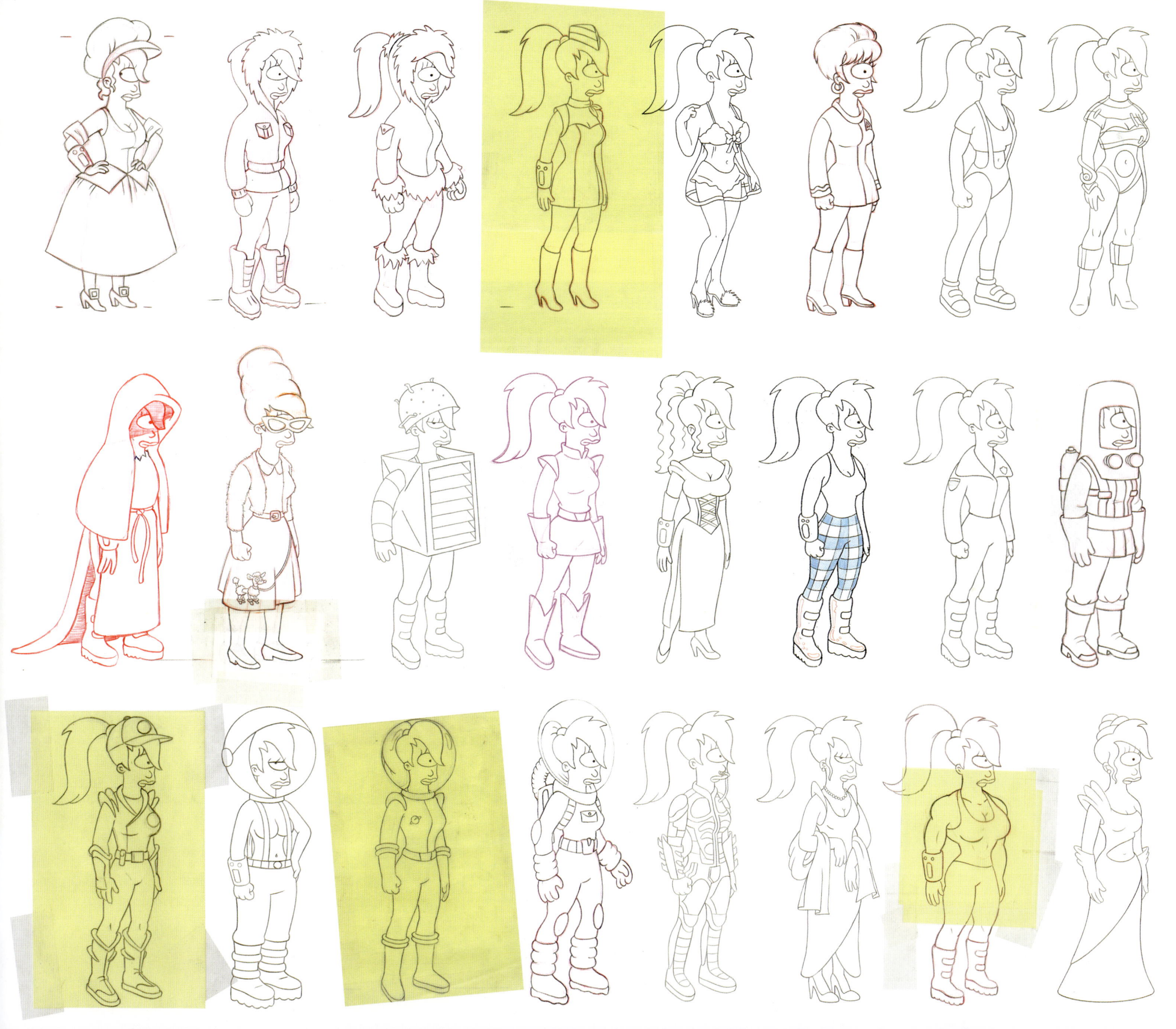

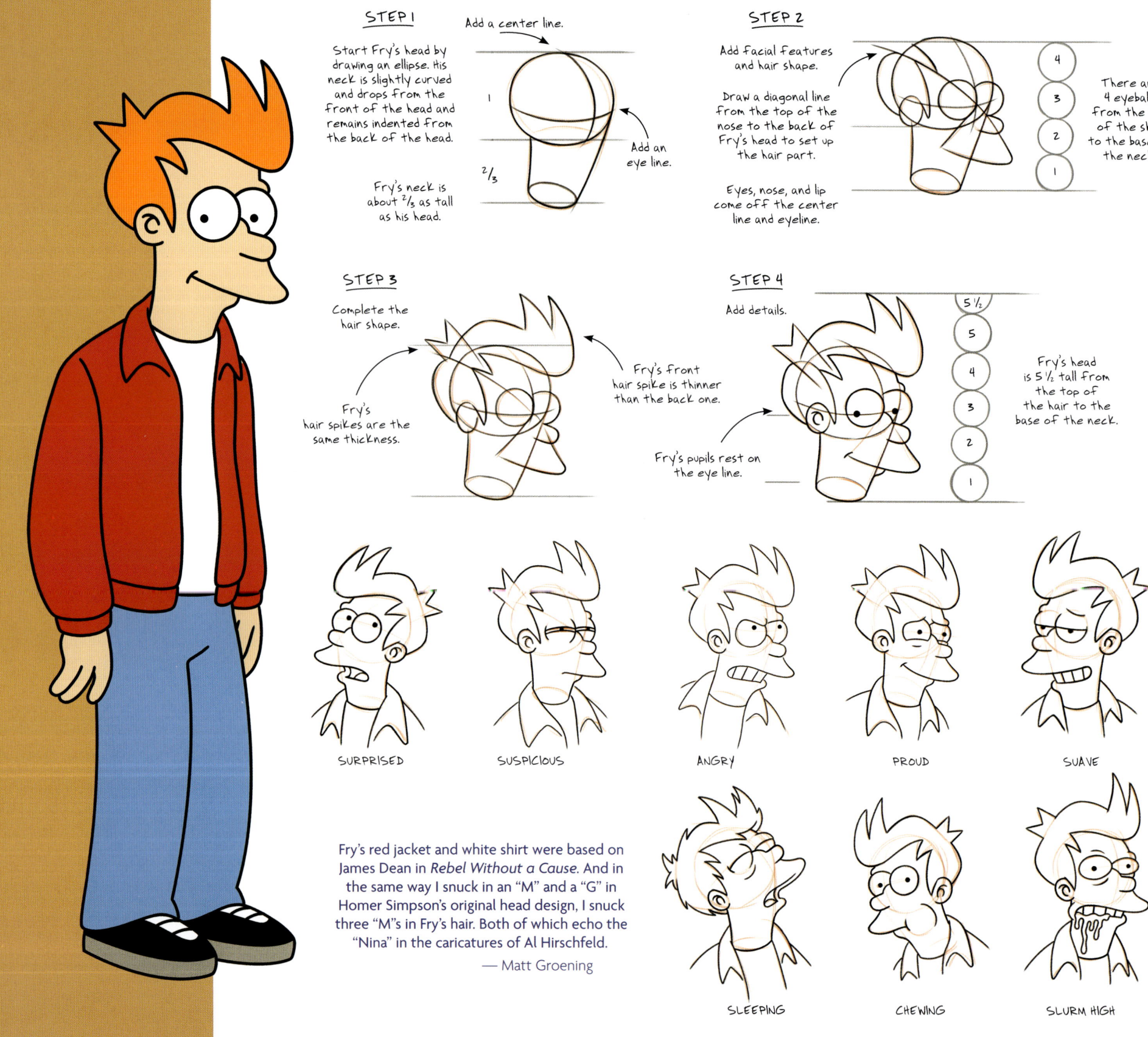

40

STEP 1

Start Fry's head by drawing an ellipse. His neck is slightly curved and drops from the front of the head and remains indented from the back of the head.

Add a center line.

Add an eye line.

1

2/3

Fry's neck is about 2/3 as tall as his head.

STEP 2

Add facial features and hair shape.

Draw a diagonal line from the top of the nose to the back of Fry's head to set up the hair part.

Eyes, nose, and lip come off the center line and eyeline.

4
3
2
1

There are 4 eyeballs from the top of the skull to the base of the neck.

STEP 3

Complete the hair shape.

Fry's hair spikes are the same thickness.

Fry's front hair spike is thinner than the back one.

STEP 4

Add details.

5 1/2
5
4
3
2
1

Fry's head is 5 1/2 tall from the top of the hair to the base of the neck.

Fry's pupils rest on the eye line.

SURPRISED

SUSPICIOUS

ANGRY

PROUD

SUAVE

Fry's red jacket and white shirt were based on James Dean in *Rebel Without a Cause*. And in the same way I snuck in an "M" and a "G" in Homer Simpson's original head design, I snuck three "M"s in Fry's hair. Both of which echo the "Nina" in the caricatures of Al Hirschfeld.

— Matt Groening

SLEEPING

CHEWING

SLURM HIGH

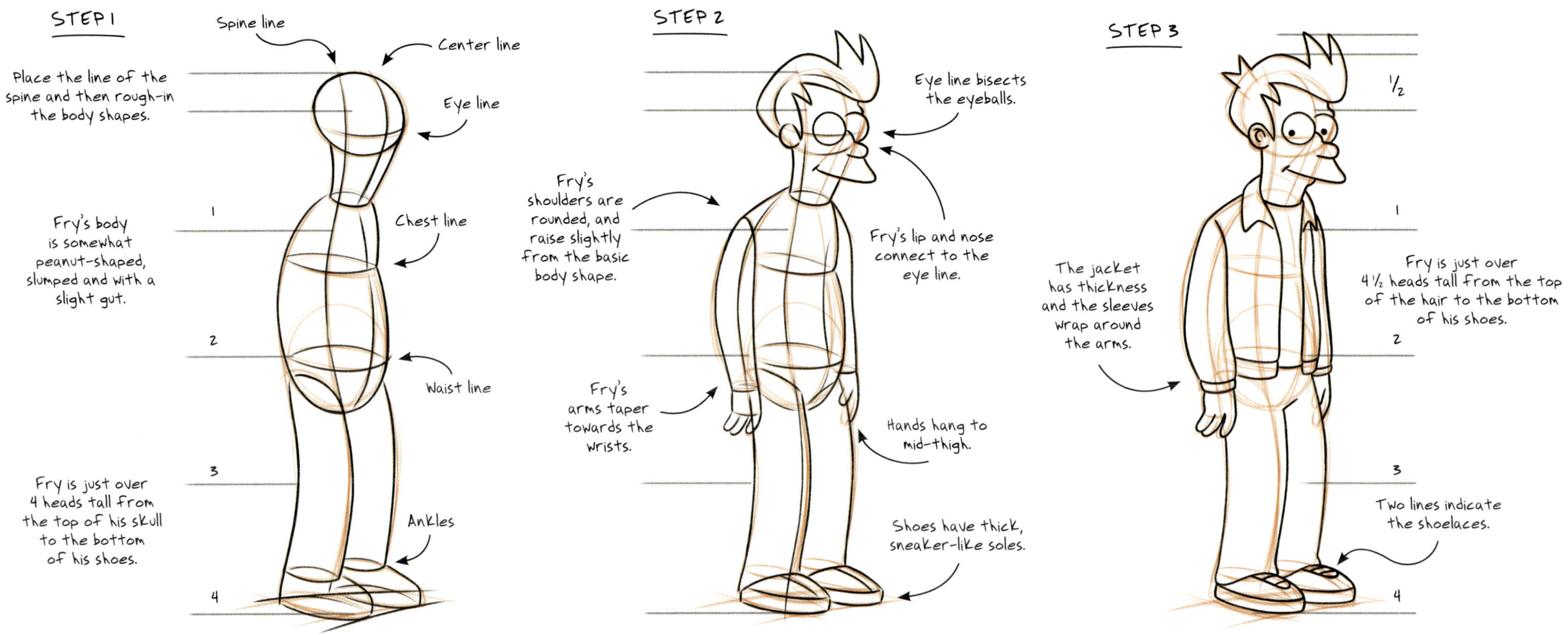

STEP 1

Place the line of the spine and then rough-in the body shapes.

Spine line

Center line

Eye line

Fry's body is somewhat peanut-shaped, slumped and with a slight gut.

Chest line

Waist line

Ankles

Fry is just over 4 heads tall from the top of his skull to the bottom of his shoes.

1

2

3

4

STEP 2

Eye line bisects the eyeballs.

Fry's shoulders are rounded, and raise slightly from the basic body shape.

Fry's lip and nose connect to the eye line.

Fry's arms taper towards the wrists.

Hands hang to mid-thigh.

Shoes have thick, sneaker-like soles.

STEP 3

The jacket has thickness and the sleeves wrap around the arms.

½

Fry is just over 4½ heads tall from the top of the hair to the bottom of his shoes.

1

2

Two lines indicate the shoelaces.

3

4

41

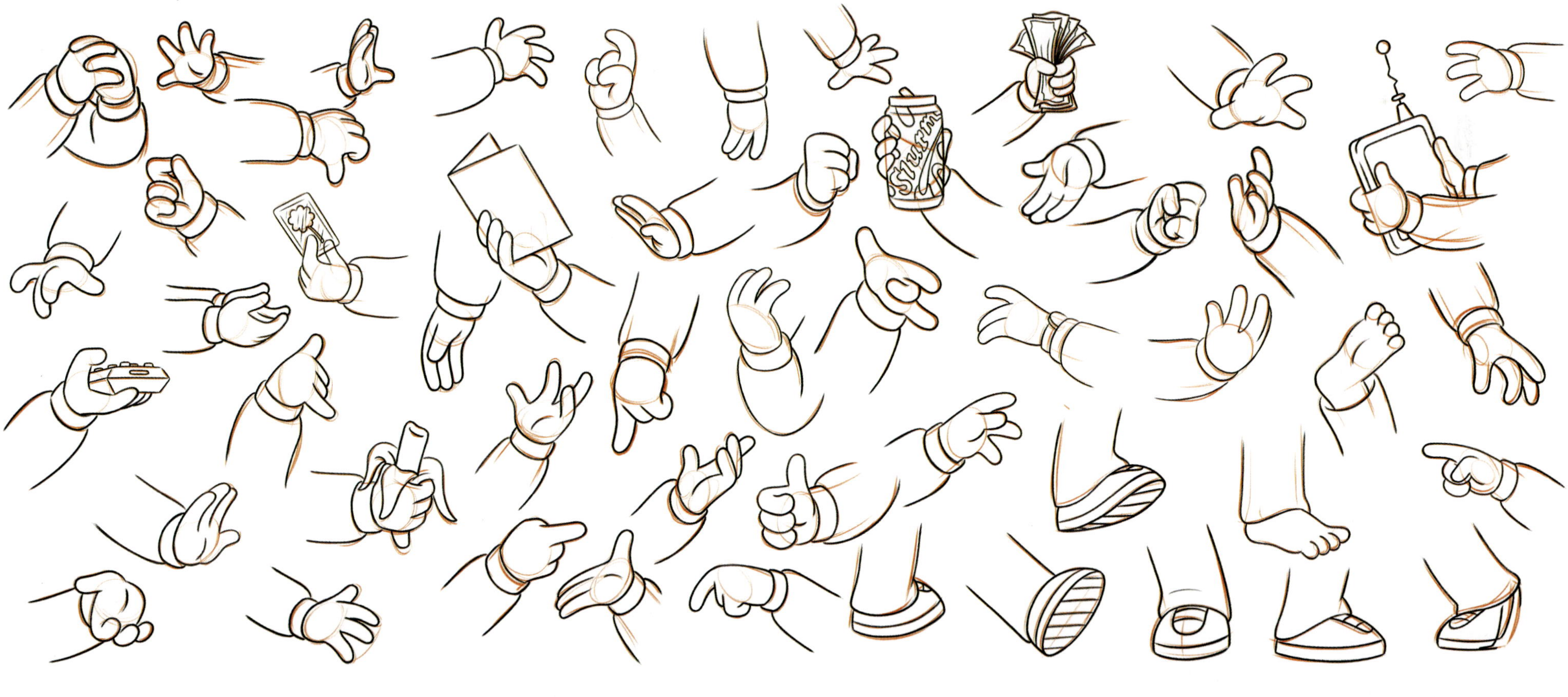

Top (from left to right):
Fry as otter (3ACV02) by Eric Keyes
Fry as dragon (5ACV12) by Karapet Keroglyan

Center:
Fry with elephant trunk (4ACV17) by Shannon O'Connor

Bottom (from left to right):
30ft-tall Fry (5ACV11) by Shannon O'Connor
Fry with pelvic cast (3ACV01) by Eric Keyes
X-Ray view Fry (2ACV11) by Eric Keyes

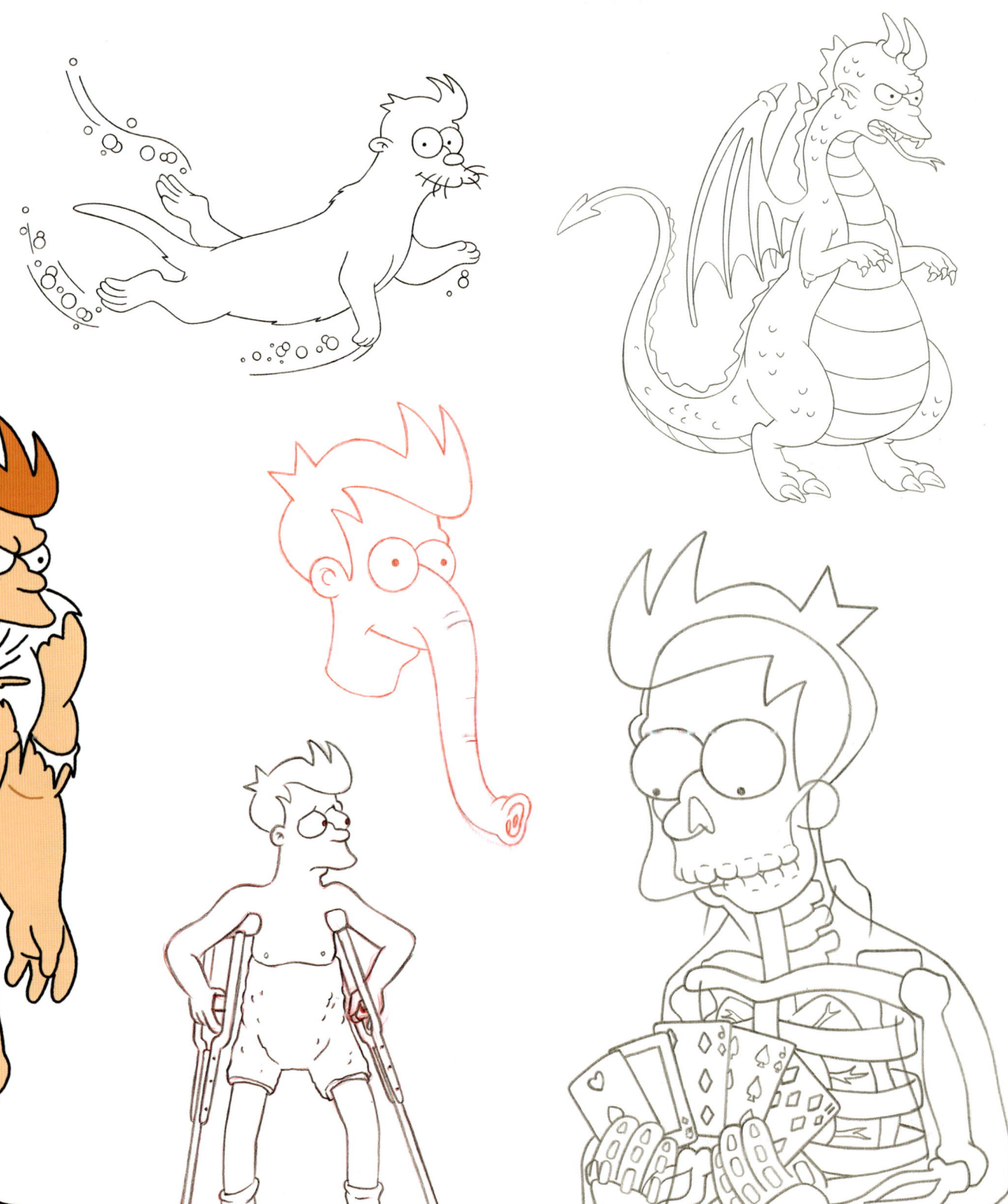

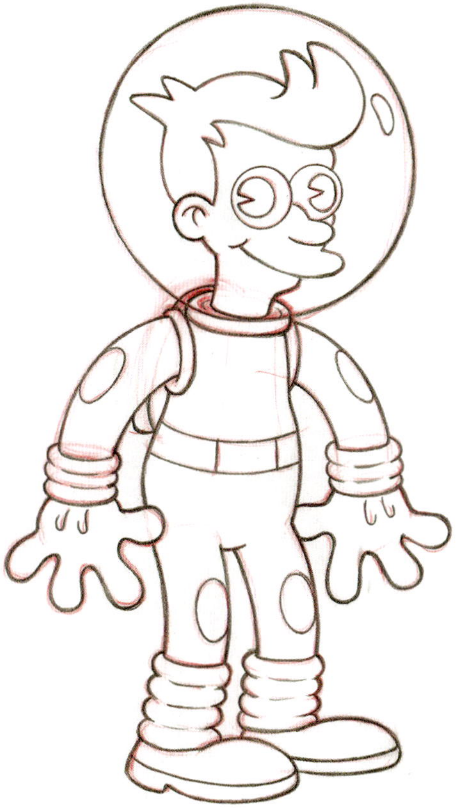

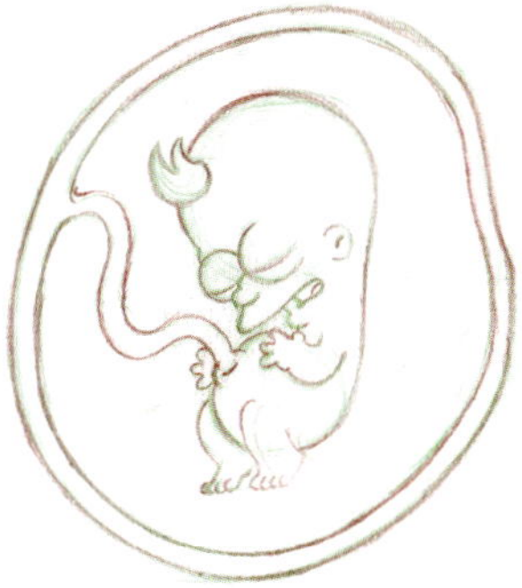

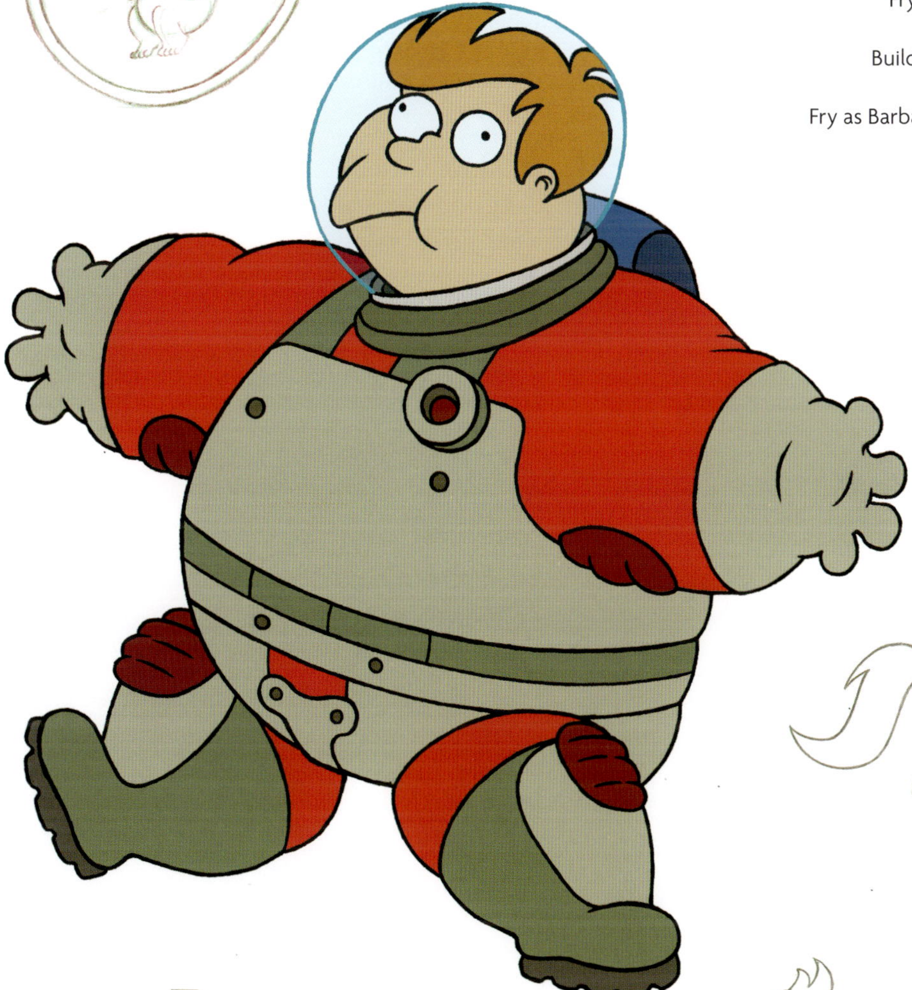

Top (from left to right):
Fleischer-style Fry (6ACV26) by Shannon O'Connor
Fetal Fry (4ACV09) by Jim Feeley
Fry in bulged space suit (7ACV07) by Shannon O'Connor

Bottom (from left to right):
Fry with tentacle through his mouth (5ACV07)
by Shannon O'Connor
Building blocks Fry (4ACV09) by Chad E. Cooper
Fry as finch (7ACV07) by Karapet Keroglyan
Fry as Barbarella pinup (6ACV20) by Karapet Keroglyan

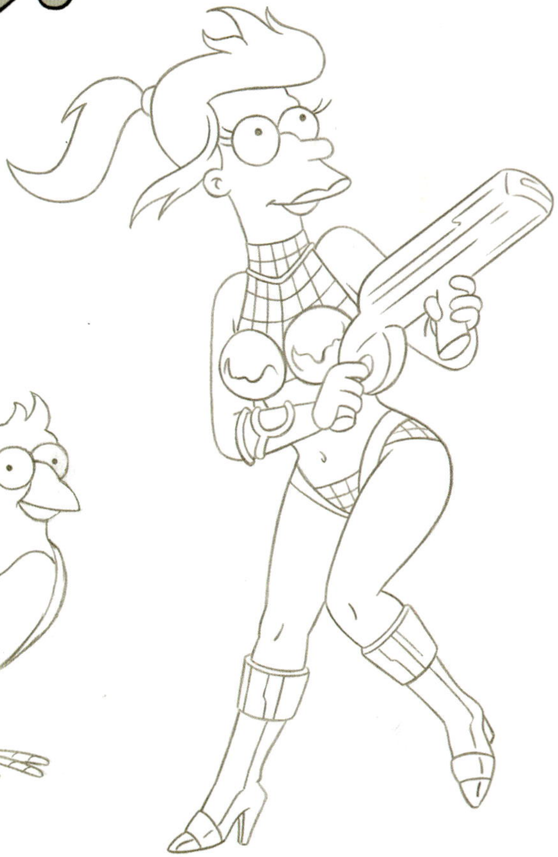

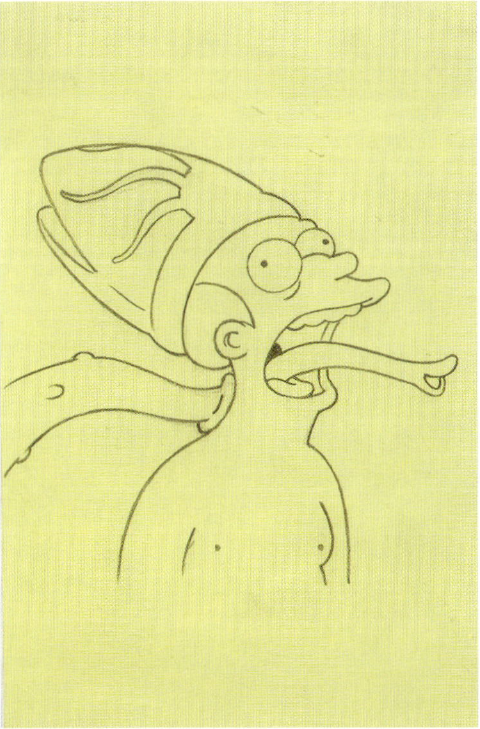

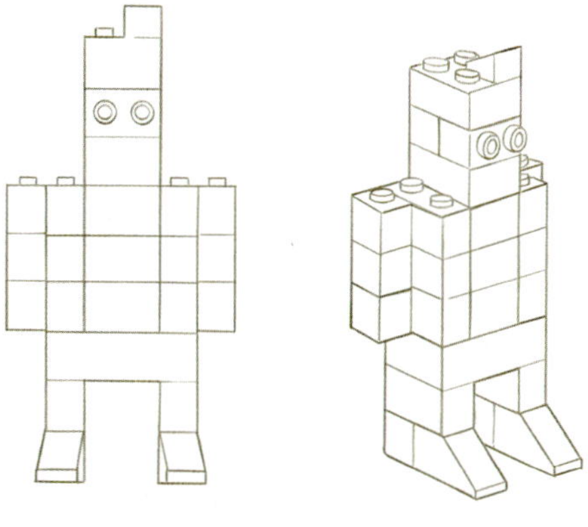

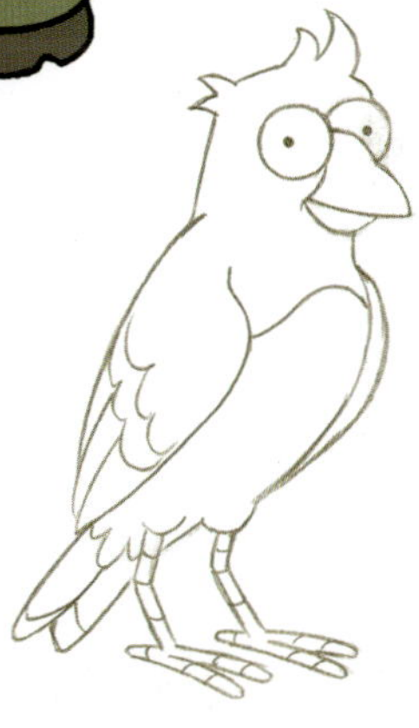

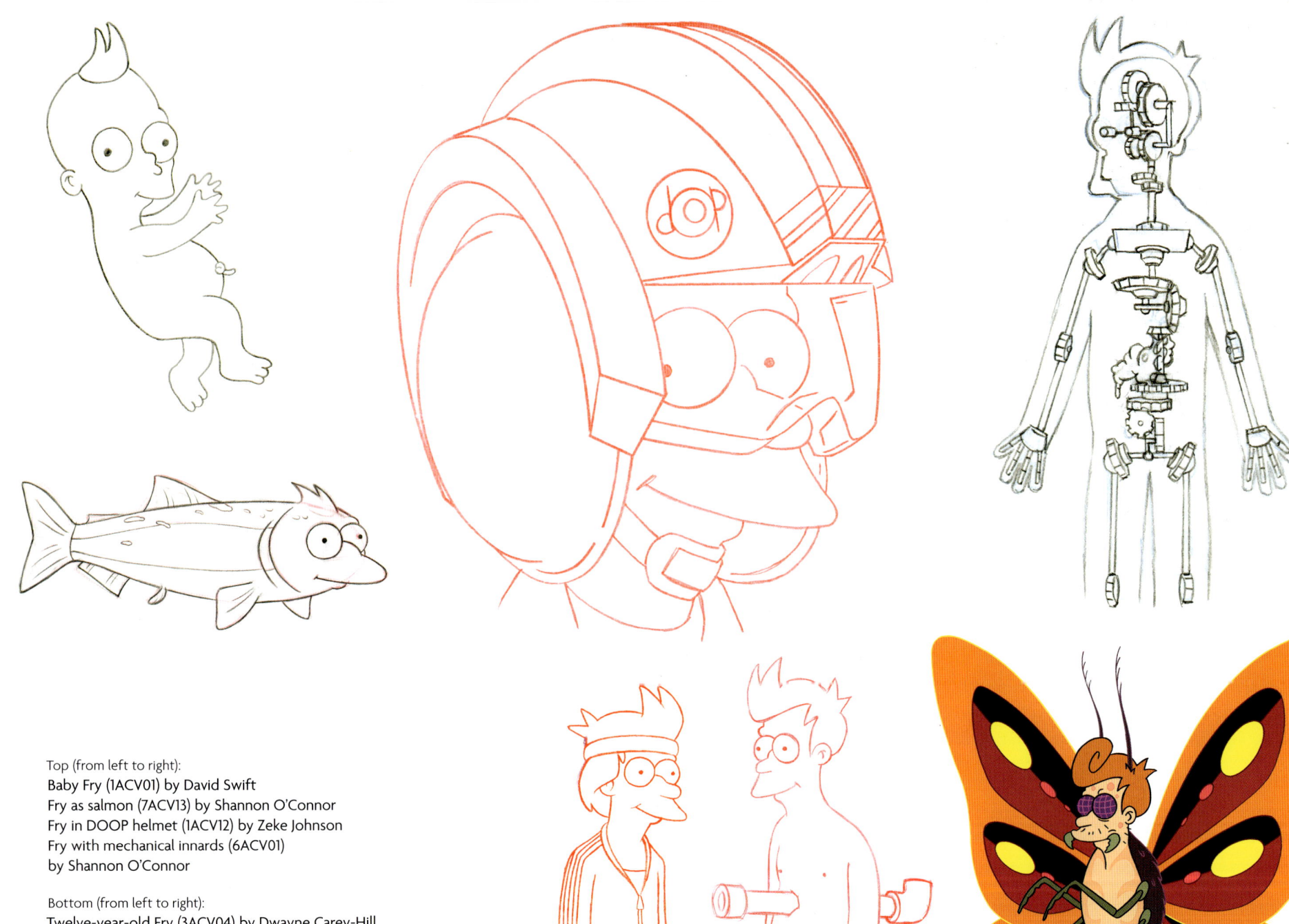

Top (from left to right):
Baby Fry (1ACV01) by David Swift
Fry as salmon (7ACV13) by Shannon O'Connor
Fry in DOOP helmet (1ACV12) by Zeke Johnson
Fry with mechanical innards (6ACV01)
by Shannon O'Connor

Bottom (from left to right):
Twelve-year-old Fry (3ACV04) by Dwayne Carey-Hill
Fry impaled by pipe (3ACV02) by Eric Keyes
Fry as giant butterfly (7ACV06) by Karapet Keroglyan

Opposite:
Fry variations by Yacine Elghorri, Jim Feeley,
Bret Haaland, Karapet Keroglyan, Eric Keyes,
Kevin M. Newman, Shannon O'Connor, David Swift,
Gregg Vanzo, and Jose Zelaya

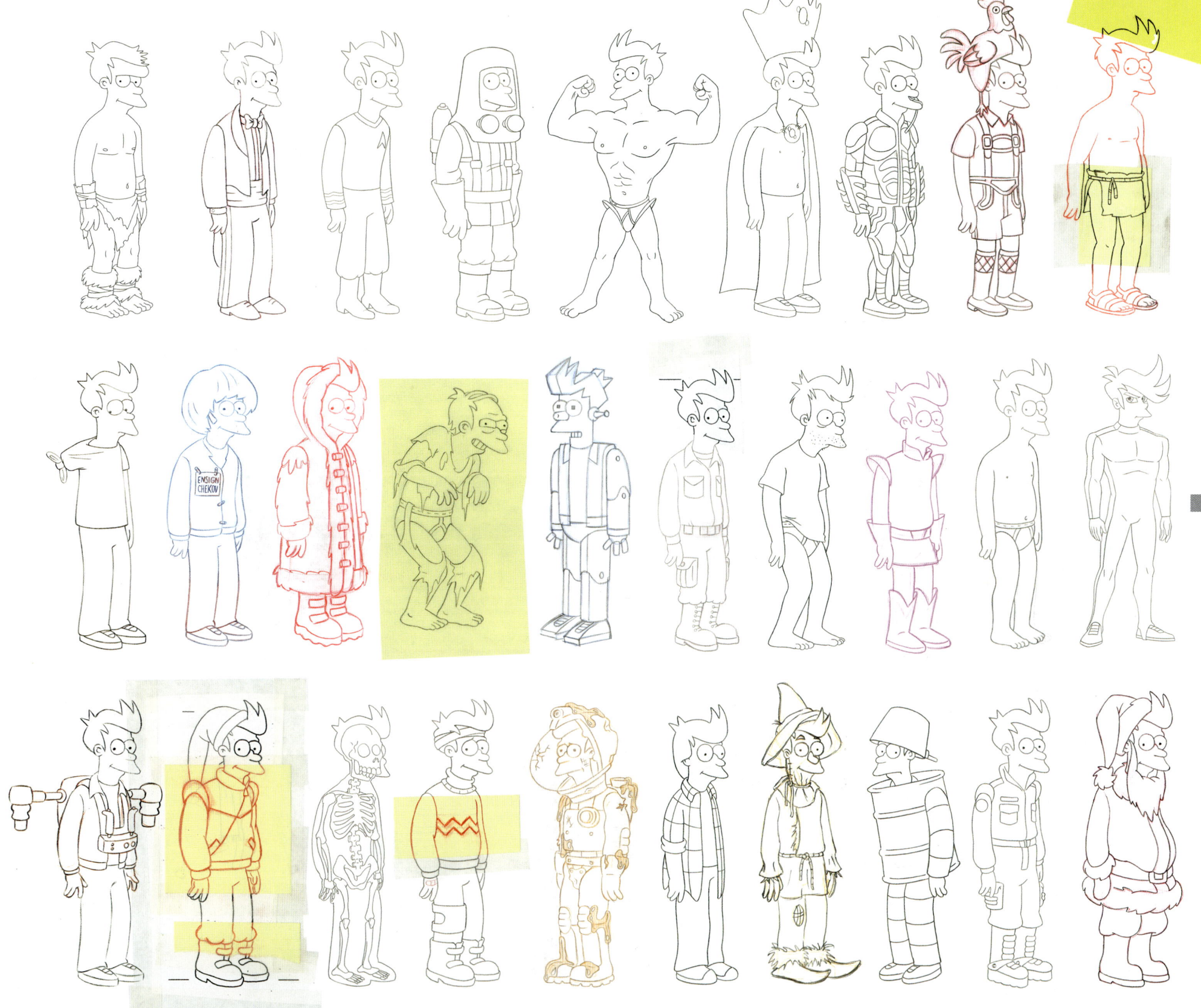

45

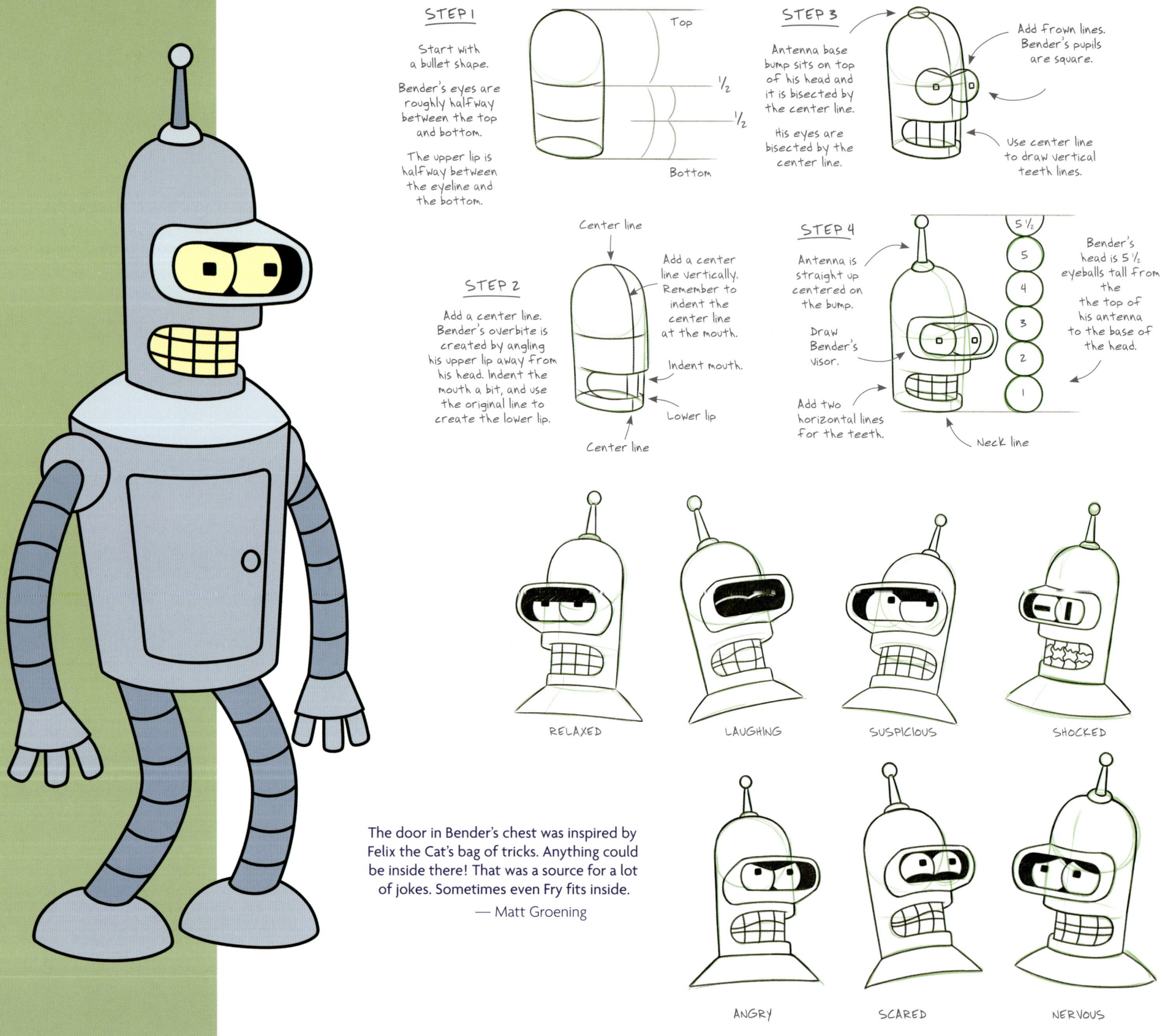

STEP 1

Start with a bullet shape.

Bender's eyes are roughly halfway between the top and bottom.

The upper lip is halfway between the eyeline and the bottom.

Top

½

½

Bottom

STEP 3

Antenna base bump sits on top of his head and it is bisected by the center line.

His eyes are bisected by the center line.

Add frown lines. Bender's pupils are square.

Use center line to draw vertical teeth lines.

STEP 2

Add a center line. Bender's overbite is created by angling his upper lip away from his head. Indent the mouth a bit, and use the original line to create the lower lip.

Center line

Add a center line vertically. Remember to indent the center line at the mouth.

Indent mouth.

Lower lip

Center line

STEP 4

Antenna is straight up centered on the bump.

Draw Bender's visor.

Add two horizontal lines for the teeth.

Neck line

5 ½
5
4
3
2
1

Bender's head is 5 ½ eyeballs tall from the the top of his antenna to the base of the head.

RELAXED

LAUGHING

SUSPICIOUS

SHOCKED

The door in Bender's chest was inspired by Felix the Cat's bag of tricks. Anything could be inside there! That was a source for a lot of jokes. Sometimes even Fry fits inside.

— Matt Groening

ANGRY

SCARED

NERVOUS

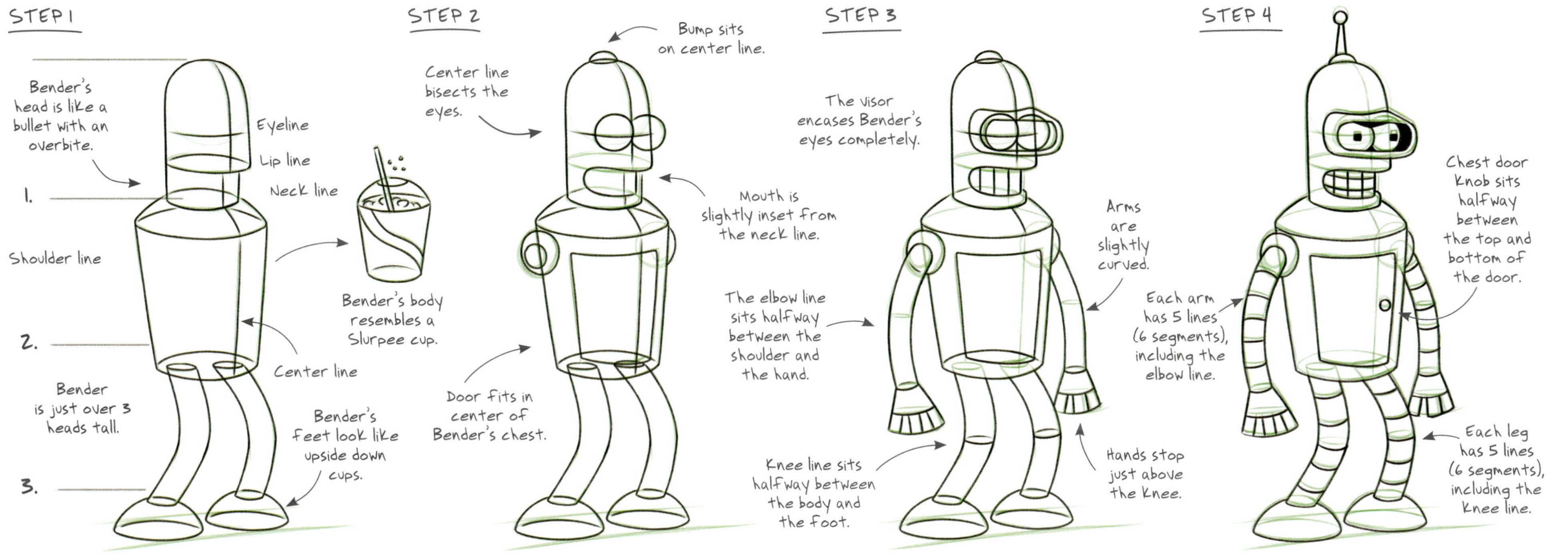

STEP 1

Bender's head is like a bullet with an overbite.

Eyeline

Lip line

Neck line

1.

Shoulder line

2.

Bender is just over 3 heads tall.

3.

Center line

Bender's feet look like upside down cups.

Bender's body resembles a Slurpee cup.

STEP 2

Bump sits on center line.

Center line bisects the eyes.

Mouth is slightly inset from the neck line.

The elbow line sits halfway between the shoulder and the hand.

Door fits in center of Bender's chest.

Knee line sits halfway between the body and the foot.

STEP 3

The visor encases Bender's eyes completely.

Arms are slightly curved.

Hands stop just above the knee.

STEP 4

Chest door knob sits halfway between the top and bottom of the door.

Each arm has 5 lines (6 segments), including the elbow line.

Each leg has 5 lines (6 segments), including the knee line.

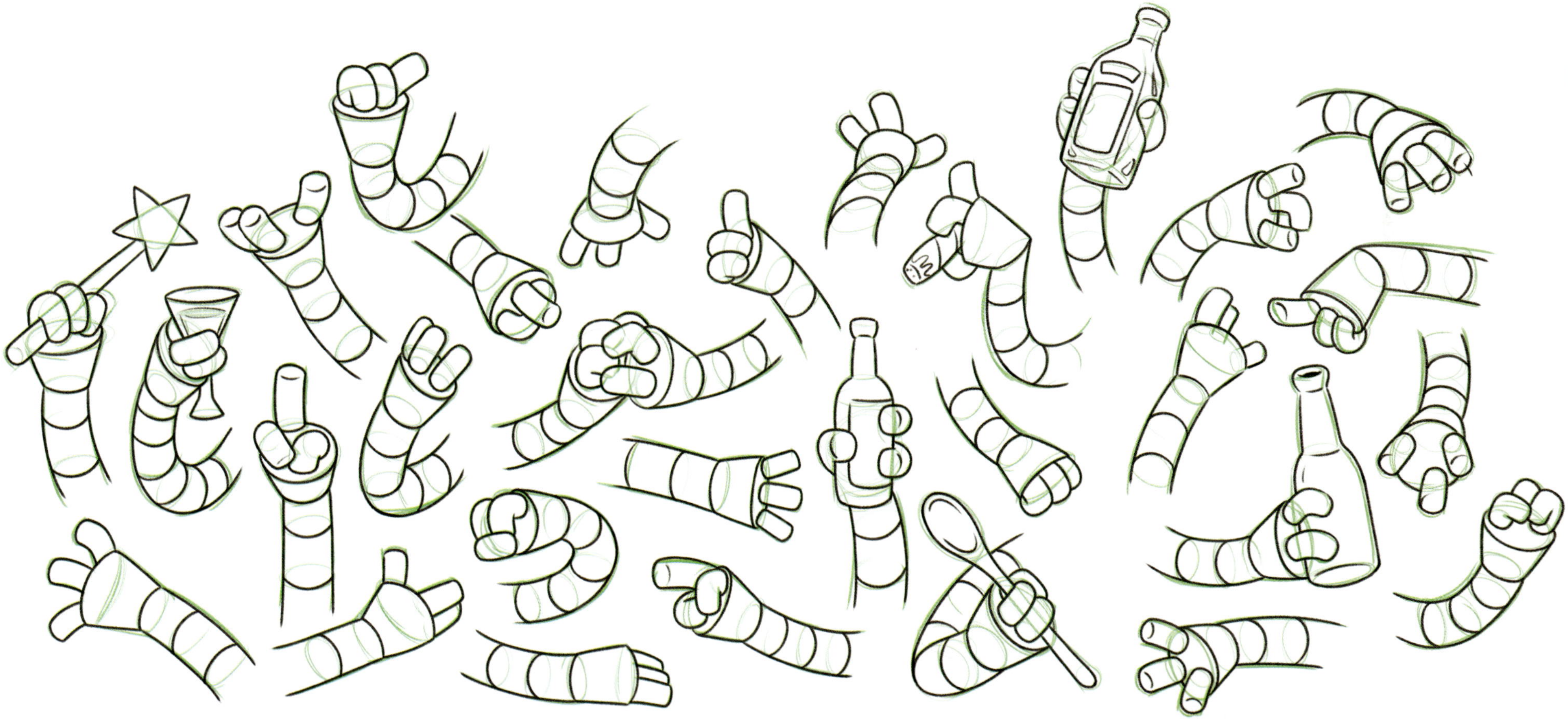

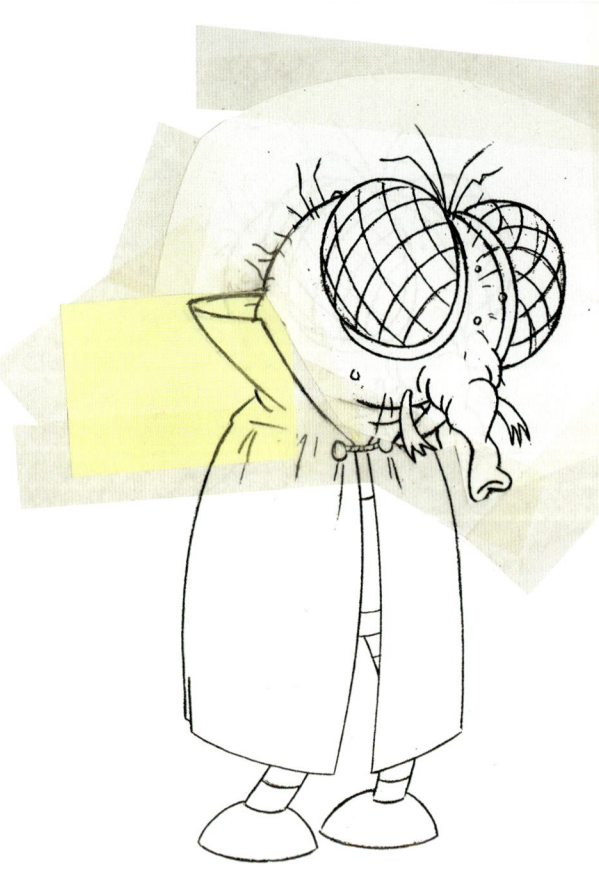

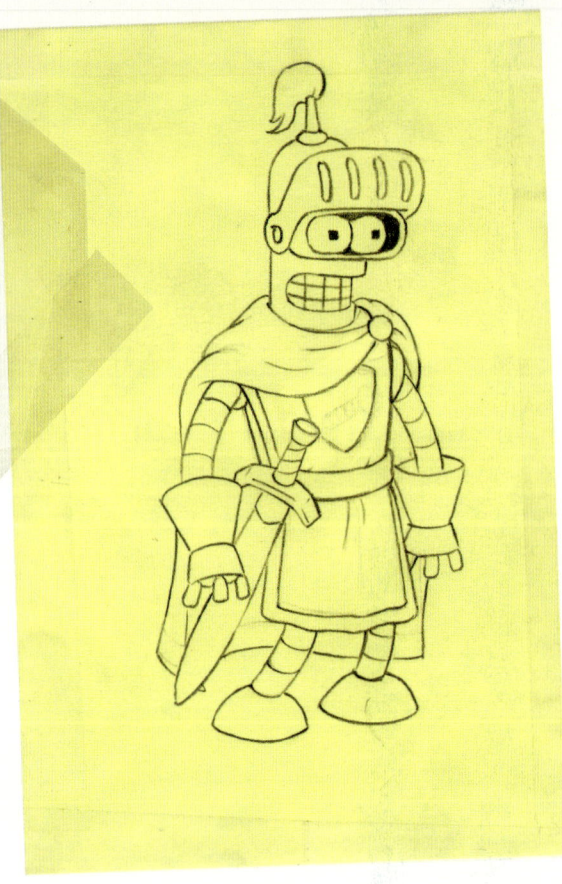

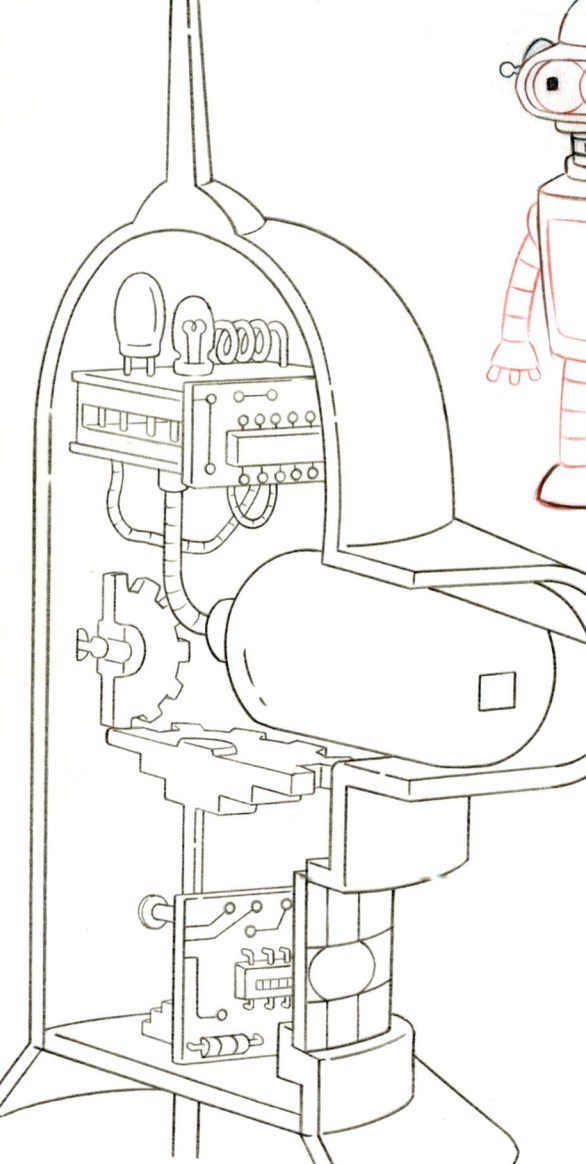

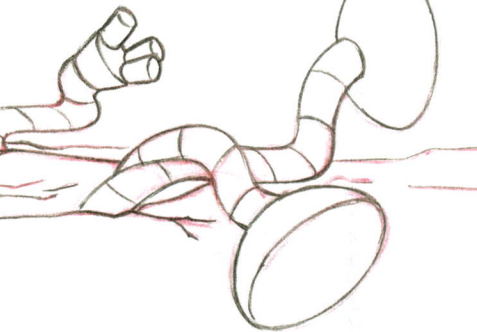

I love working with Bender and Zoidberg. They're both very interesting physically. So much animation comes down from vaudeville and there's a lot of rough-and-tumble Three Stooges physical comedy with those two. Inventing crazy dances for Bender to do is always fun.

— Crystal Chesney-Thompson

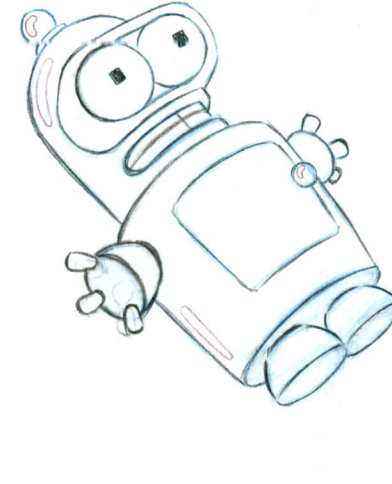

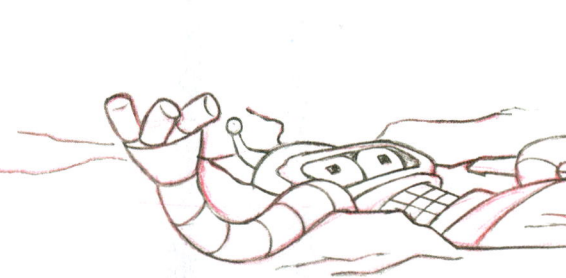

Top (from left to right):
Bender in fly mask (2ACV19) by Kevin M. Newman
Bender as knight (5ACV11) by Karapet Keroglyan
Little Bender (4ACV09) by Jose Zelaya

Middle:
Baby Bender (4ACV09) by Jose Zelaya
Cross section of Bender's head (6ACV18). Artist unknown.

Bottom:
Crushed Bender (7ACV08) by Shannon O'Connor

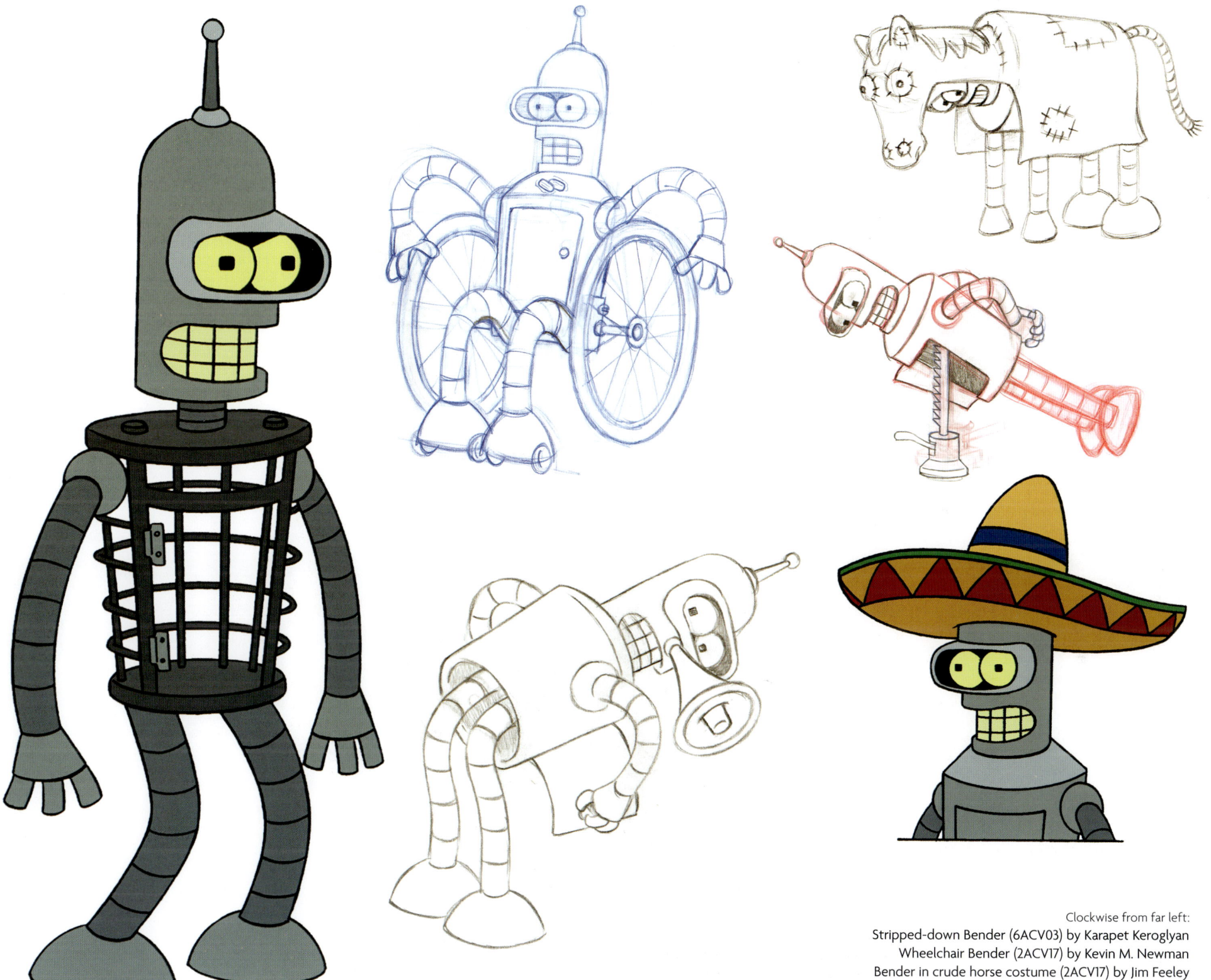

Clockwise from far left:
Stripped-down Bender (6ACV03) by Karapet Keroglyan
Wheelchair Bender (2ACV17) by Kevin M. Newman
Bender in crude horse costume (2ACV17) by Jim Feeley
Bender with jack in chest (2ACV08) by Anna Chambers
Bender with sombrero (6ACV06) by Jose Zelaya
Bender missing ass plate and with horn nose (4ACV18) by Jim Feeley

Bender as sports car (2ACV03) by DJ Kang

Opposite:
Bender variations by Anna Chambers, Jim Feeley, Peter Gomez, Bret Haaland, Ron Hughart, Karapet Keroglyan, Eric Keyes, Kevin M. Newman, Shannon O'Connor, David Swift, and Jose Zelaya

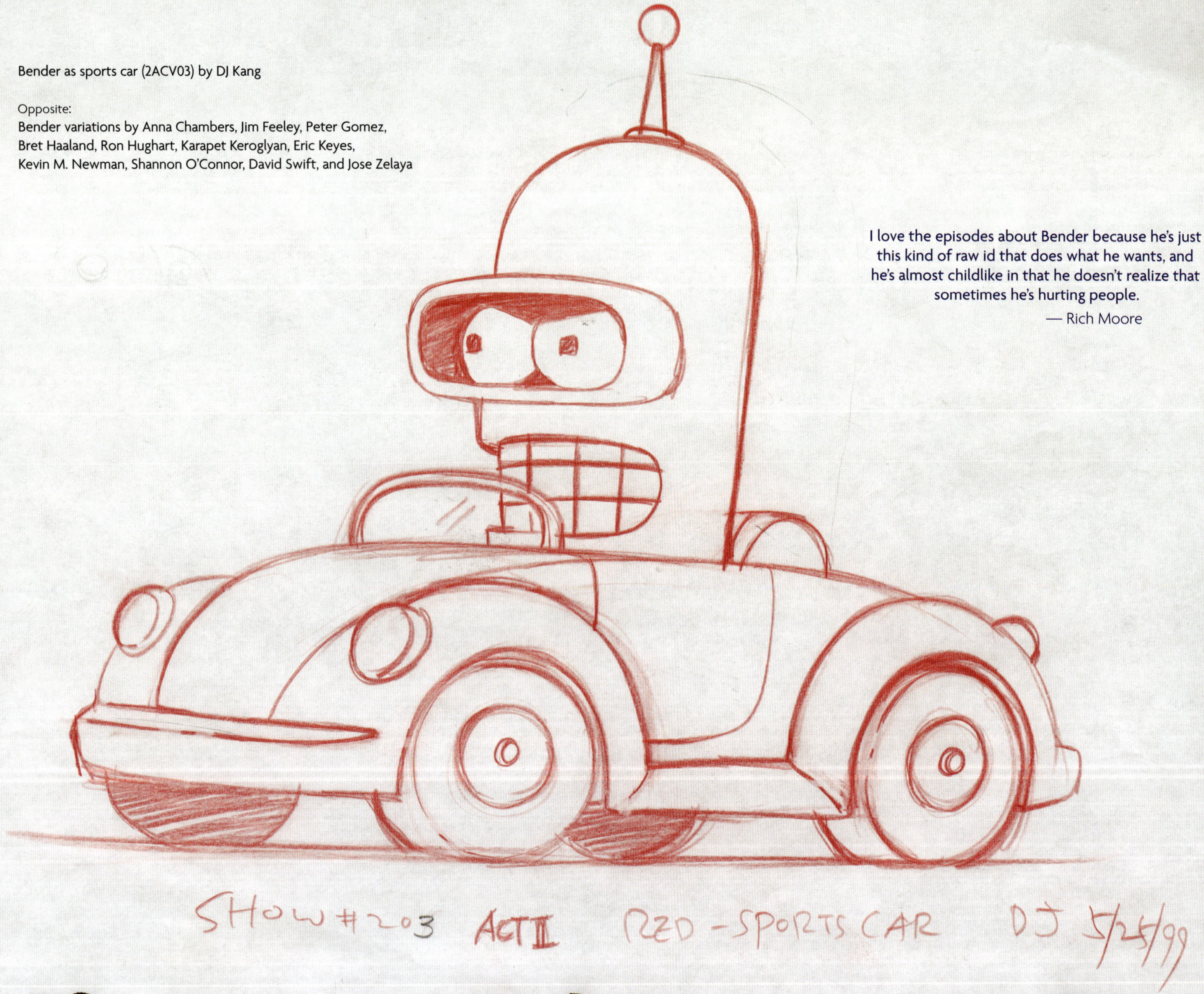

I love the episodes about Bender because he's just this kind of raw id that does what he wants, and he's almost childlike in that he doesn't realize that sometimes he's hurting people.
— Rich Moore

SHOW #203 ACT II RED-SPORTS CAR DJ 5/25/99

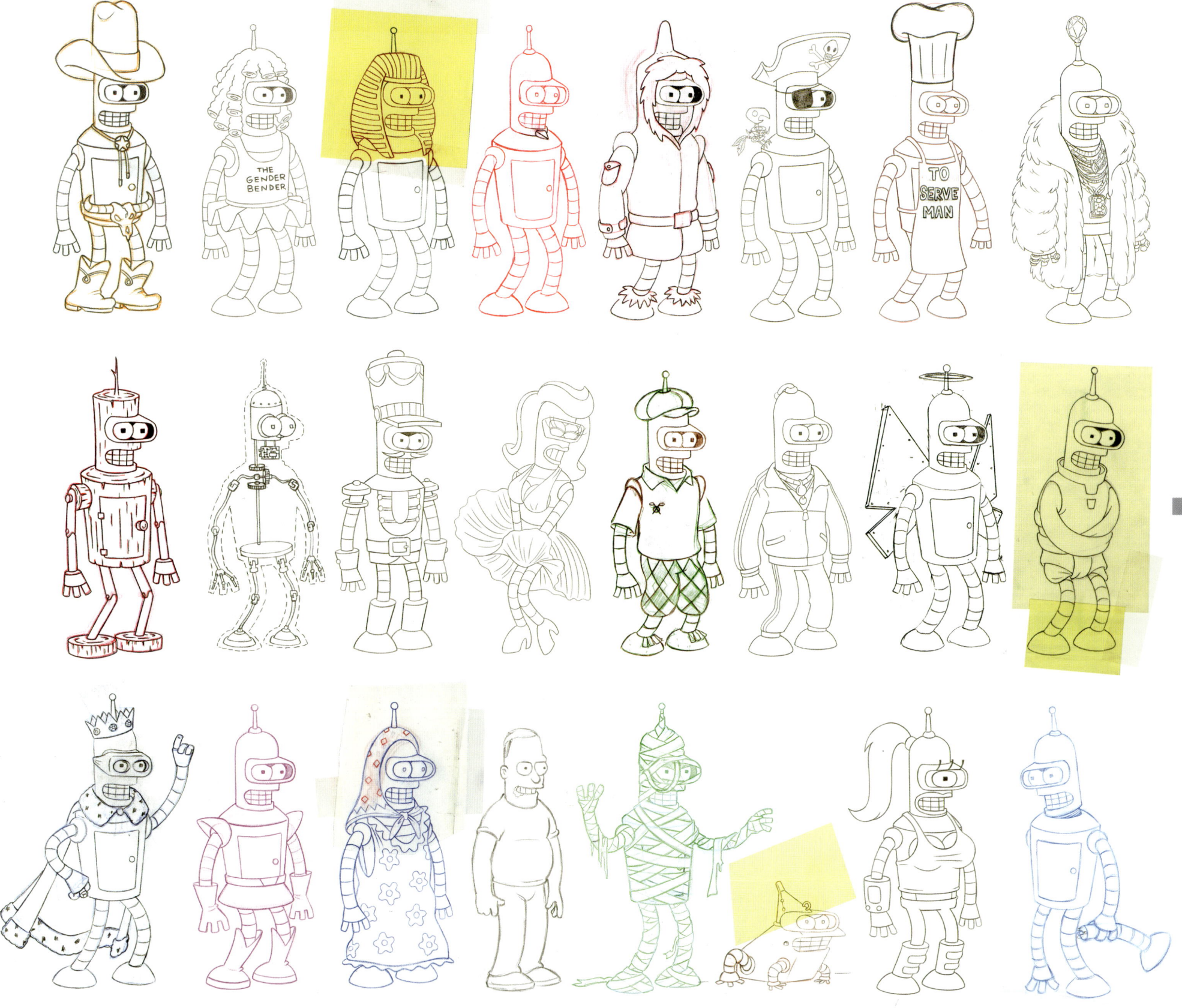

Top (from left to right):
Hermes variations
by Jim Feeley, Kevin M. Newman,
and Shannon O'Connor

Bottom (from left to right):
Amy variations
by Jim Feeley, Kevin M. Newman,
Shannon O'Connor, and Jose Zelaya

Opposite, top (from left to right):
Professor variations
by Jim Feeley, Kevin M. Newman,
Shannon O'Connor, and Jose Zelaya

Opposite, bottom (from left to right):
Scruffy variations
by Yacine Elghorri, Jim Feeley,
Kevin M. Newman, and Shannon O'Connor

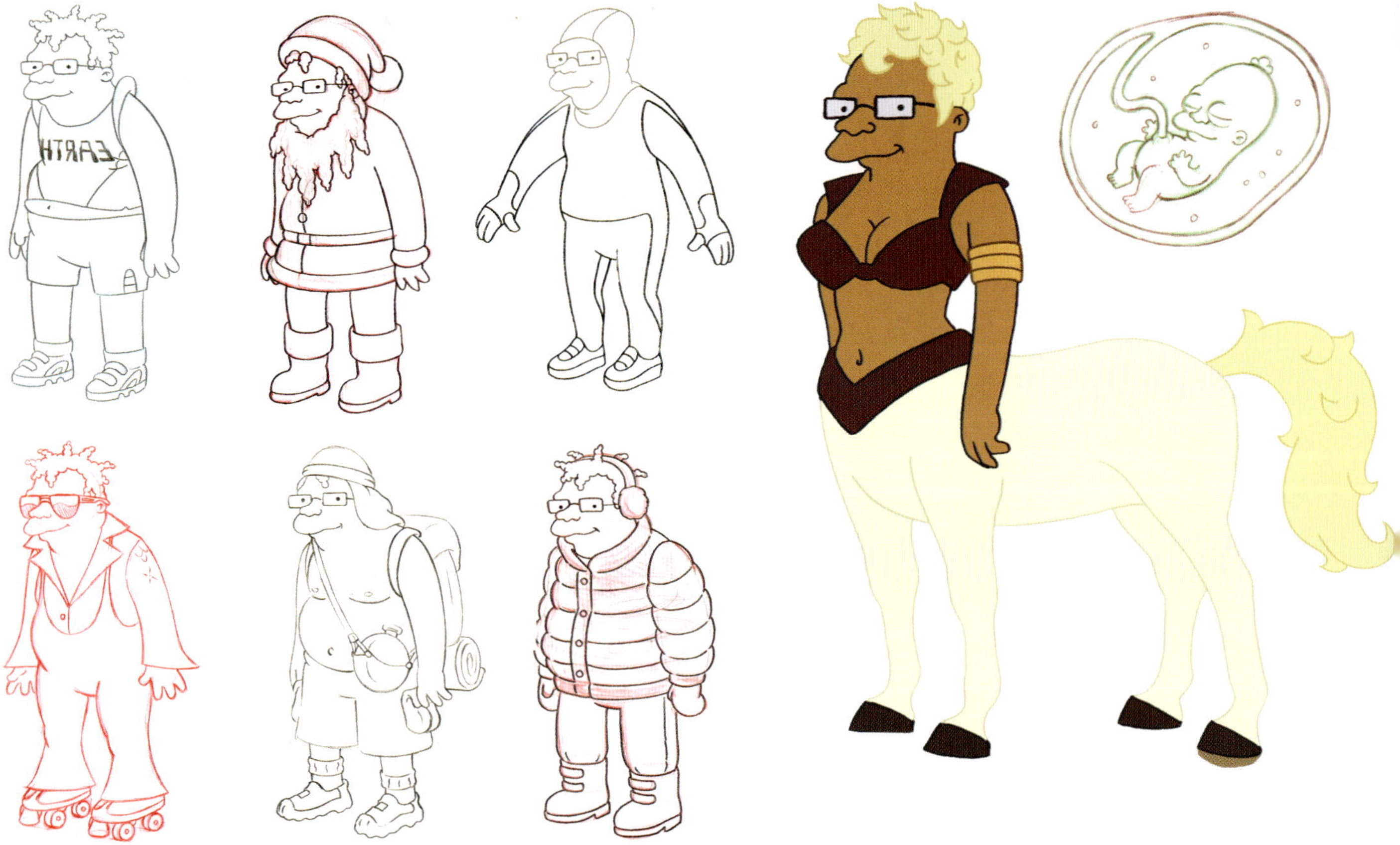

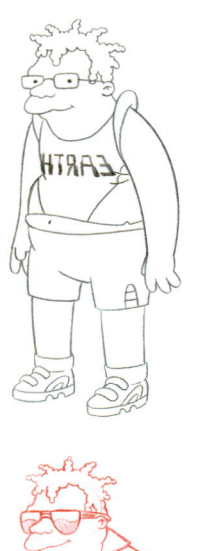

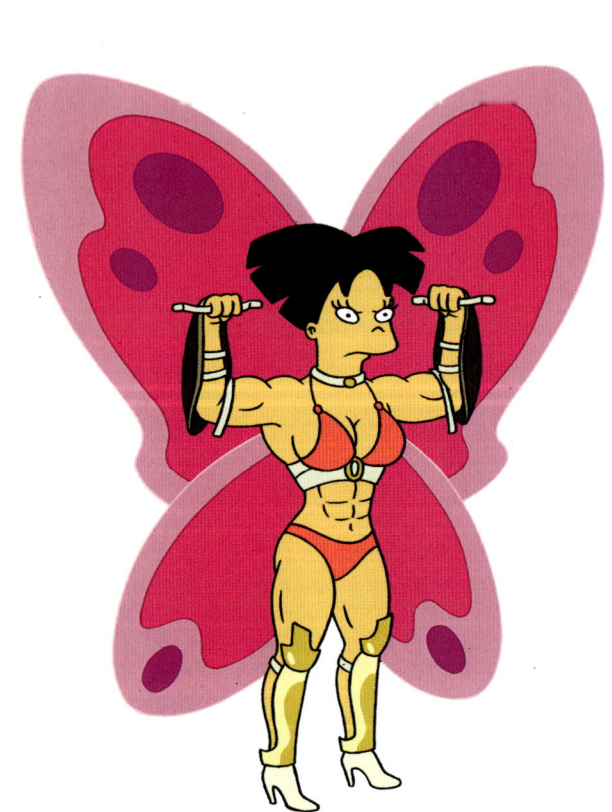

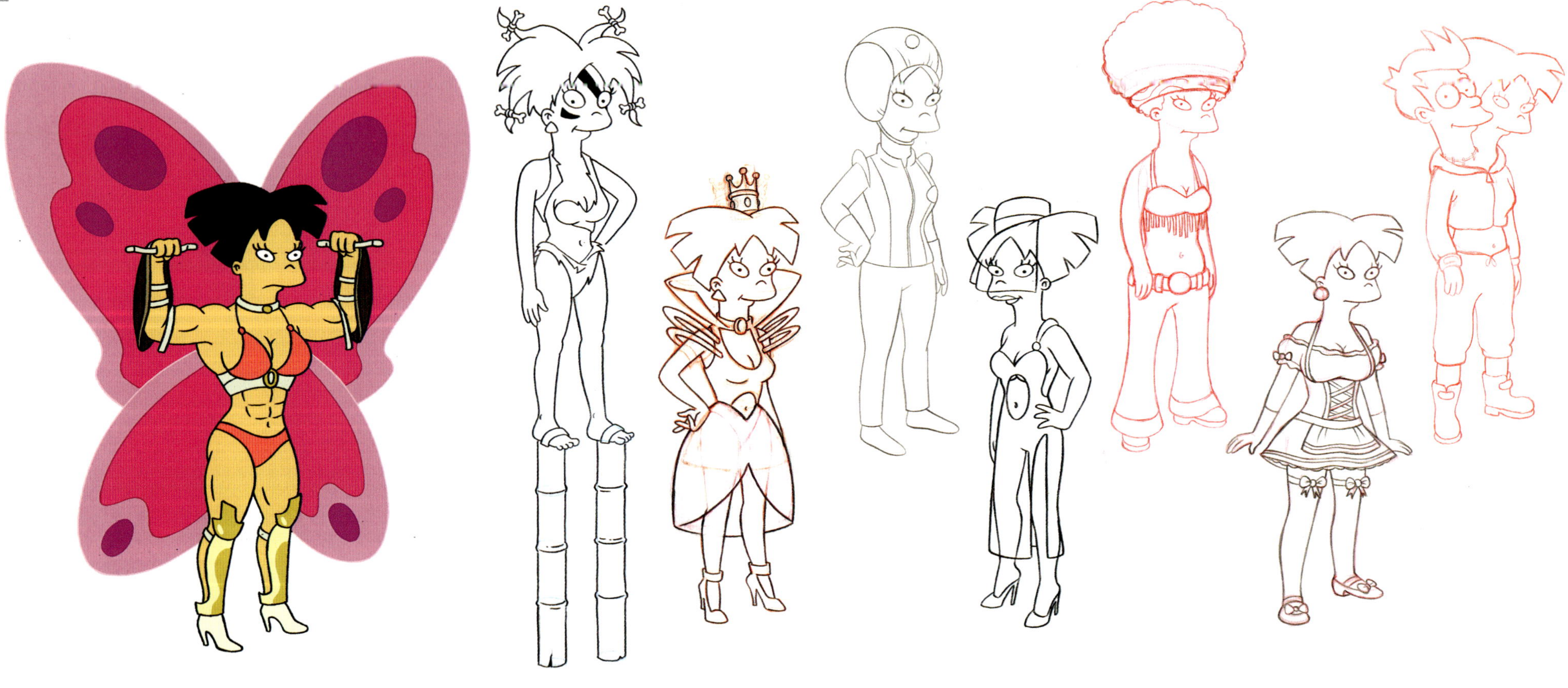

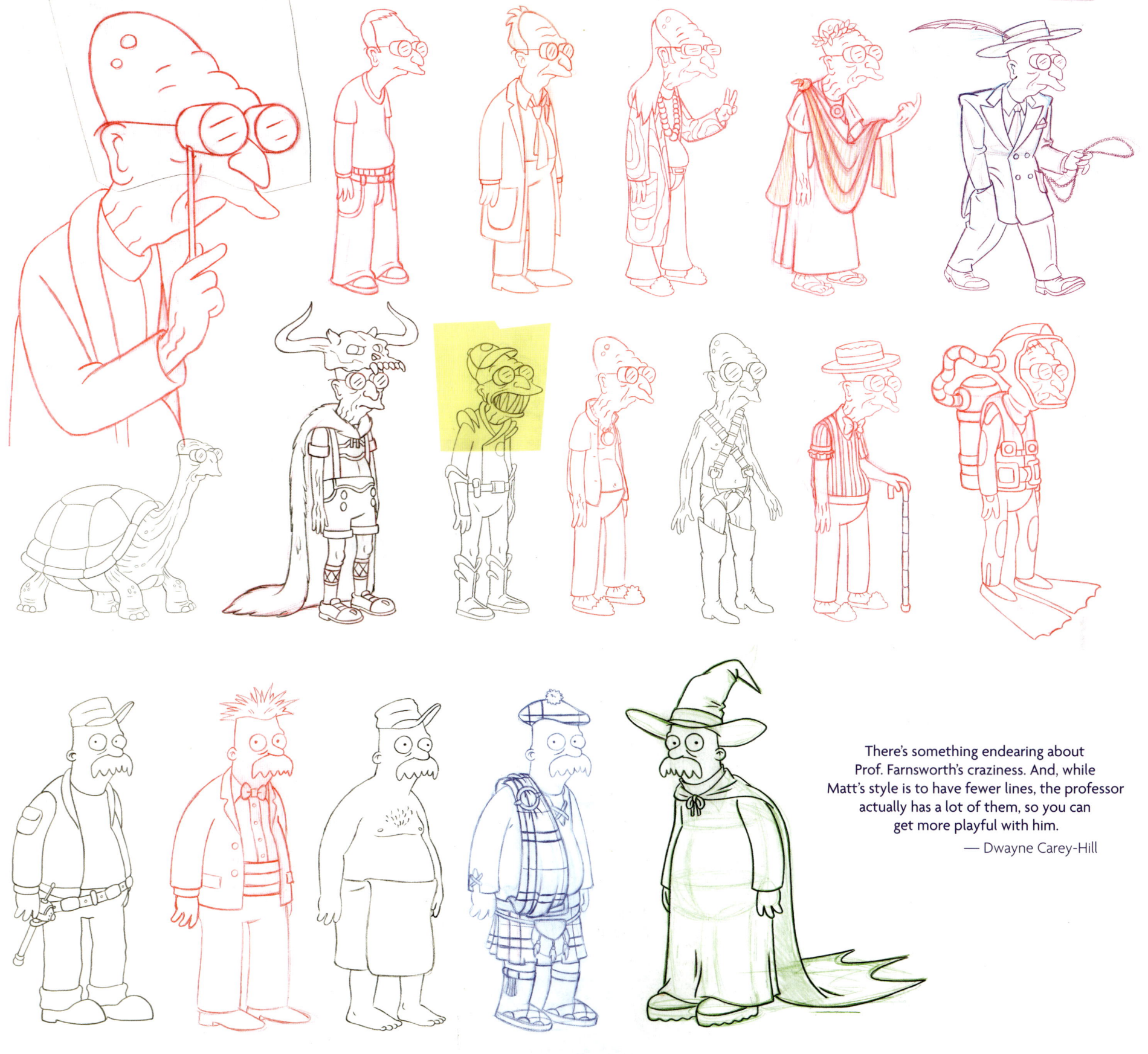

There's something endearing about Prof. Farnsworth's craziness. And, while Matt's style is to have fewer lines, the professor actually has a lot of them, so you can get more playful with him.

— Dwayne Carey-Hill

53

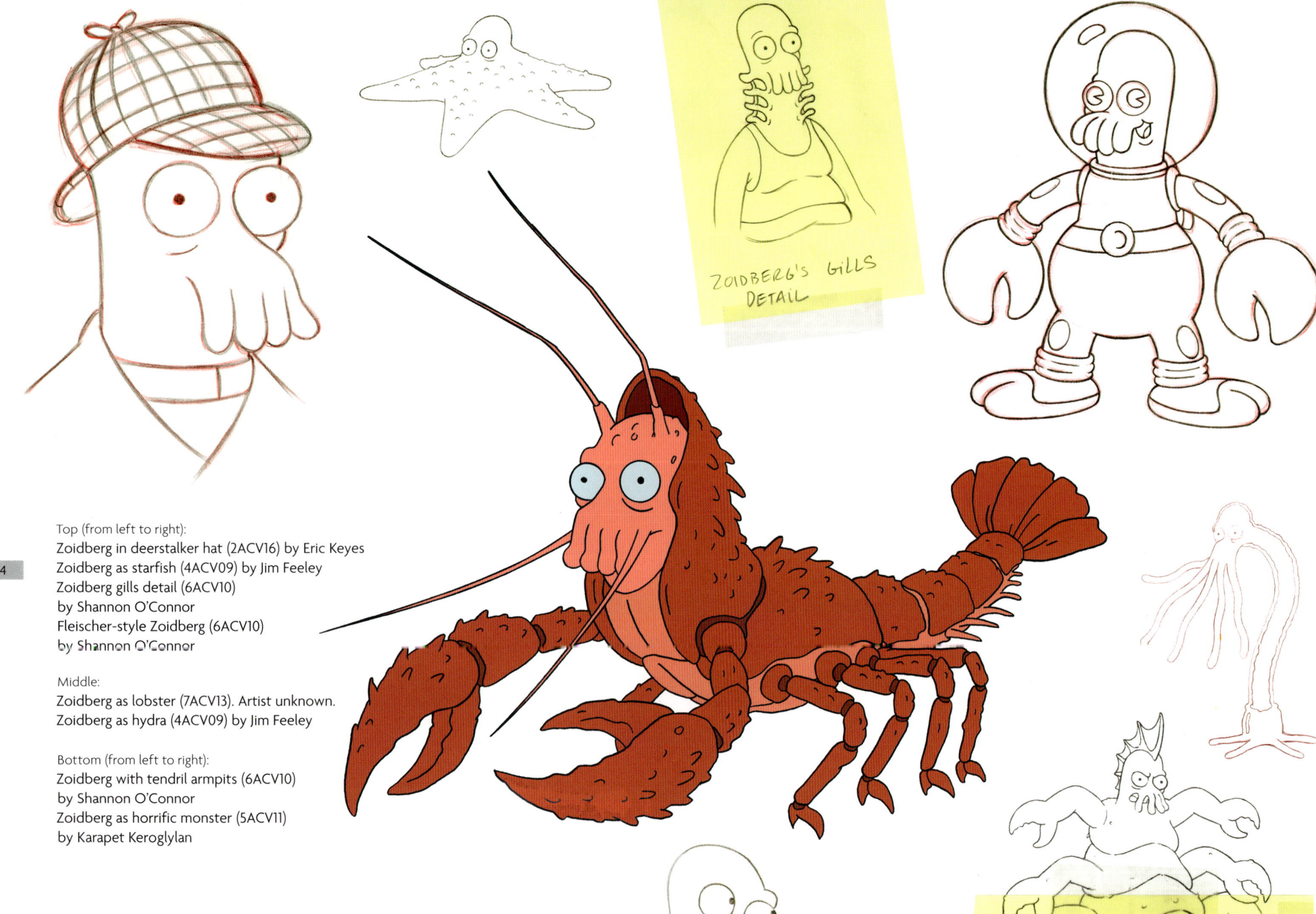

Top (from left to right):
Zoidberg in deerstalker hat (2ACV16) by Eric Keyes
Zoidberg as starfish (4ACV09) by Jim Feeley
Zoidberg gills detail (6ACV10)
by Shannon O'Connor
Fleischer-style Zoidberg (6ACV10)
by Shannon O'Connor

Middle:
Zoidberg as lobster (7ACV13). Artist unknown.
Zoidberg as hydra (4ACV09) by Jim Feeley

Bottom (from left to right):
Zoidberg with tendril armpits (6ACV10)
by Shannon O'Connor
Zoidberg as horrific monster (5ACV11)
by Karapet Keroglylan

Character designers sometimes use these yellow
sticky-notes to revise an existing drawing. Rather than
re-draw the whole thing, you put a sticky-note over the part
you want to revise. Like this Zoidberg with all the lobster claws
and segments; there's probably a different Zoidberg
underneath the yellow sticky-note.
— Bill Morrison

ZOIDBERG'S GILLS DETAIL

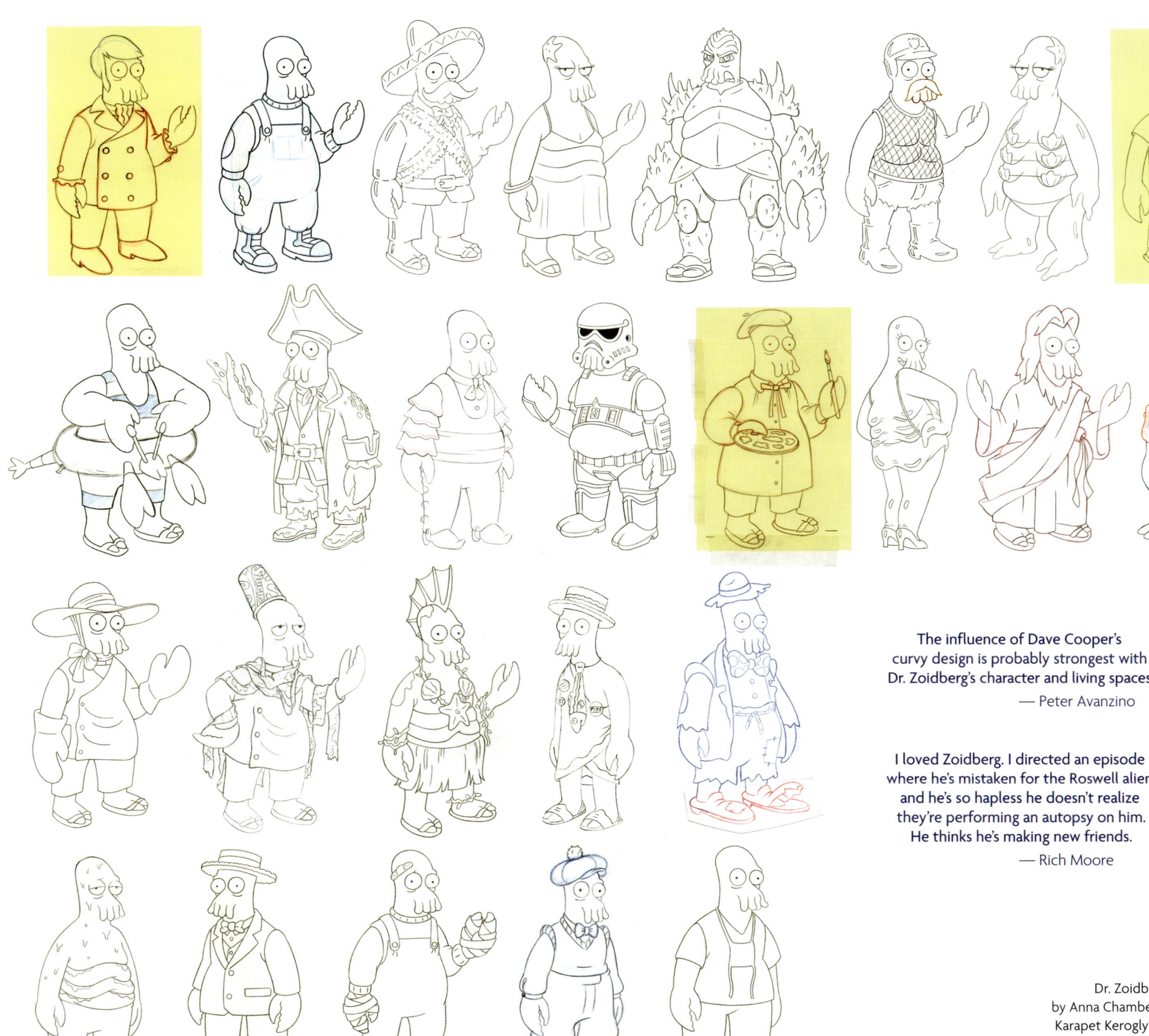

The influence of Dave Cooper's curvy design is probably strongest with Dr. Zoidberg's character and living spaces.

— Peter Avanzino

I loved Zoidberg. I directed an episode where he's mistaken for the Roswell alien and he's so hapless he doesn't realize they're performing an autopsy on him. He thinks he's making new friends.

— Rich Moore

Dr. Zoidberg variations by Anna Chambers, Jim Feeley, Karapet Keroglyan, Eric Keyes, Kevin M. Newman, Shannon O'Connor, David Swift, and Jose Zelaya

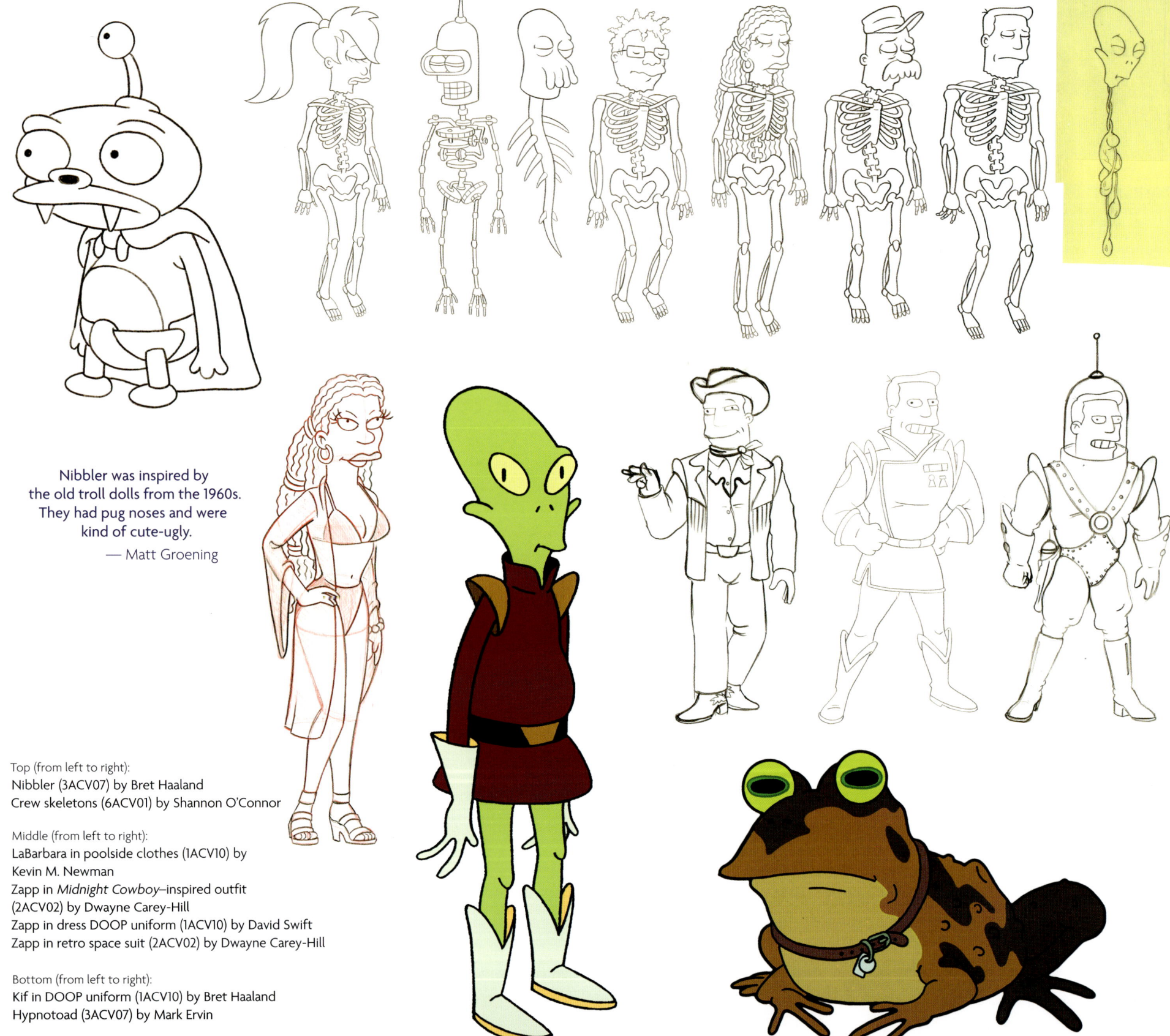

Nibbler was inspired by
the old troll dolls from the 1960s.
They had pug noses and were
kind of cute-ugly.

— Matt Groening

Top (from left to right):
Nibbler (3ACV07) by Bret Haaland
Crew skeletons (6ACV01) by Shannon O'Connor

Middle (from left to right):
LaBarbara in poolside clothes (1ACV10) by
Kevin M. Newman
Zapp in *Midnight Cowboy*–inspired outfit
(2ACV02) by Dwayne Carey-Hill
Zapp in dress DOOP uniform (1ACV10) by David Swift
Zapp in retro space suit (2ACV02) by Dwayne Carey-Hill

Bottom (from left to right):
Kif in DOOP uniform (1ACV10) by Bret Haaland
Hypnotoad (3ACV07) by Mark Ervin

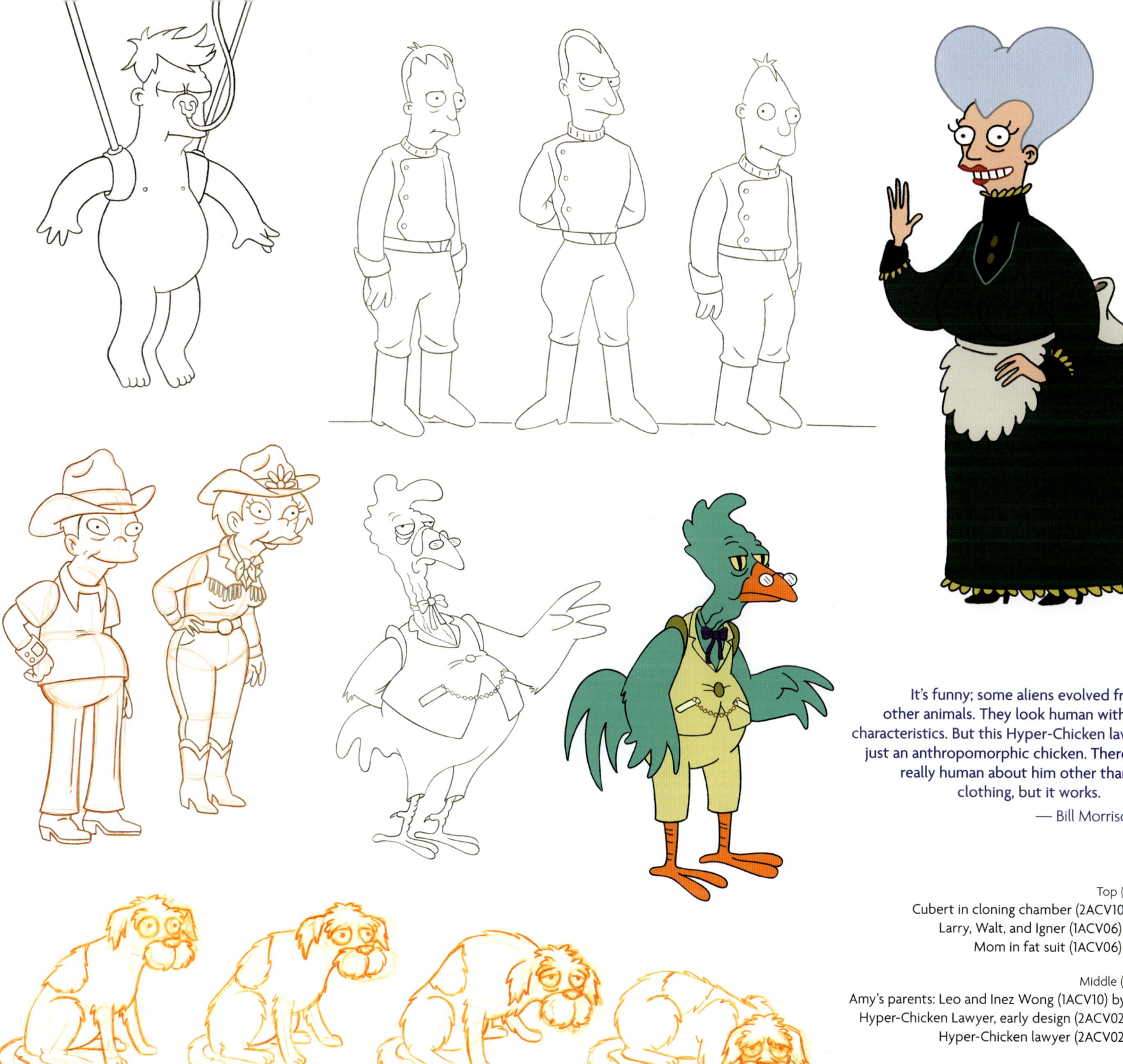

It's funny; some aliens evolved from other animals. They look human with animal characteristics. But this Hyper-Chicken lawyer is really just an anthropomorphic chicken. There's nothing really human about him other than the clothing, but it works.

— Bill Morrison

Top (from left to right):
Cubert in cloning chamber (2ACV10) by Rich Moore
Larry, Walt, and Igner (1ACV06) by Gregg Vanzo
Mom in fat suit (1ACV06) by Gregg Vanzo

Middle (from left to right):
Amy's parents: Leo and Inez Wong (1ACV10) by Kevin Newman
Hyper-Chicken Lawyer, early design (2ACV02) by Rich Moore
Hyper-Chicken lawyer (2ACV02) by Rich Moore

Bottom:
Seymour's aging cycle (4ACV07) by Jim Feeley

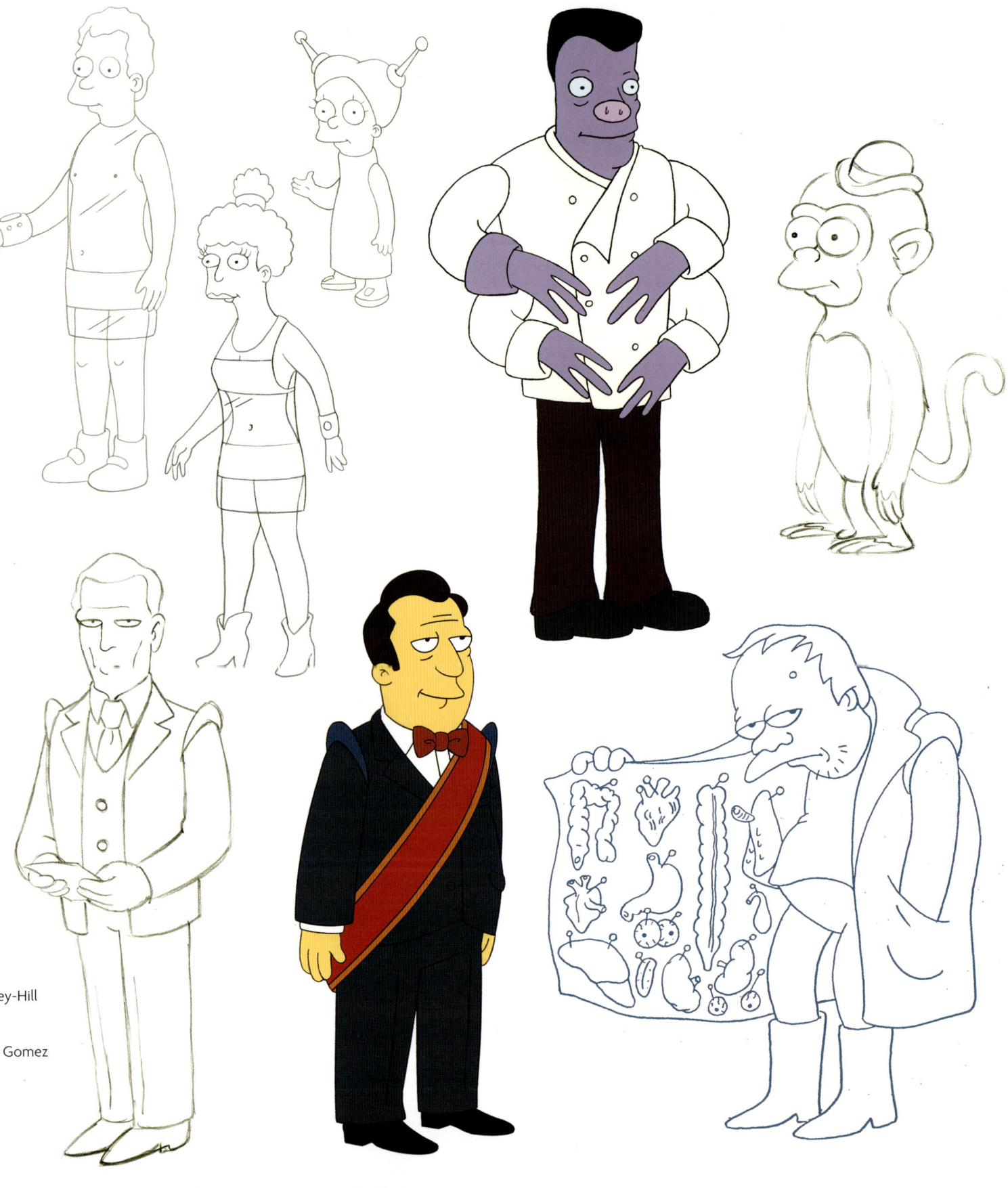

These were some of the oldest original designs we did for the show, going back to the pilot. One idea Matt had was that people walk around in transparent body sleeves with censor bars, but I think it's only in the pilot. We were still trying to figure out the look of the future.

— Rich Moore

Top (from left to right):
30th Century citizens (1ACV01)
by Dwayne Carey-Hill and Rich Moore
Elzar (1ACV07) by David Swift
Guenter (1ACV07) by Bret Haaland

Bottom (from left to right):
Dean Vernon (1ACV11) by Bret Haaland
Mayor Poopenmeyer (6ACV12)
by David Swift
Shady Guy (1ACV07) by Yacine Elgharri
and Rich Moore

Opposite page, top (from left to right):
Mr. Panucci early designs (1ACV01)
by David Swift, Rich Moore
Panucci Pizza twelve-year-old boy (1ACV01)
by Rich Moore
Luna Park patrons (1ACV02) by Dwayne Carey-Hill

Opposite page, bottom (from left to right):
Horrible Gelatinous Blob (1ACV02) by Peter Gomez
Decapodian female (1ACV06)
by David Swift and Gregg Vanzo
Nightclub patrons (1ACV04)
by Dwayne Carey-Hill and Yacine Elghorri

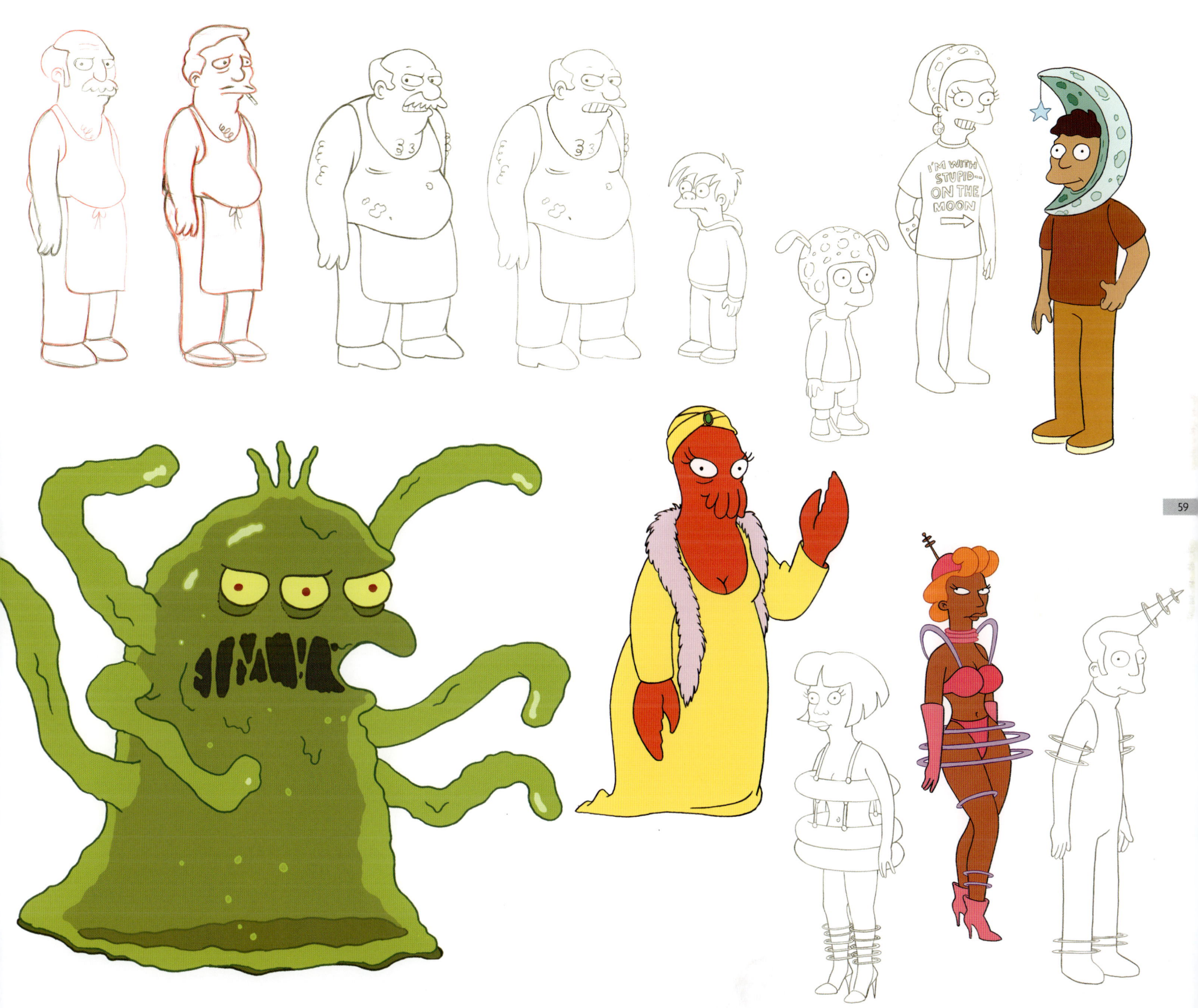

Top::
Umbriel (2ACV12) by Eric Keyes

Middle (from left to right):
General (3ACV19) by Jim Feeley
Slurms McKenzie (1ACV13) by Kevin M. Newman
Amazonian (3ACV01) by Kevin M. Newman

Bottom (from left to right):
Grunka-Lunkas (1ACV13) by Matt Groening
and Kevin M. Newman
Worm Leader (3ACV02) by Jim Feeley

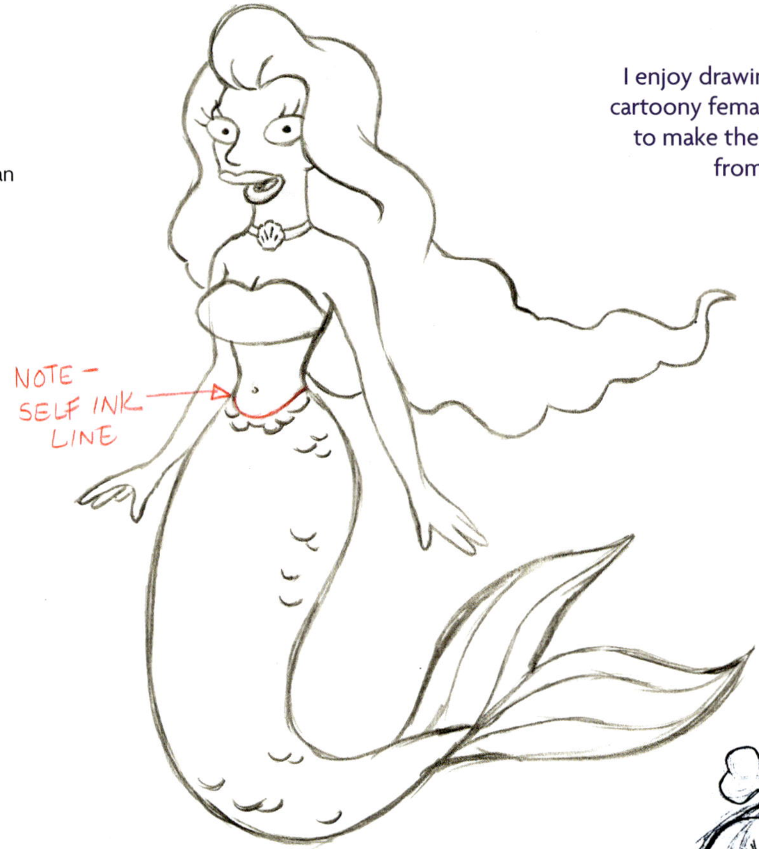

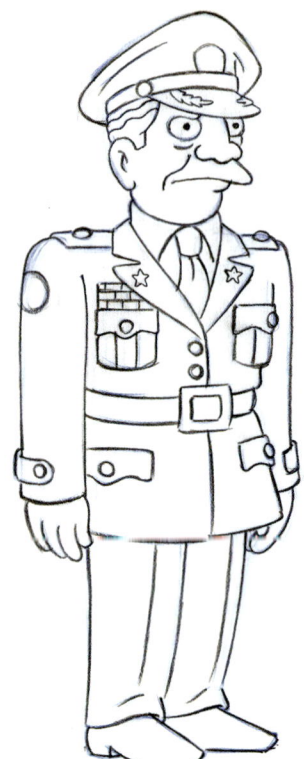

NOTE —
SELF INK
LINE

I enjoy drawing women, but a lot of times really cartoony female characters get sort of cliché. I try to make their acting and gestures feel natural from a feminine point of view.

— Crystal Chesney-Thompson

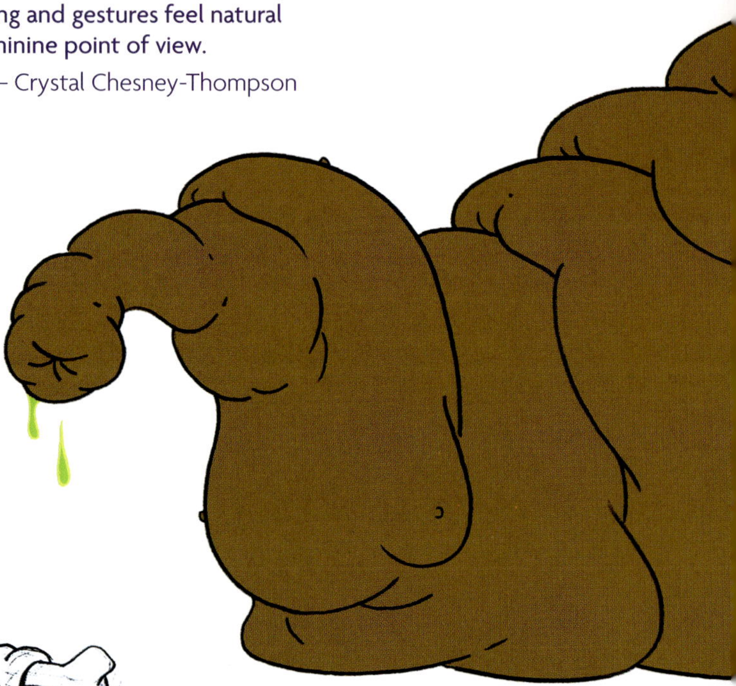

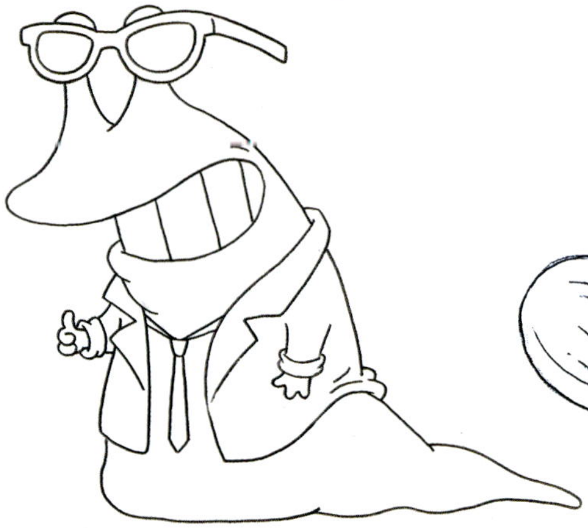

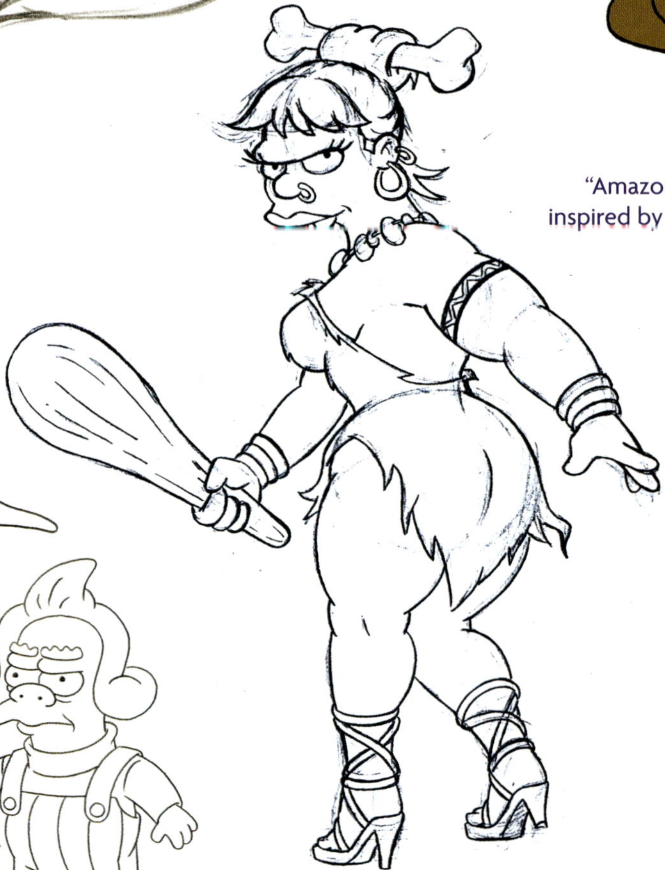

The giant women in "Amazon Women in the Mood" were inspired by R. Crumb. And yes, we wanted to arouse Robert Crumb.

— Matt Groening

Like *The Simpsons,* we'd do satires of movies and TV shows. Rather than a chocolate factory, these Grunka-Lunka characters work in a Slurm factory making this highly addictive soda from the horrible excretions of a giant worm. This was a seminal episode where both the writing and the visuals really started to click.

— Rich Moore

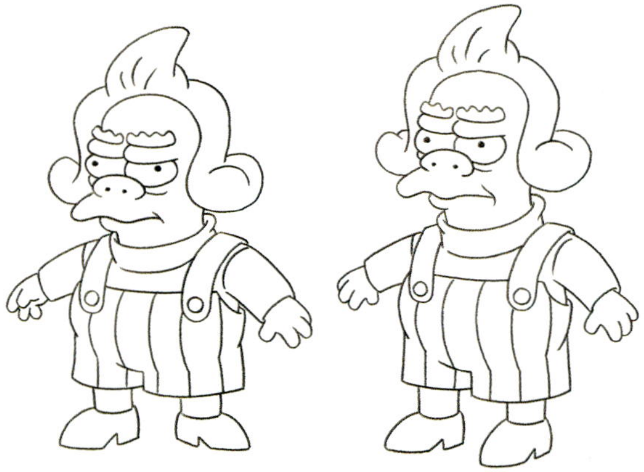

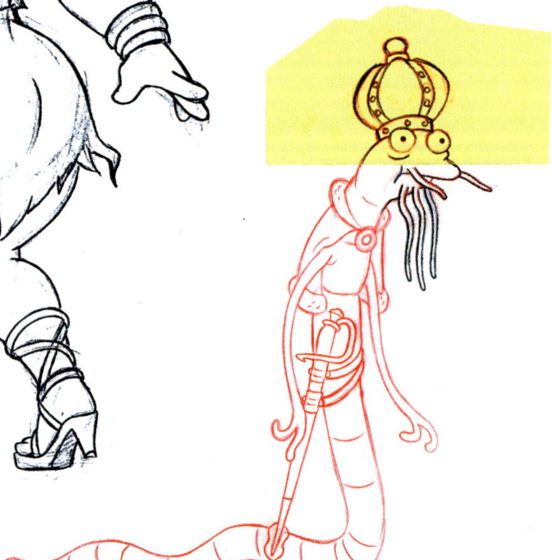

60

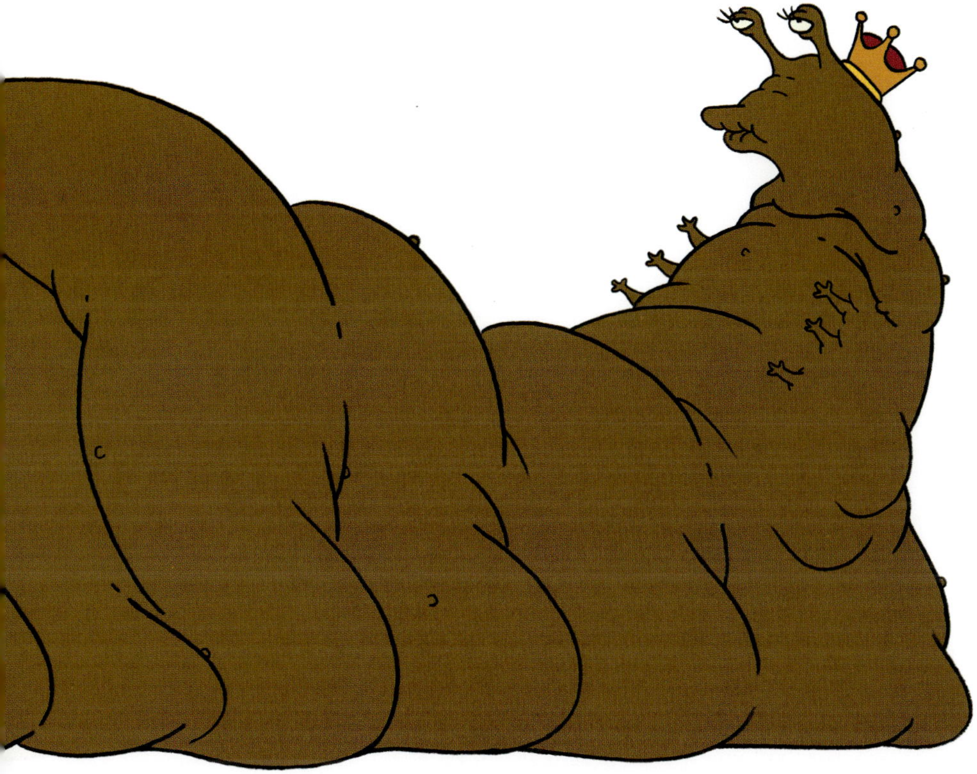

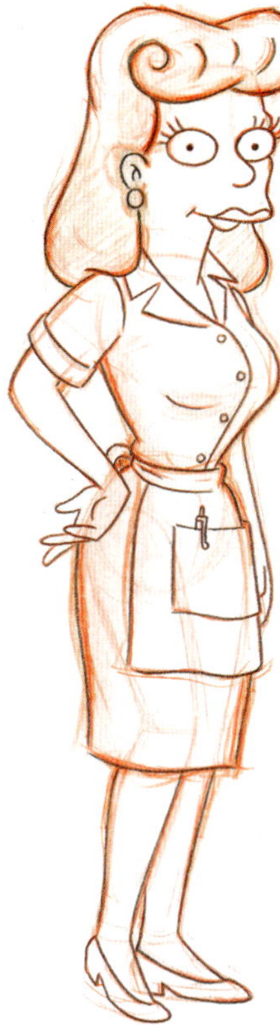

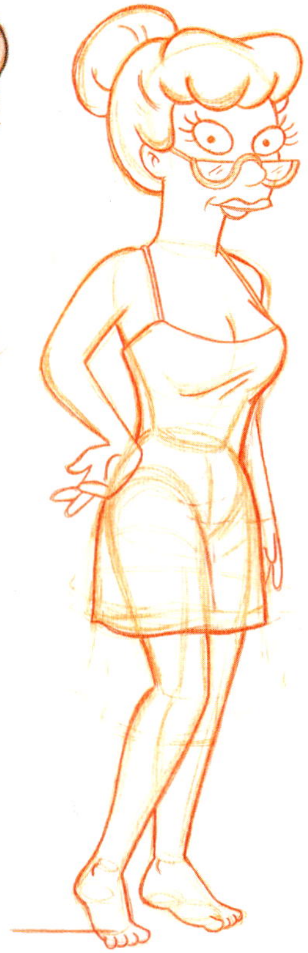

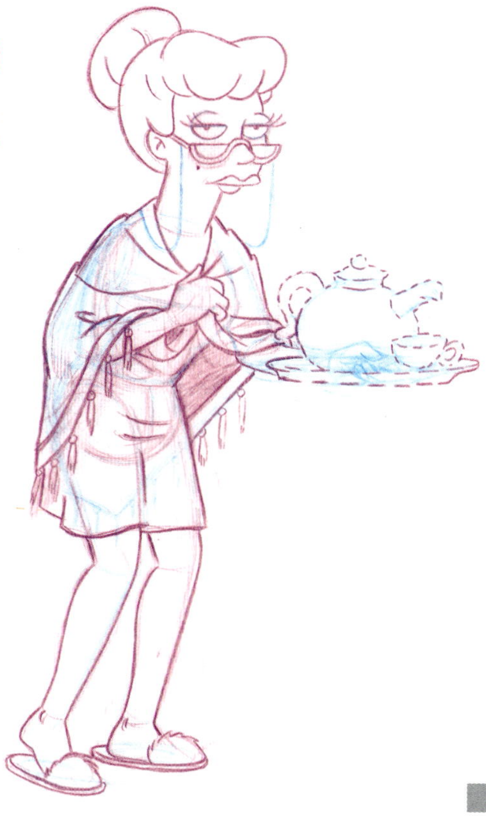

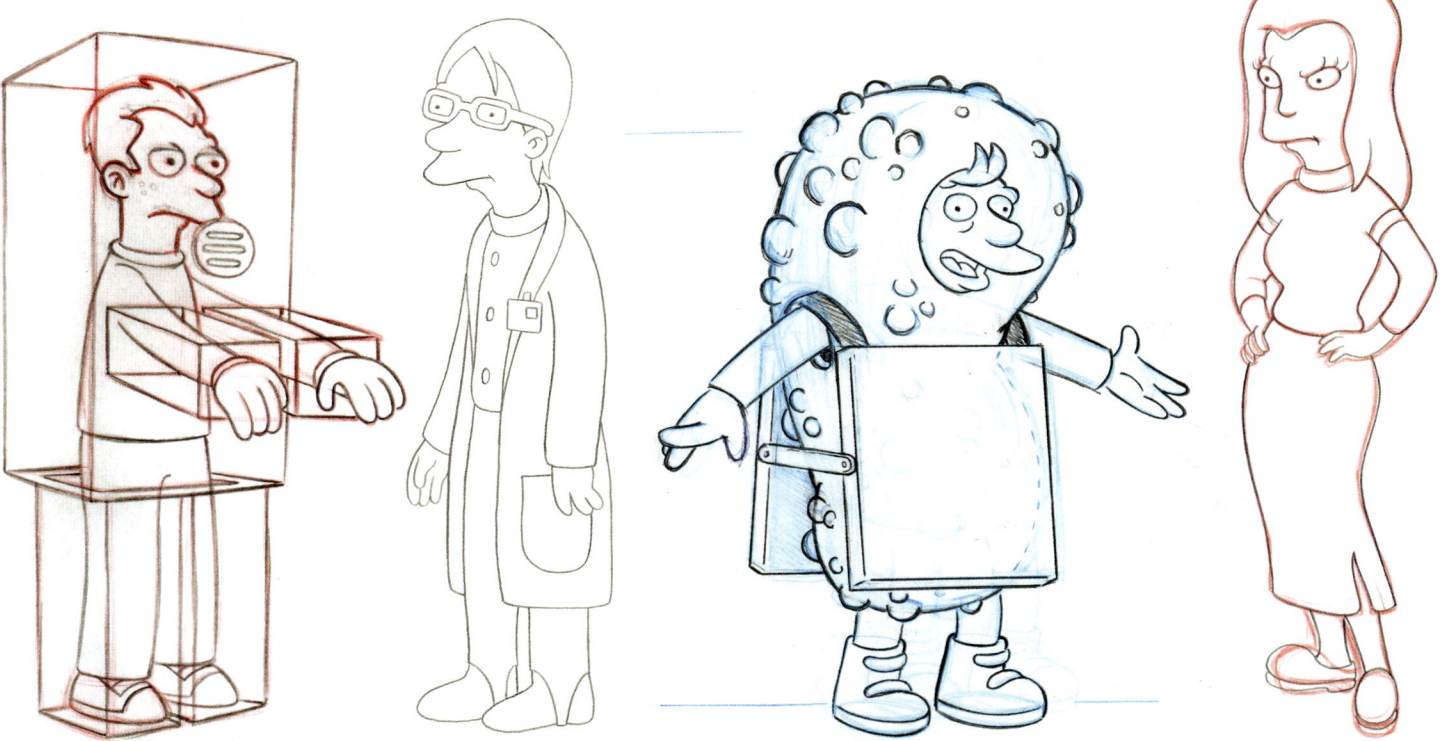

61

Top (from left to right):
Slurm Queen (1ACV13)
by Kevin M. Newman
Mildred (3ACV19) by Bill Morrison
Mildred with granny glasses (3ACV19)
by Kevin M. Newman
Mildred with shawl (3ACV19)
by Kevin M. Newman

Bottom:
Cashier encased in
bullet-proof plexiglass (2ACV17)
by Rich Moore and Bill Morrison
Cryo lab technician (1ACV01) by Rich Moore
Poppler mascot (2ACV15) by Kevin M. Newman
Michelle (1ACV01) by David Swift

What kid doesn't want to see the head of Grover Cleveland or George McGovern?

— Rich Moore

Not to mention the luxuriant eyebrows of Michael Dukakis or the bristling ears of Ross Perot.

— Matt Groening

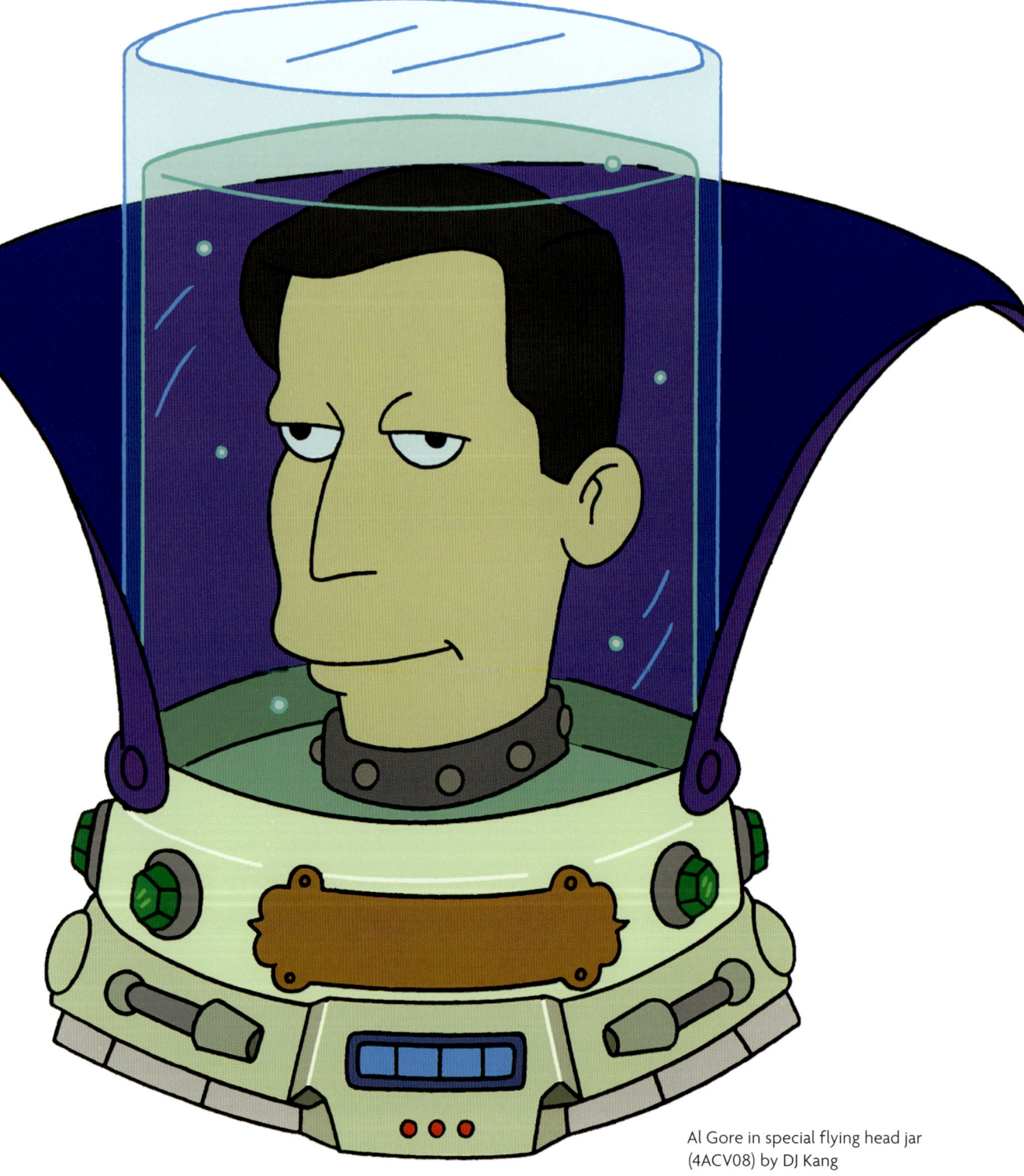

Al Gore in special flying head jar
(4ACV08) by DJ Kang

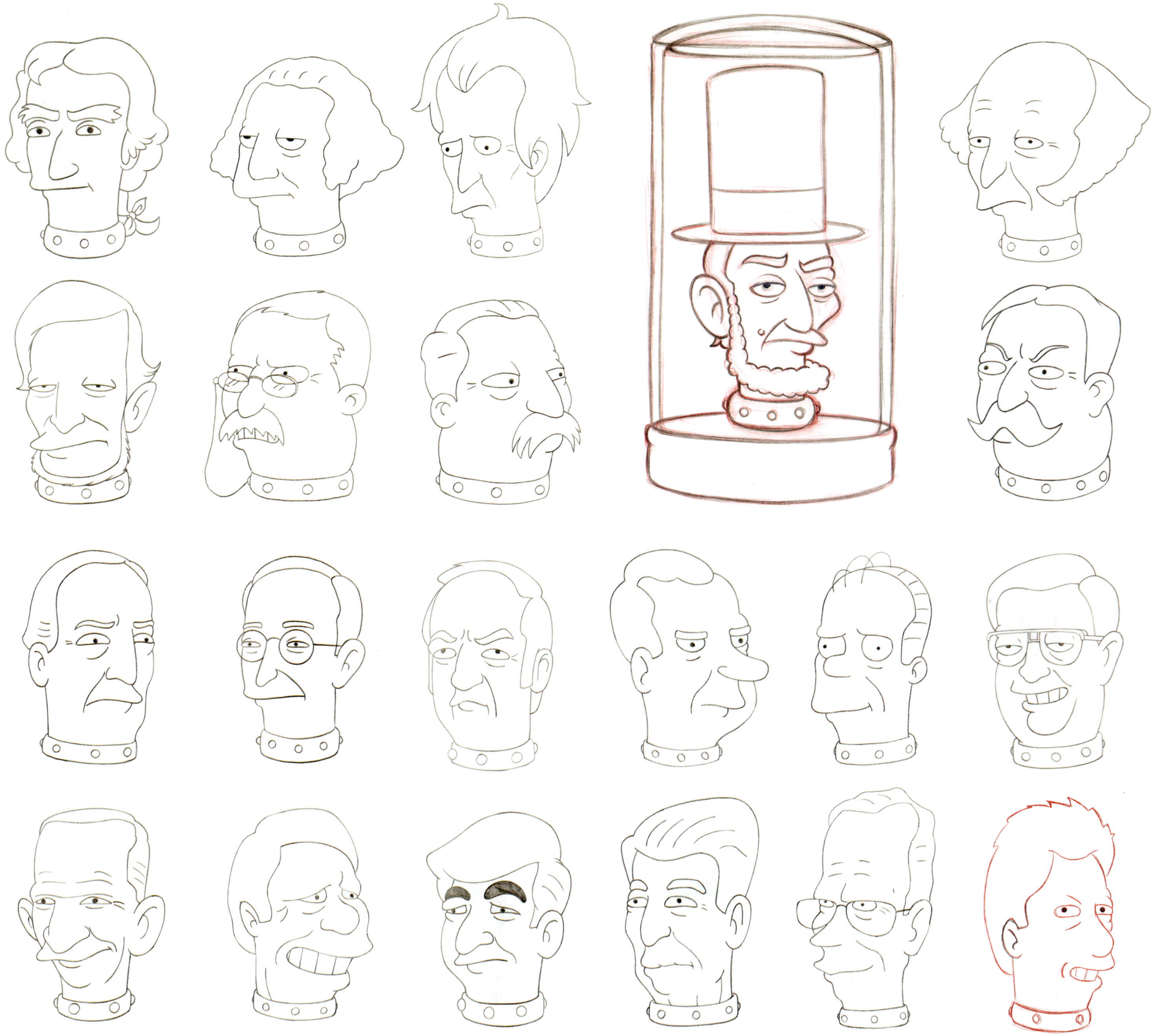

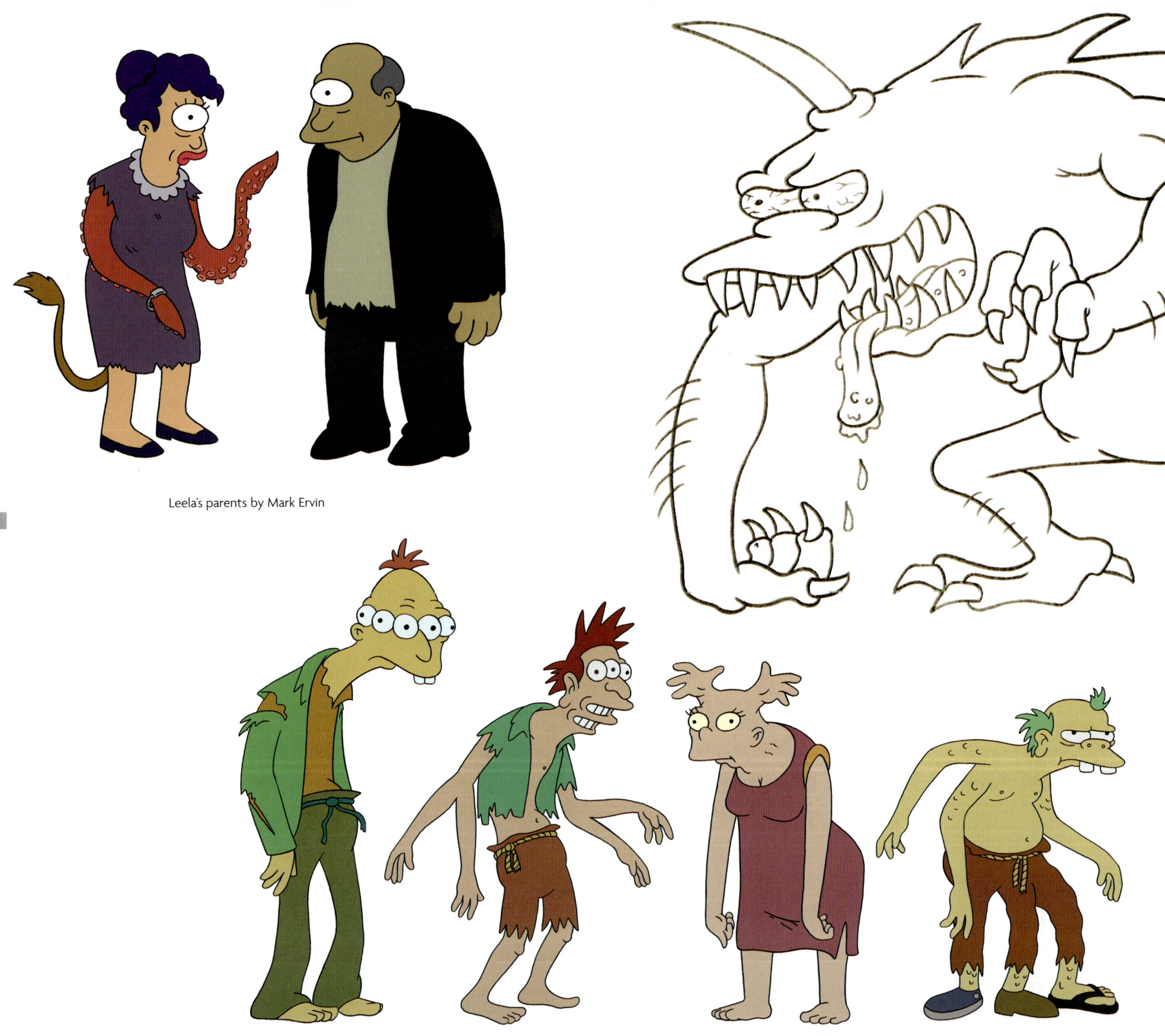

Leela's parents by Mark Ervin

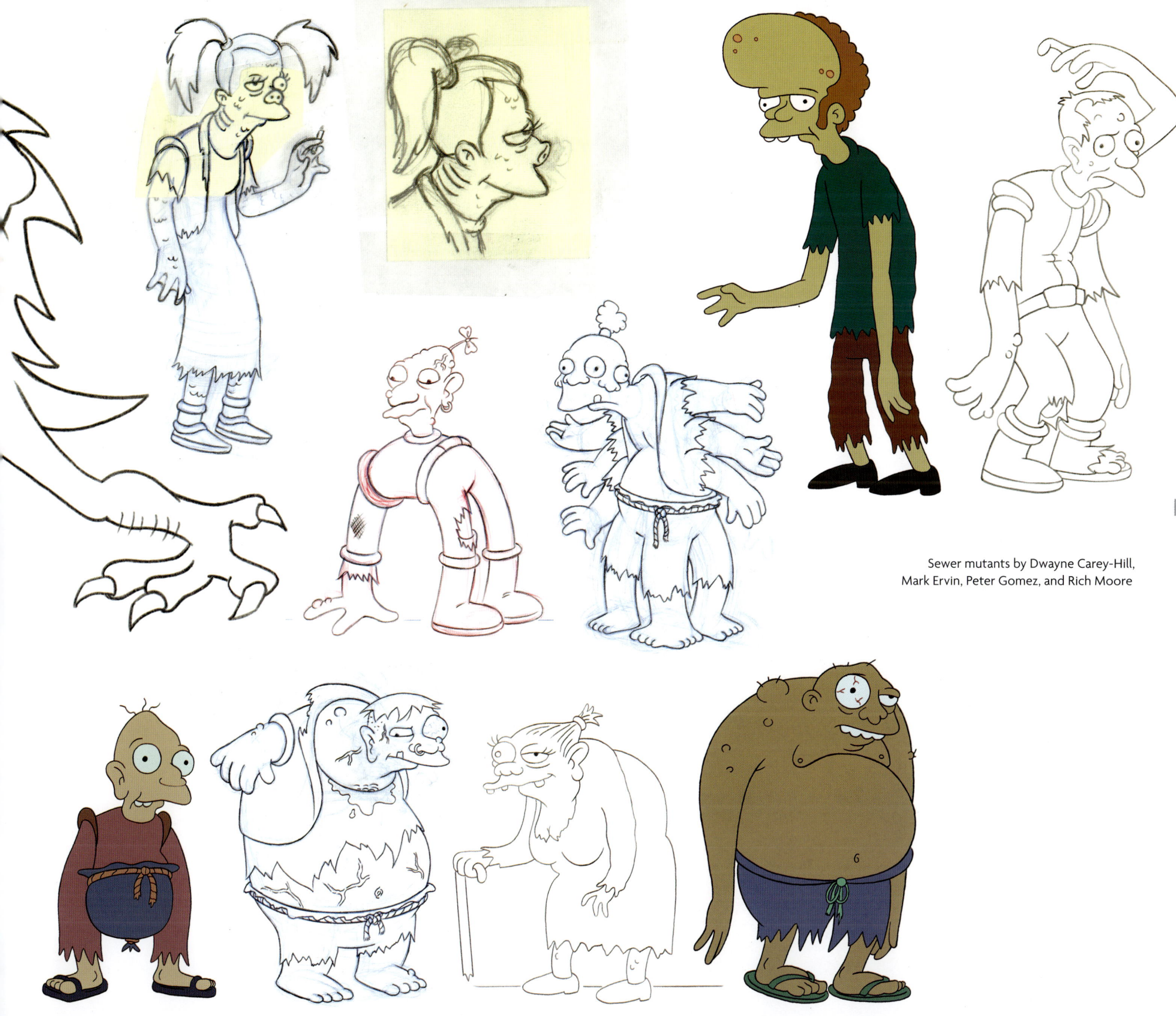

65

Sewer mutants by Dwayne Carey-Hill,
Mark Ervin, Peter Gomez, and Rich Moore

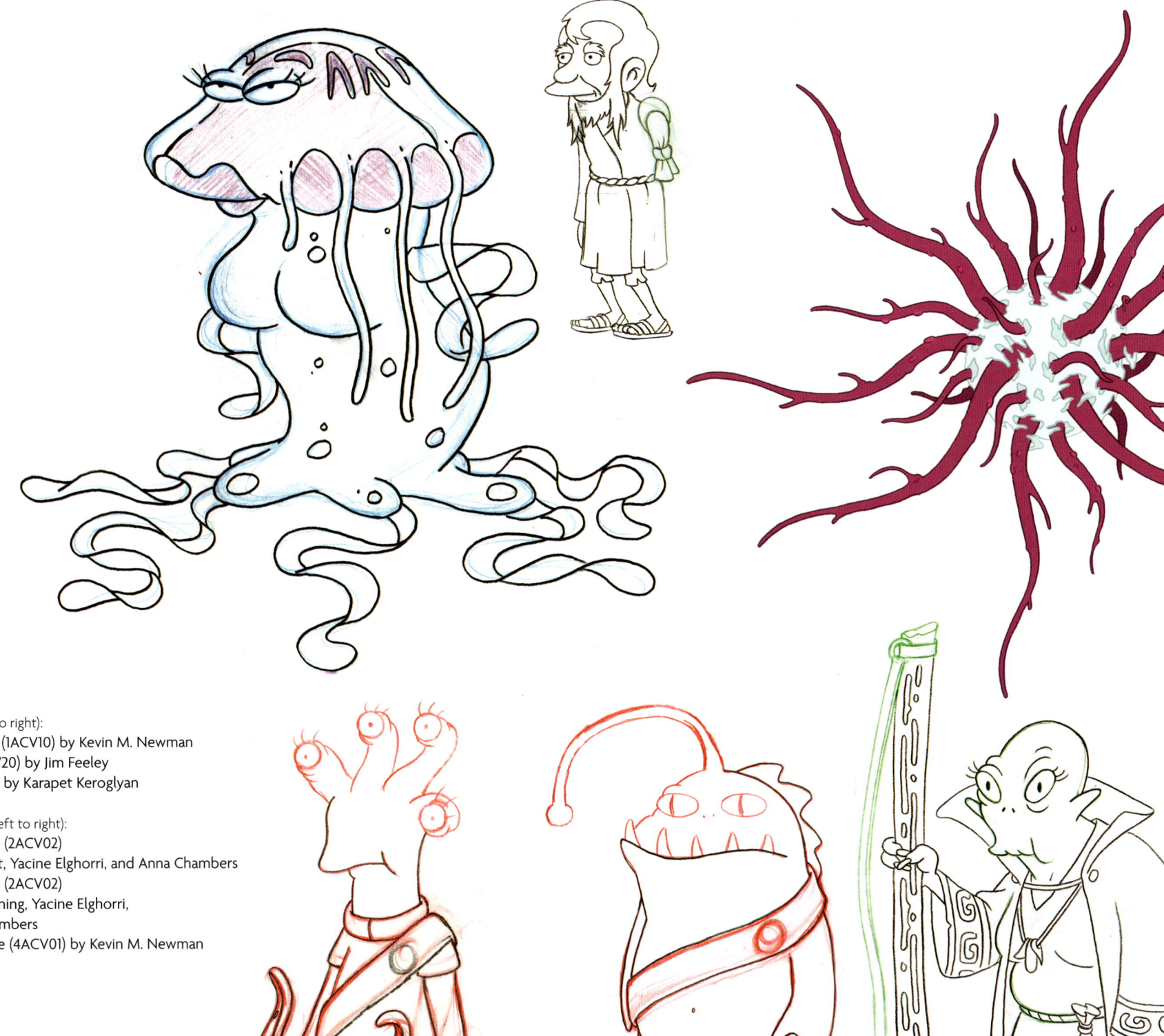

Top (from left to right):
Busty jellyfish (1ACV10) by Kevin M. Newman
Malachi (3ACV20) by Jim Feeley
Yivo (5ACV06) by Karapet Keroglyan

Bottom (from left to right):
Alien delegate (2ACV02)
by David Swift, Yacine Elghorri, and Anna Chambers
Alien delegate (2ACV02)
by Matt Groening, Yacine Elghorri,
and Anna Chambers
Grand Midwife (4ACV01) by Kevin M. Newman

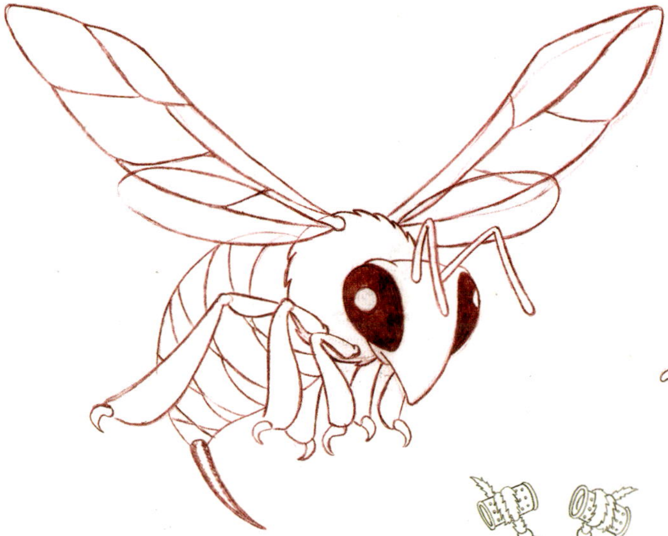

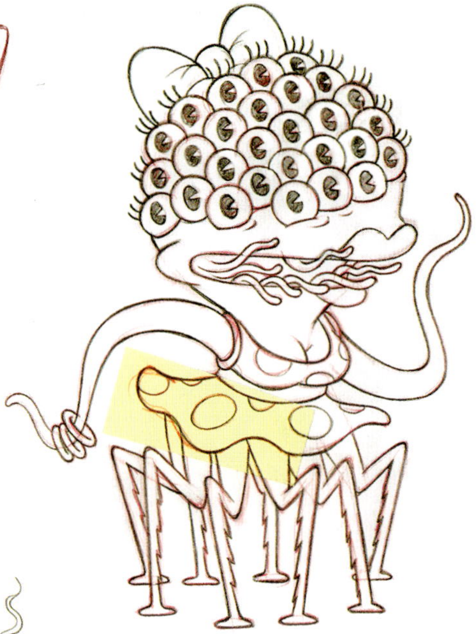

Top (from left to right):
Space bee (4ACV12)
by Shannon O'Connor and Jim Feeley
Fleischer-style alien (6ACV26)
by Shannon O'Connor

Center:
Master Fong (2ACV08) by Anna Chambers
Female Centipede (2ACV06) by Eric Keyes

Bottom (from left to right):
Asteroid creature (5ACV15) by Karapet Keroglyan
Nudar (5ACV02) by Eric Keyes
Flying Brain (3ACV07) by Kevin M. Newman
Emperor Bont (1ACV07) by Yacine Elghorri

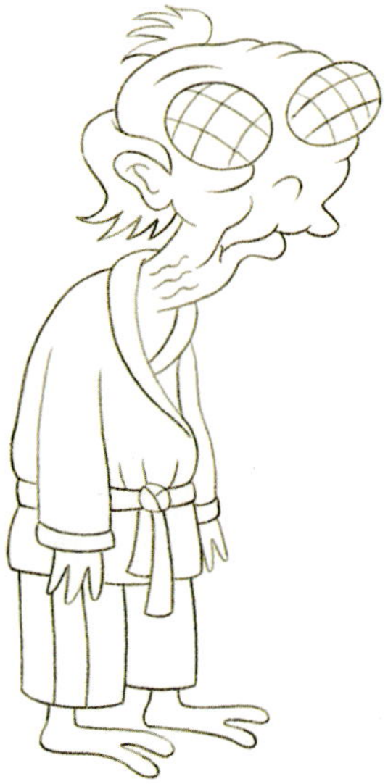

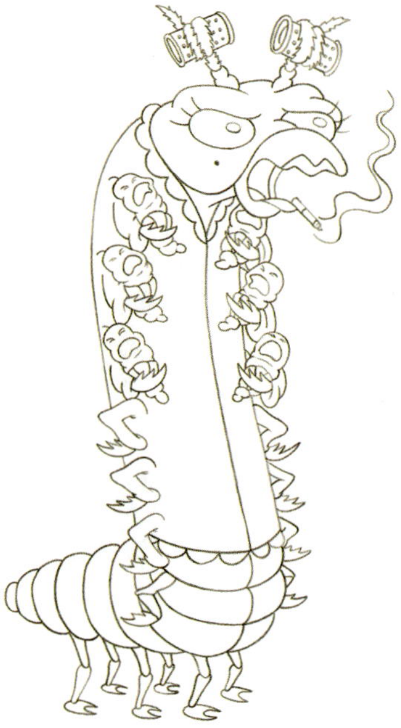

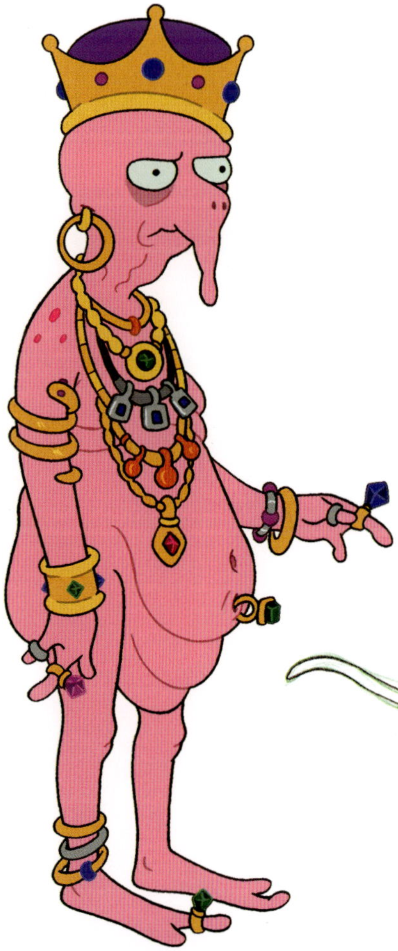

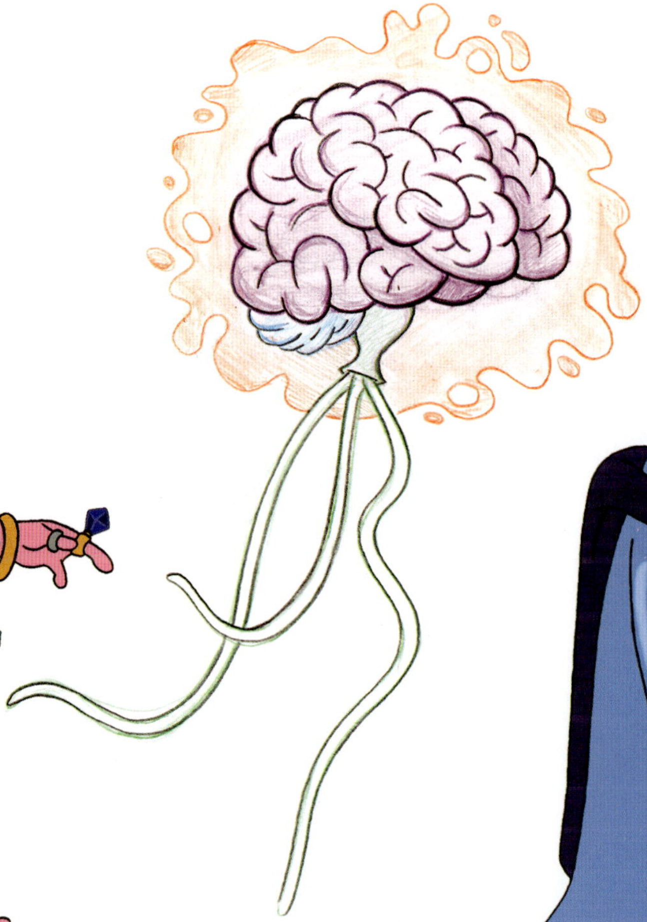

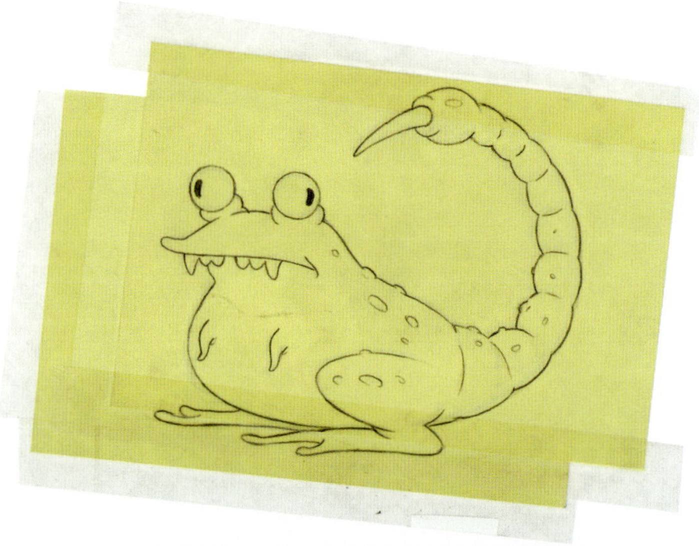

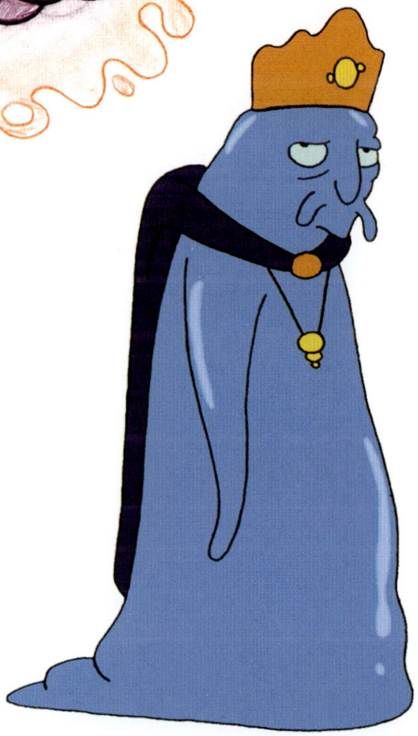

TAKEOFF: MECHANICAL ADVANTAGES

Claudia Katz: The first season was such a big world to build. And, at that time, the world was not at your fingertips. I had some reference books, and Matt was collecting books. All we did was troll bookstores. Any time I went to New York or anywhere else, I'd look for architecture books, picture books, design books. Matt found some books on water towers that really inspired him.

Matt Groening: People have mentioned that the Planet Express building was modeled on the Harvard Lampoon building, but it was also very much influenced by photographs of various water towers and other industrial buildings by Bernd and Hilla Becher. Among the many books we collected, we gave those books to the designers to use as reference. Everything was still books in those days.

Rich Moore: We've got the show. Fantastic! But we don't have time to celebrate because we're already behind. We need to hire fast and we couldn't hire anyone from the other studios working with Fox. At that time, that's everyone in primetime animation. Rough Draft was only about 15–20 people. We needed a crew of 100-plus, so we were going to have to train every single one of them ourselves. We went to CalArts and hired a bunch of their graduating class. Using what we'd learned on *The Simpsons*, Gregg Vanzo and I showed them what we needed them to do. We assigned them jobs. "You're background designers; you do this. You're character designers; you do that." Assembling the team and training a fresh, brand-spanking-new crop of animators from the ground up was a proud moment for all of us. Since then, some of

the people we trained moved onto other things and really helped the industry a lot. Some are still with us working on the show.

Dwayne Carey-Hill: On *Futurama*, I started officially as a character layout artist. But the character layout can't start until the storyboards are done. There weren't any backgrounds, character designs, or essentially anything. So, I was tasked with drawing incidentals, celebrity heads, and robots. Rich Moore gave me a mannequin lineup of empty, hollow bodies to work on top of and said, "Draw, just draw characters, anything you like." I asked how many. "As many as you can draw. We have a world to fill." So, for probably the first three, four weeks—all day, every day—I just drew random people.

> ### "Draw, just draw characters, anything you like." I asked how many. "As many as you can draw. We have a world to fill."
>
> — Dwayne Carey-Hill

Crystal Chesney-Thompson: The big studios have everything very compartmentalized. One department is separate from another department. If work needs doing in a particular department, they hire outside people to come in specifically to do that particular work. At Rough Draft, I started in layout. When things shifted to storyboards, I learned storyboards. Then they asked, "Do you want to learn how to time the storyboards?" You bet! I learned timing and then became an assistant director. Working someplace else, I don't know if I'd have gotten to do layout boards, timing, storyboards, editing, directing—all the different aspects of an episode's creation. That's really cool.

Dwayne Carey-Hill: At Rough Draft, there's always been a nurturing encouragement to work hard, adjust to the changing demands, and acquire new skills as the work progresses, which is invaluable on a show and for the artist.

Crystal Chesney-Thompson: Once you know the whole process, it becomes quite manageable to tackle just about anything.

Rich Moore: Early on, we believed we could do this show better than anyone because we had technology that integrates CG and 2D while making both feel they exist in the same universe. *The Simpsons* is a comedy about a suburban family. *Futurama* is a comedy about a workplace family traveling through outer space. So, it needs to look better than *The Simpsons*. A genre like science fiction demands the art direction be heavier and more consistent, otherwise it doesn't feel like science fiction.

We all knew going in that the writing and the jokes take center stage. We were there to support that with beautiful designs, dynamic animation, great color, and a kind of a scope that *The Simpsons* didn't have, because, as a domestic comedy, it doesn't have to be

art directed within an inch of its life. At the same time, *Futurama* needs to be in Matt's style, which is all about shape and form. Once you get into Matt's wavelength of what makes good design, you start to learn that it's all about comedy. It's all about humility, and making the characters feel like underdogs, putting them behind the eight ball. This goes against what a lot of animation designers are taught, or what they believe: that their characters should always look cool. But what makes Matt's characters cool is that they're so *uncool*. And with Matt, that is deliberate. That is part of his process. Matt's style reads beautifully in silhouette, and each character has a unique attribute that identifies them. You don't get them confused with any other cartoon or comic character.

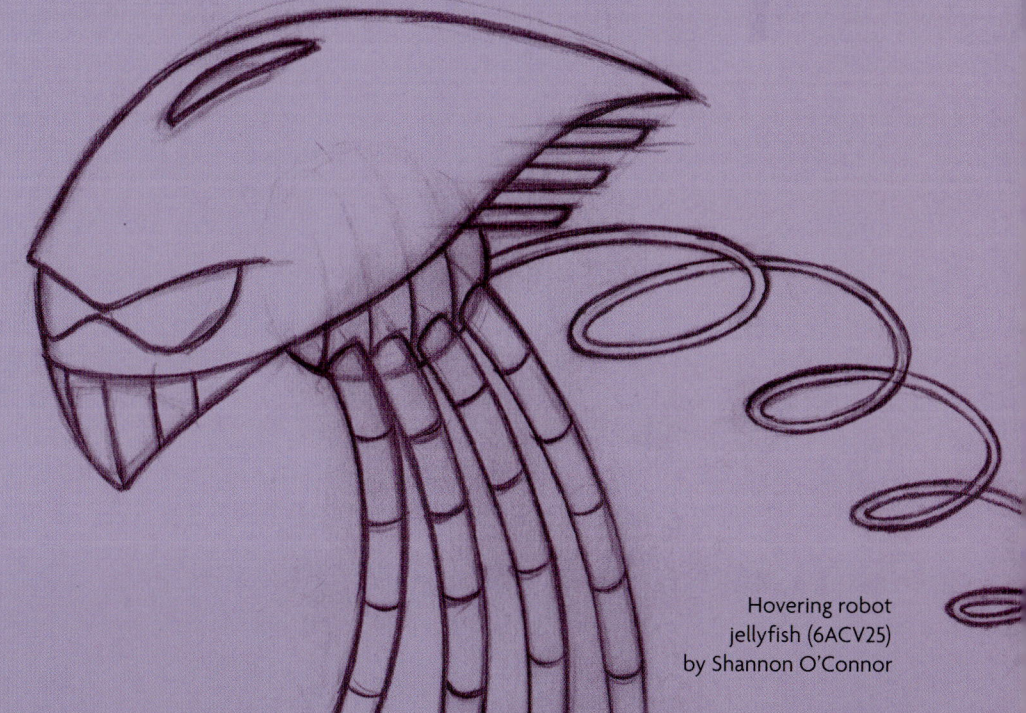

Hovering robot jellyfish (6ACV25) by Shannon O'Connor

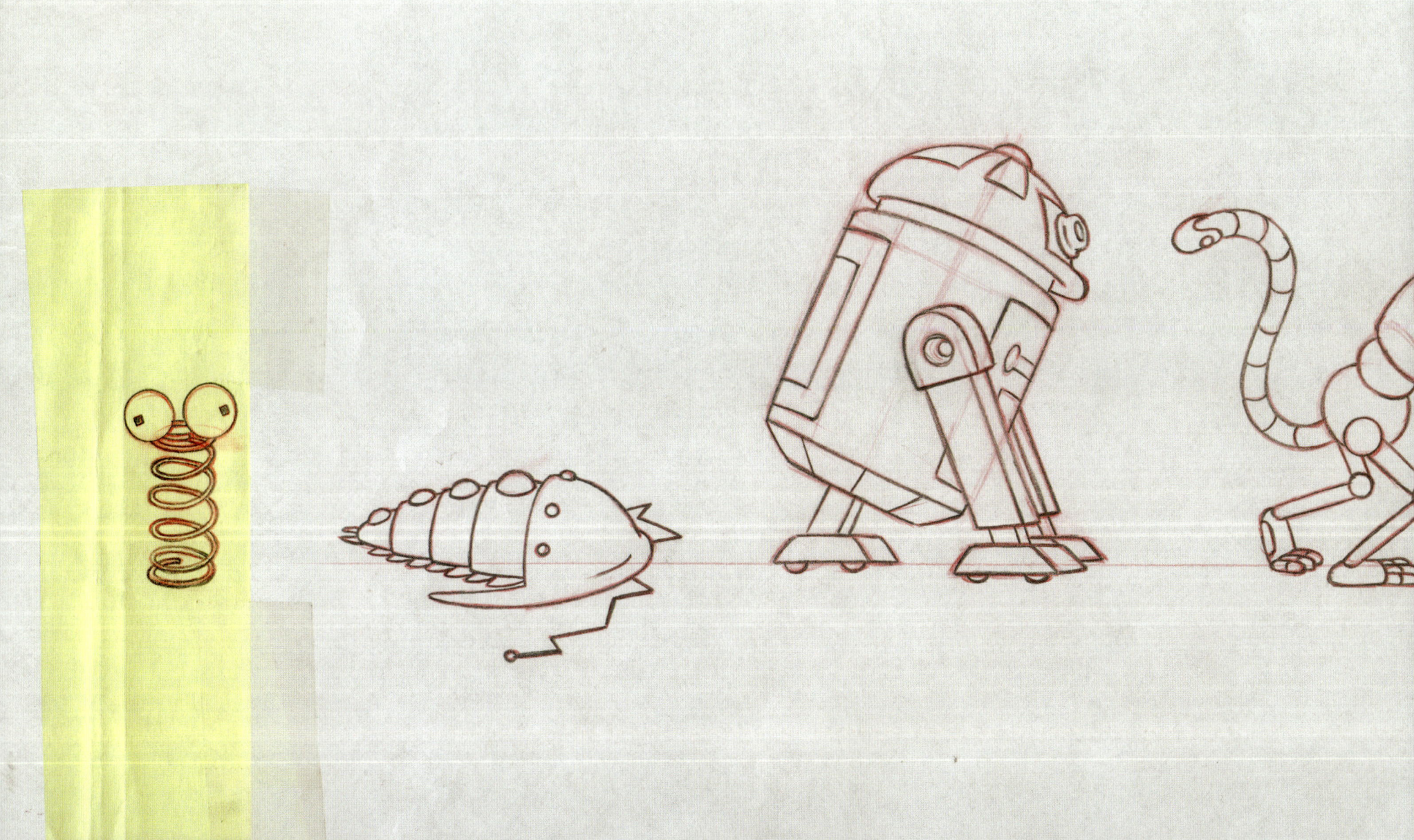

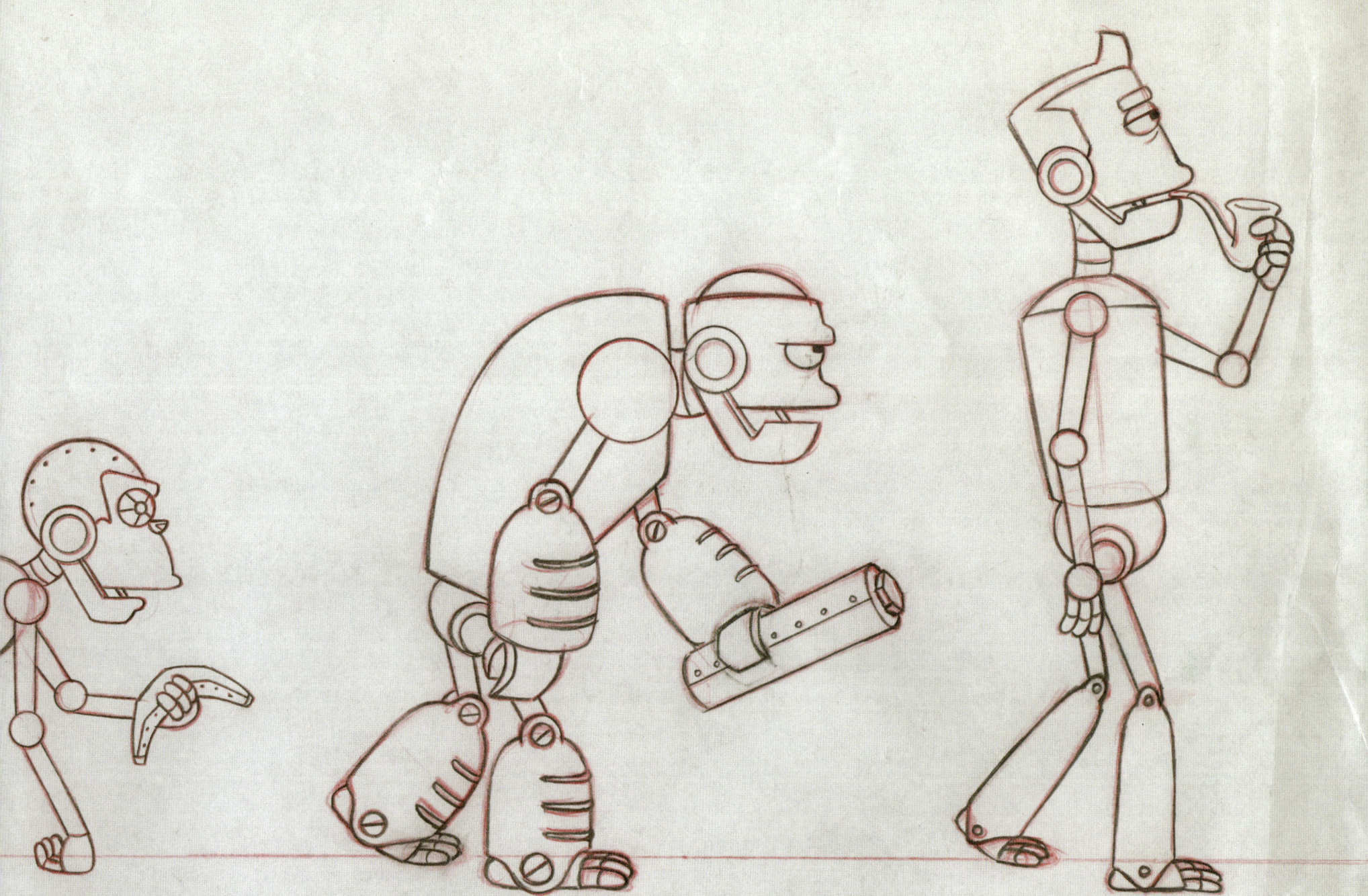

Evolution of Robot (6ACV09)
by Shannon O'Connor

Pocket Pal was originally one of the main characters we designed for the pitch, though he wasn't really used until Season 5. Matt's idea was just a AA battery with arms and legs. In an earlier design his head is just a light bulb. Just a little bulb.

— Bill Morrison

Pocket Pal, with his Mickey-style gloves and a Simpsons TV rabbit ear antenna on top, was inspired by Gyro Gearloose's Little Helper. I thought he was going to be a big hit (sniff).

— Matt Groening

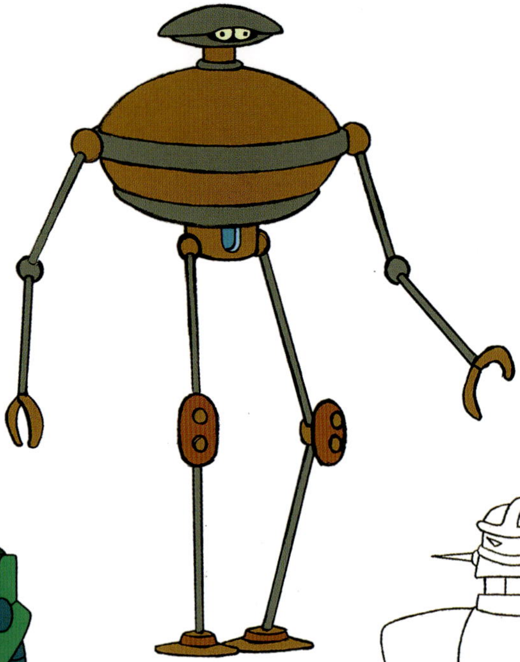

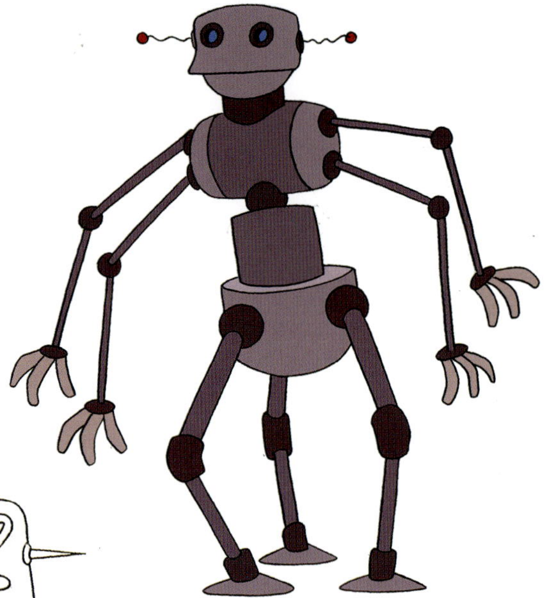

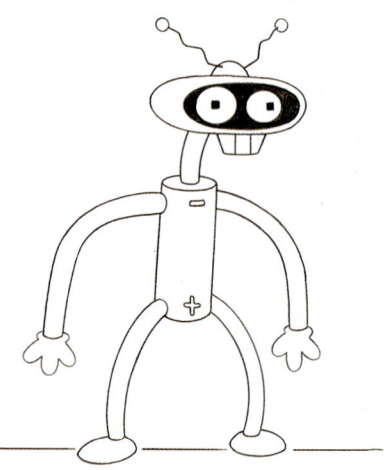

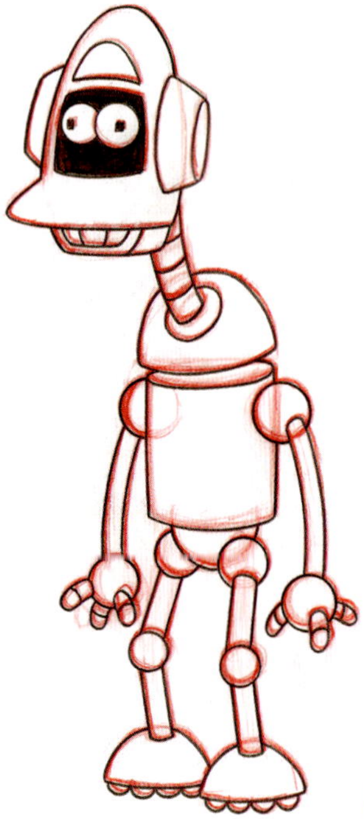

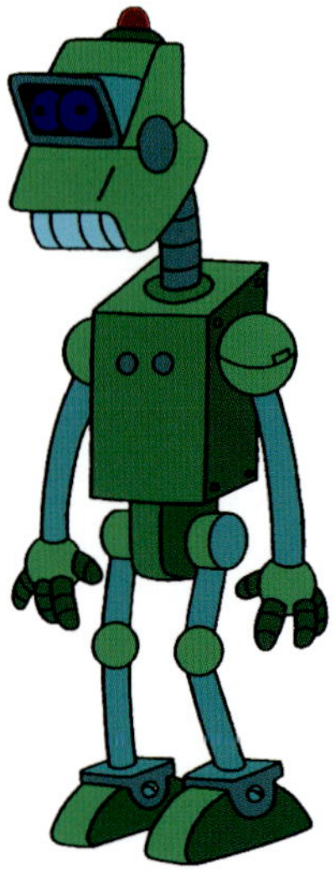

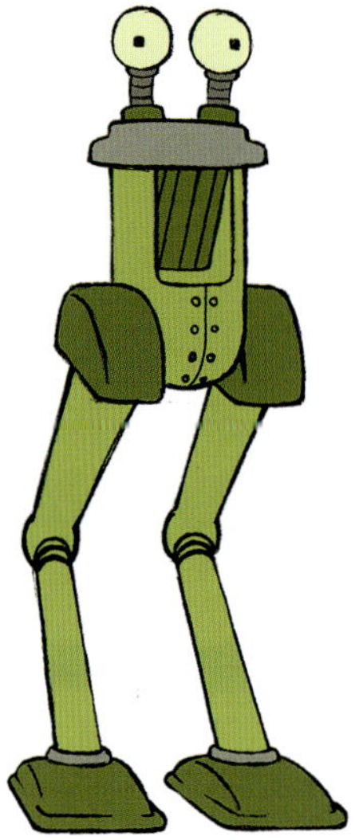

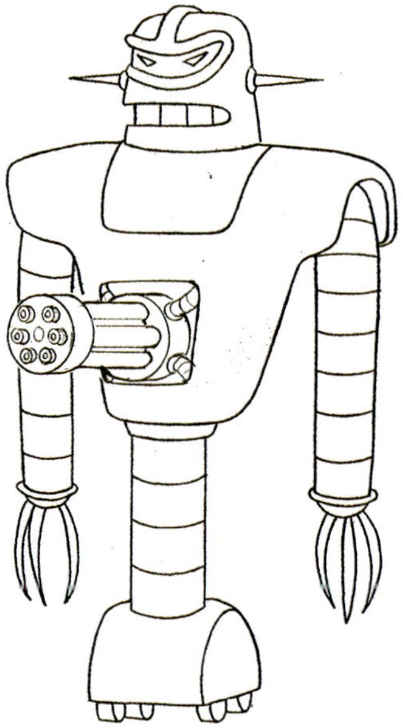

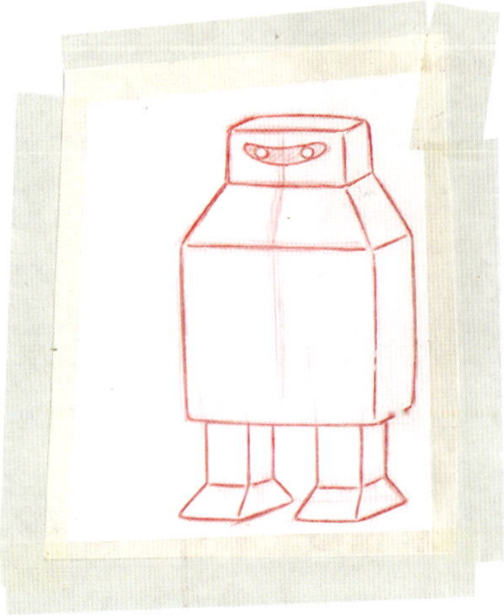

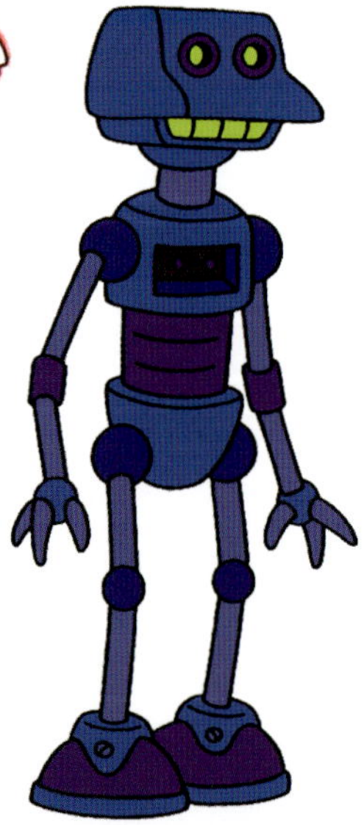

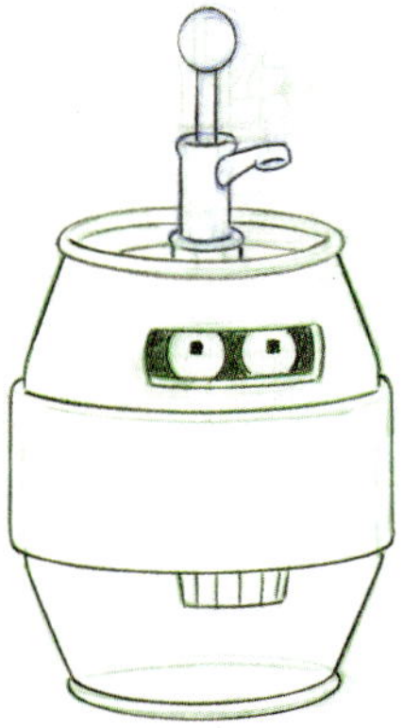

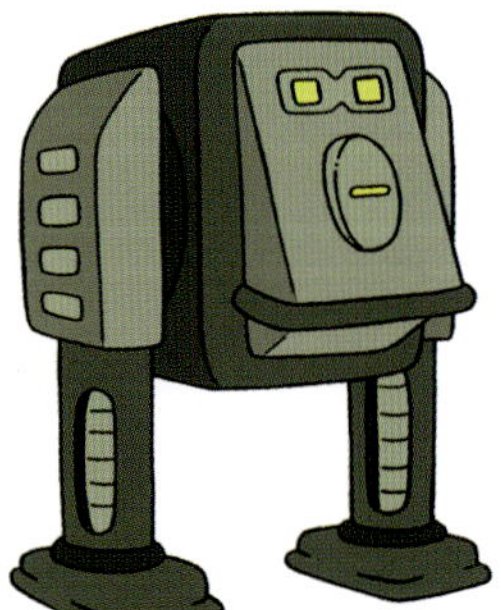

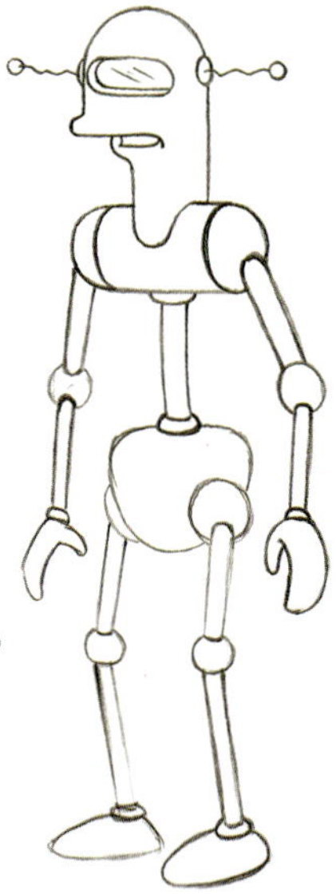

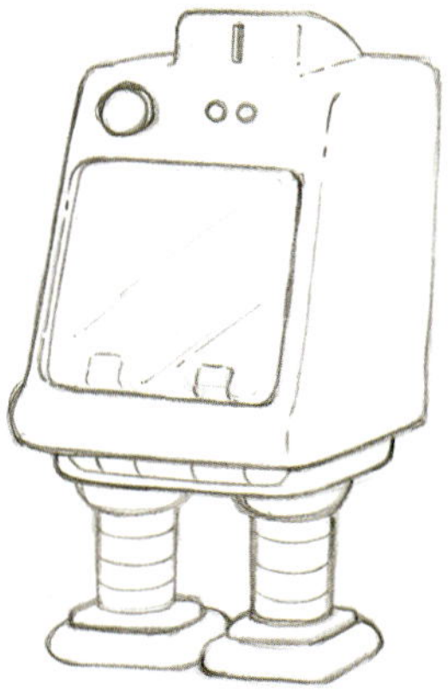

Top (from left to right):
Generic robot (1ACV07) by Dwayne Carey-Hill
Piano player robot (1ACV04) by Brian Sheesley

Middle (from left to right):
Pocket Pal (5ACV06) by Matt Groening
Generic robot (1ACV09) by Kevin M. Newman
Generic robot (1ACV01) by Kevin M. Newman
Generic robot (1ACV01) by Dwayne Carey-Hill
Corpsatron (1ACV04) by Brian Sheesley
Boxy robot (1ACV07) by Dwayne Carey-Hill

Bottom (from left to right):
Generic robot (1ACV01) by Kevin M. Newman
Keg-like robot (4ACV08) by Jim Feeley
Generic robot (1ACV01) by Dwayne Carey-Hill
Generic robot (1ACV01) by Dwayne Carey-Hill
Newspaper vending robot (7ACV03) by Dwayne Carey-Hill

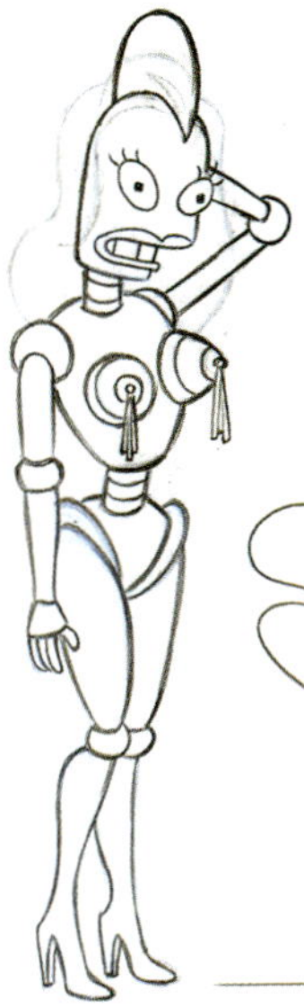

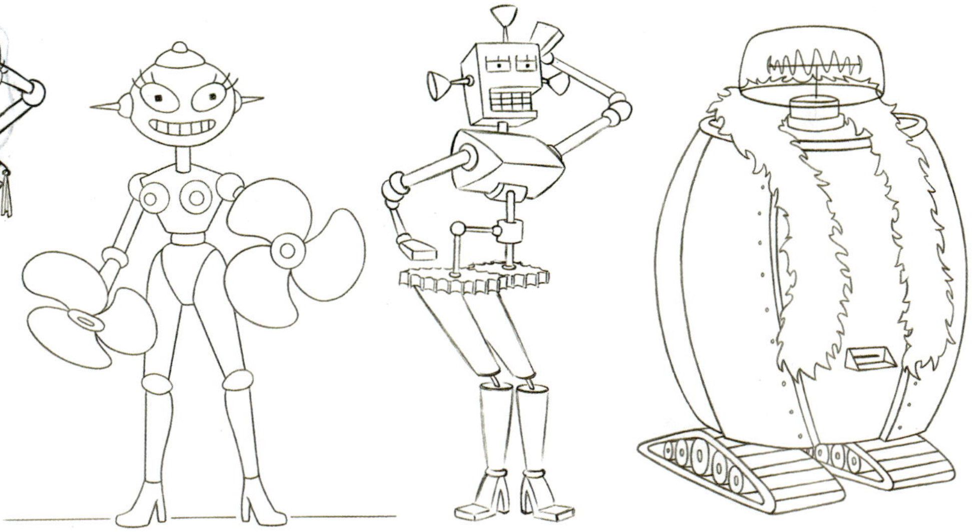

All these robots either have multiple or no antennas coming out of their heads. If there was another robot in the show with just a single antenna, it would be a mistake. Bender is the only one.

— Bill Morrison

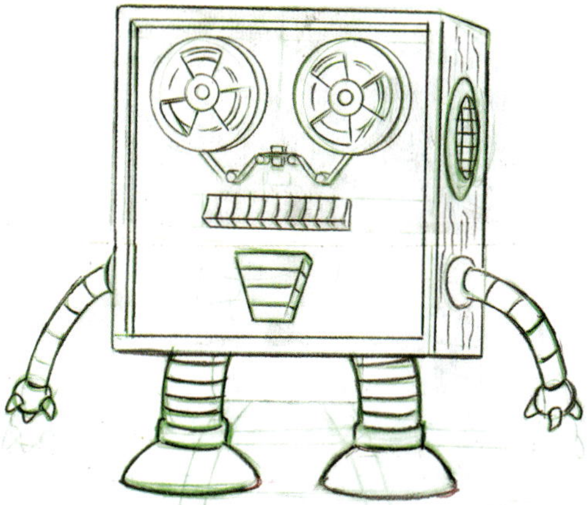

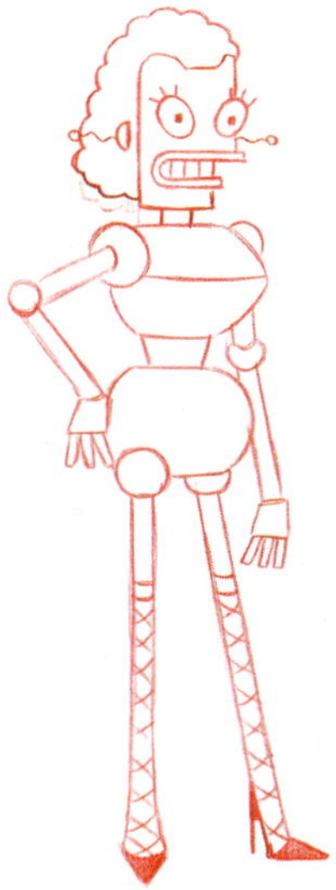

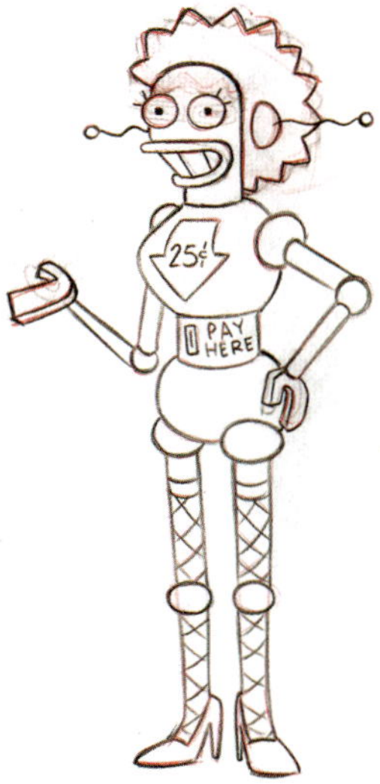

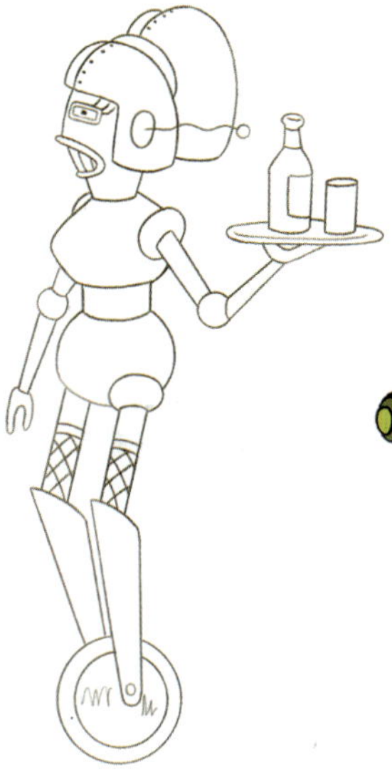

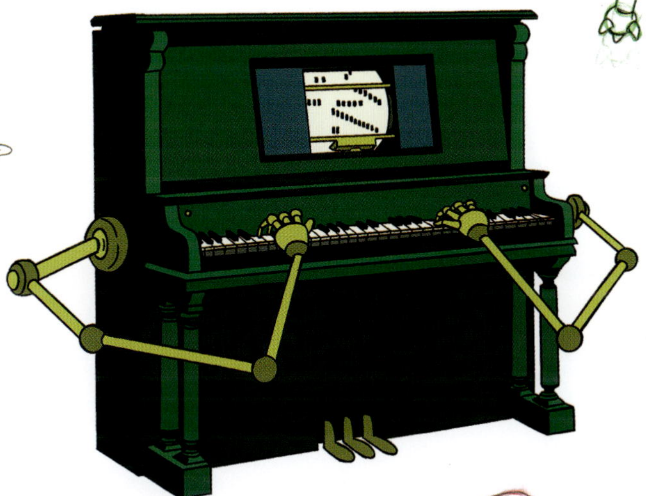

Top (from left to right):
Stripper robot with tassels (1ACV09)
by Kevin M. Newman and Rich Moore
Stripper robots (2ACV06) by Eric Keyes
Reel-to-reel robot (4ACV08) by Jim Feeley

Middle (from left to right):
Bimbo robot (2ACV08) by Eric Keyes
Hooker robot (2ACV07) by Rich Moore
Hooker robot 5000 (2ACV06) by Chris Sauve
Player-piano robot (6ACV14) by Timothy Hwang

Bottom (from left to right):
Robot maid (5ACV10) by Karapet Keroglyan
Robot dinosaur skeletons (6ACV09)
by Shannon O'Connor

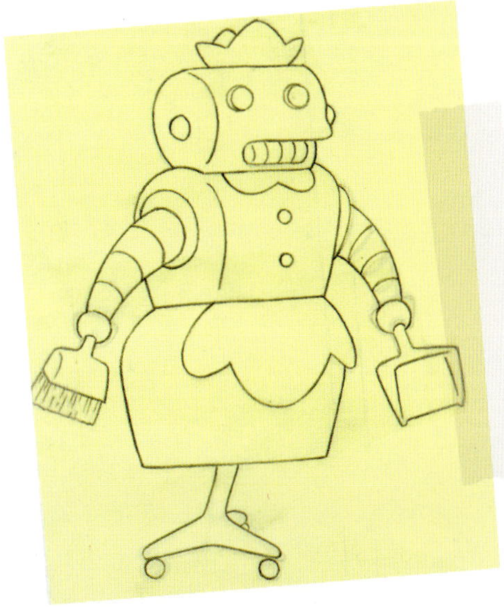

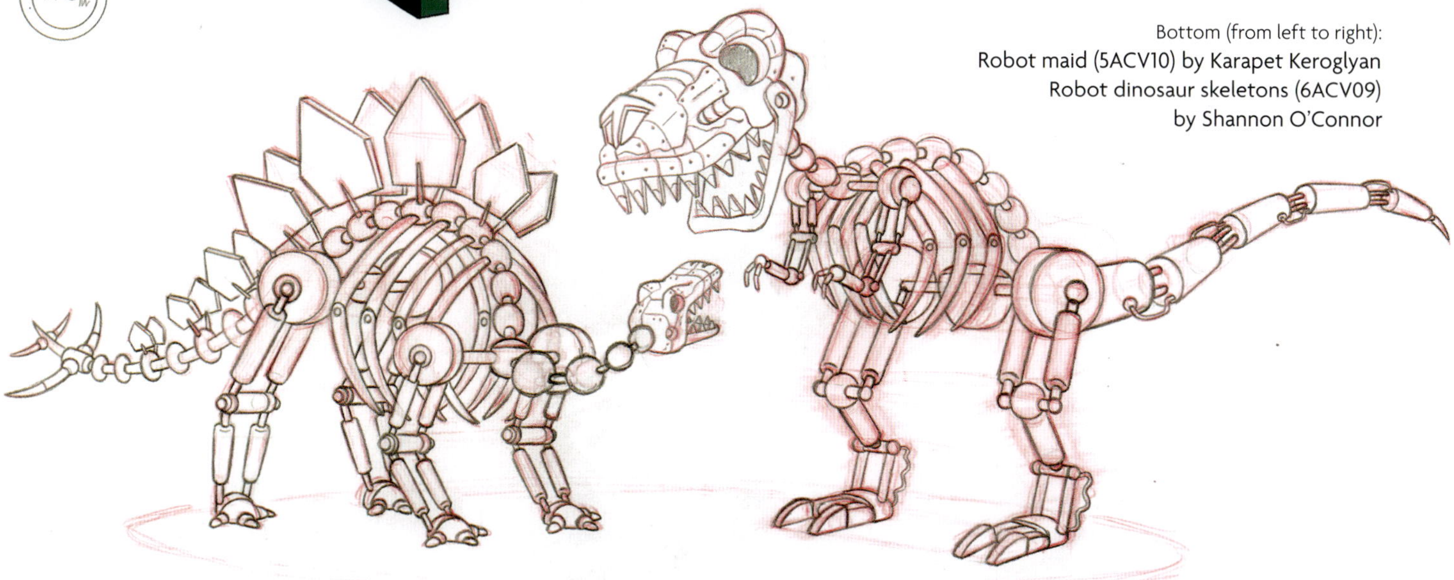

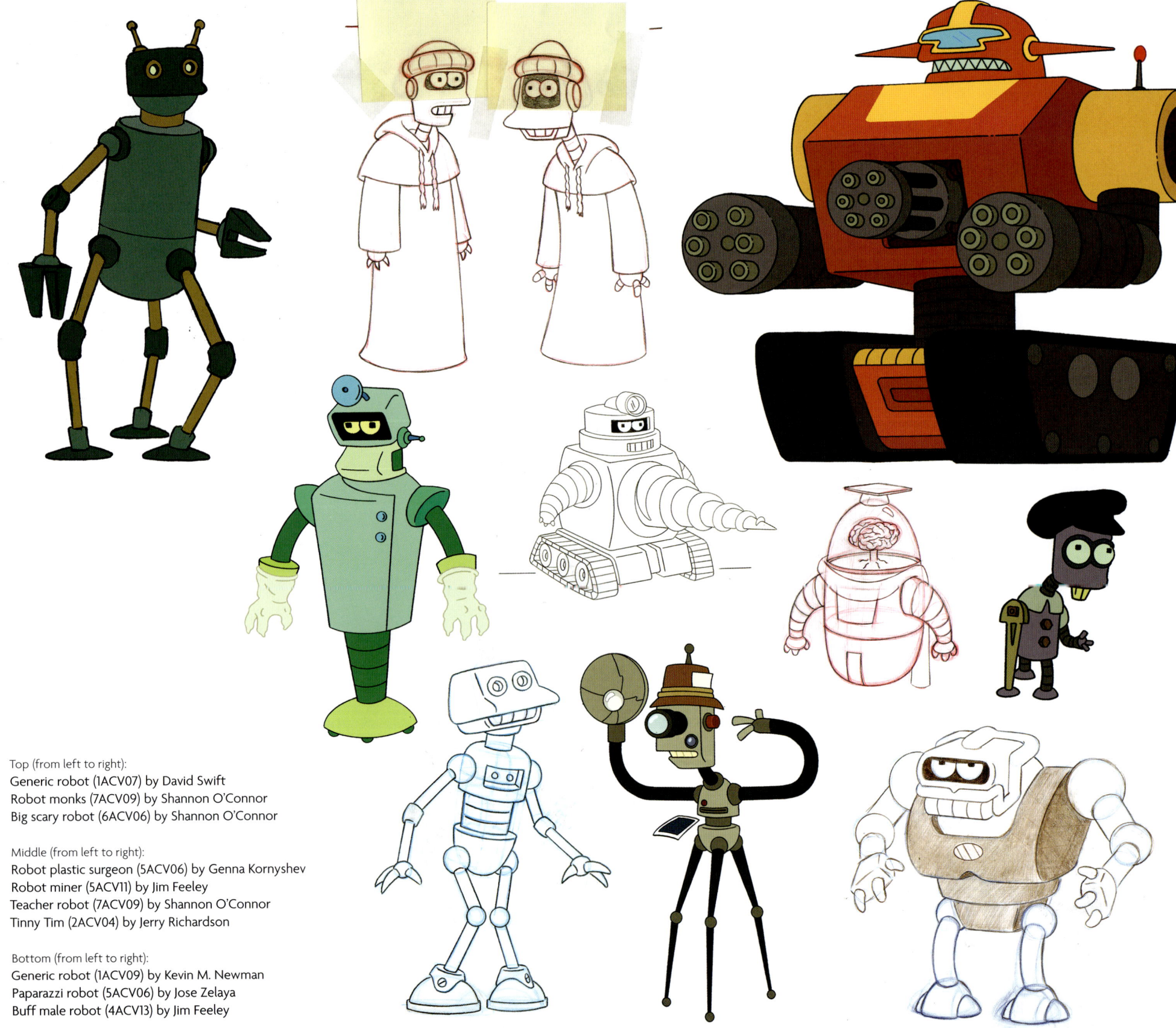

74

Top (from left to right):
Generic robot (1ACV07) by David Swift
Robot monks (7ACV09) by Shannon O'Connor
Big scary robot (6ACV06) by Shannon O'Connor

Middle (from left to right):
Robot plastic surgeon (5ACV06) by Genna Kornyshev
Robot miner (5ACV11) by Jim Feeley
Teacher robot (7ACV09) by Shannon O'Connor
Tinny Tim (2ACV04) by Jerry Richardson

Bottom (from left to right):
Generic robot (1ACV09) by Kevin M. Newman
Paparazzi robot (5ACV06) by Jose Zelaya
Buff male robot (4ACV13) by Jim Feeley

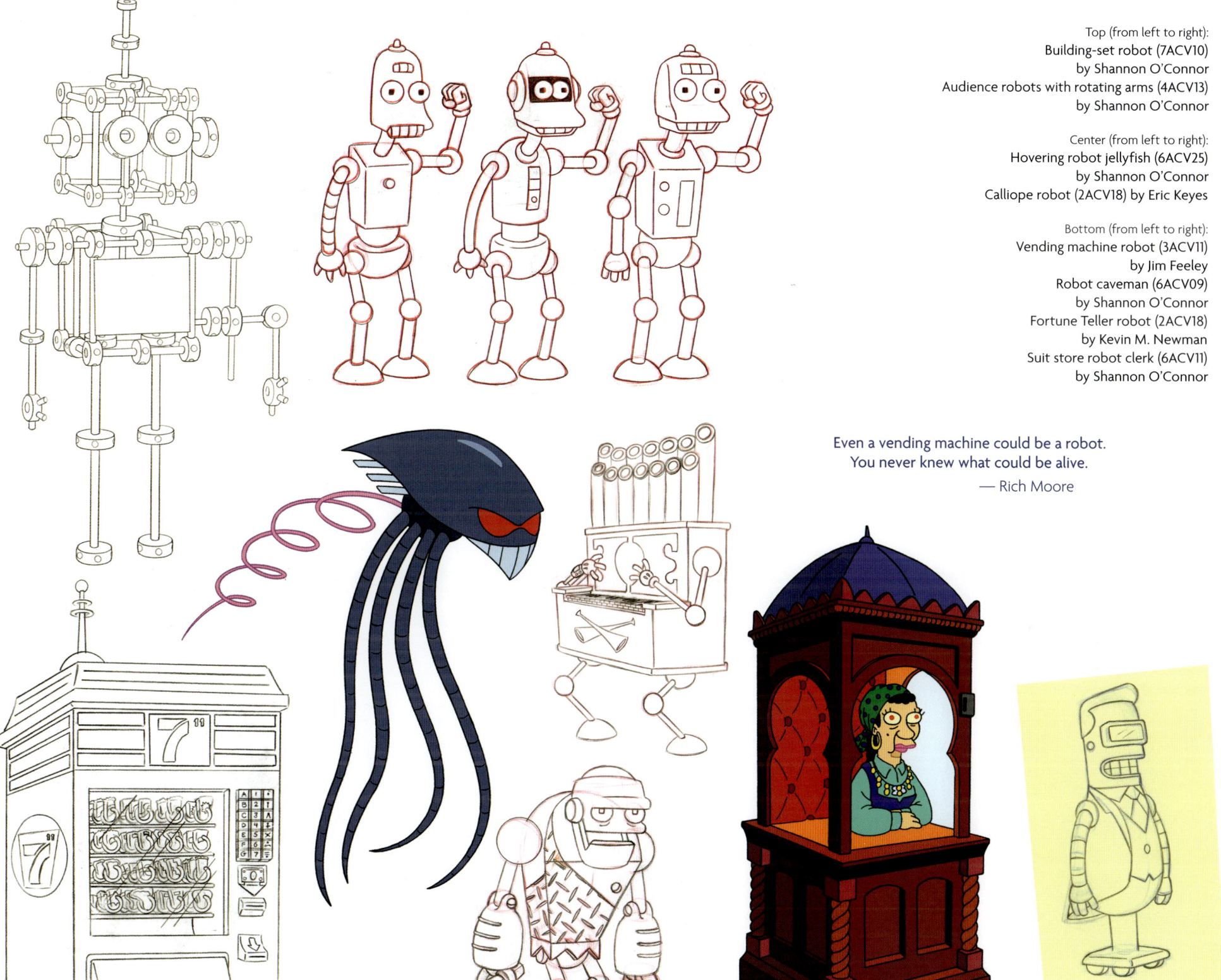

Top (from left to right):
Building-set robot (7ACV10)
by Shannon O'Connor
Audience robots with rotating arms (4ACV13)
by Shannon O'Connor

Center (from left to right):
Hovering robot jellyfish (6ACV25)
by Shannon O'Connor
Calliope robot (2ACV18) by Eric Keyes

Bottom (from left to right):
Vending machine robot (3ACV11)
by Jim Feeley
Robot caveman (6ACV09)
by Shannon O'Connor
Fortune Teller robot (2ACV18)
by Kevin M. Newman
Suit store robot clerk (6ACV11)
by Shannon O'Connor

Even a vending machine could be a robot.
You never knew what could be alive.
— Rich Moore

Following pages:
Robot Cemetery (7ACV07) by Maurice Morgan

75

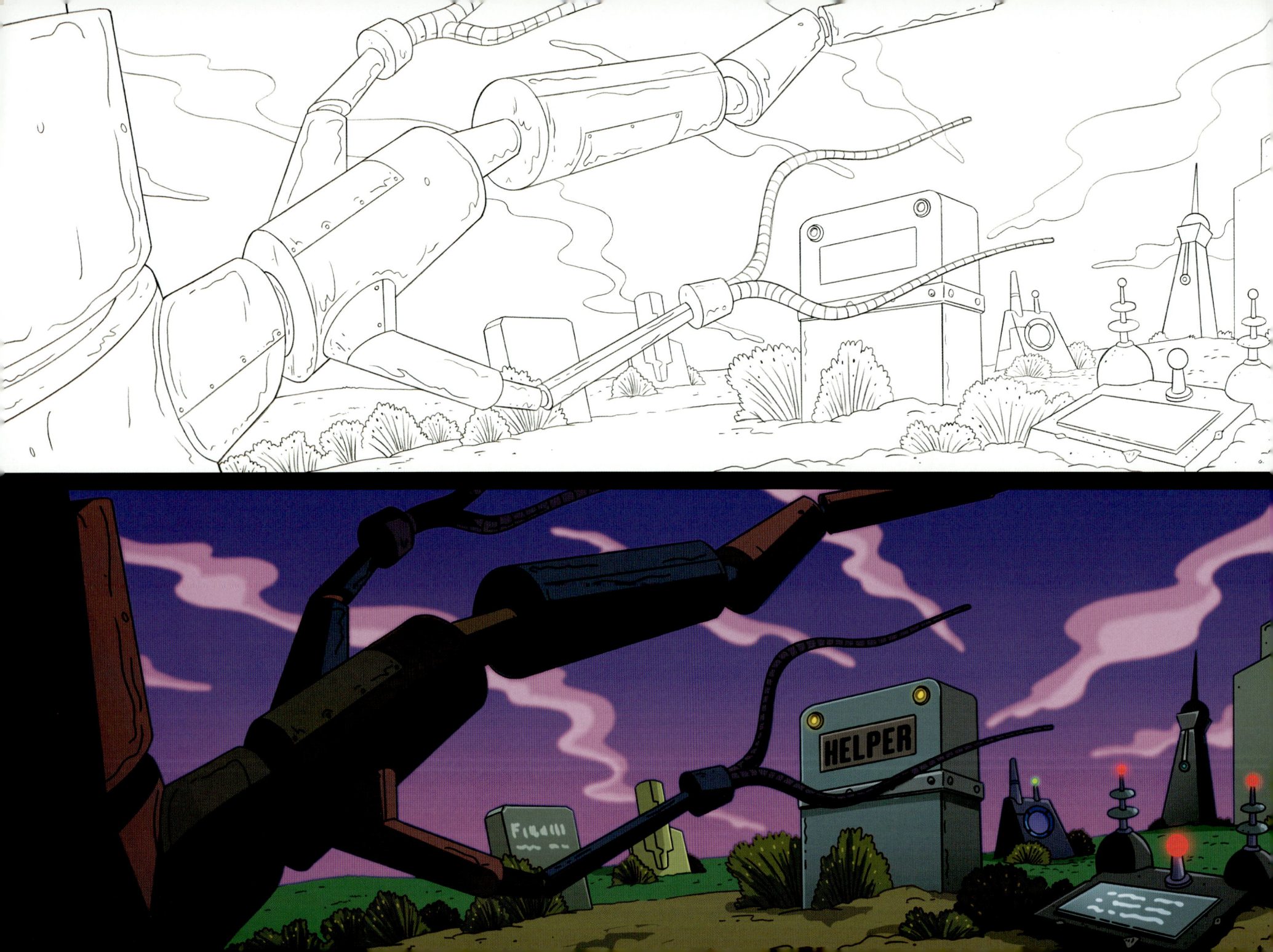

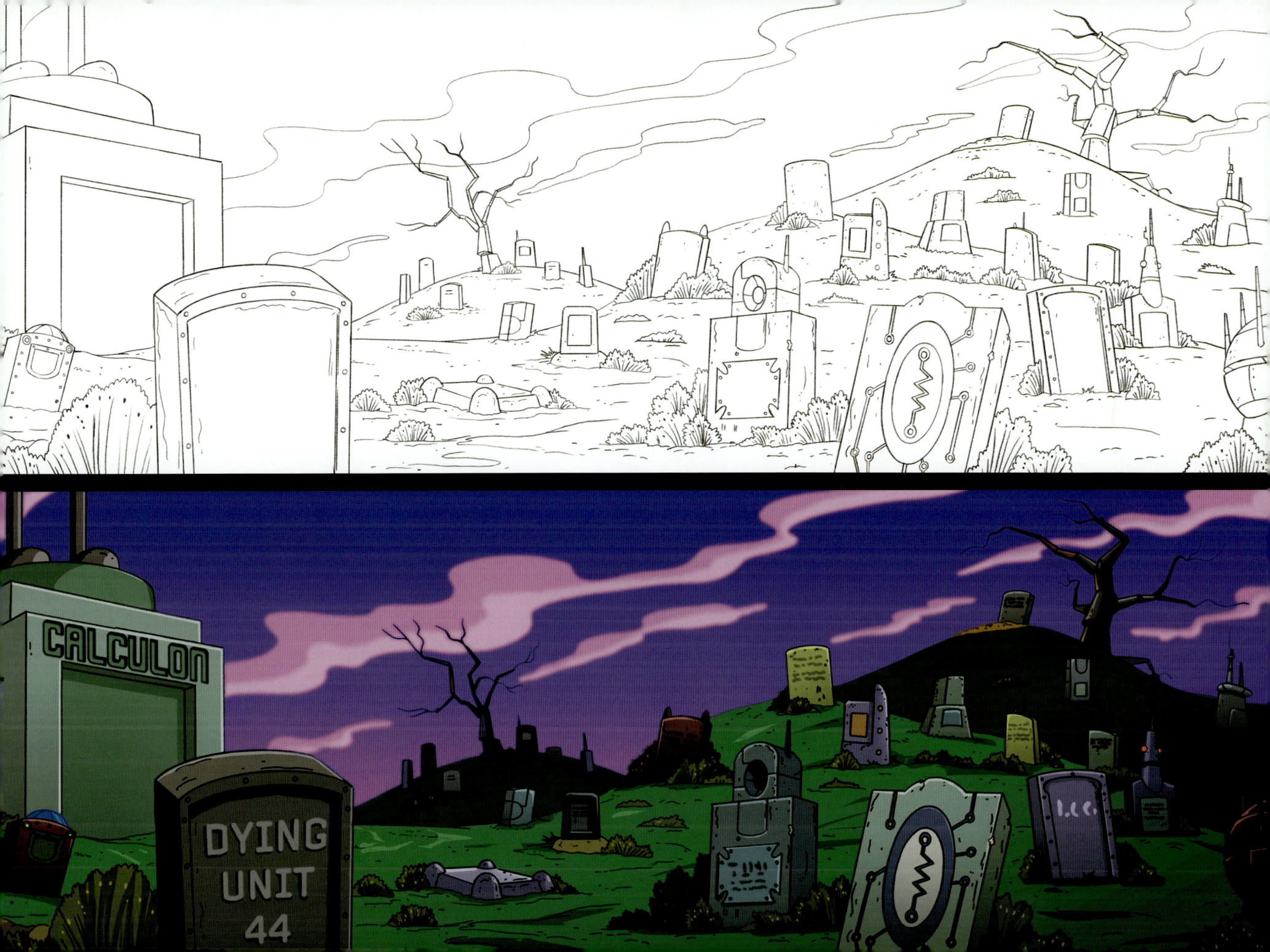

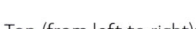

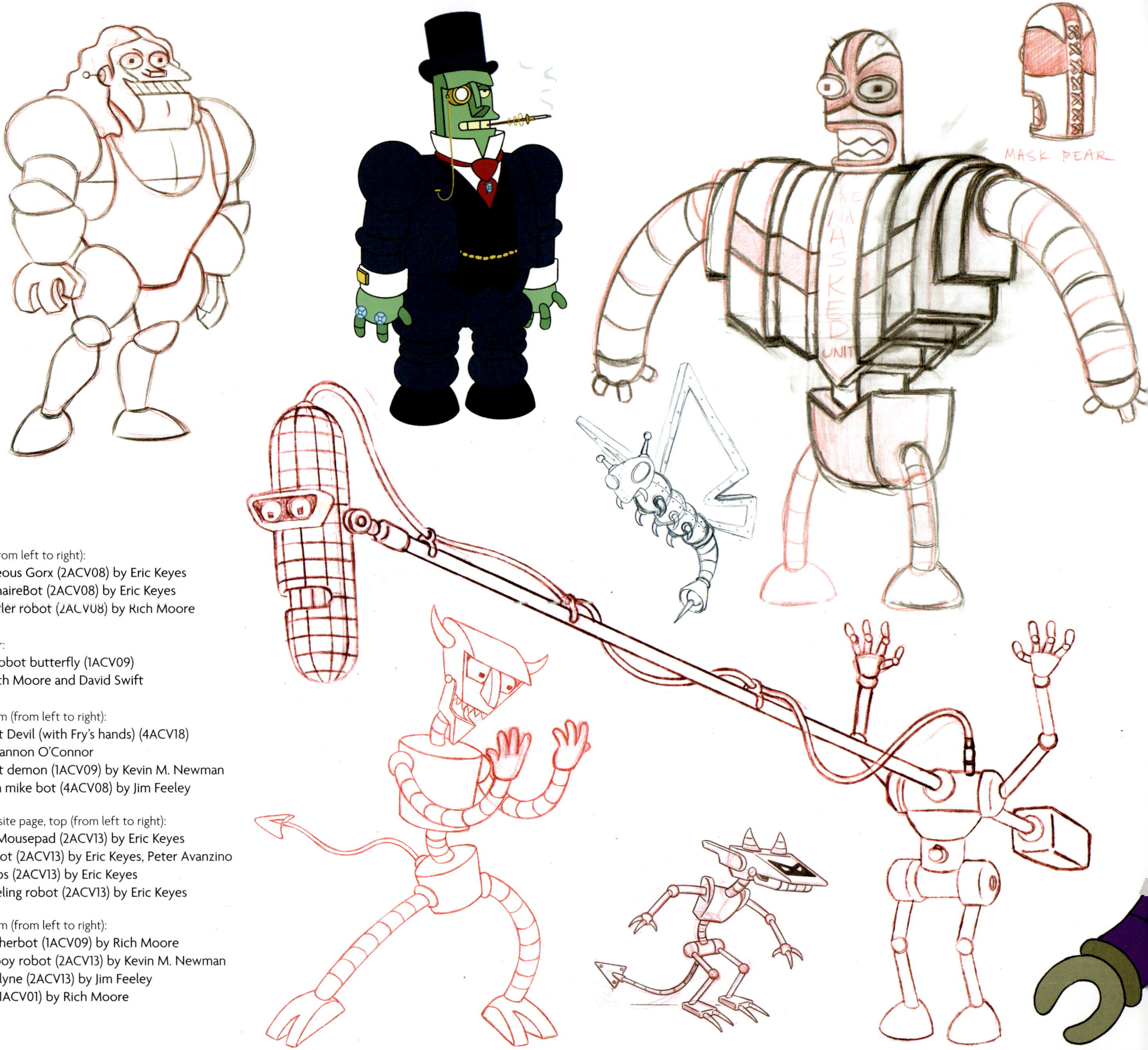

Top (from left to right):
Gorgeous Gorx (2ACV08) by Eric Keyes
BillionaireBot (2ACV08) by Eric Keyes
Wrestler robot (2ACV08) by Rich Moore

Center:
Hell robot butterfly (1ACV09)
by Rich Moore and David Swift

Bottom (from left to right):
Robot Devil (with Fry's hands) (4ACV18)
by Shannon O'Connor
Robot demon (1ACV09) by Kevin M. Newman
Boom mike bot (4ACV08) by Jim Feeley

Opposite page, top (from left to right):
Joey Mousepad (2ACV13) by Eric Keyes
Donbot (2ACV13) by Eric Keyes, Peter Avanzino
Clamps (2ACV13) by Eric Keyes
Groveling robot (2ACV13) by Eric Keyes

Bottom (from left to right):
Preacherbot (1ACV09) by Rich Moore
Cowboy robot (2ACV13) by Kevin M. Newman
Anglelyne (2ACV13) by Jim Feeley
URL (1ACV01) by Rich Moore

MASK REAR

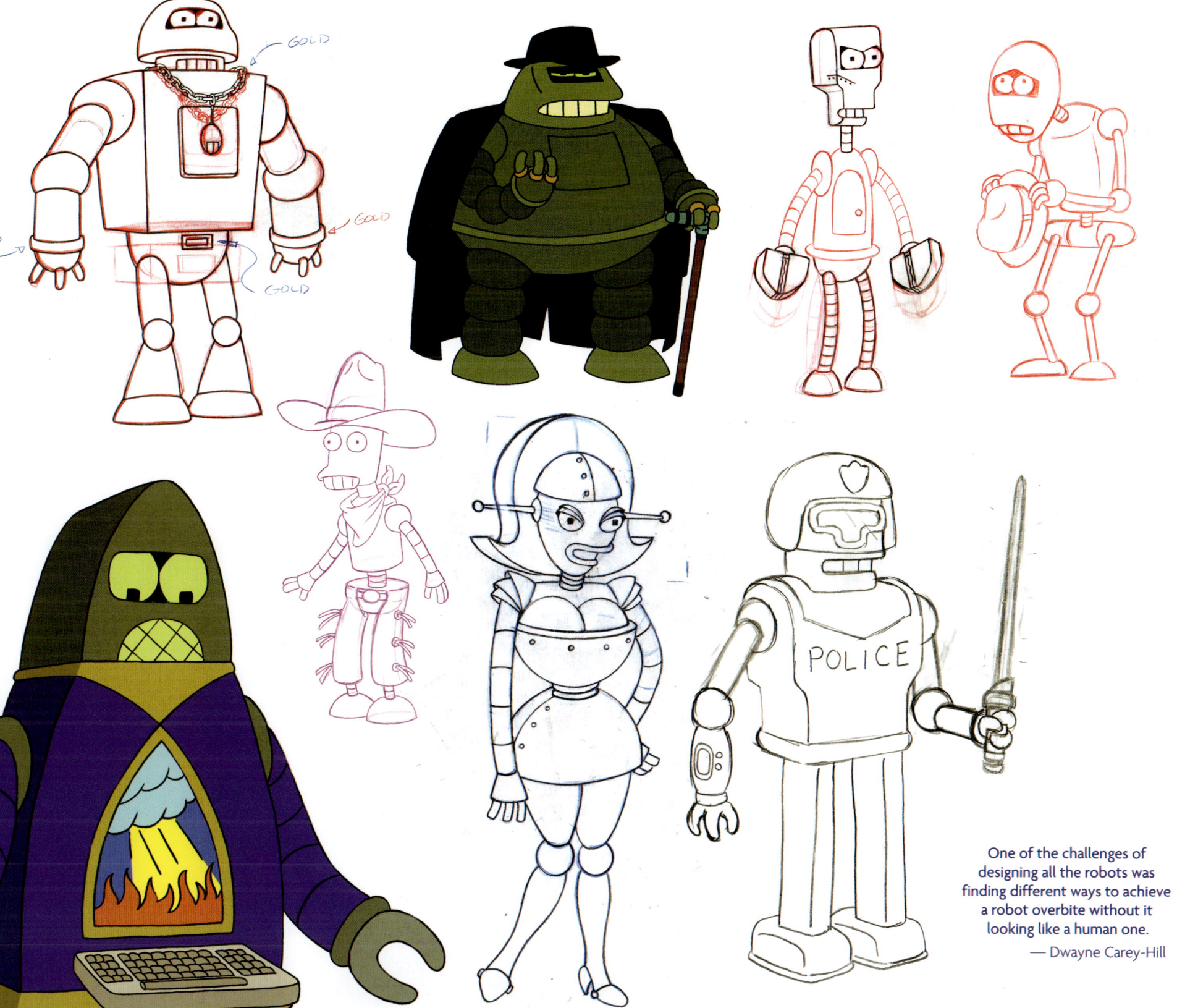

GOLD
GOLD
GOLD

POLICE

One of the challenges of designing all the robots was finding different ways to achieve a robot overbite without it looking like a human one.

— Dwayne Carey-Hill

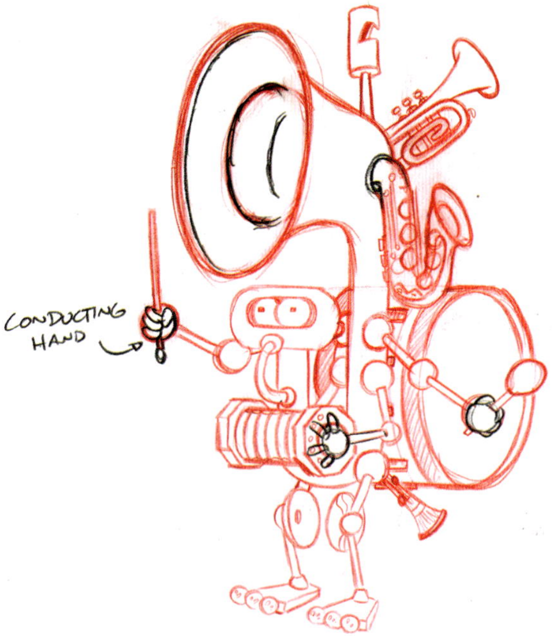

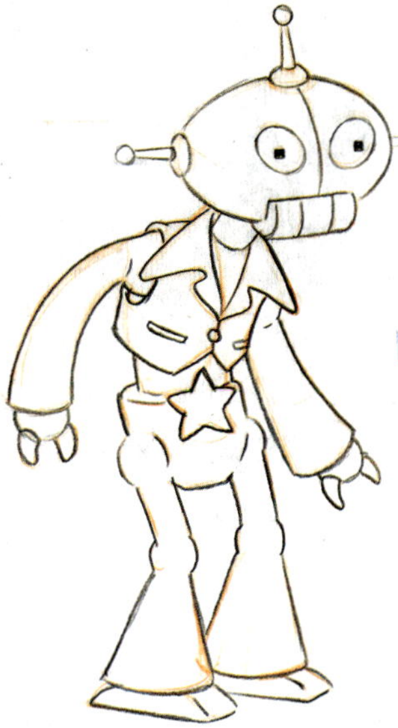

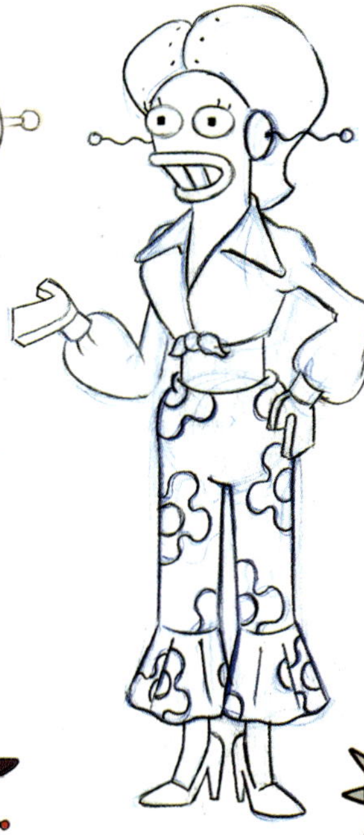

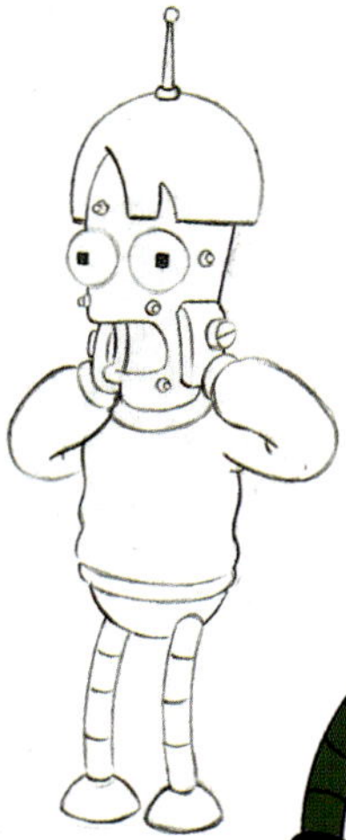

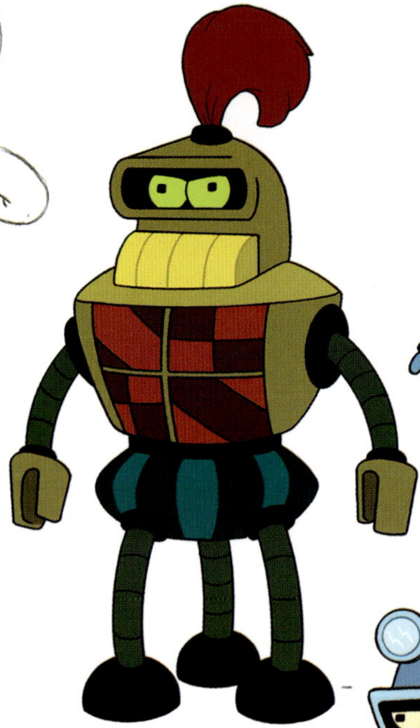

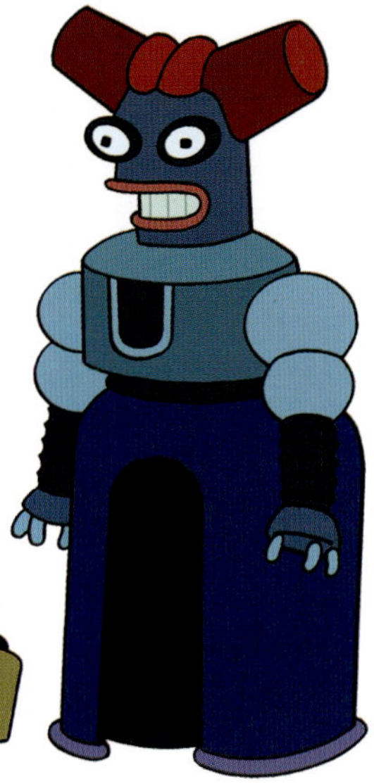

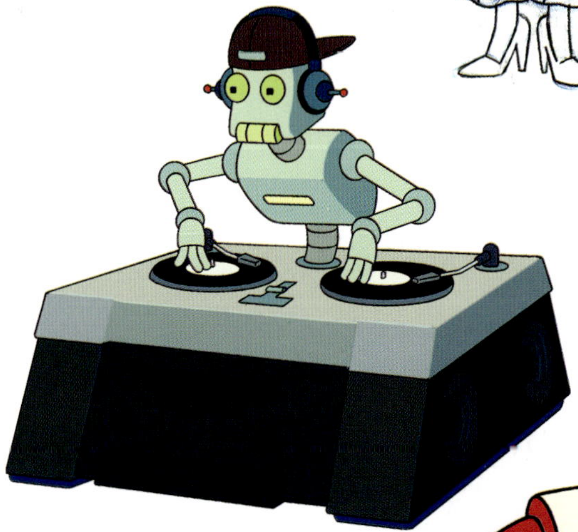

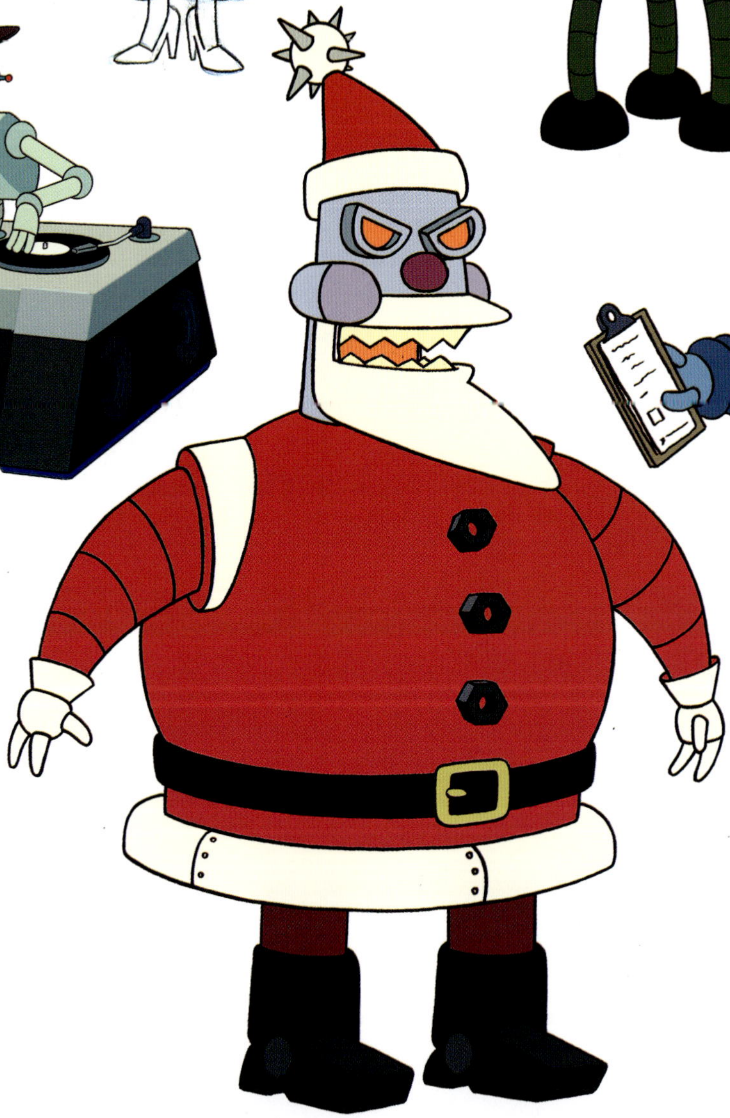

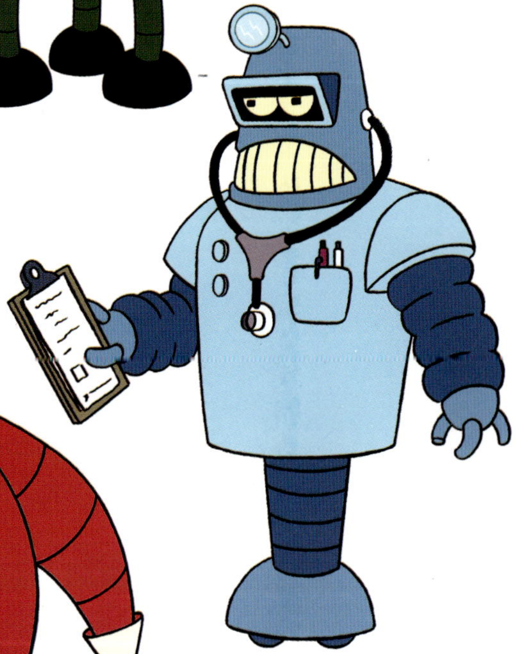

Top (from left to right):
One-bot band (2ACV13) by Eric Keyes
Robot in 1970's clothes (4ACV06) by Jim Feeley
Robot in 1970's clothes (4ACV06) by Jim Feeley
Macaulay Cul-Con (4ACV06) by Jim Feeley
Medieval robot knight (5ACV11) by Jim Feeley
Medieval robot incidental (5ACV11) by Jim Feeley

Bottom (from left to right):
DJ robot (6ACV12) by Jim Feeley
Robot Santa (2ACV04) by Kevin M. Newman
Robot doctor (2ACV01) by Mark Ervin

Opposite page, top (from left to right):
Robot Elder (1ACV05) by Dwayne Carey-Hill
Robot in human costume (1ACV05) by Dwayne Carey-Hill and Rich Moore
Robot general (1ACV05) by Dwayne Carey-Hill and Rich Moore
Trans-sex robot (1ACV13) by Ron Hughart and David Swift
Trans-sex robot X-Ray view (1ACV13) by Ron Hughart and David Swift

Opposite page, center (from left to right):
Robot pizza chef (1ACV06) by Gregg Vanzo
Execu-Tor (2ACV18) by Eric Keyes

Opposite page, bottom (from left to right):
Hellbot soldier (5ACV08) by Jim Feeley
All My Circuits actor robot (1ACV03) by David Swift
Hellbot pirate (5ACV08) by Jim Feeley

CONDUCTING HAND

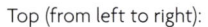

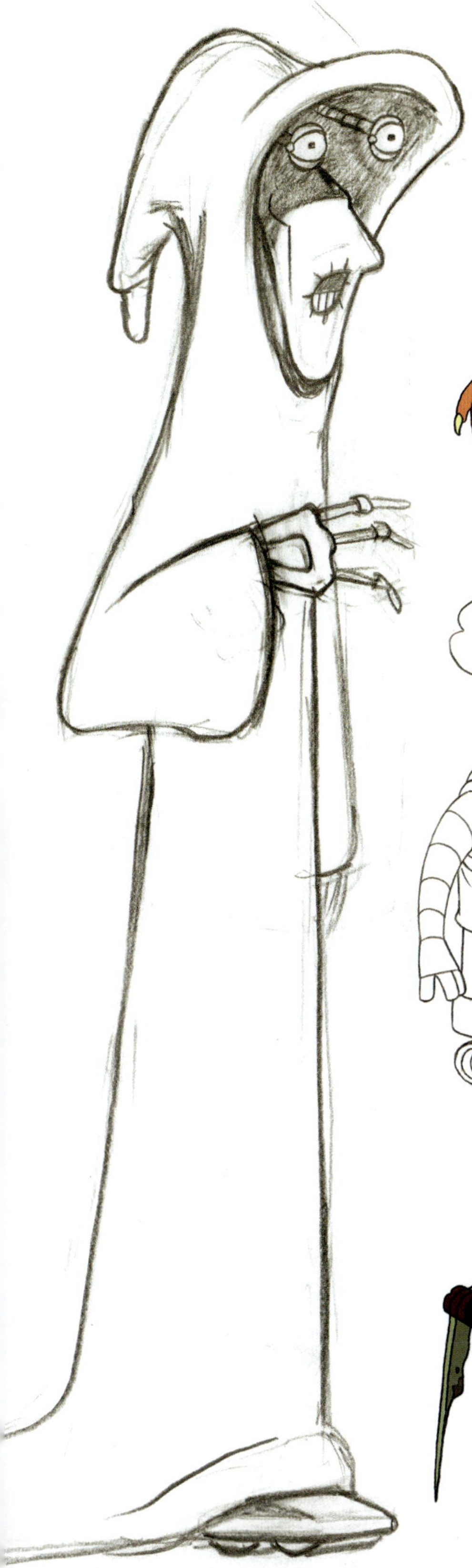

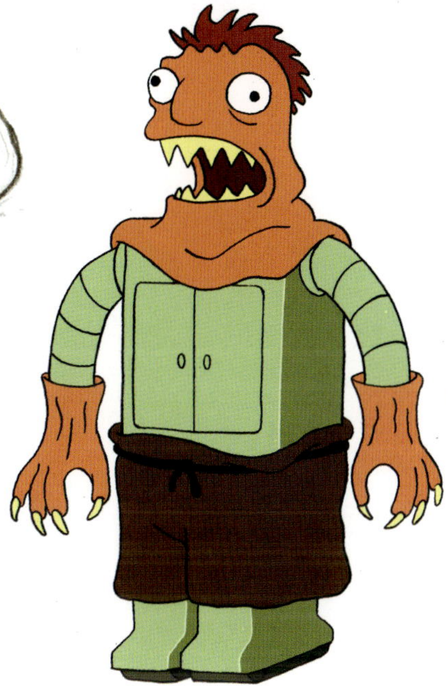

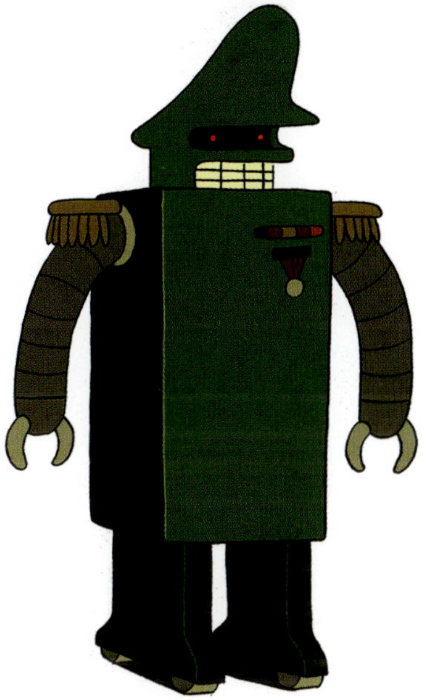

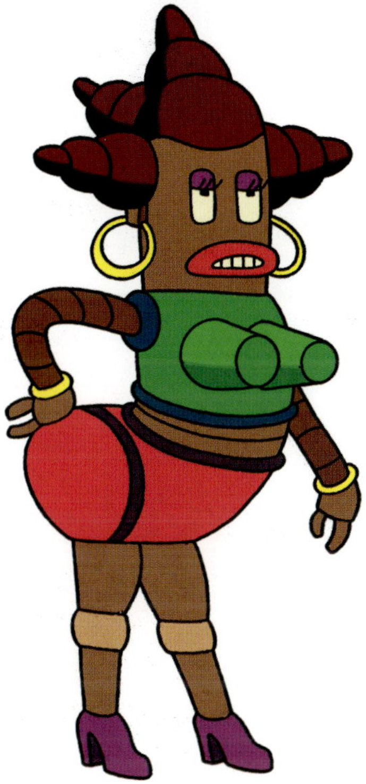

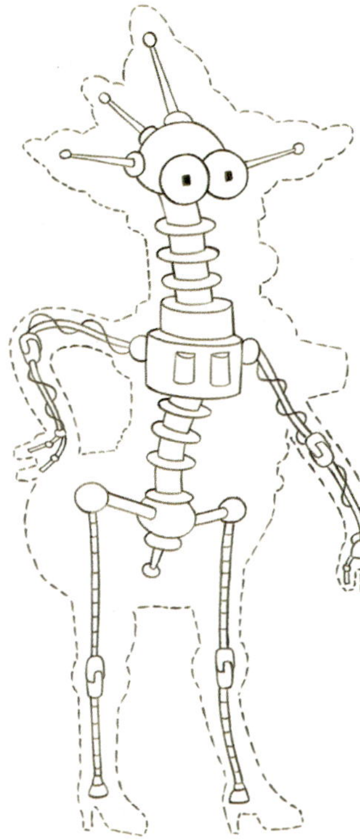

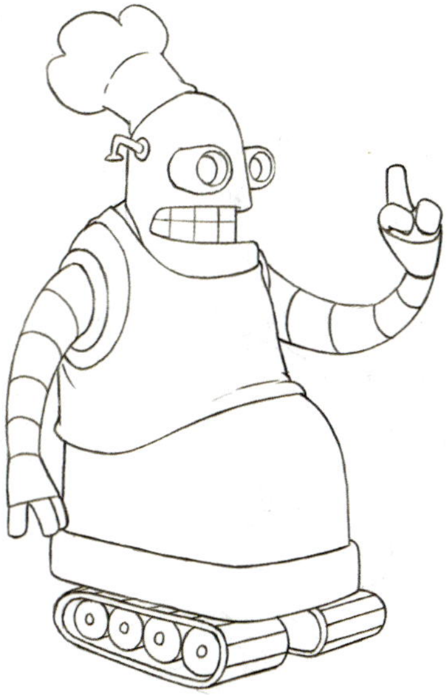

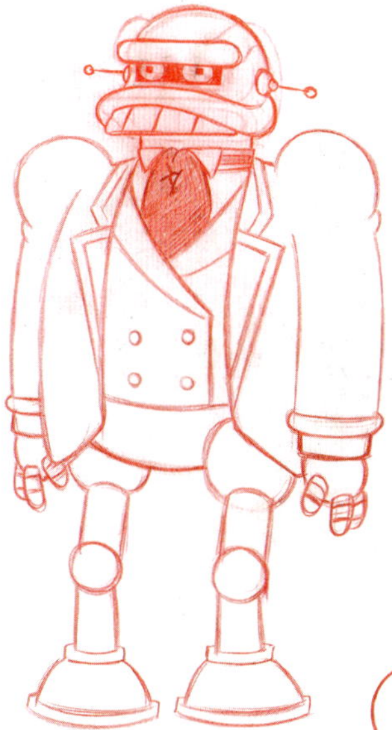

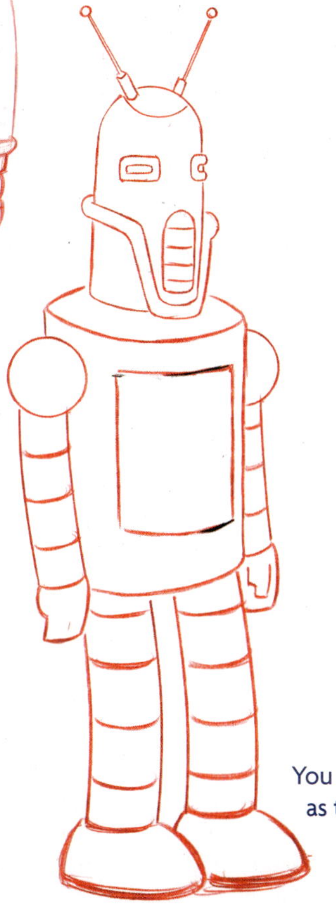

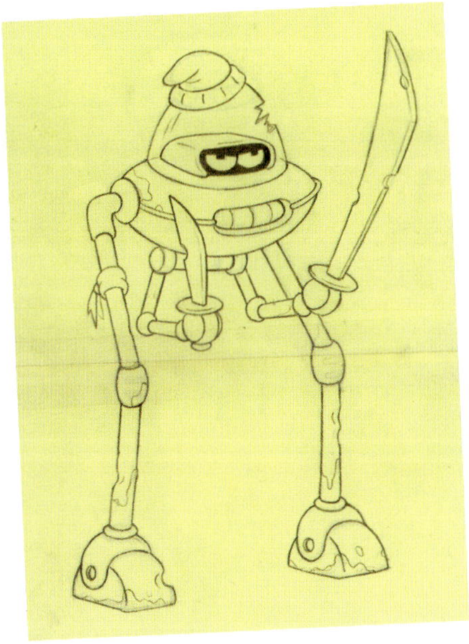

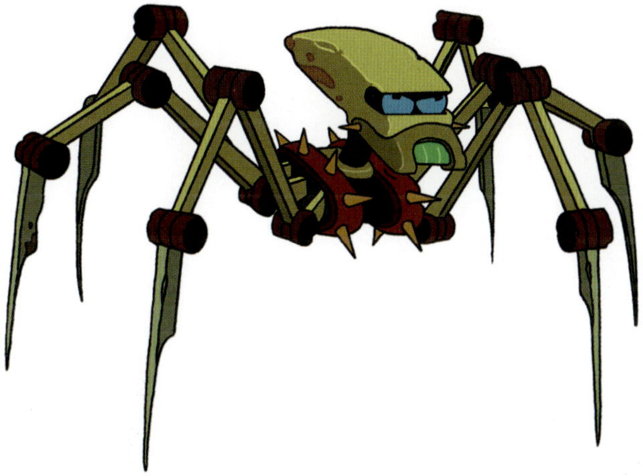

This robot was a really old one.
You can kind of tell. They got more detailed
as the show went on. Just finding our way
at this point with this guy.

— Rich Moore

CLIMBING TO ALTITUDE: DESTINATION GRATIFICATION

Matt Groening: What I'm really impressed by is how quickly, from the very first episode, Rough Draft had the look of the show, and it was consistent. You can watch the first episode and, unlike most cartoons, it really looks like what the show ended up being.

Rich Moore: When you're creating a world in animation, it should feel like it has some history to it. To achieve that, it shouldn't look like it's all designed by the same person. For instance, you might design an older building in New New York depicting a certain style, then add newer buildings with different architectural styles. The same with the cars and the clothes. Everything will have the overall feel of Matt's style, but there isn't one dominant aesthetic. Lots of great designers with their own definitive and distinct styles worked on *Futurama*, which lent a nice realism and sense of history to New New York.

Gregg Vanzo: The show was an ongoing process because we would concentrate on building what we needed right away for that script. Then the next episode would come and we'd build out a little more. That first season we were constantly building the city with the idea that we were going to keep coming back to it and use it a lot. As it turned out, in a lot of our future episodes we leave the city behind and end up going to lots of other different planets.

Every new planet, every new location the Planet Express crew visits, requires a lot of research. One planet might be based on Polynesian spirit lodges, another might be an Amazon village.

The designers need to research what each place might look like. What style is it in? The crazy intricate locations and civilizations that they create are grounded in diligent research so they convey authenticity. The design of a new location feels right to the viewer when it echoes things in our world that seem familiar. Once cleaned up and painted by Samantha Harrison's color crew they look gorgeous.

Rich Moore: I asked the color stylist, Samantha Harrison, if they had a name for the look of the color on *Futurama*. She called it "saturated tertiaries," meaning it's mostly not primary colors, like red, yellow, or blue. And it's not secondary colors, like green, orange, and purple. Tertiaries are this kind of gold or olive or taupe color, that often are described as neutral. You'll usually see them as a soft bed that other colors rest on. But in *Futurama*, Samantha wants those to be the highlight colors, the main colors, so she saturates them. When you look at the color of the show, it's these great tertiary colors that are just pumped. This is what gives the show it's unique look that's recognizable as *Futurama*.

Samantha Harrison: The challenge with color is that the characters are flat and the backgrounds are flat. So, in this world you're trying not to share the colors because things are passing over one another. Color-wise, the way the show looks is really flat with no gradations. For instance, when the *Planet Express* ship crashes into the Space Beehive (page 104) there are yellows on yellows within the dripping honey. There's a gradation there with color, but it's completely flat. Each shape is flat. At the very end of the process a Photoshop artist comes in, and

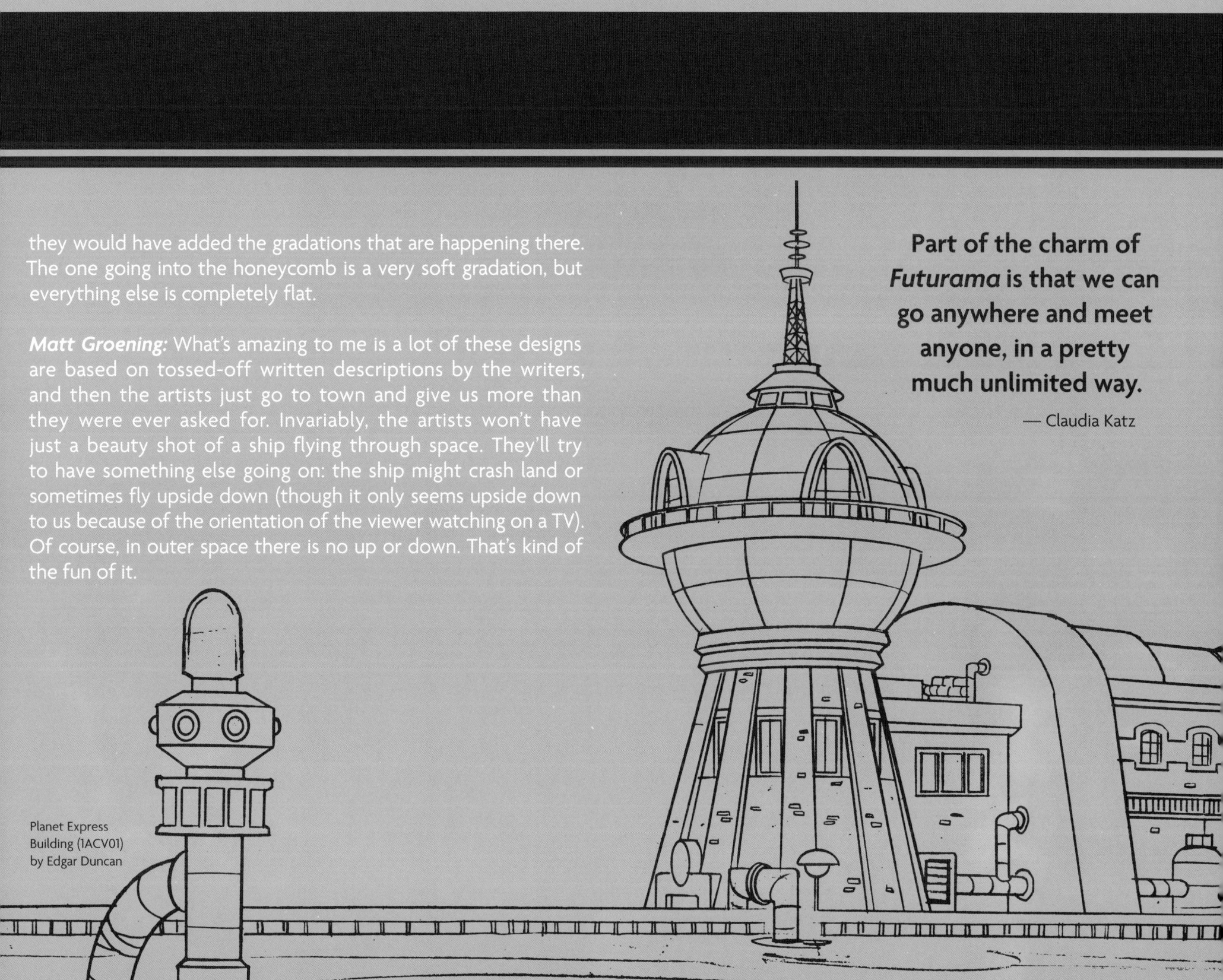

they would have added the gradations that are happening there. The one going into the honeycomb is a very soft gradation, but everything else is completely flat.

Matt Groening: What's amazing to me is a lot of these designs are based on tossed-off written descriptions by the writers, and then the artists just go to town and give us more than they were ever asked for. Invariably, the artists won't have just a beauty shot of a ship flying through space. They'll try to have something else going on: the ship might crash land or sometimes fly upside down (though it only seems upside down to us because of the orientation of the viewer watching on a TV). Of course, in outer space there is no up or down. That's kind of the fun of it.

Planet Express
Building (1ACV01)
by Edgar Duncan

Part of the charm of *Futurama* is that we can go anywhere and meet anyone, in a pretty much unlimited way.

— Claudia Katz

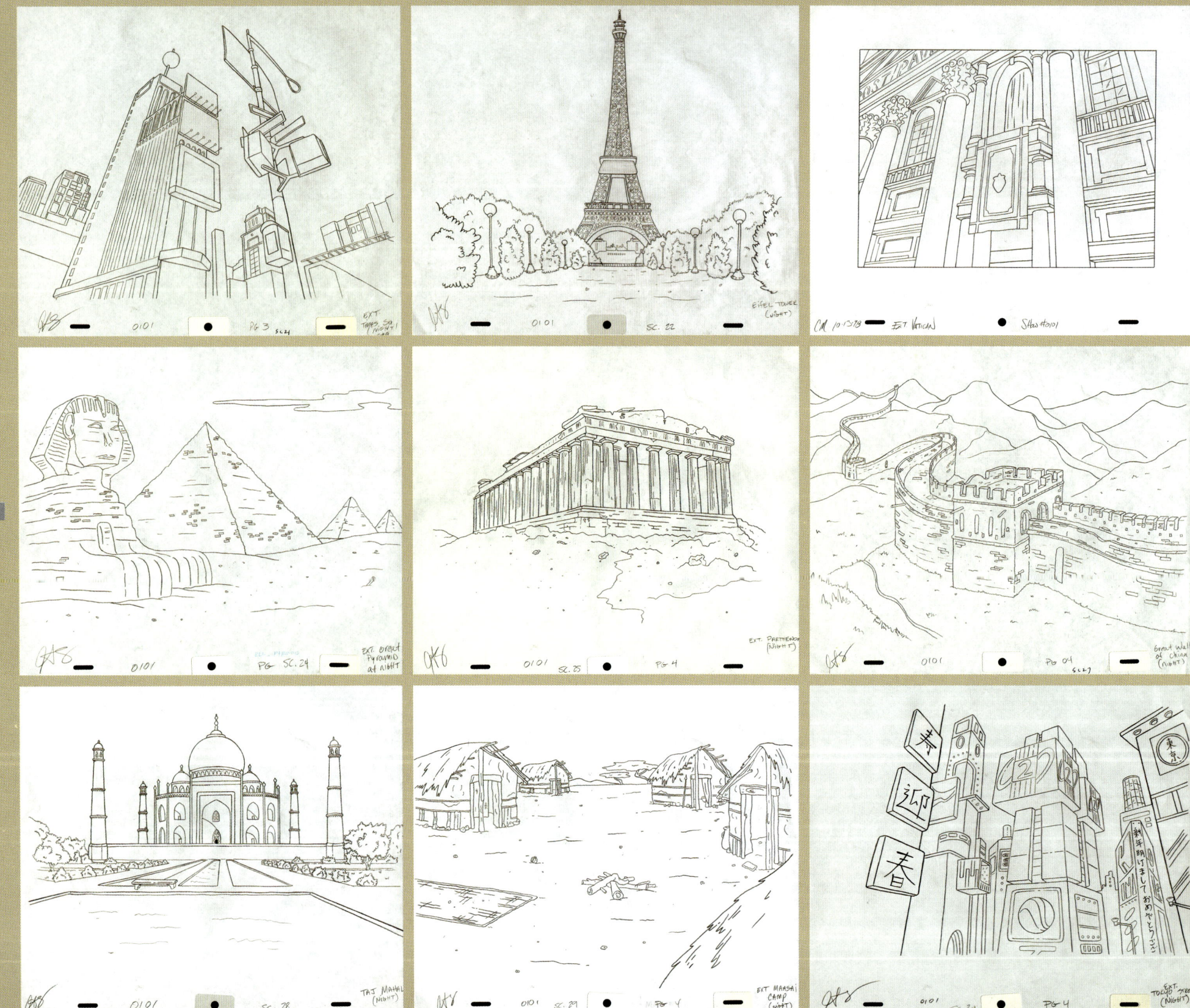

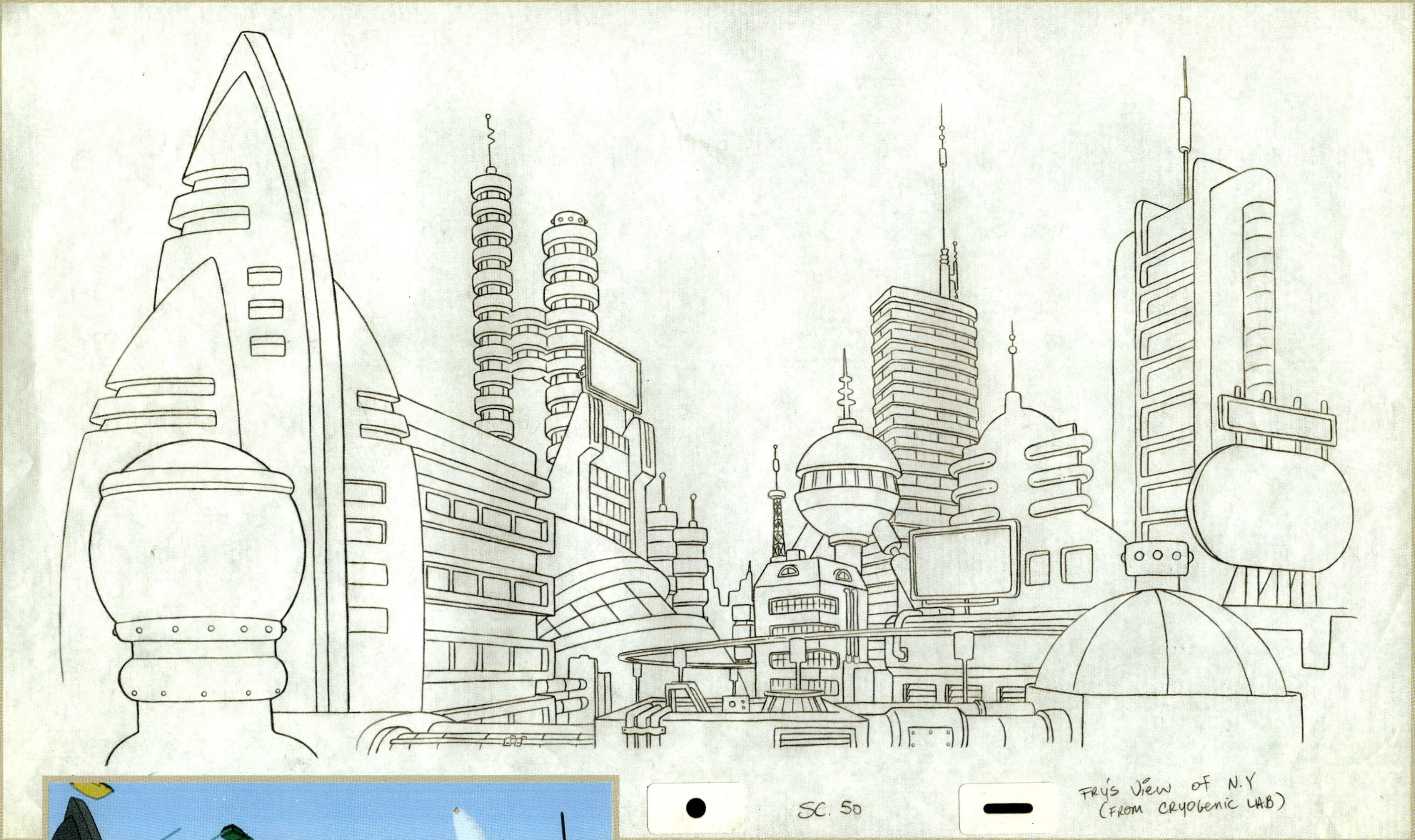

SC. 50

FRY's View OF N.Y
(FROM CRYOGENIC LAB)

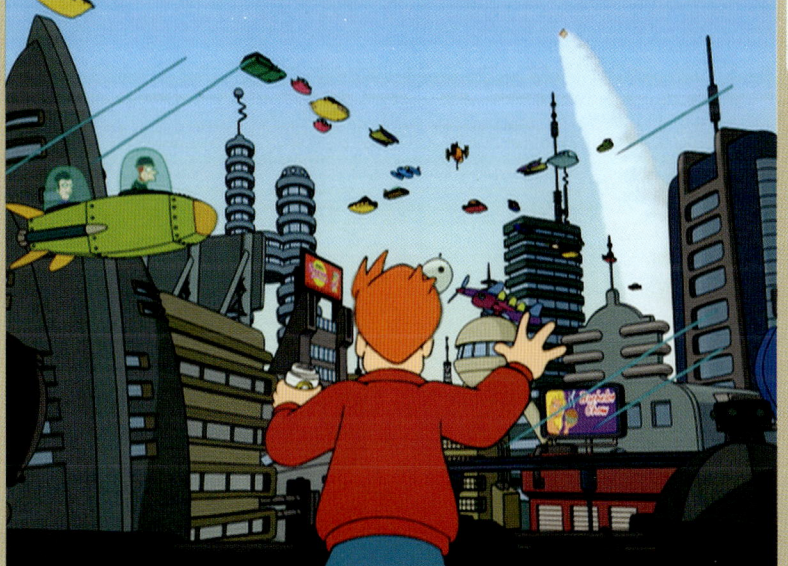

Above:
Fry's view of New New York from cryogenic lab (1ACV01) by Edgar Duncan

Opposite (from left to right, top to bottom):
Countdown sequence locations: Times Square, the Eiffel Tower, the Vatican, Great Pyramid of Giza, the Parthenon, the Great Wall of China, the Taj Mahal, Masai Camp, and Tokyo Street (1ACV01) by Debbie Silver

Reverse spread:
Cryogenic lab (1ACV01) by John Krause

When we visited Matt's studio, this artwork was one of the first things Matt showed us of New New York. I loved this art so much I decided to make this Fry's first vision, the first thing he sees when he wakes up in the future.

— Rich Moore

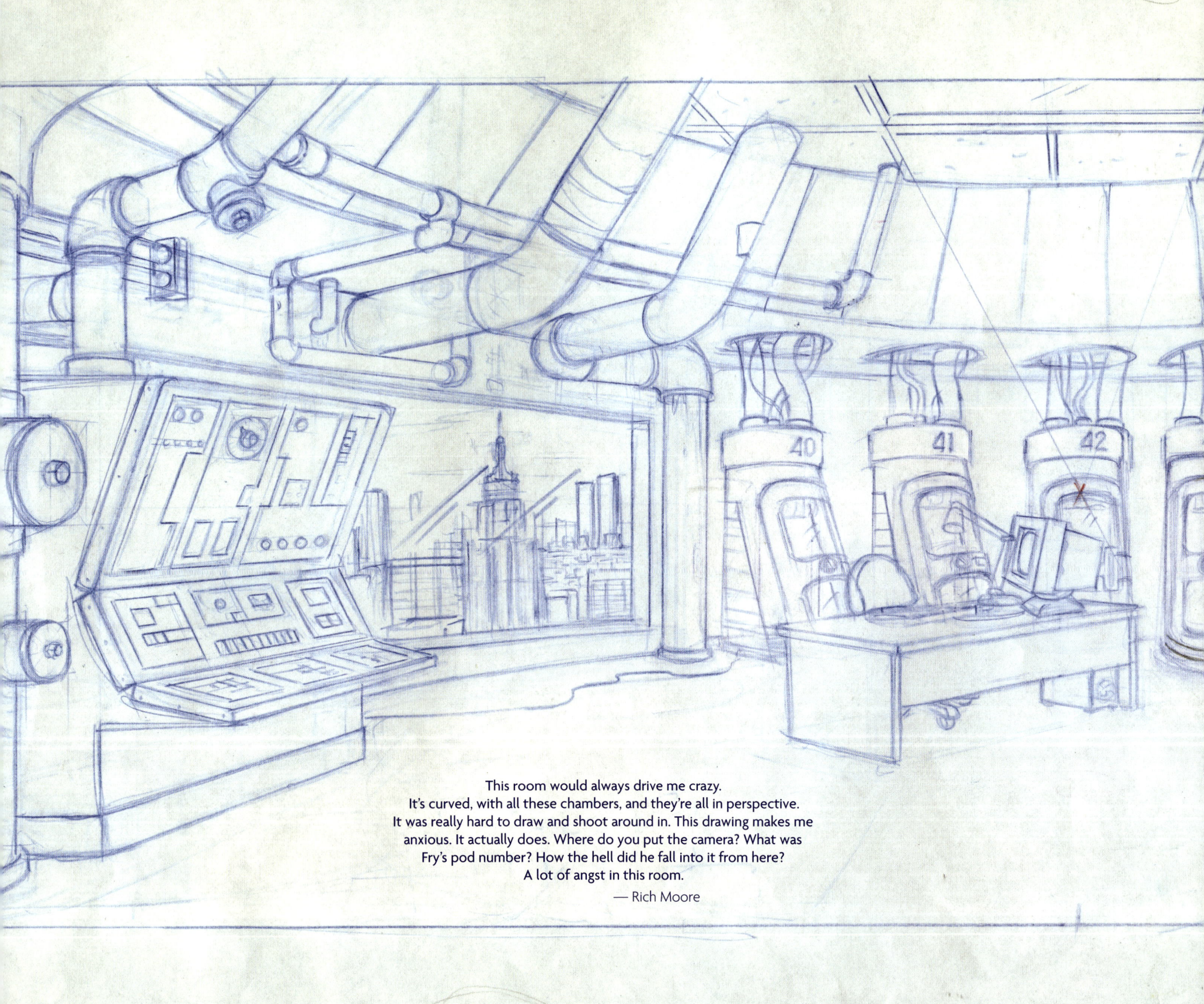

This room would always drive me crazy.
It's curved, with all these chambers, and they're all in perspective.
It was really hard to draw and shoot around in. This drawing makes me
anxious. It actually does. Where do you put the camera? What was
Fry's pod number? How the hell did he fall into it from here?
A lot of angst in this room.

— Rich Moore

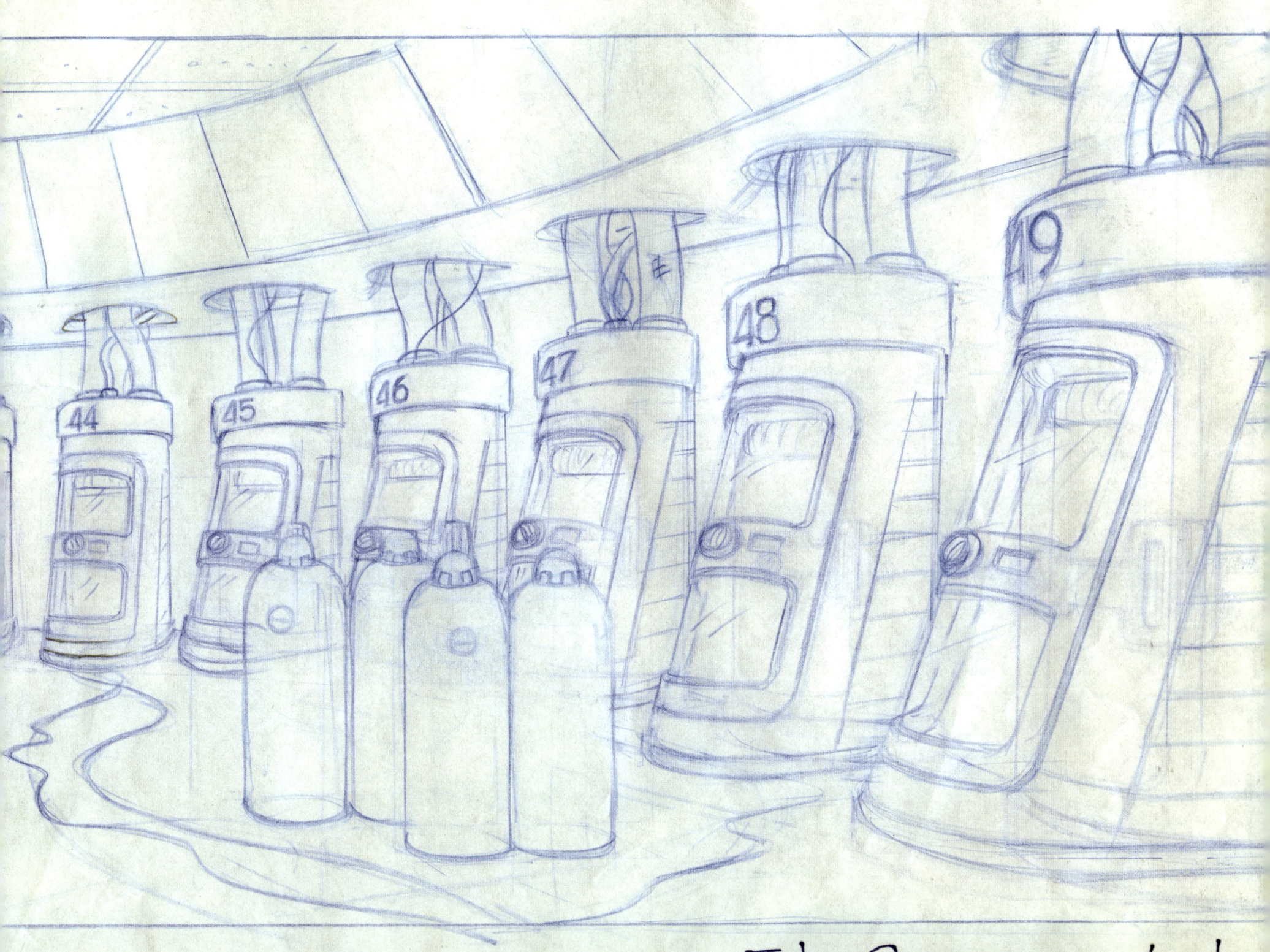

Int. Cryogenic Lab

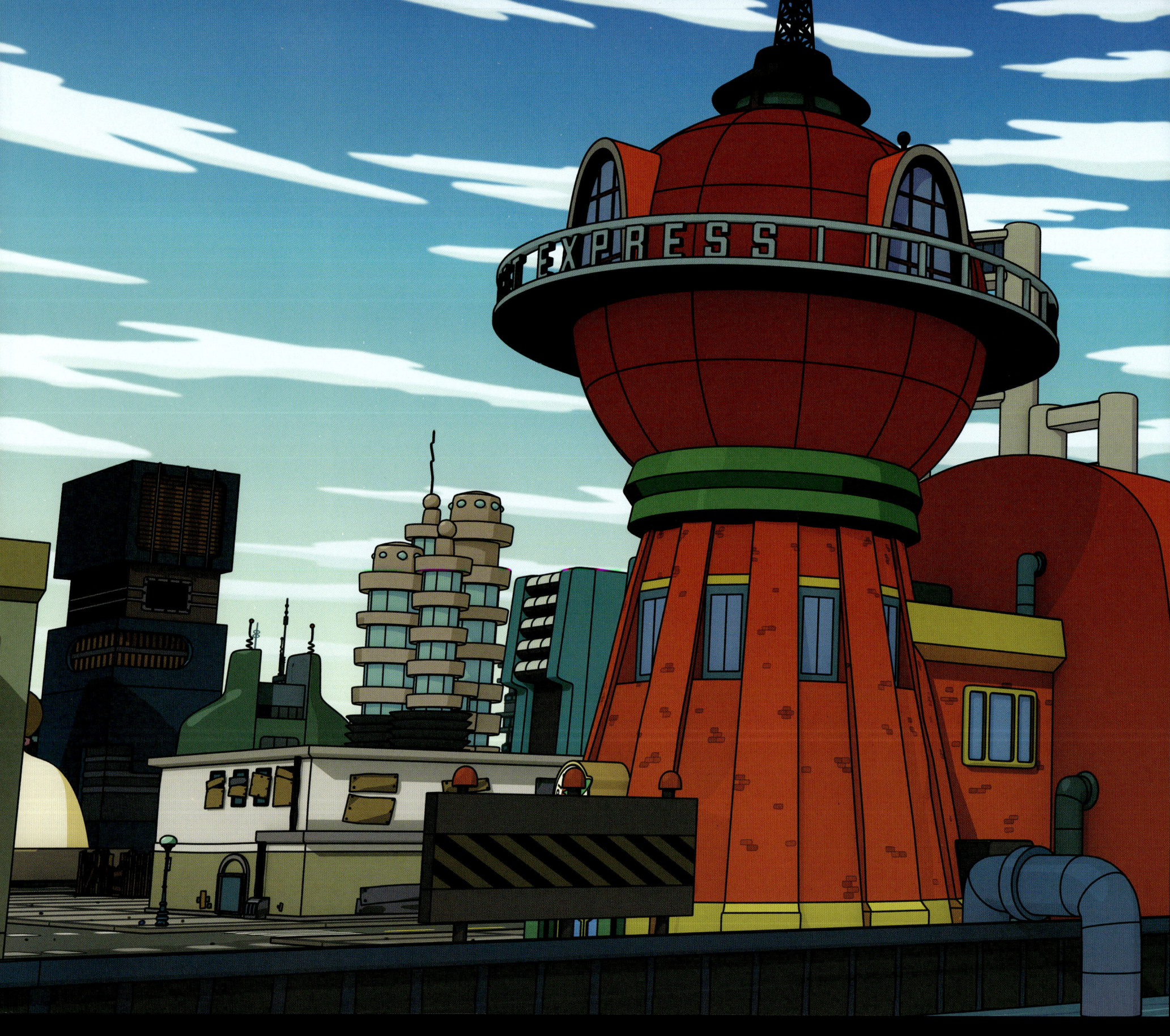

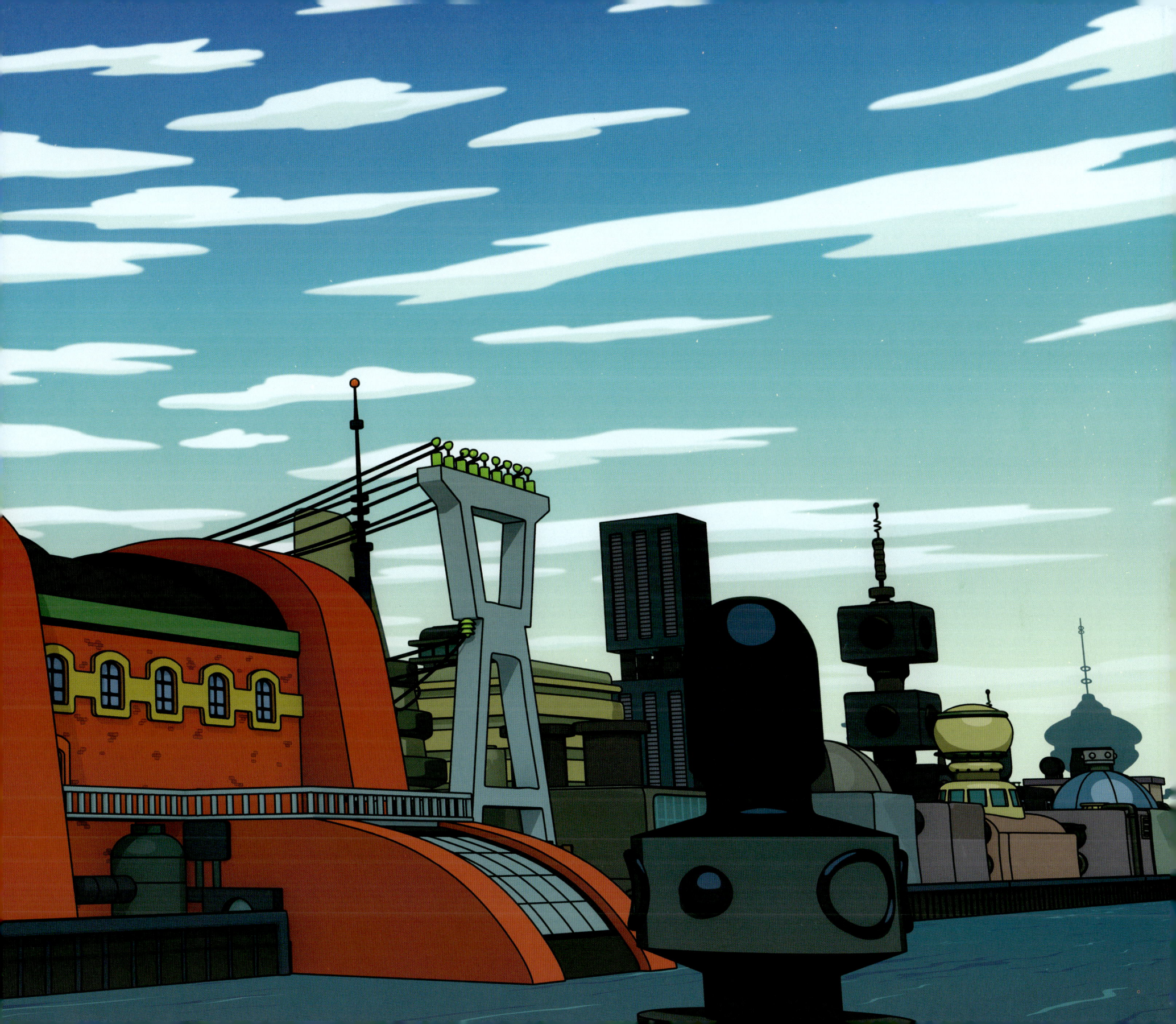

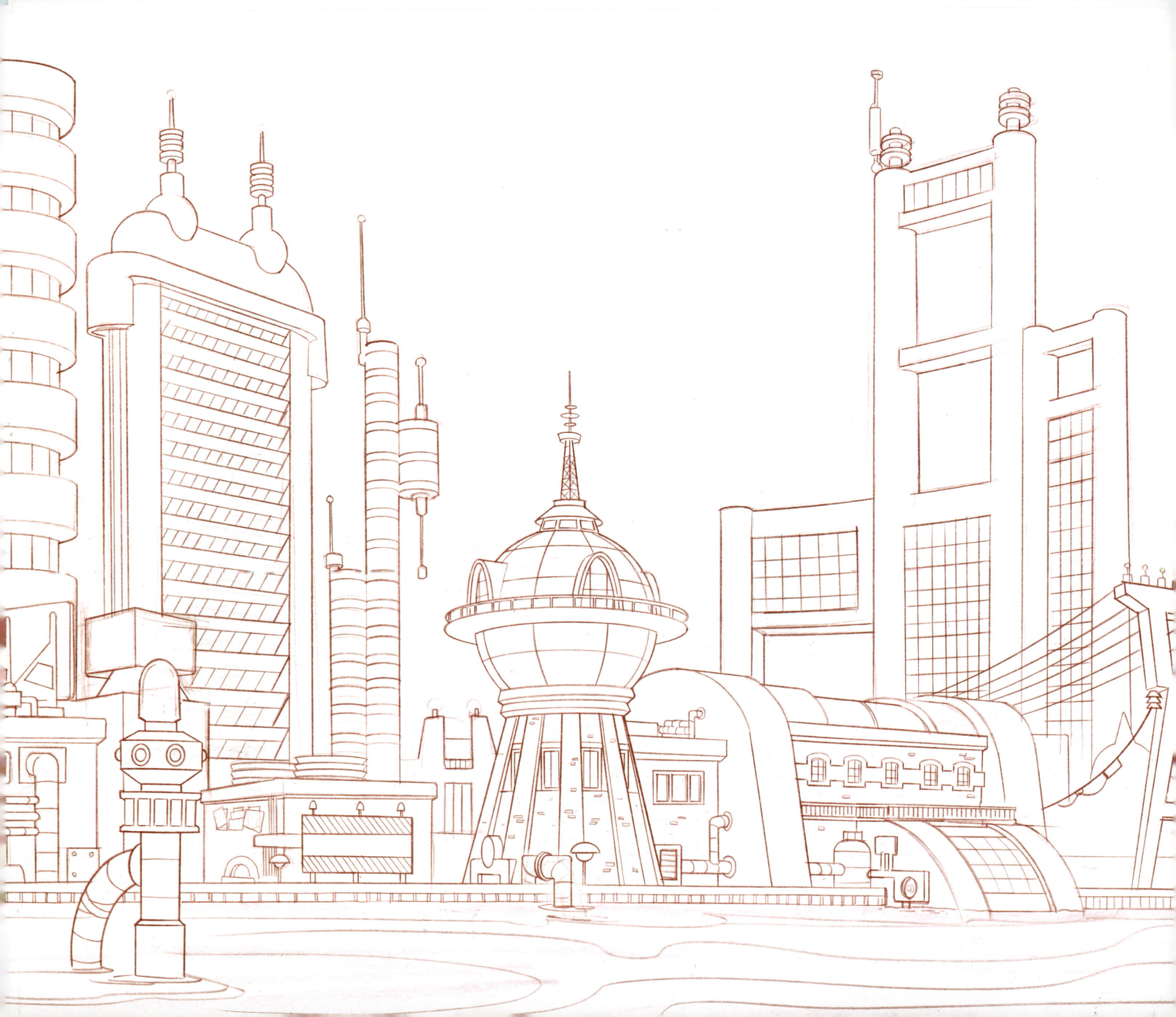

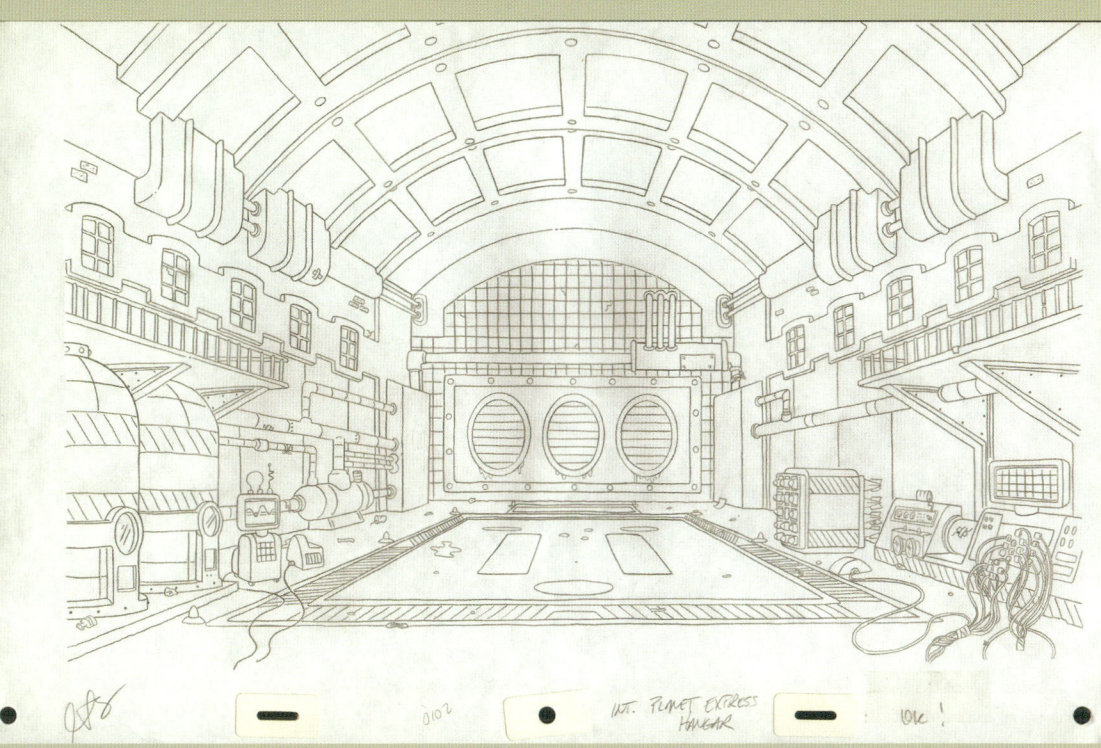

Previous spread:
Planet Express Building 3D rendering
by Eric Whited

This page, top to bottom:
Hangar with Roof Closed (1ACV02) by Edgar Duncan
Hangar Close-Up Shot (1ACV02) by Edgar Duncan

Opposite:
Planet Express Building (1ACV01) by Edgar Duncan

I grew up being a giant 1939 World's Fair
fan because I'm from Queens, so leaning
into that retro, streamlined design
seemed kind of perfect.
— Claudia Katz

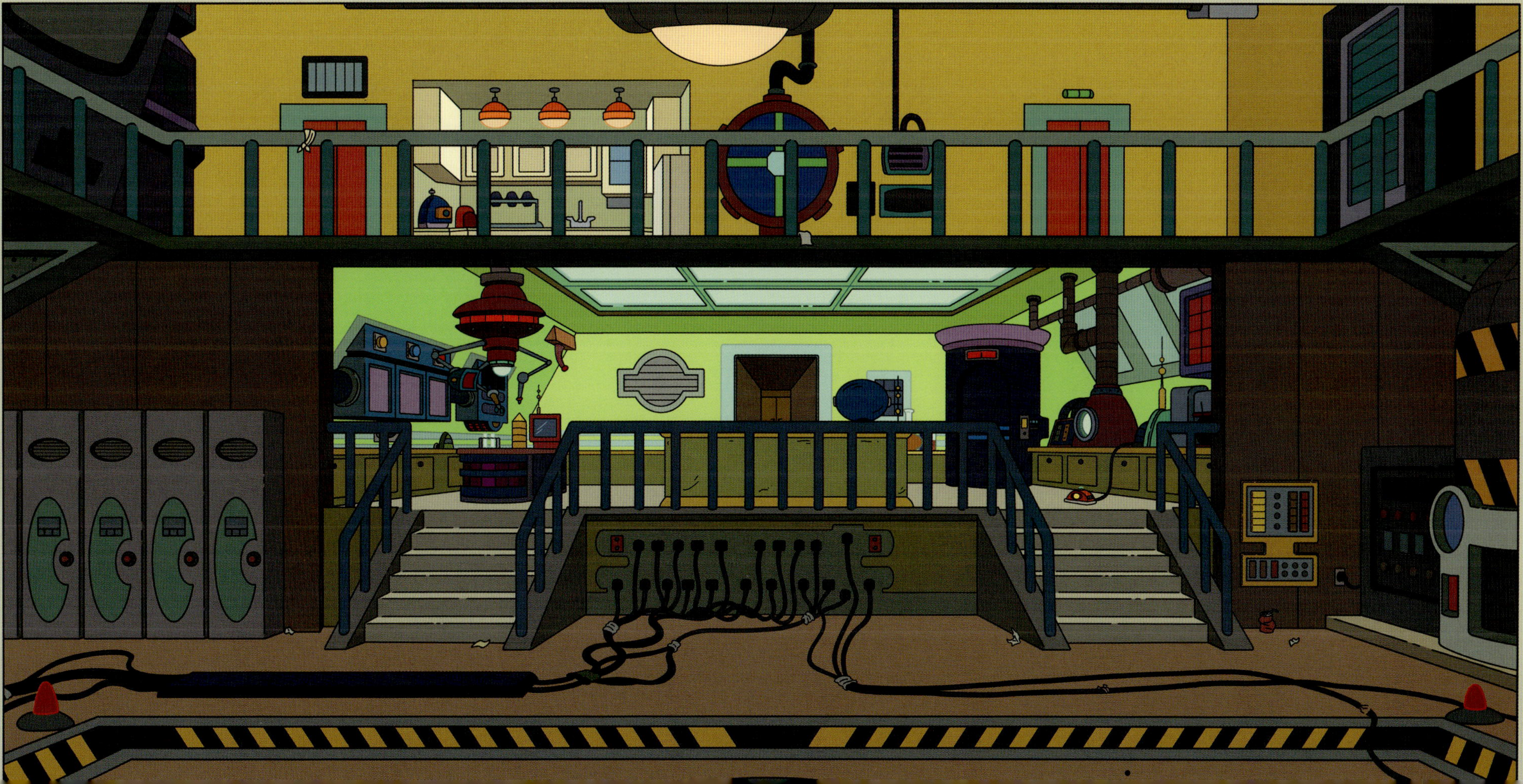

The Planet Express building exists to support the writing and ideas in the scripts. Any part of that building can become whatever it needs to become because things were designed to be adjustable.

— Crystal Chesney-Thompson

Everything exists to support the story. If we need something, we put it in. If we don't, it disappears or is replaced with something else.

— Dwayne Carey-Hill

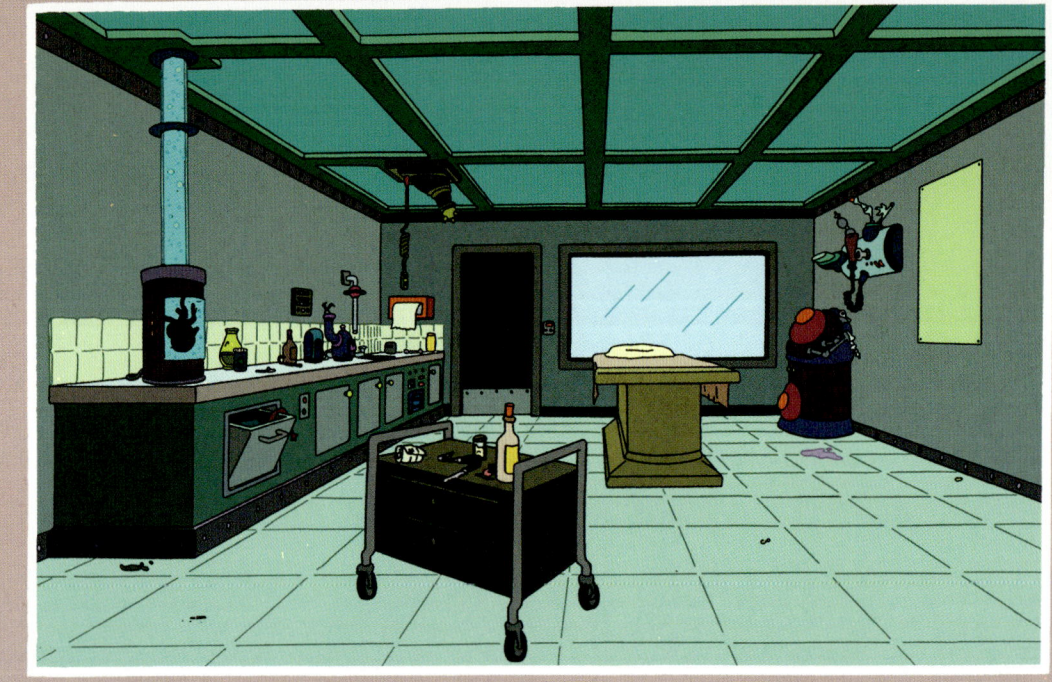

Top:
Dr. Zoidberg's laboratory (1ACV01) by Debbie Silver

Bottom:
Planet Express living room (1ACV01) by Edgar Duncan

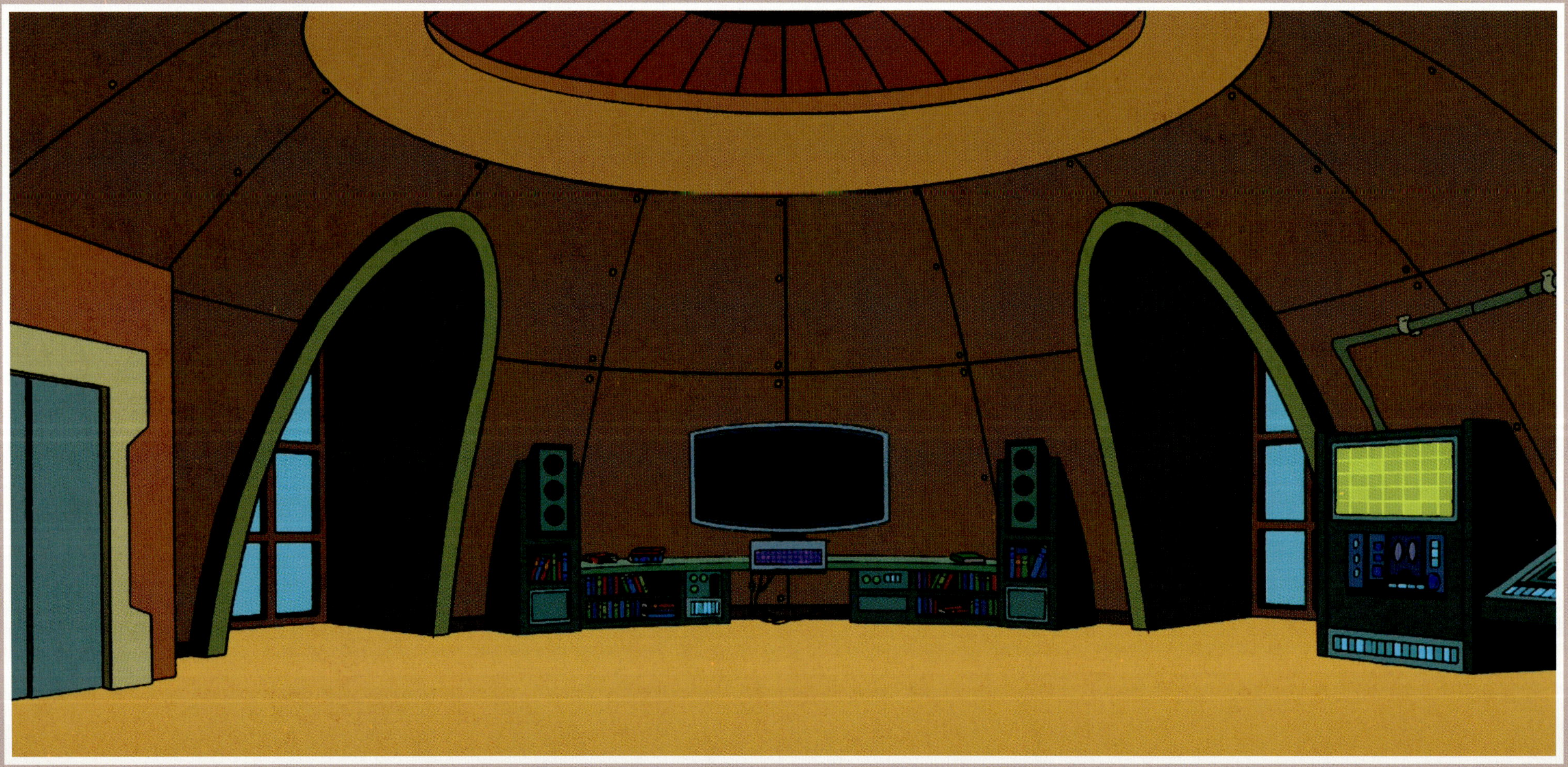

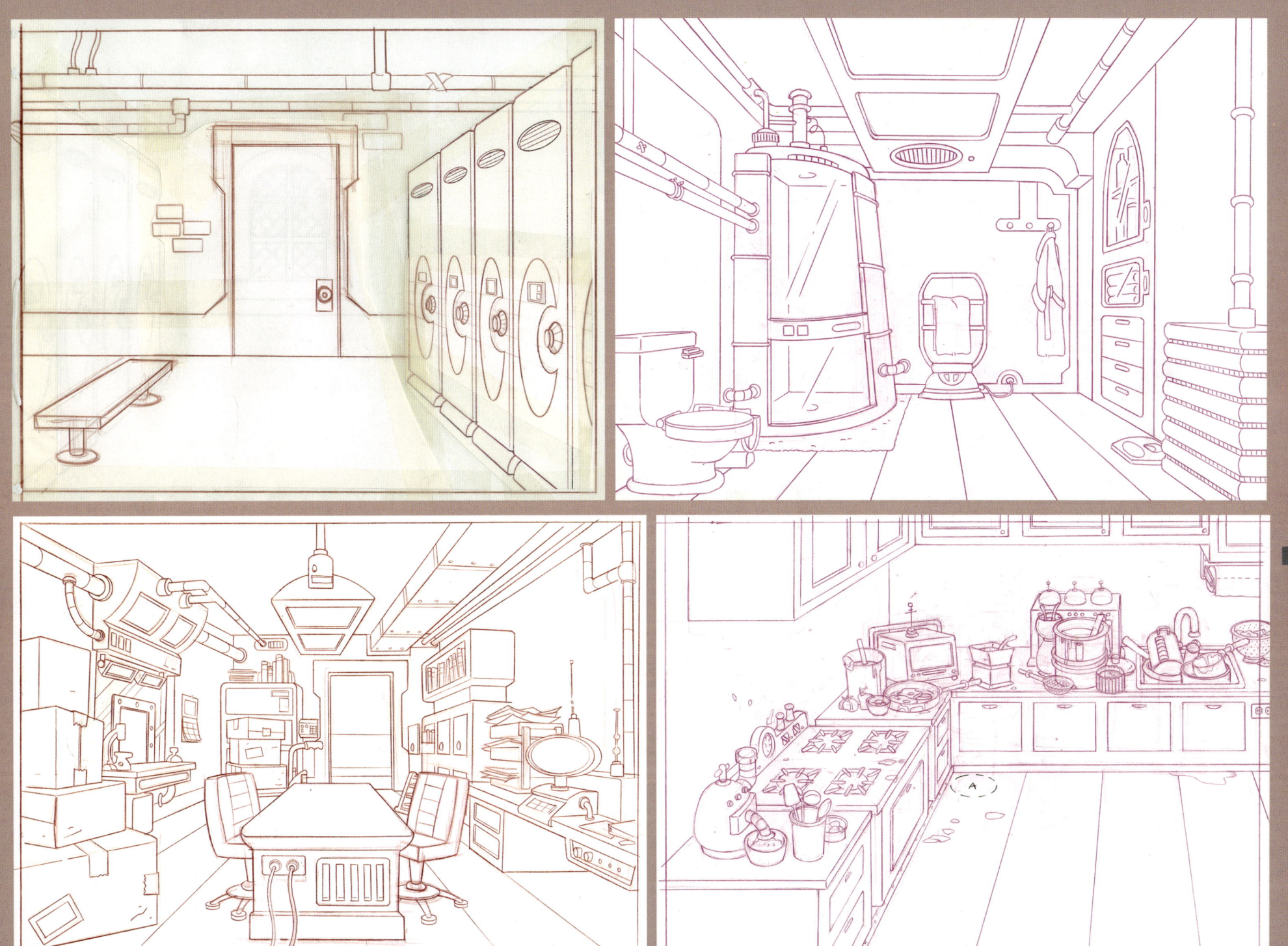

Clockwise from top left:
Planet Express locker room (2ACV11) by Edgar Duncan
Planet Express showers (6ACV09) by Debbie Silver
Planet Express kitchen (1ACV03) by Debbie Silver
Hermes' office (1ACV02) by Edgar Duncan

Right:
Mutant sewer (6ACV12)
by Chad E. Cooper

Opposite:
Underground cavern (4ACV04)
by Edgar Duncan

Bottom:
NNY cityscape (4ACV04).
Artist unknown.

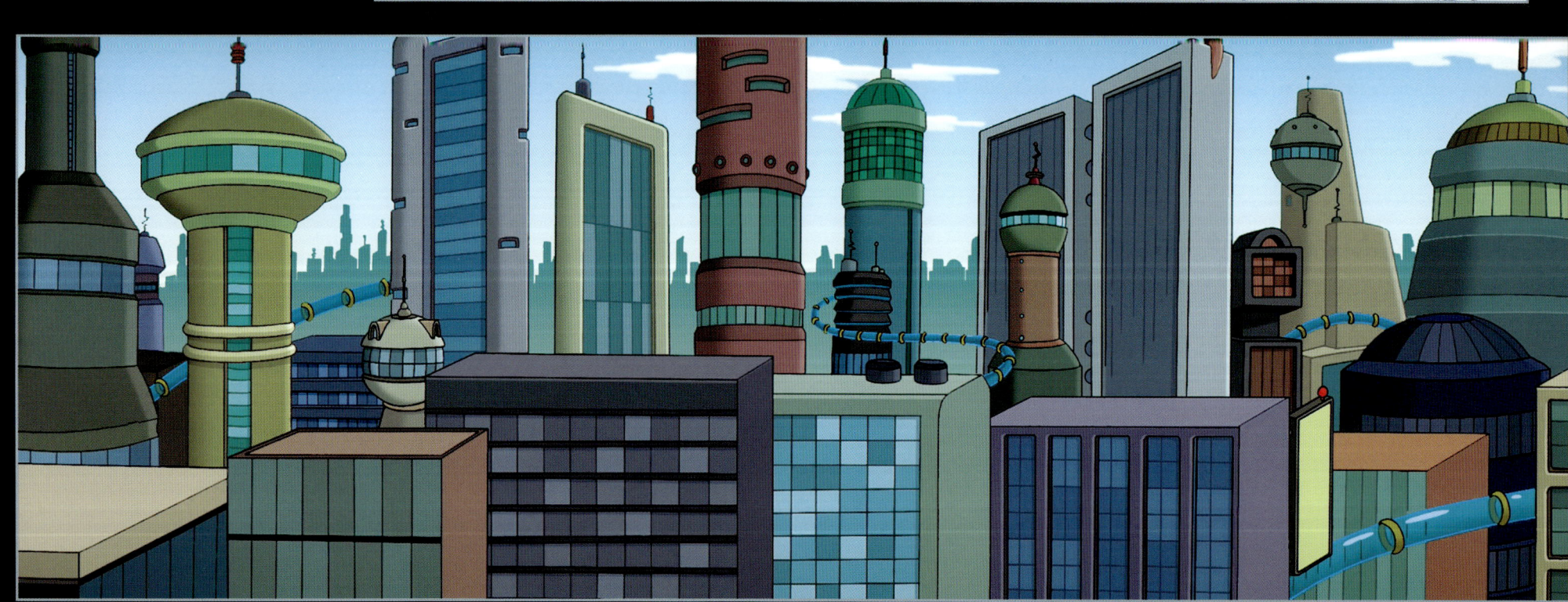

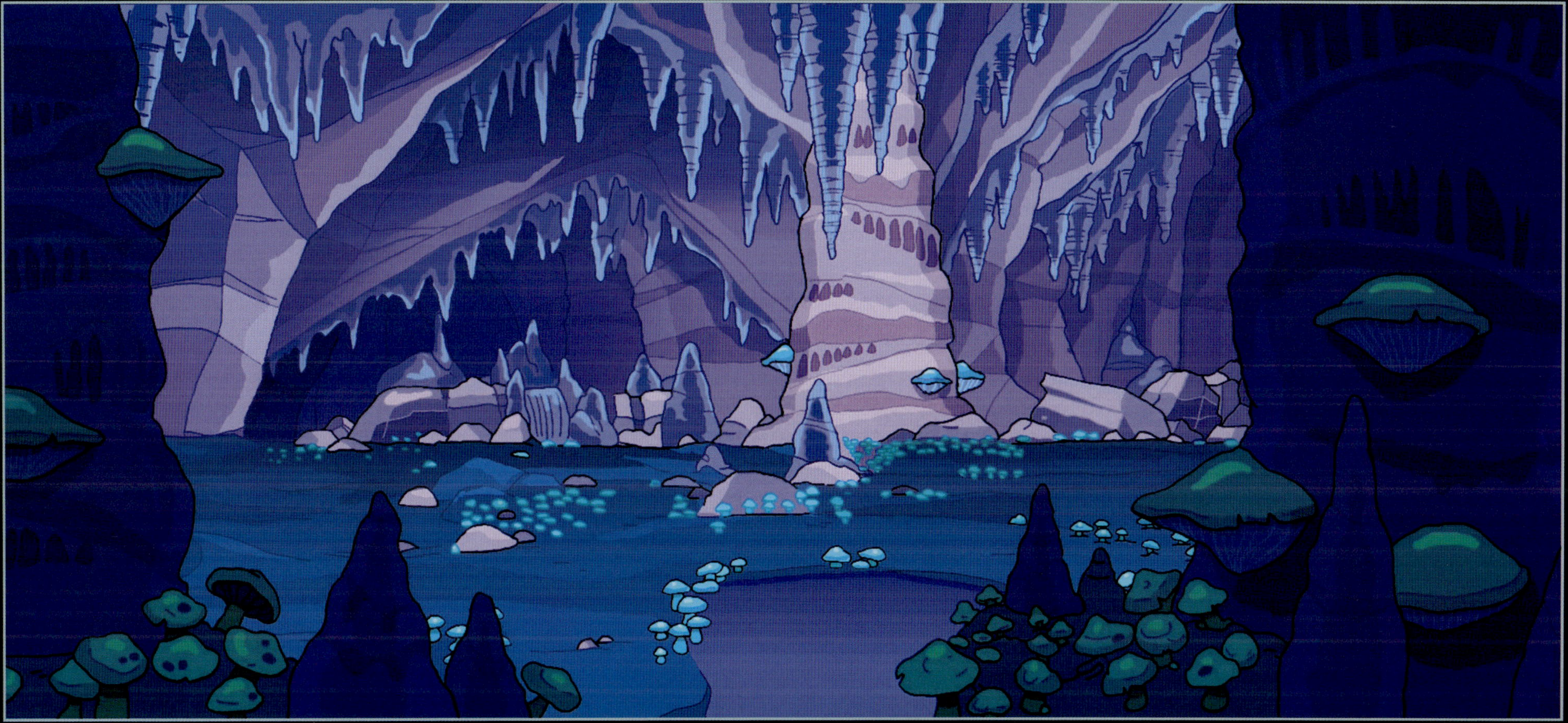

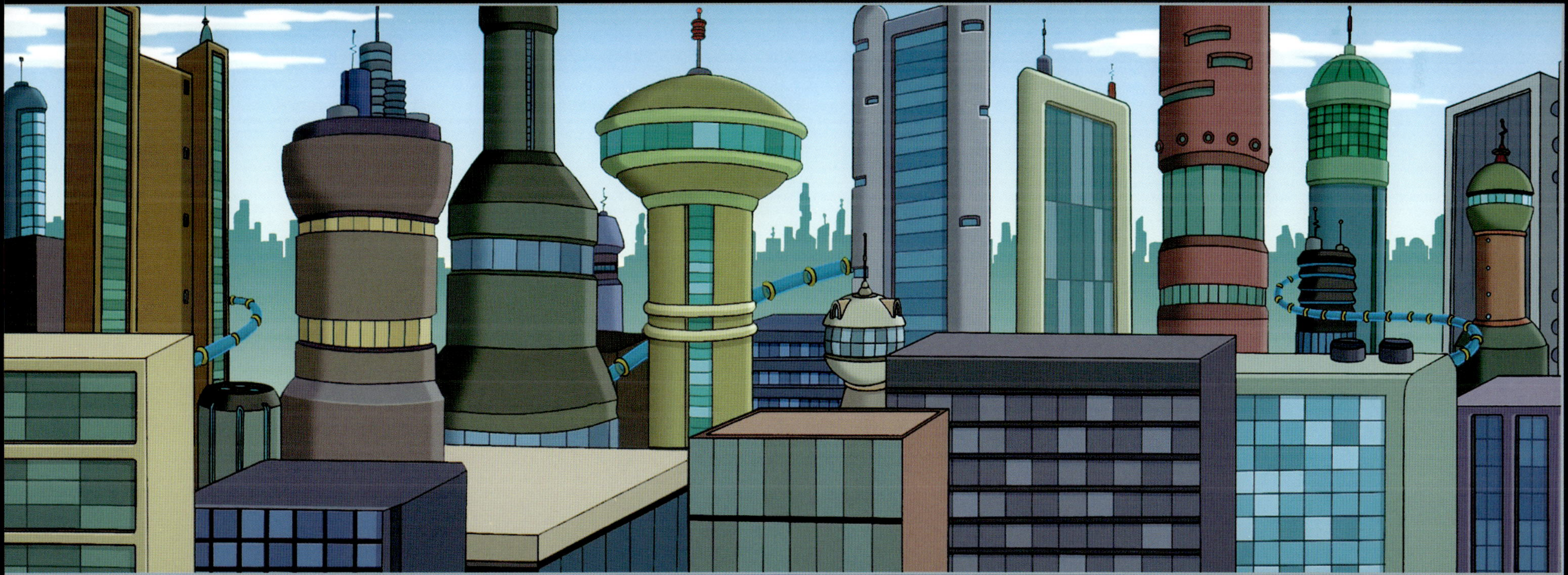

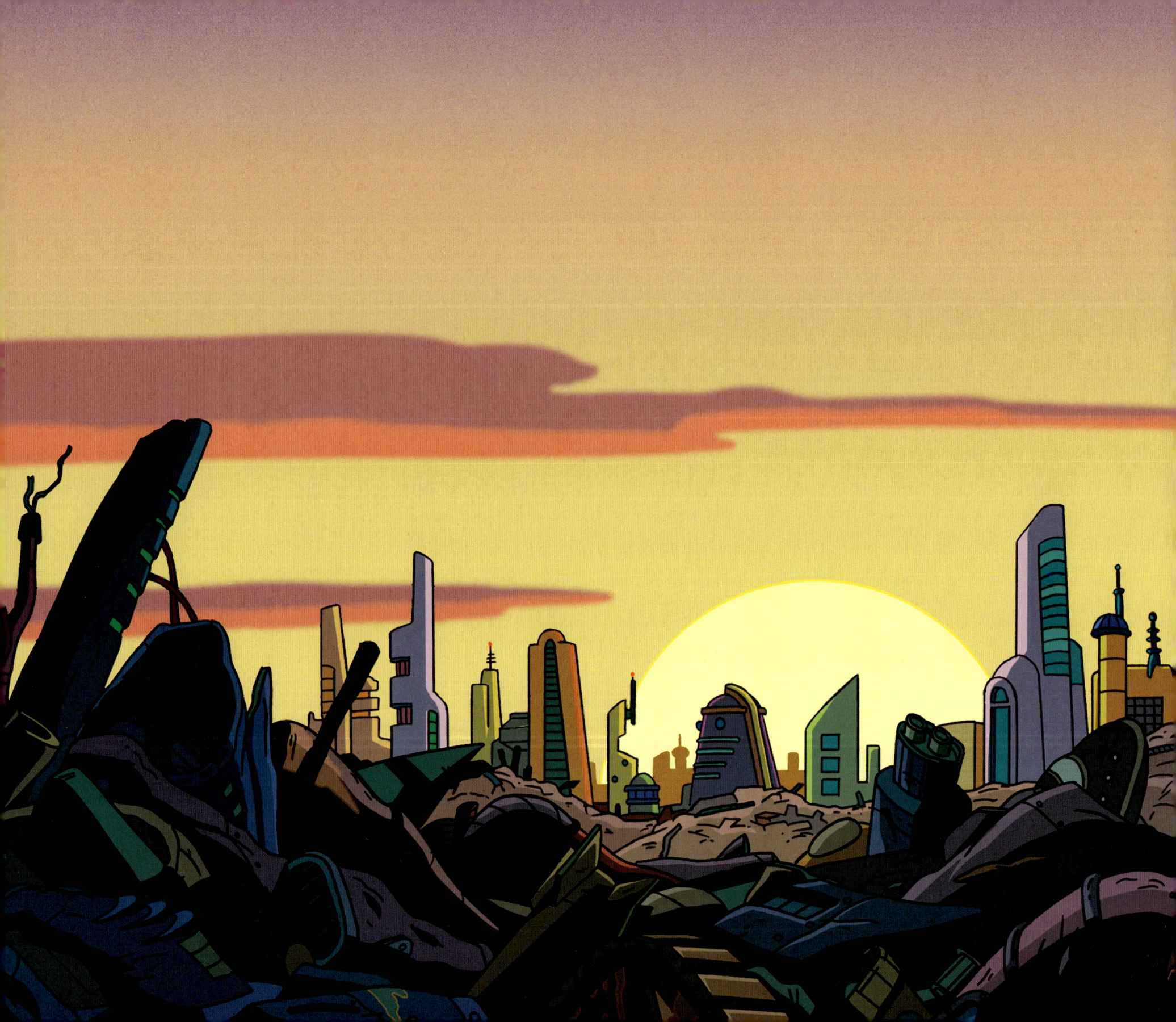

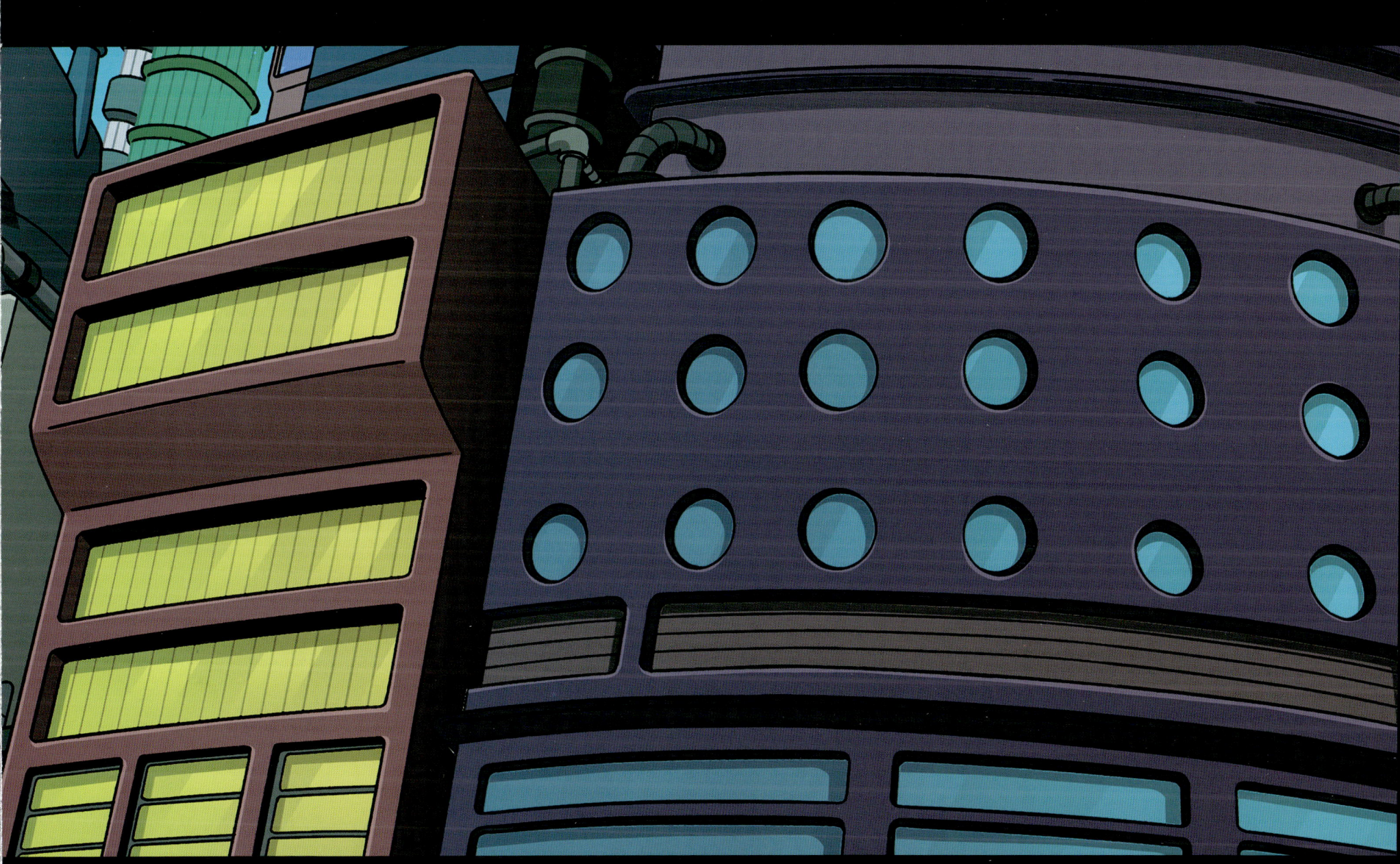

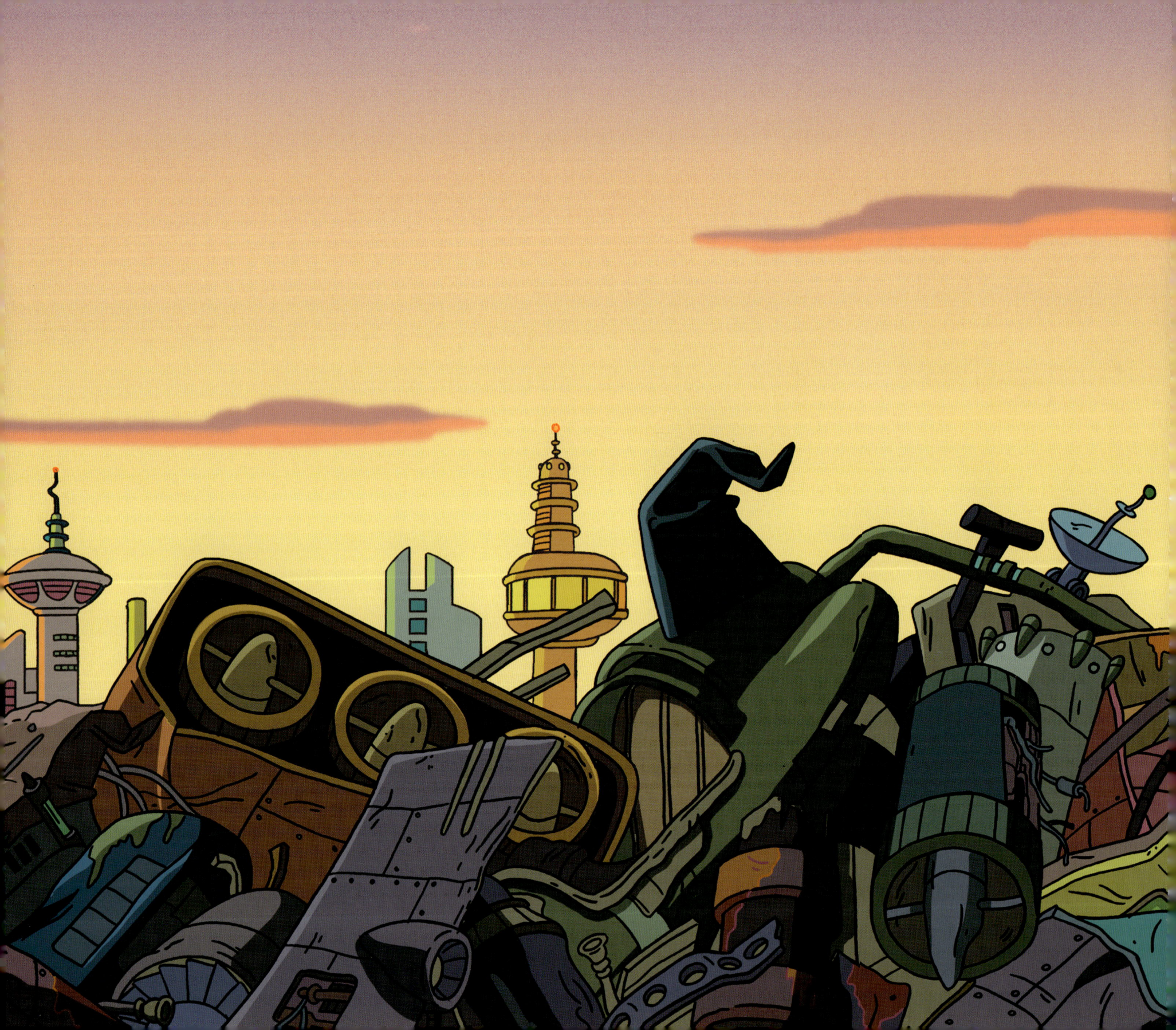

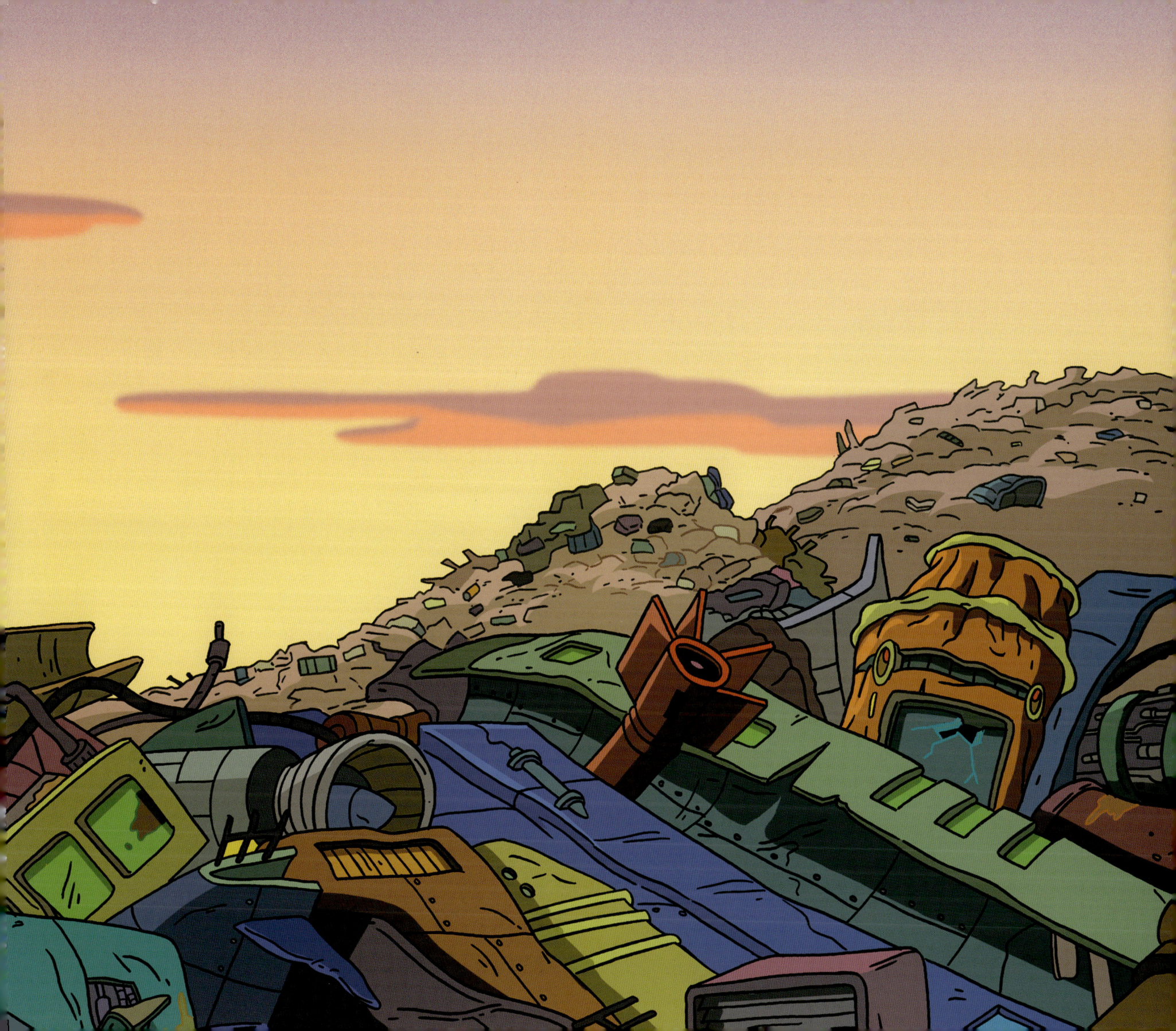

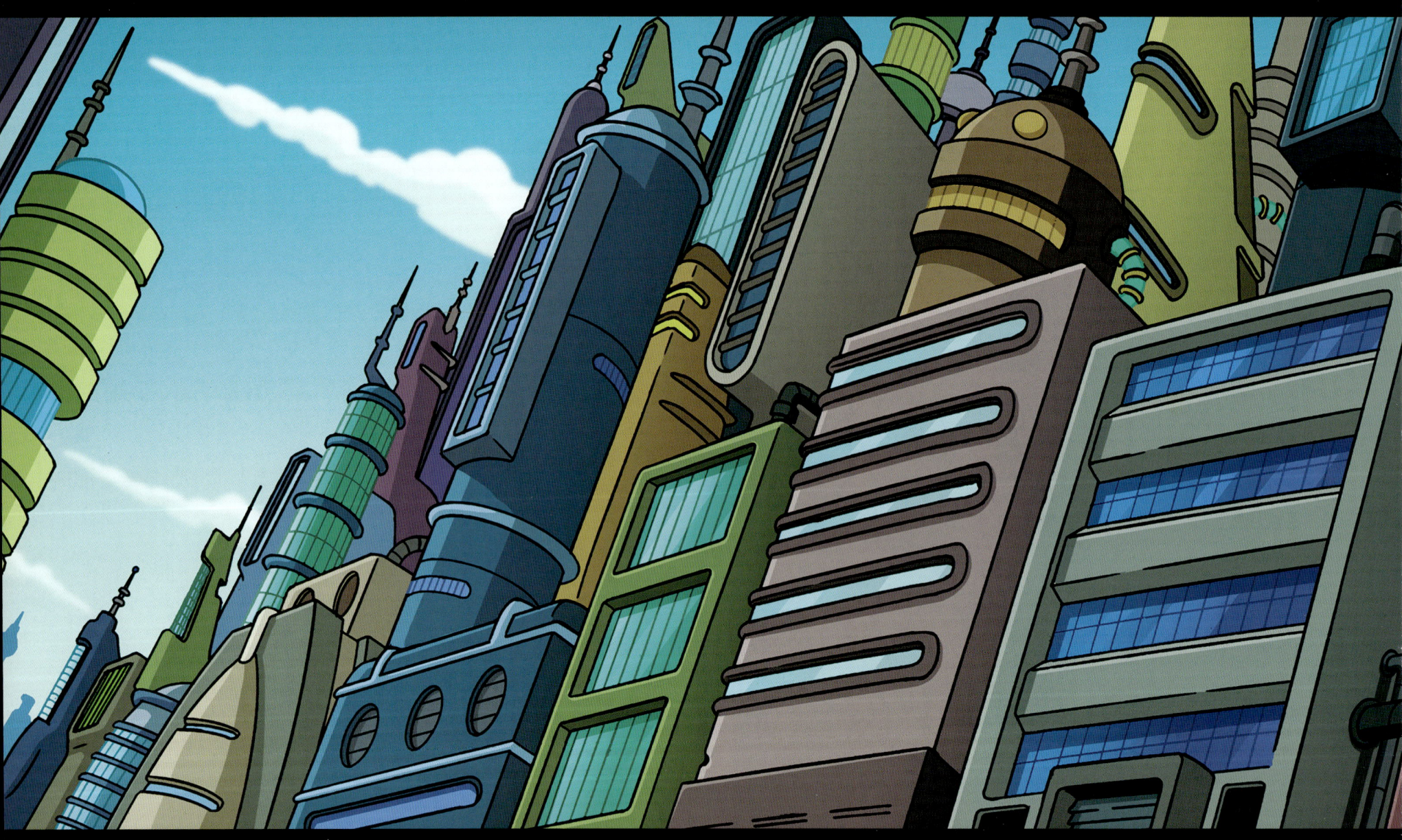

New New York buildings (7ACV15)
by Nam Suk Cho

Previous spread:
New New York Junkyard (7ACV15)
by Alen Esmaelian

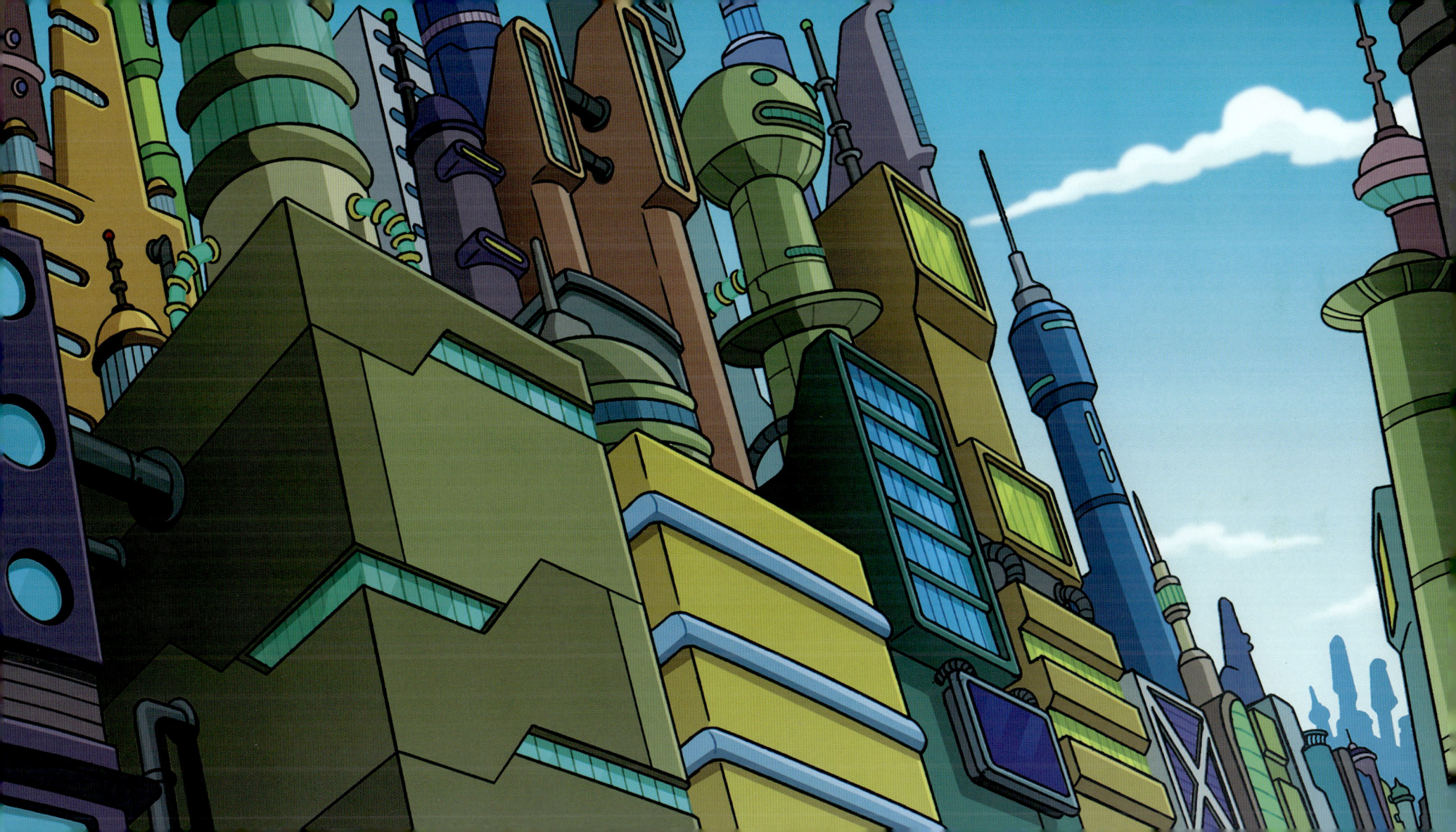

I was very impressed with the original
look the animators gave to New New York.
After *Futurama* was first off the air, I visited
Shanghai and that's what the skyline looks like.
It's amazing!

— Matt Groening

Clockwise:
Panucci's Pizza (4ACV07) by Debbie Silver
Panucci's Pizza over time, final shot (4ACV07) by Debbie Silver
Panucci's Pizza interior (1ACV01) by John Krause

Opposite (cockwise from left):
Top city view (5ACV07) by Zeke Johnson
Improbable apartment (1ACV03) by Zeke Johnson
Planet Express ship brain (4ACV03) by Jeff Mertz

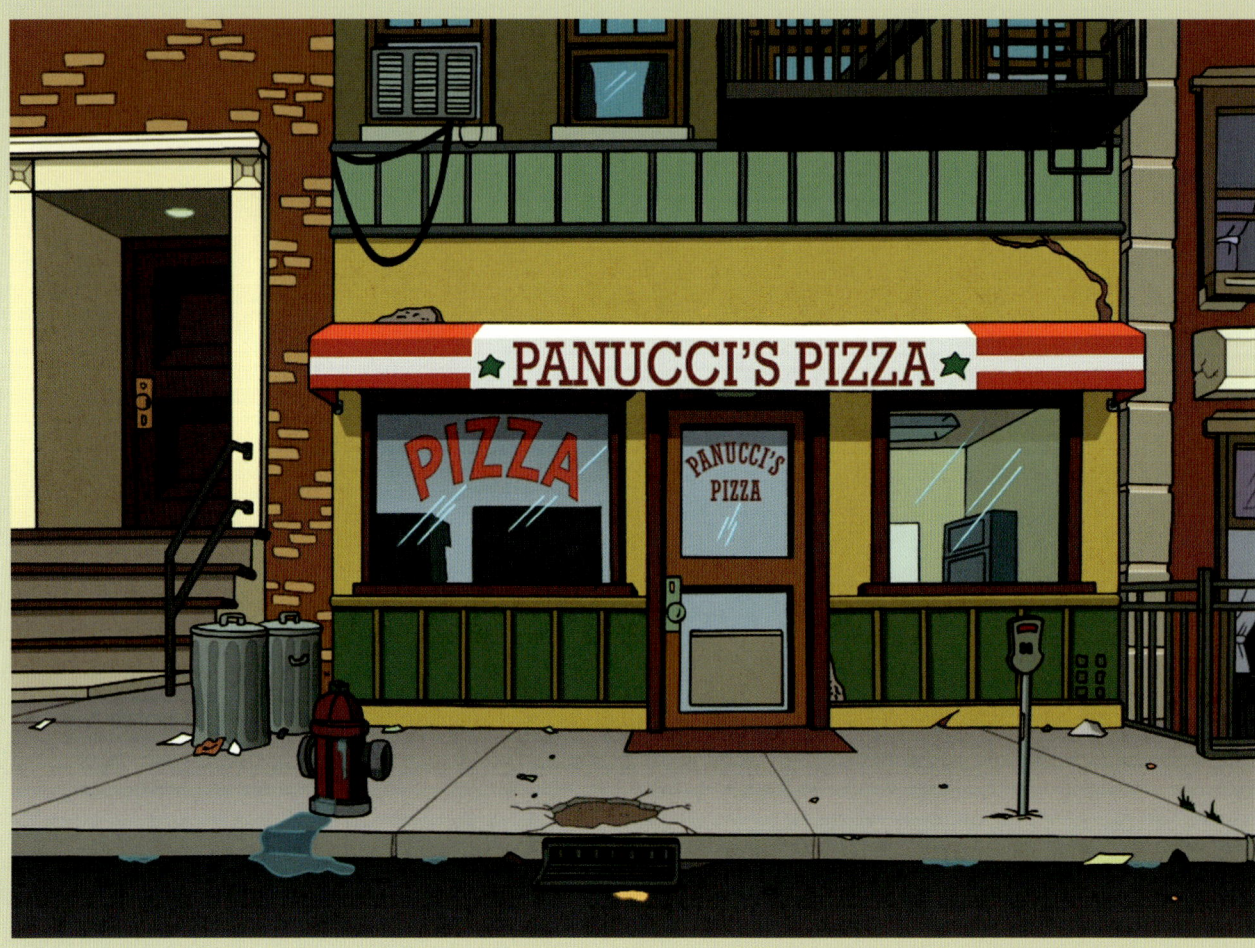

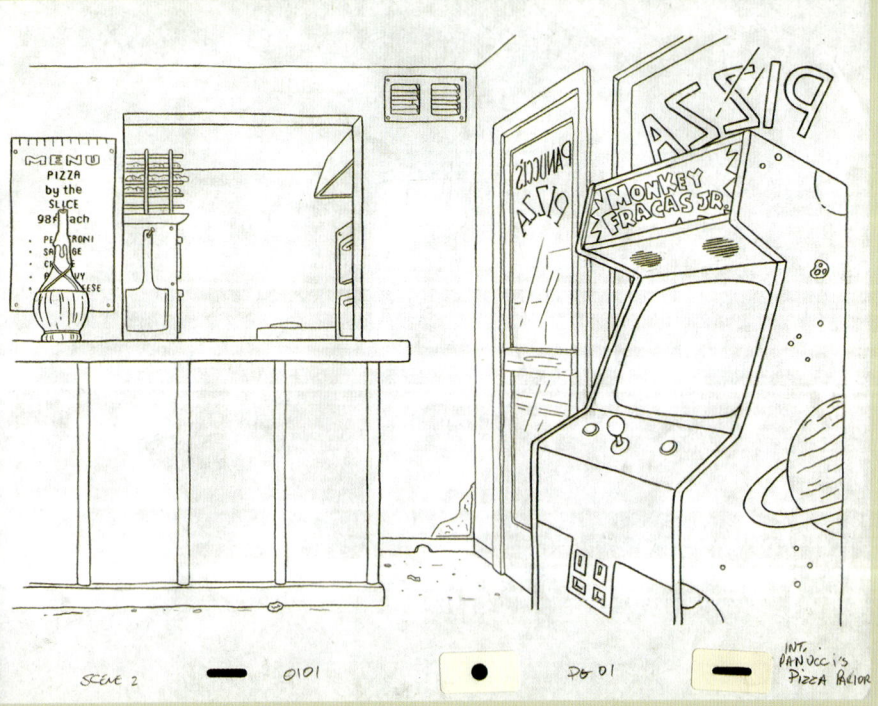

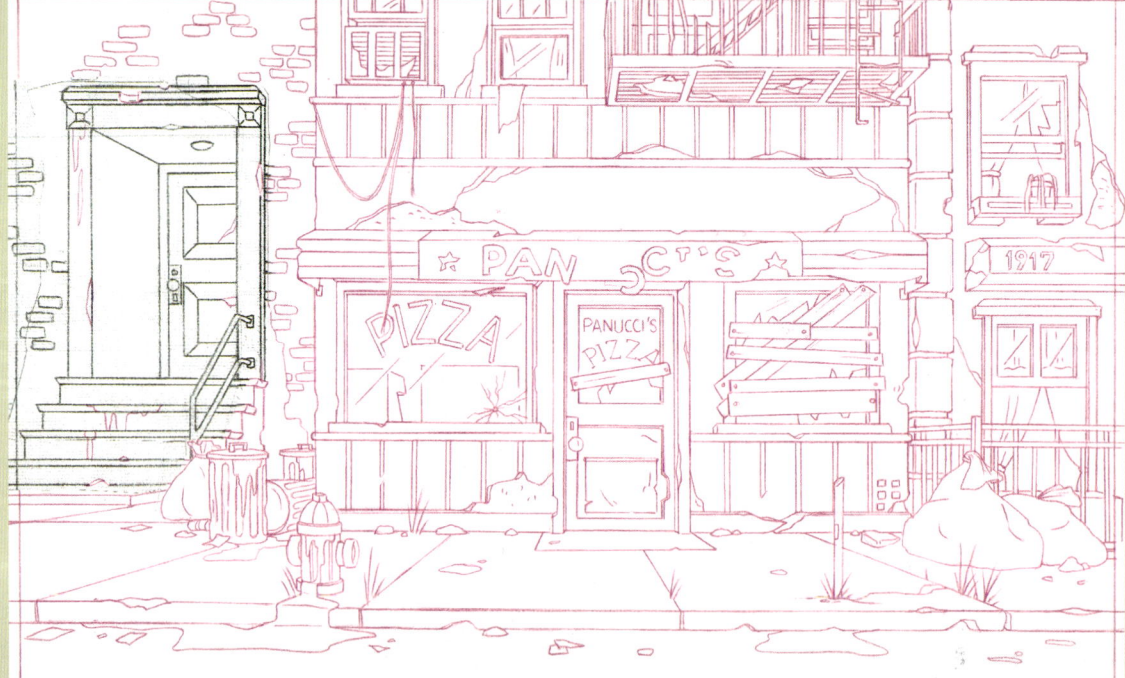

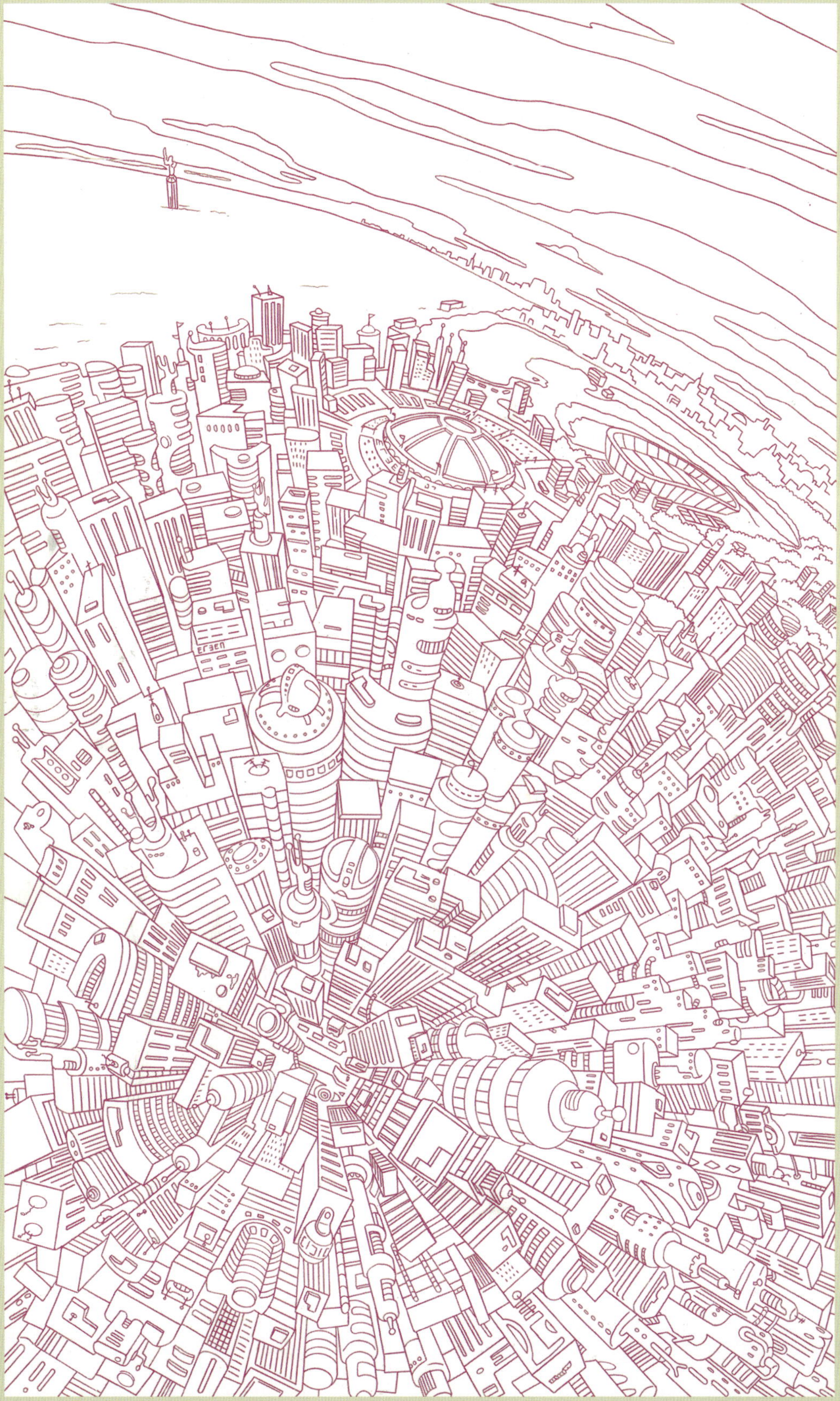

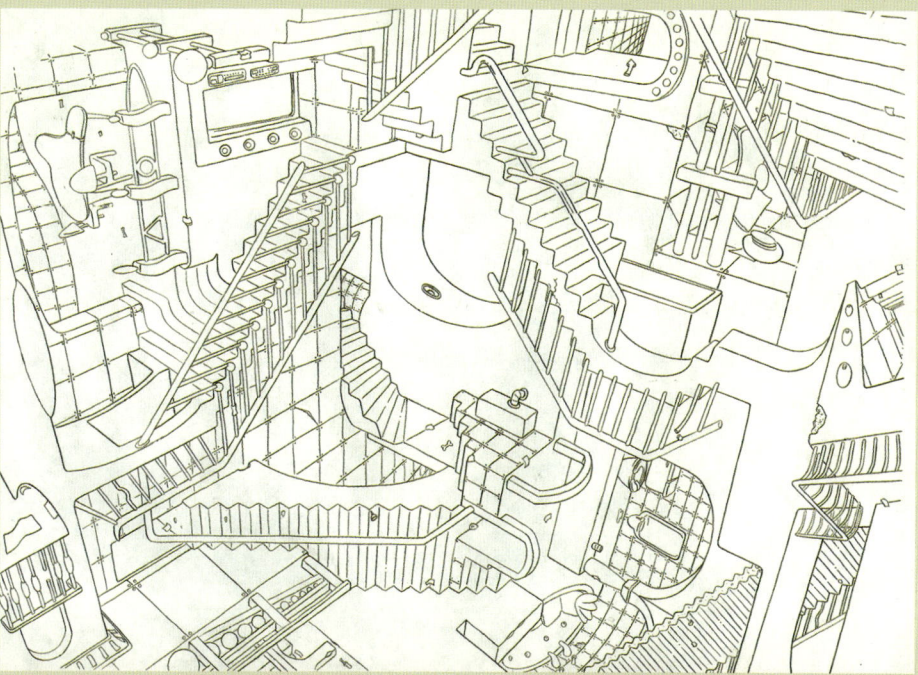

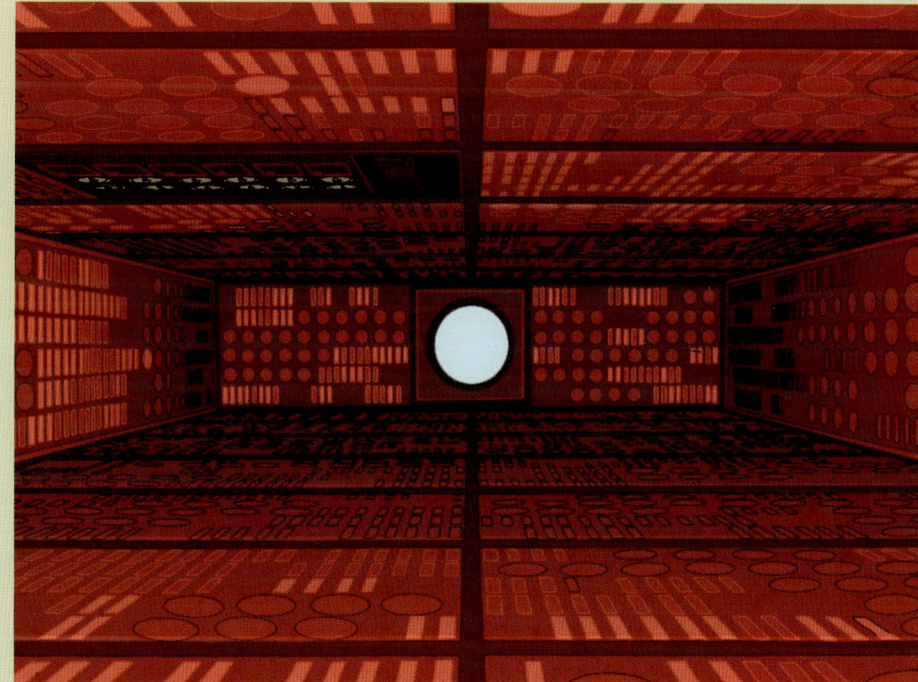

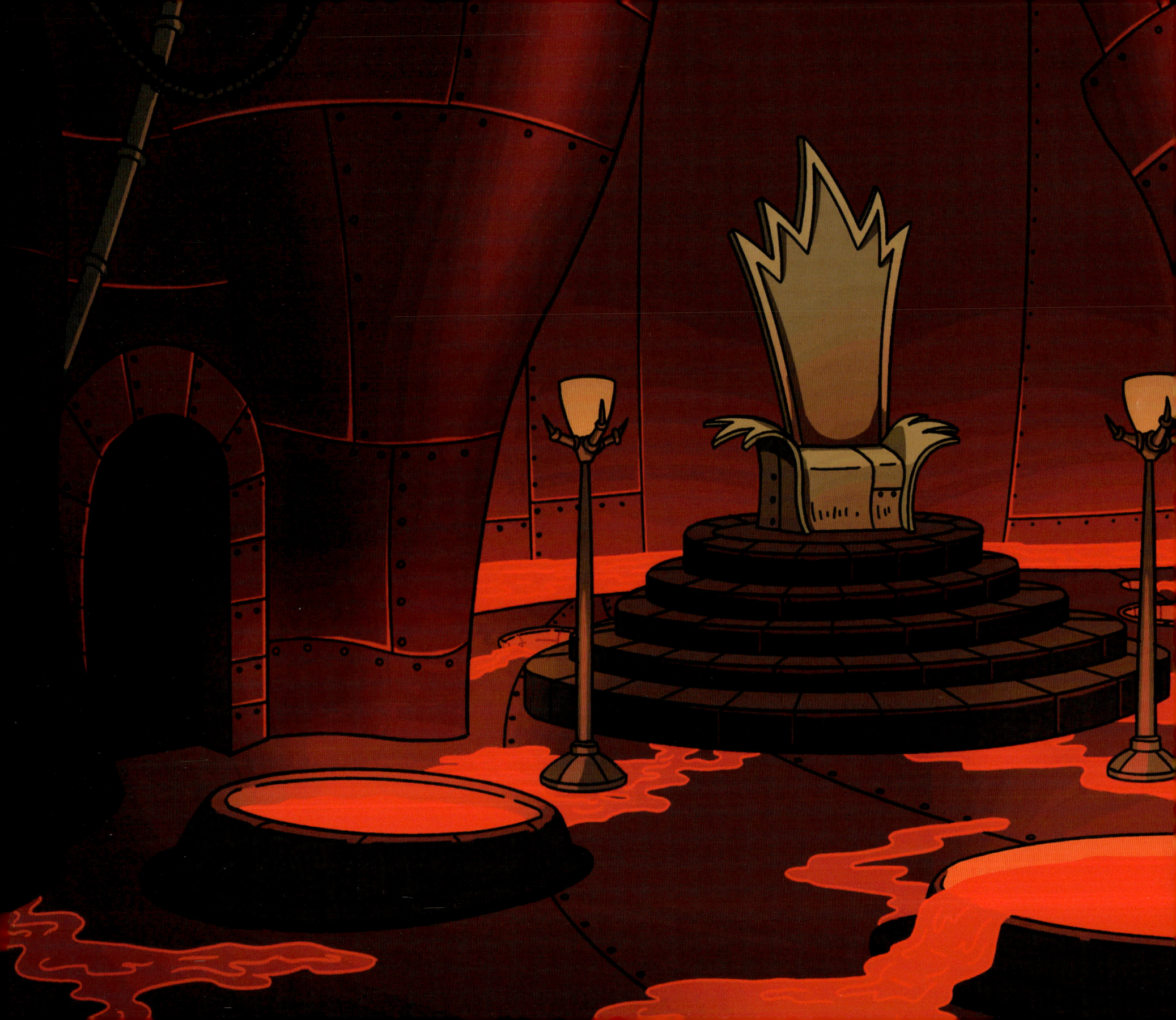

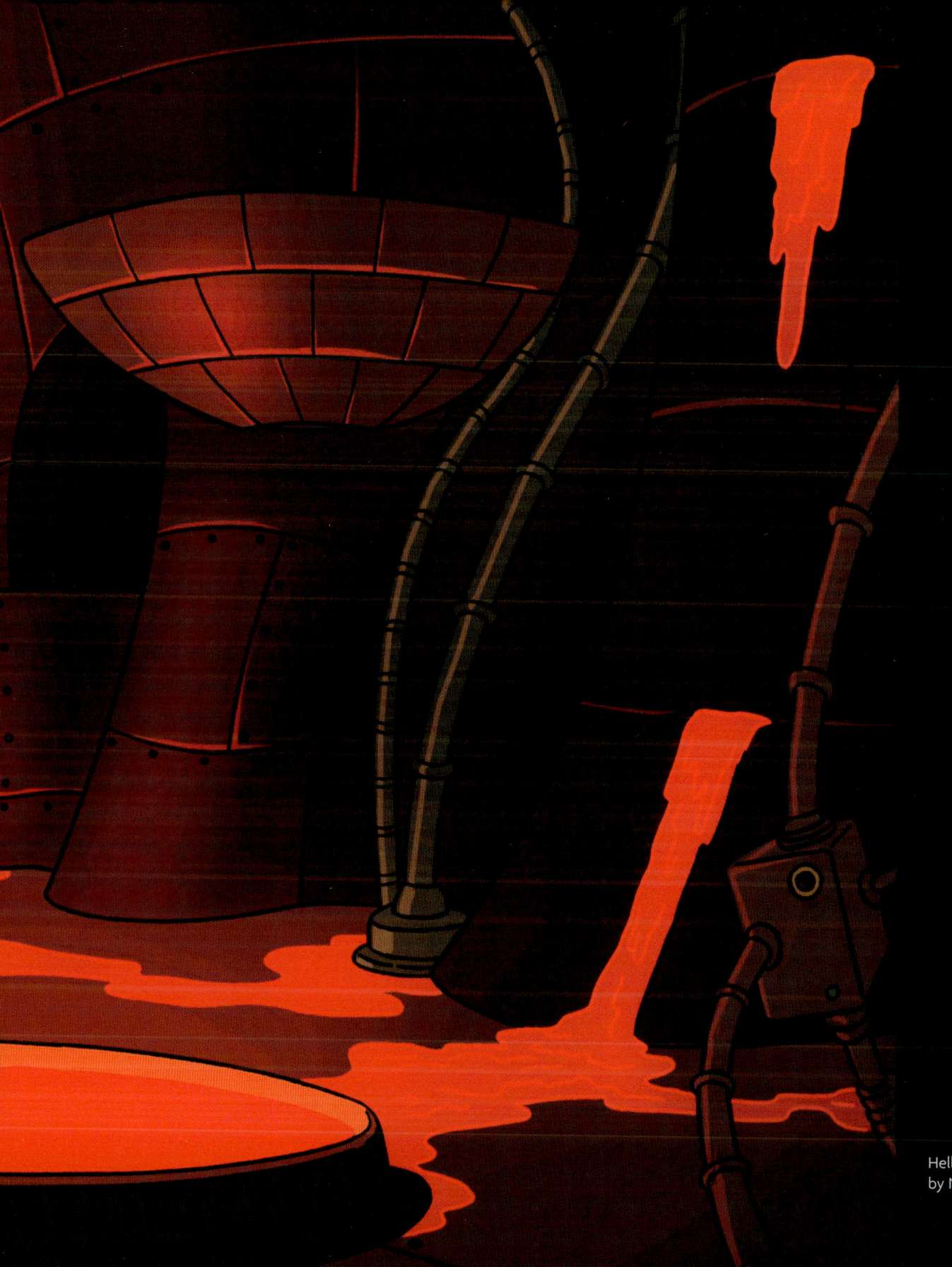

In our mythology,
Robot Hell is not a supernatural place.
It's an actual geographical location below
Coney Island created to keep robots
in line and to make them feel guilty.

— Matt Groening

It's interesting making something
look like it's glowing, but it's still flat.
It's really fun to do.

— Gregg Vanzo

Hell throne room (1ACV09)
by Nam Suk Cho

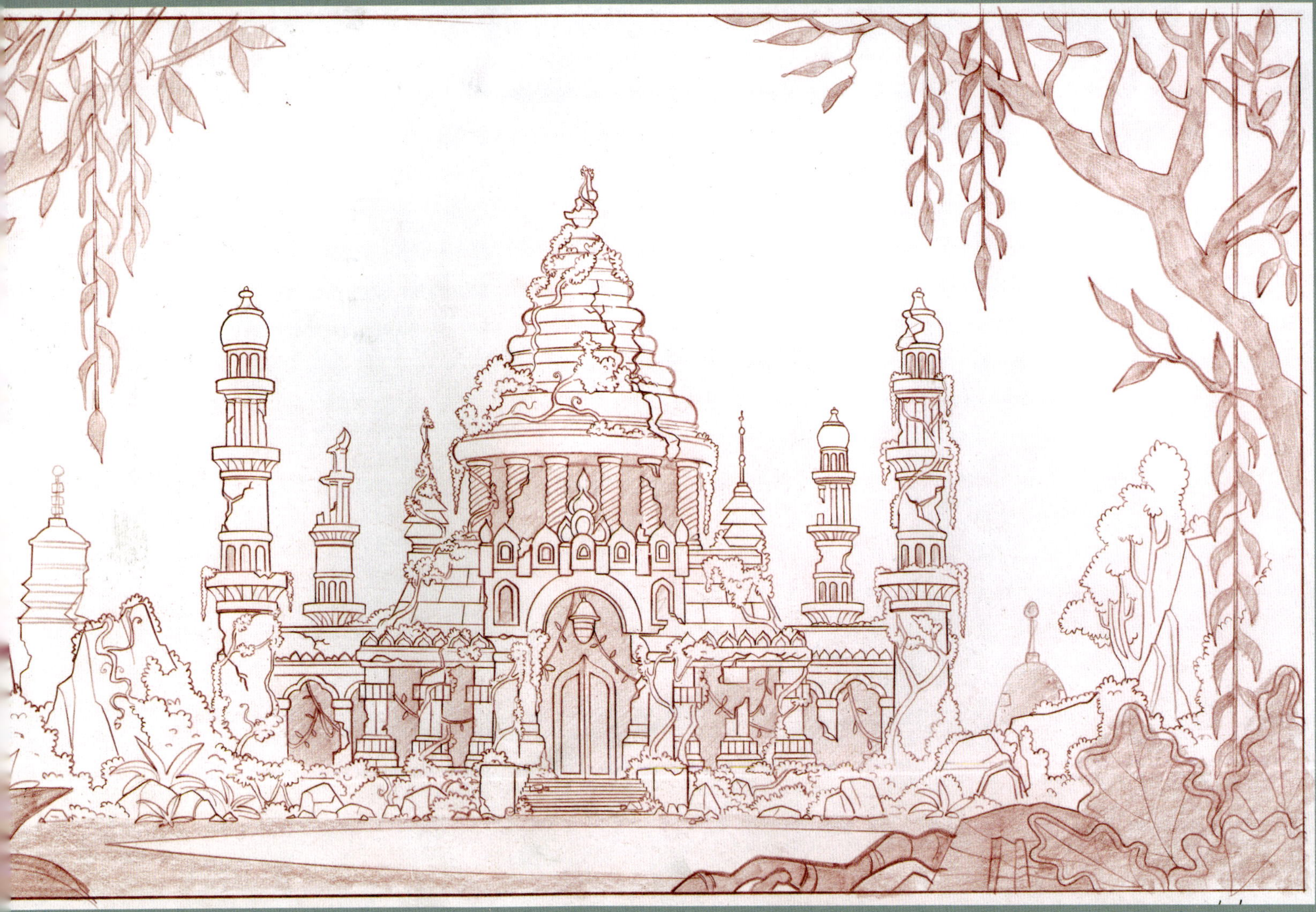

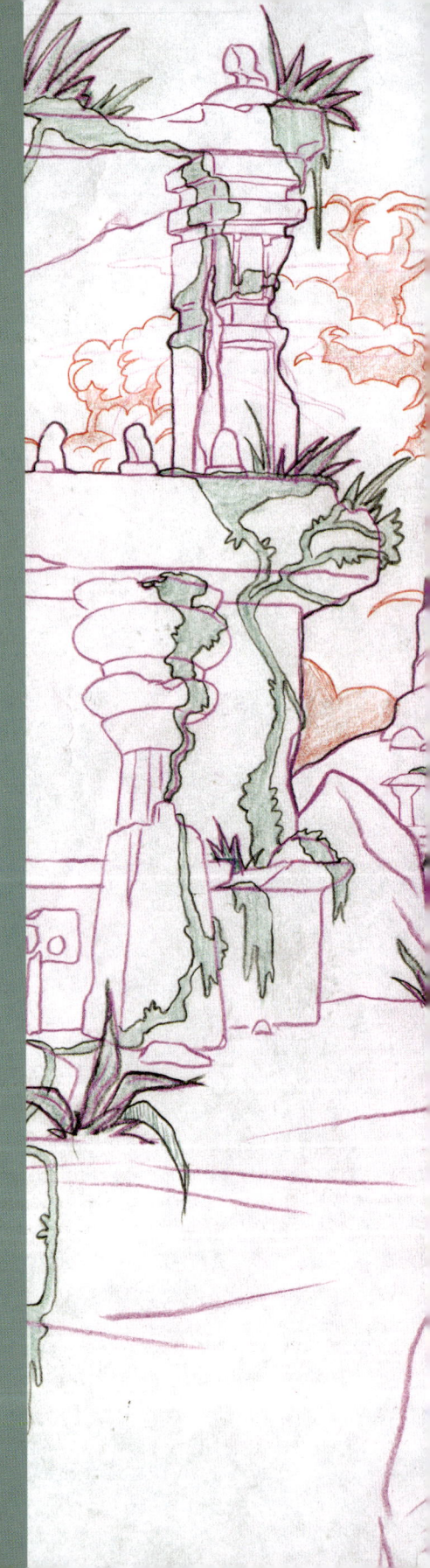

We had this great effects animator on the show, which was weird.
On an animated TV show you didn't often have an effects animator, but we had one.
And David Lee was just so good with these natural environmental elements, like clouds
and fire and explosions. He had a great way of simplifying them to where it's still
complex, but simple enough that it belongs in Matt's universe.

— Rich Moore

Above:
Planet Cyclopia, Alkazar's Castle (2ACV09) by Edgar Duncan

Right:
Planet Cyclopia ruined city (2ACV09) by Debbie Silver

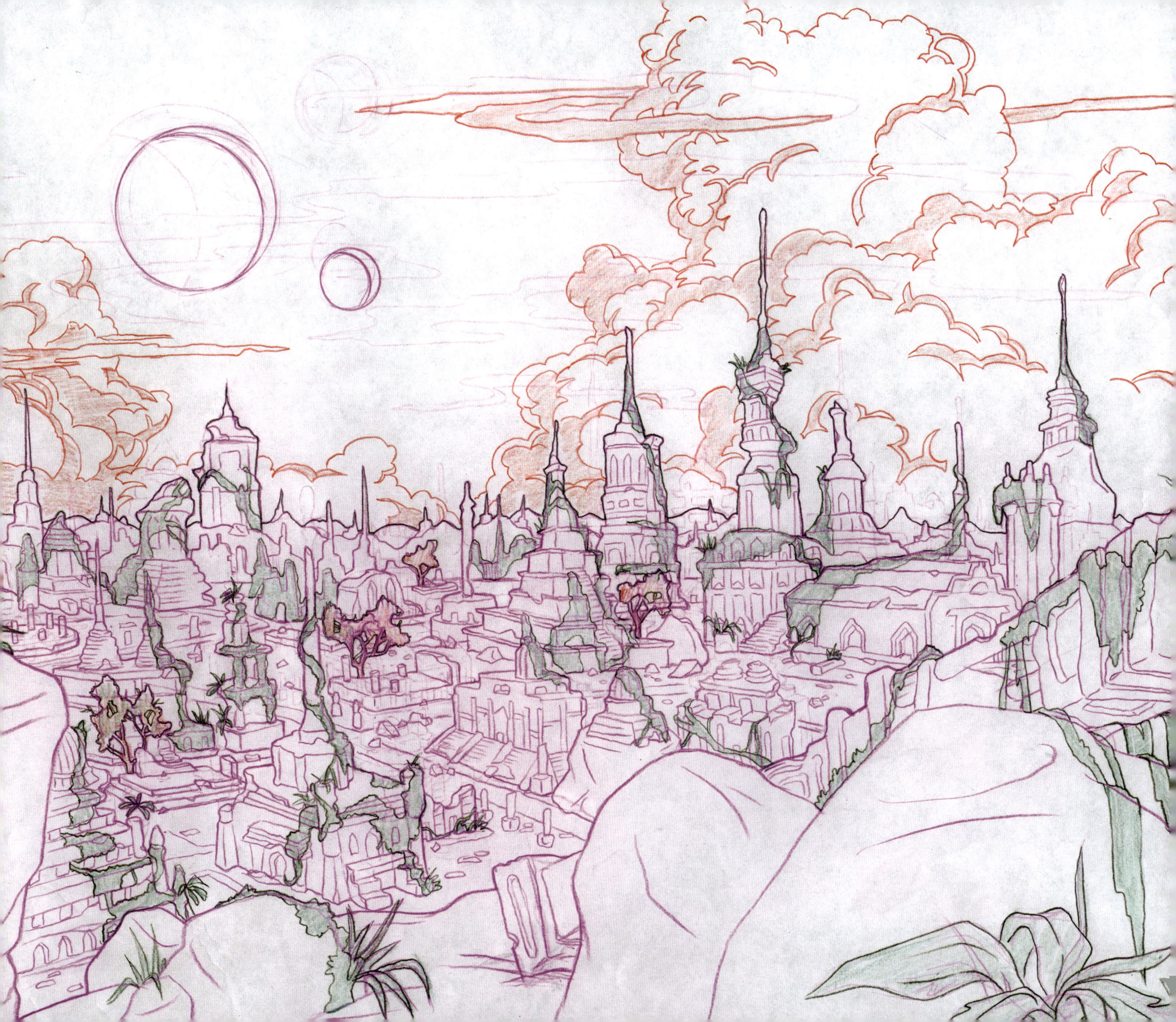

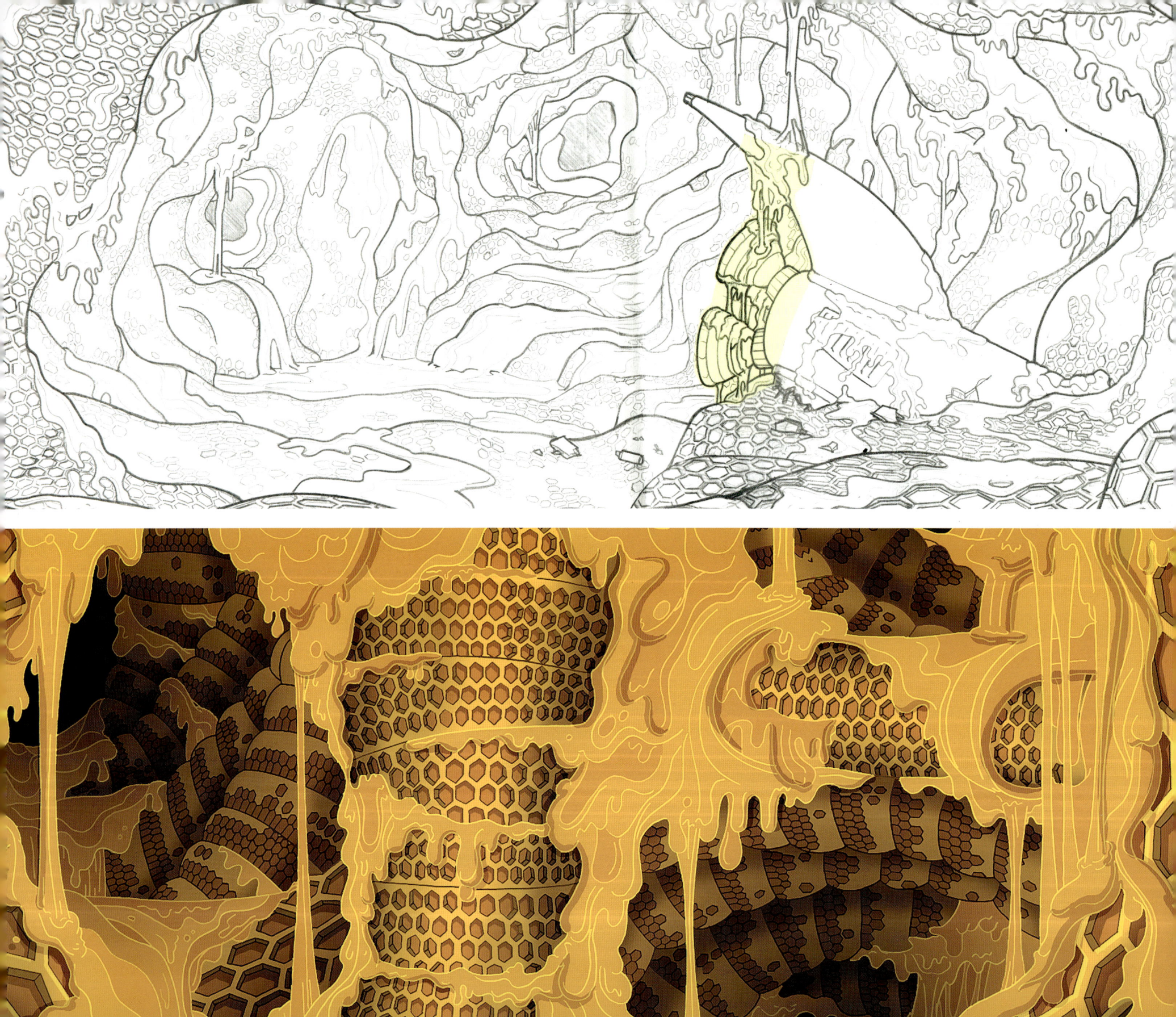

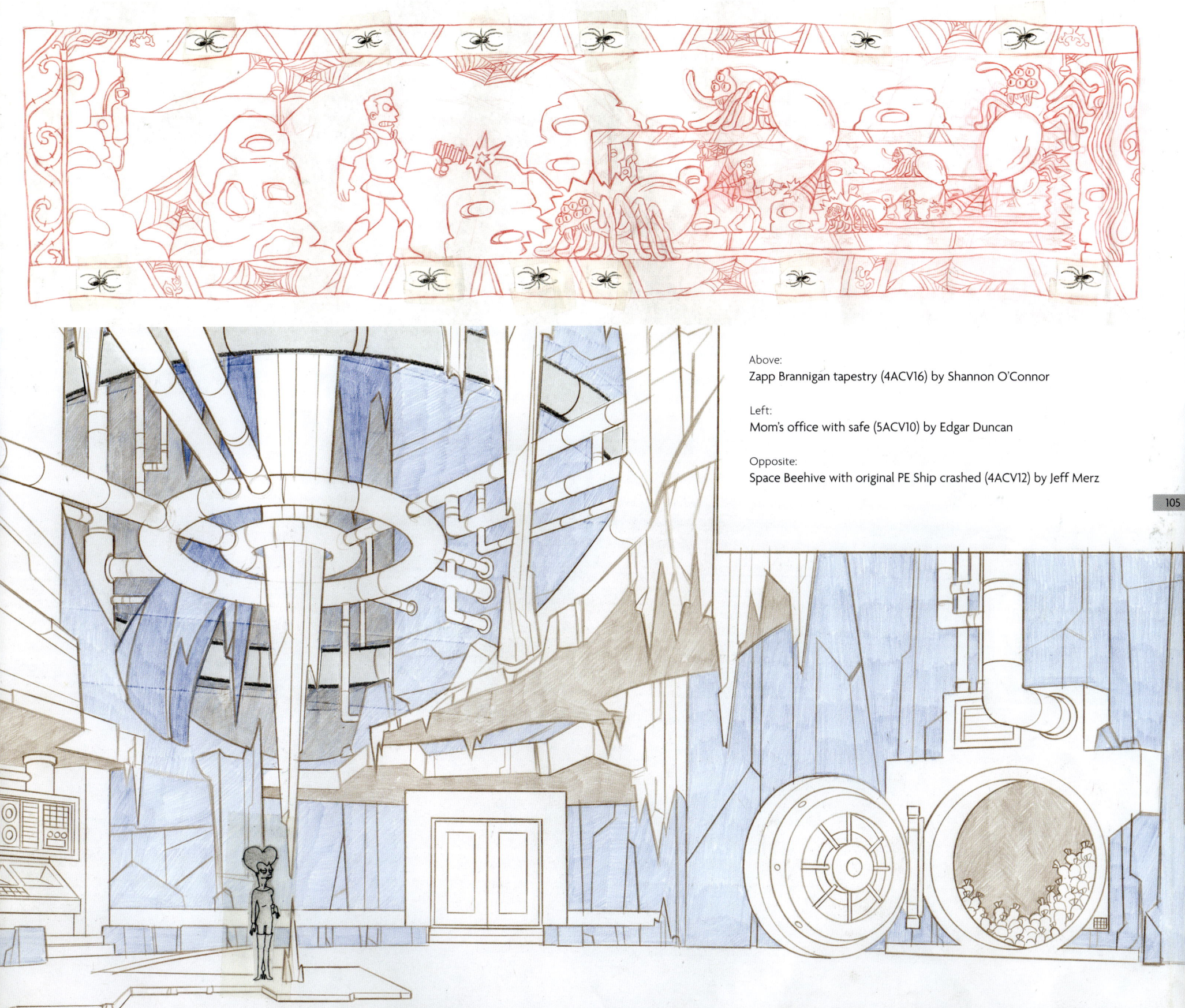

Above:
Zapp Brannigan tapestry (4ACV16) by Shannon O'Connor

Left:
Mom's office with safe (5ACV10) by Edgar Duncan

Opposite:
Space Beehive with original PE Ship crashed (4ACV12) by Jeff Merz

105

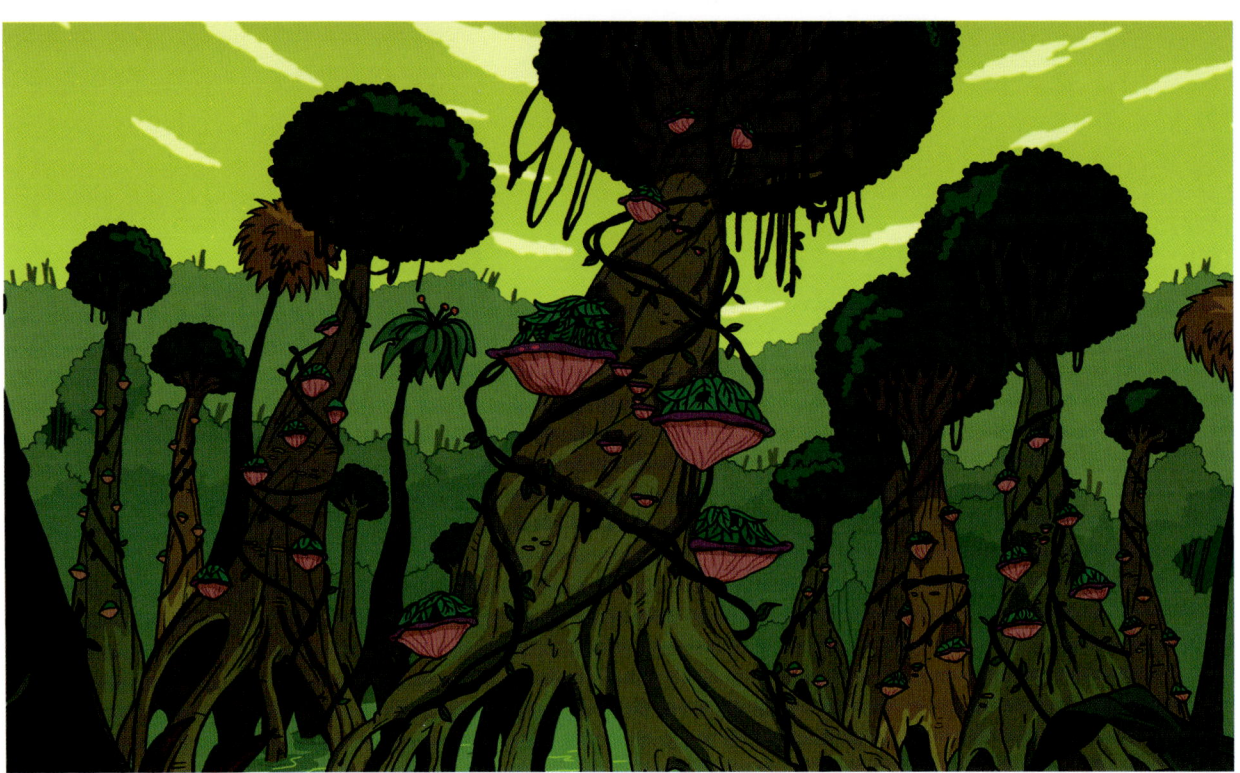

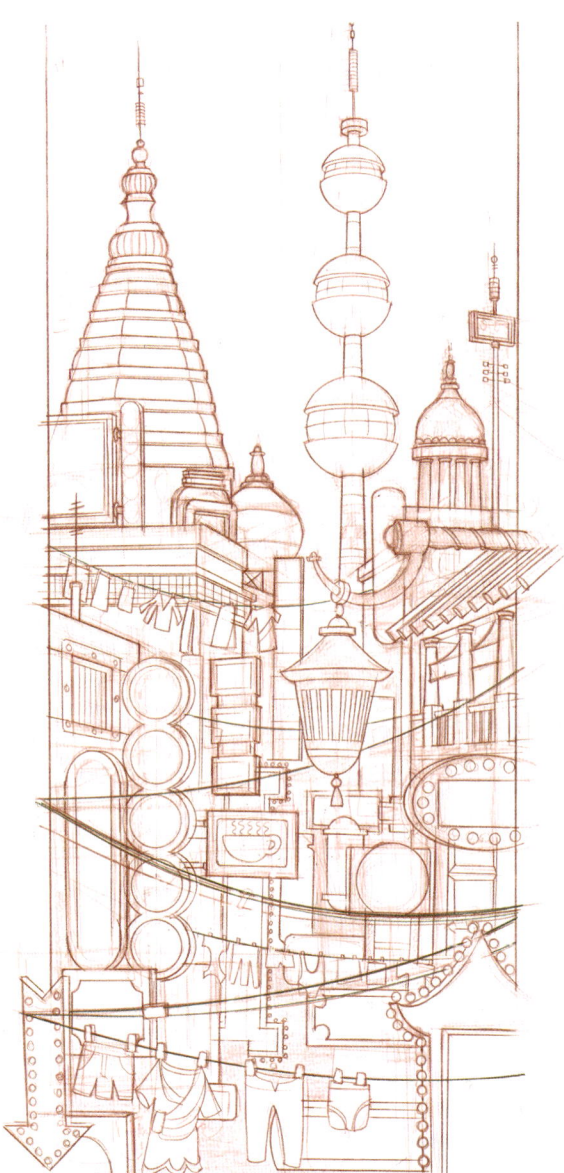

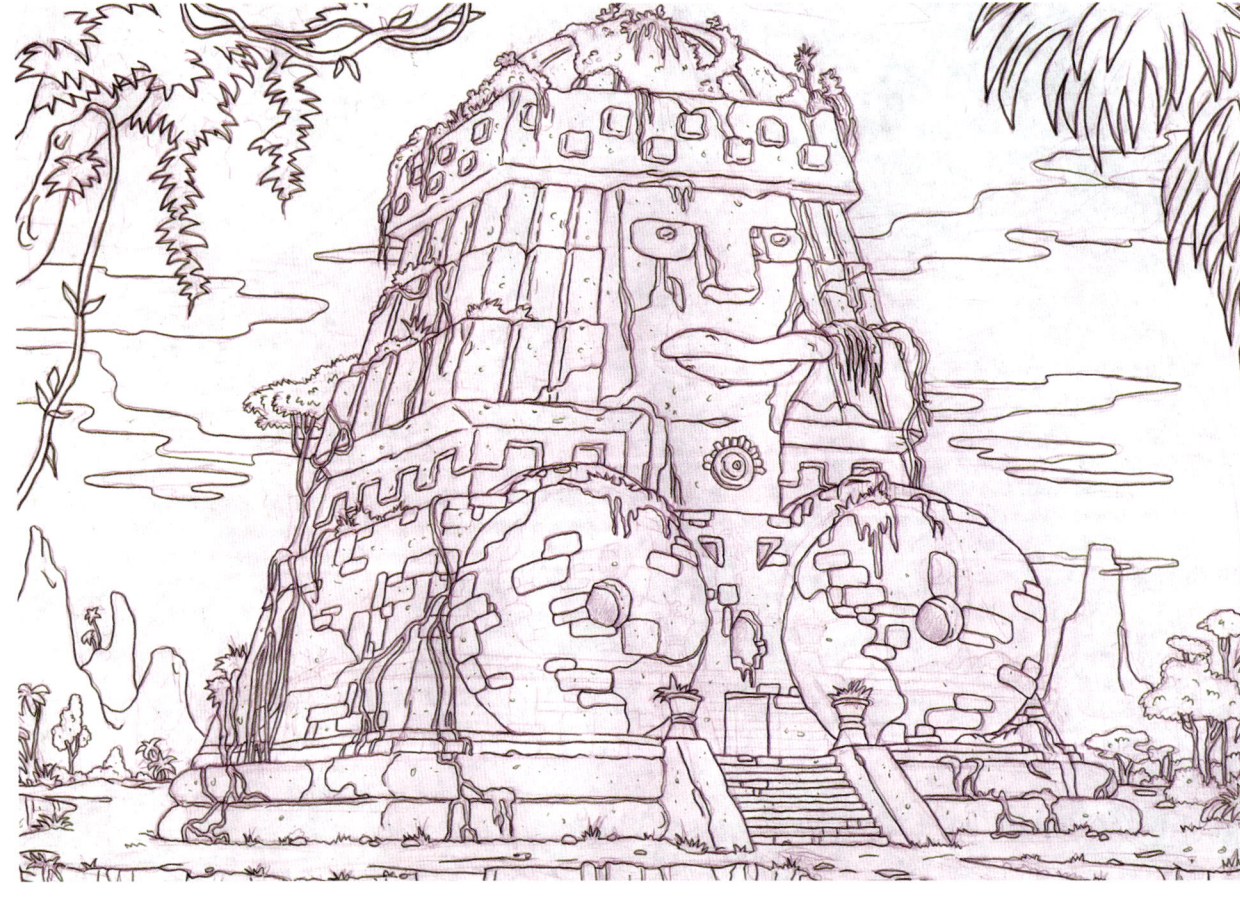

Clockwise:
Little Neptune (1ACV07) by Edgar Duncan
Kif's parents' treehouse (7ACV06) by Alen Esmaelian
Amazonia Fem Temple (3ACV01) by Debbie Silver

Opposite:
Trisol harem room (1ACV07) by Debbie Silver

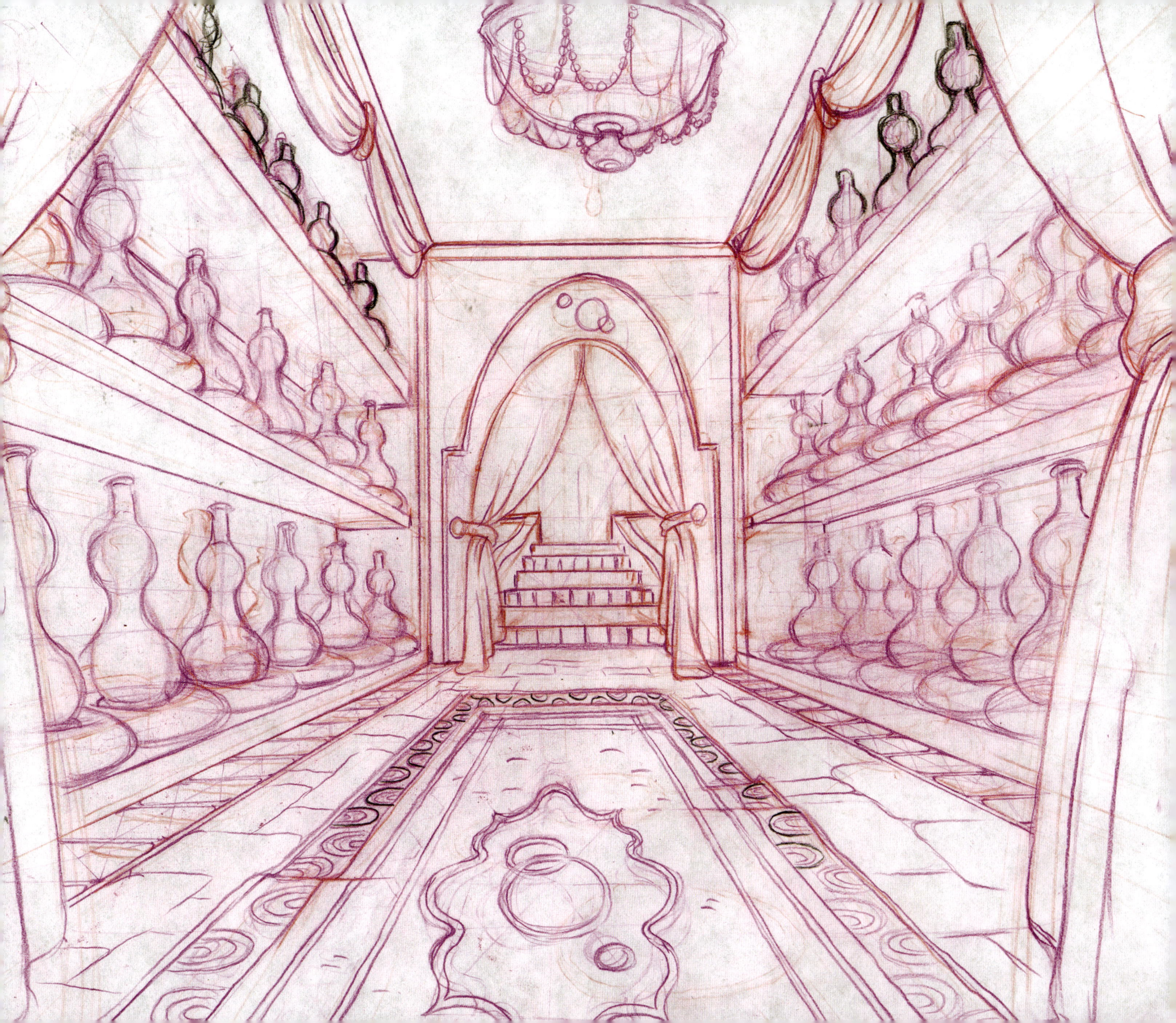

CRUISING SPEED:
ANOTHER DIMENSION ACHIEVED

Scott Vanzo is the director of computer graphics at Rough Draft. He directs the composite crew as well as the 3D crew, developing effects that are hard to produce using traditional animation. Rough Draft usually employs a crew of about three or four 3D artists for *Futurama*. Eric Whited is the lead 3D artist and usually does the cracking of the look as far as the 3D is concerned. They've both worked on *Futurama* through every single season, regarding each return of the show as a welcome homecoming.

Over the years, the show has gone through a host of different technical changes, which is a welcome challenge to Scott and Eric.

Scott Vanzo: When we first started working on the show, I don't think any other studios were doing cell-shaded 3D for television. There was probably some done for movies, but we might have been the first to actually do it for episodic television—for animated shows. We had to figure out how it all worked and how to get the best out of the tools that were there.

Cell-shaded animation allows Rough Draft to integrate the look of 3D elements with 2D elements, extending the storytelling they are able to do. The 3D tools create better-looking images when animating complicated things, like moving vehicles, for instance. So many lines have to be rendered very precisely because the viewer can quickly tell if the laws of perspective are being violated. It's a challenge for traditional animation artists; the vehicle might jitter or distort when making a turn. 3D doesn't have that problem, allowing the crew to add effects like galaxies, explosions, and the ability to travel through different environments and dimensions that lend themselves to a 3D space.

Eric Whited: Once a specific effect has been rendered in 3D it becomes an asset that can be reused in multiple instances without having someone have to redraw every frame, like a smoke effect or something.

Over the years, a library of these assets has been built up, allowing directors working on a particular sequence to dip into the back-catalog of effects, vehicles, and backgrounds. This is particularly helpful with background detail. For instance, since most of the ships and vehicles have been modeled in 3D, directors can easily throw traffic into a scene. It's a fairly straightforward process to bring in those assets the director wants and to animate them through the same demos in 3D.

Scott Vanzo: Most of the main characters have been modeled in 3D to be used as stand-ins, so they're recognizable in the distance inside of a vehicle or something like that. But generally, all the characters are strictly kept in 2D for acting purposes—more emotional expression. Being mechanical rather than organic, Bender is the exception and 3D might be used more liberally, for instance, in a dance sequence or if he's flying off somewhere.

Eric Whited: One of the challenges with new technology is filling in holes that you didn't have to worry about previously. Other concerns are texturing your signs and sets to make sure they've been up-rezzed. With higher definition, more details might be needed that weren't necessary before.

Some challenges come directly from the writers, many with advanced science degrees, who sometimes ask the animators to visually express theoretical phenomenon.

Scott Vanzo: At least once a year the showrunner, David Cohen, will bring us something like that. The directors scratch their heads a bit and scrape together any information David may have told them—*Is it an observed physical phenomenon or a theoretical phenomenon? Are there illustrations or descriptions of what*

it might look like? By now we're used to it and just kind of roll with it. We'll also talk to the supervising director, Peter Avanzino, until we come up with an idea. Then Eric and I talk and Eric hammers something out that looks like it might work in 3D. I take it to the director for notes. We work some more. Then we'll send a version to Matt and David. It goes through a lot of stages so it can be improved before we put it through twenty or thirty scenes.

Eric Whited: Sometimes you can pull from past experience, but a lot of times you're starting with the concept. And because of the situation or the procedure for that particular case, you're having to address new technical problems that arise for each instance. It's really satisfying when you can successfully work through a new challenge like that. It just adds to your skill set and creates assets for the library.

As technology advances, we've switched from one rendering software to another. We retool and improve what we're able to do.

—Scott Vanzo

The title sequence, originally directed by Mike Smith, was re-engineered three times, going from standard definition to high definition to 4K.

— Scott Vanzo

This page, top:
3D animation for opening sequence by Conan Low

Bottom:
3D animation for opening sequence by Eric Whited

Opposite, top:
3D grid of platforms with transparency showing people hooked to tubes and 3D hovering patrolmen by Eric Whited

Opposite, bottom:
3D generated Benders (6ACV15) by Scott Vanzo

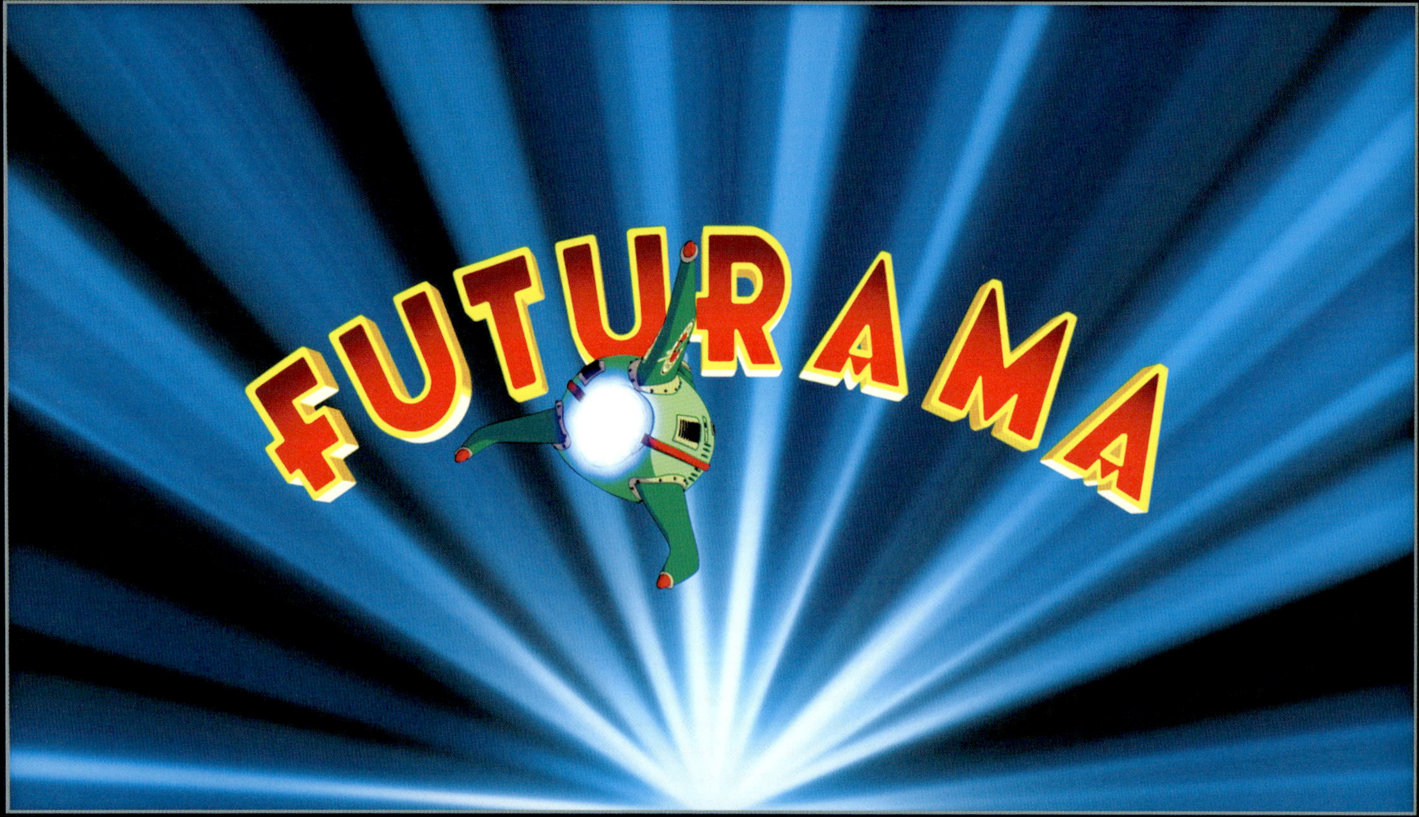

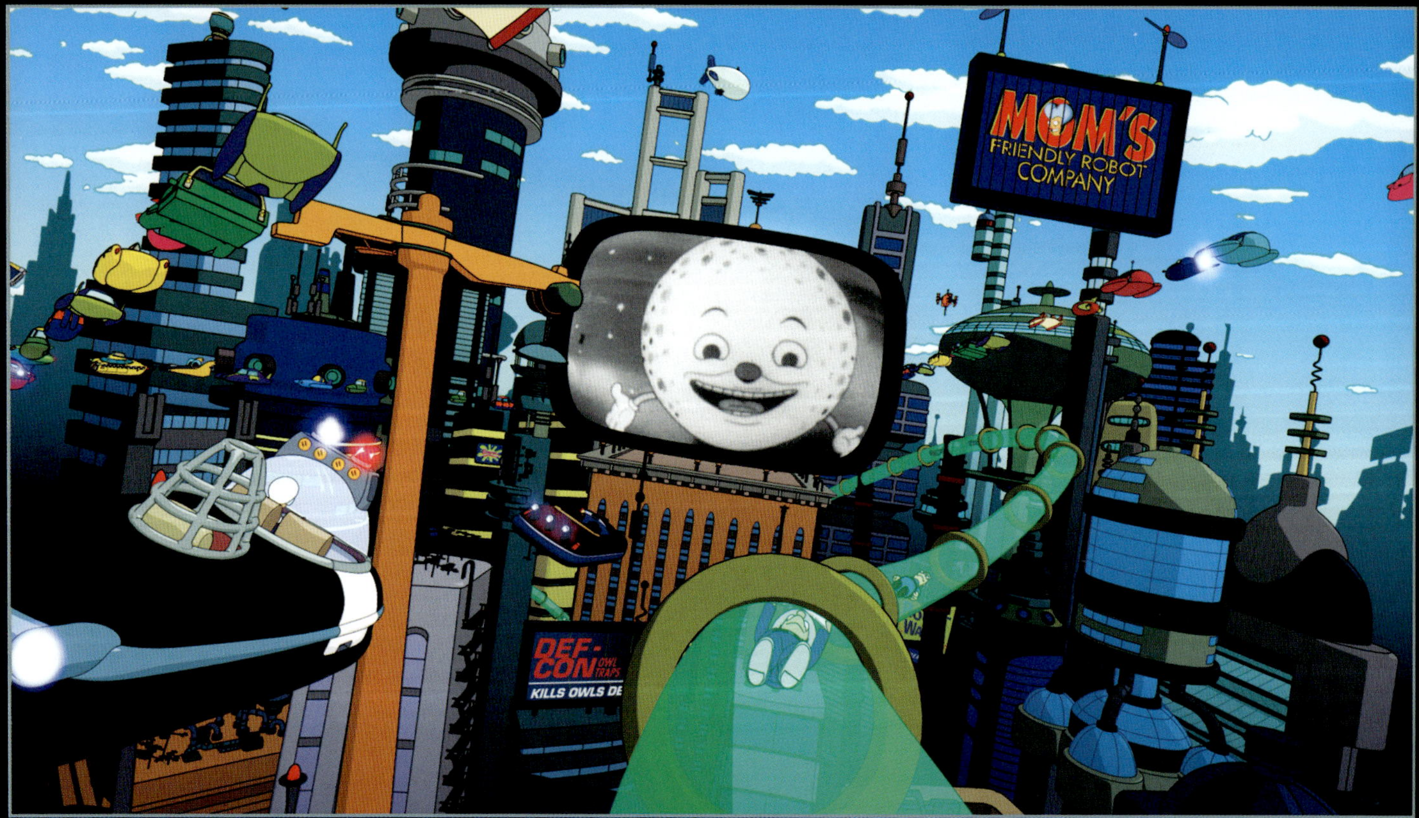

A lot of times when we redo things the director will ask for new buildings to be inserted. We put Mom's building in this last pass, and redid the 3D characters shooting through the tubes because at 4K the older models just don't hold up.

— Eric Whited

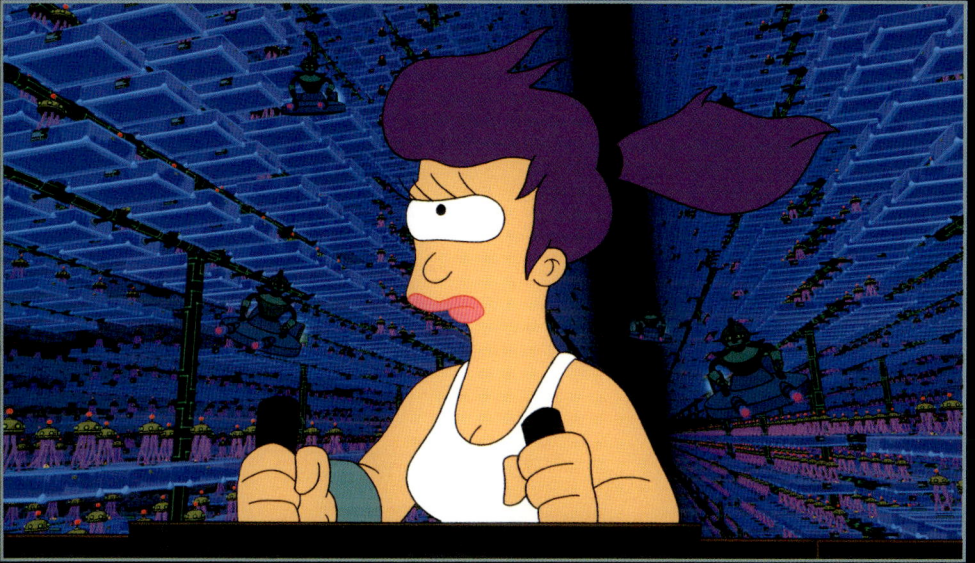

The Near-Death Star was a Matrix parody. We had rows and rows of old people in stacks of trays with tubes going in every direction, almost to infinity.
— Eric Whited

Eric had to figure out how to not only generate the huge number of rows and trays without breaking the computer, but also layer everything properly—with vehicles moving between the layers. It got kind of complicated.
— Scott Vanzo

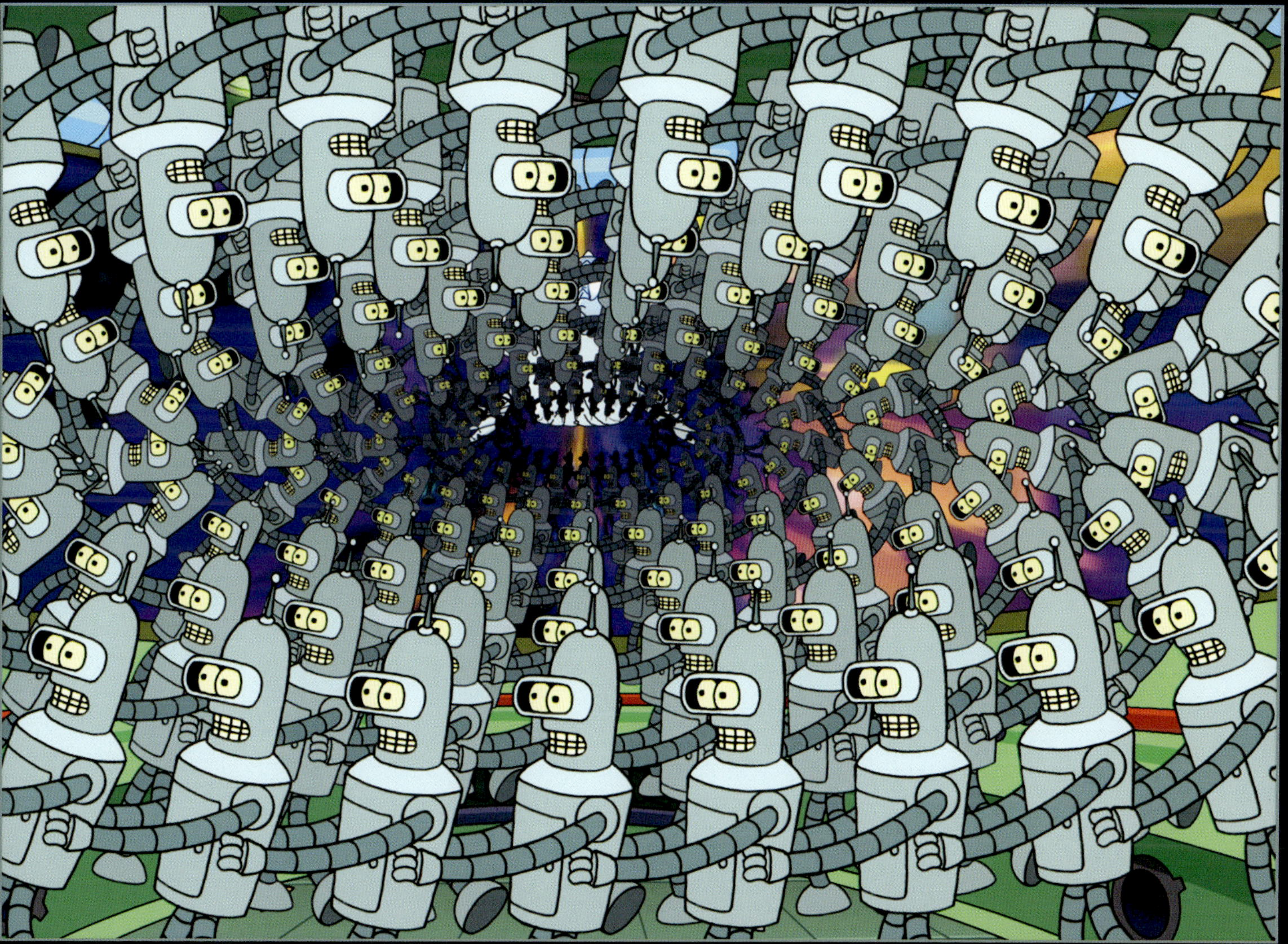

Another time we rendered thousands upon thousands of Benders.
— Eric Whited

Toward the end, a puff of smoke blows toward camera, enveloping it, and we see the smoke is filled with a myriad of different, smaller floating Benders tumbling around one other.
— Scott Vanzo

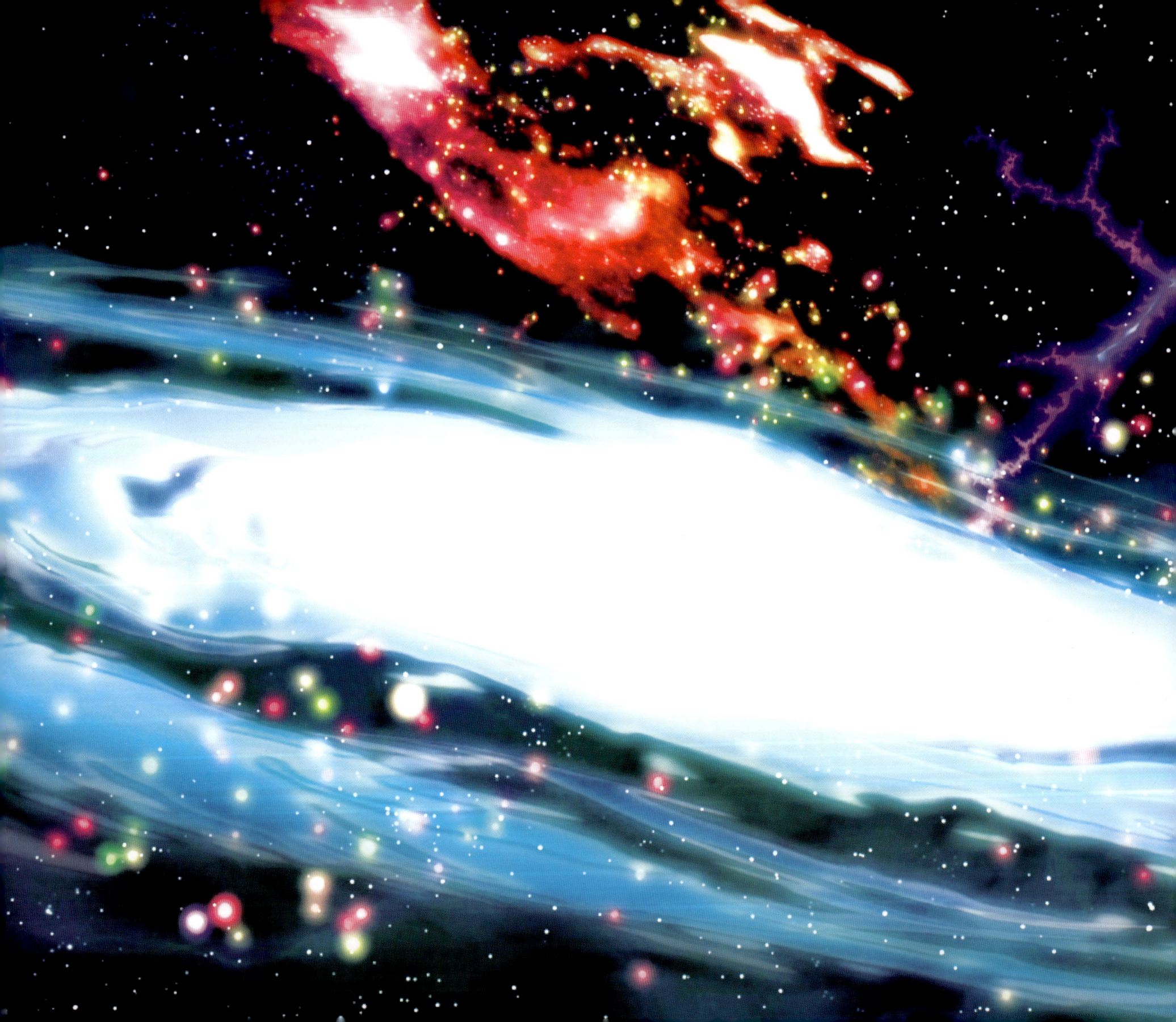

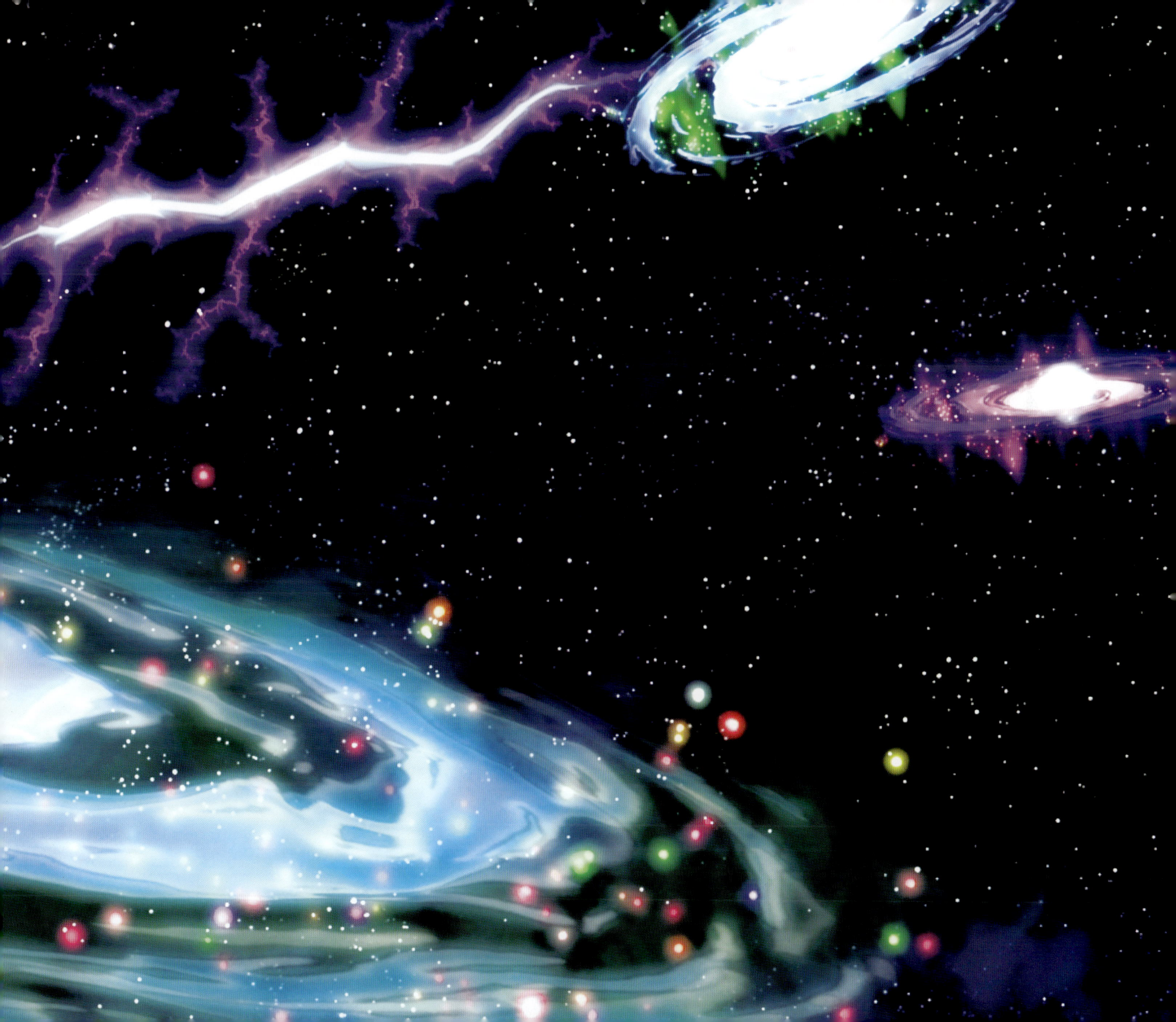

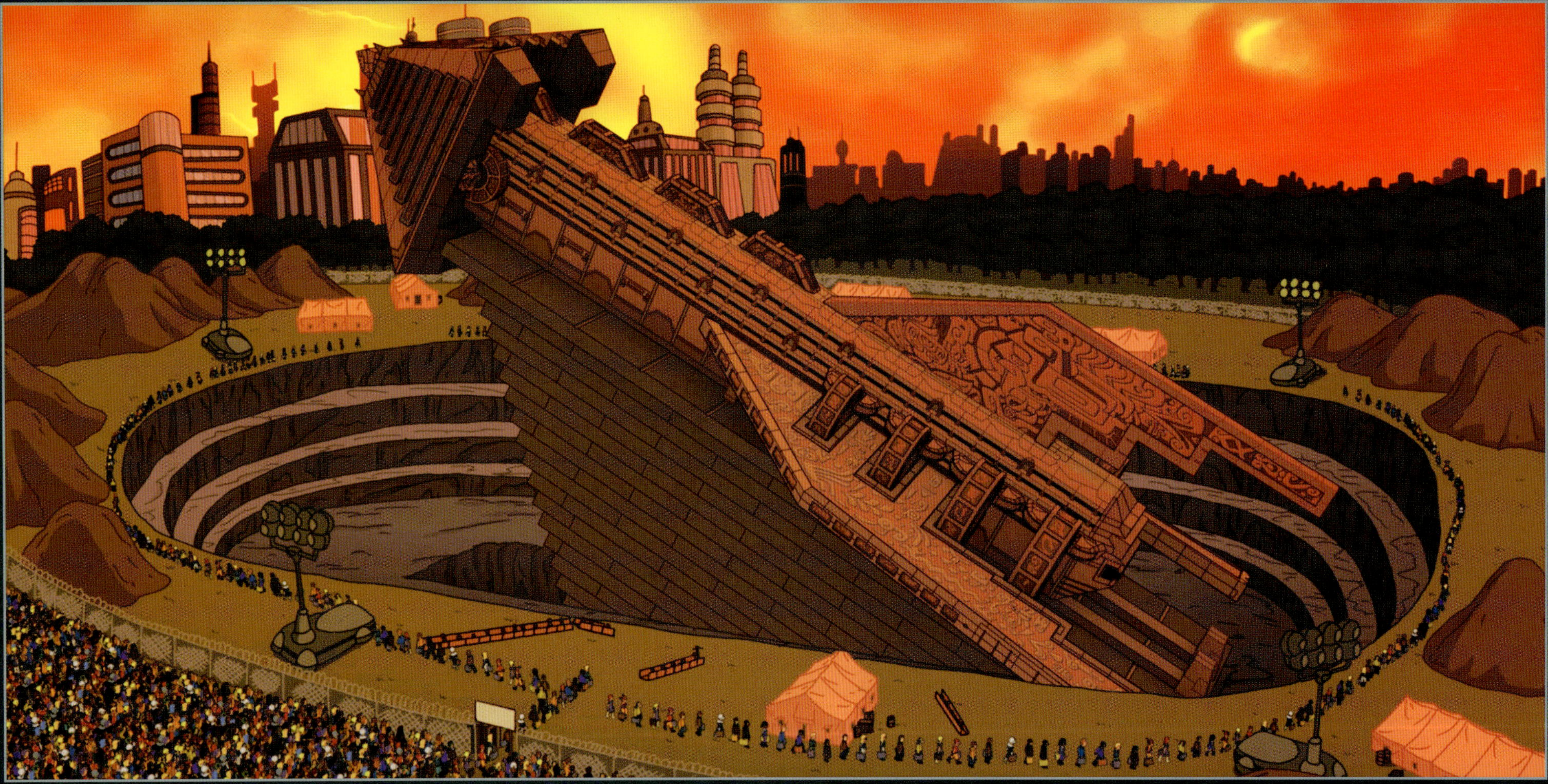

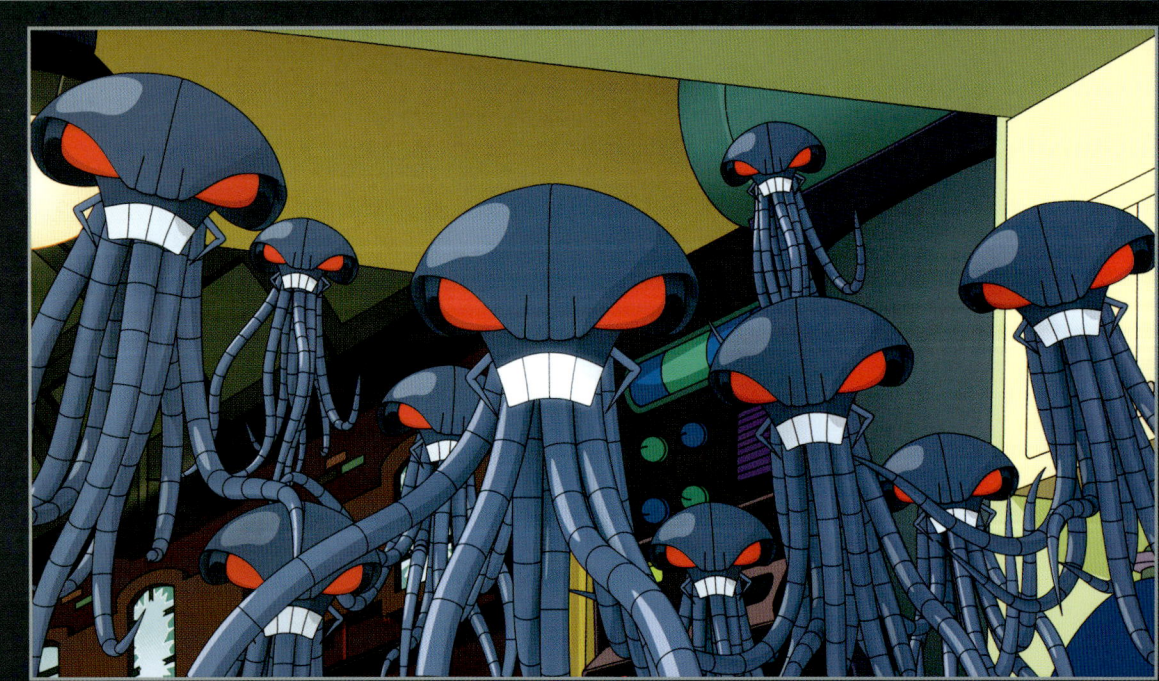

The color department has quite a profound impact on the look of the show. When this Aztec-style ship takes off, the whole world gets cast in a red light, like it was Armageddon. Everybody was fleeing the planet. It was actually very beautiful. The skies were all fiery orange.

— Scott Vanzo

Previous spread:
Eerie cosmic rip anomaly (5ACV04) by Eric Whited

Above:
Stone space ship and 3D crowd (7ACV02) by B. Shimbe Shim

Right:
Robot hover jellyfish (6ACV25) by B. Shimbe Shim

Opposite:
Example of 3D (the sun) and 2D animation combined in a scene (7ACV18) by Eric Whited

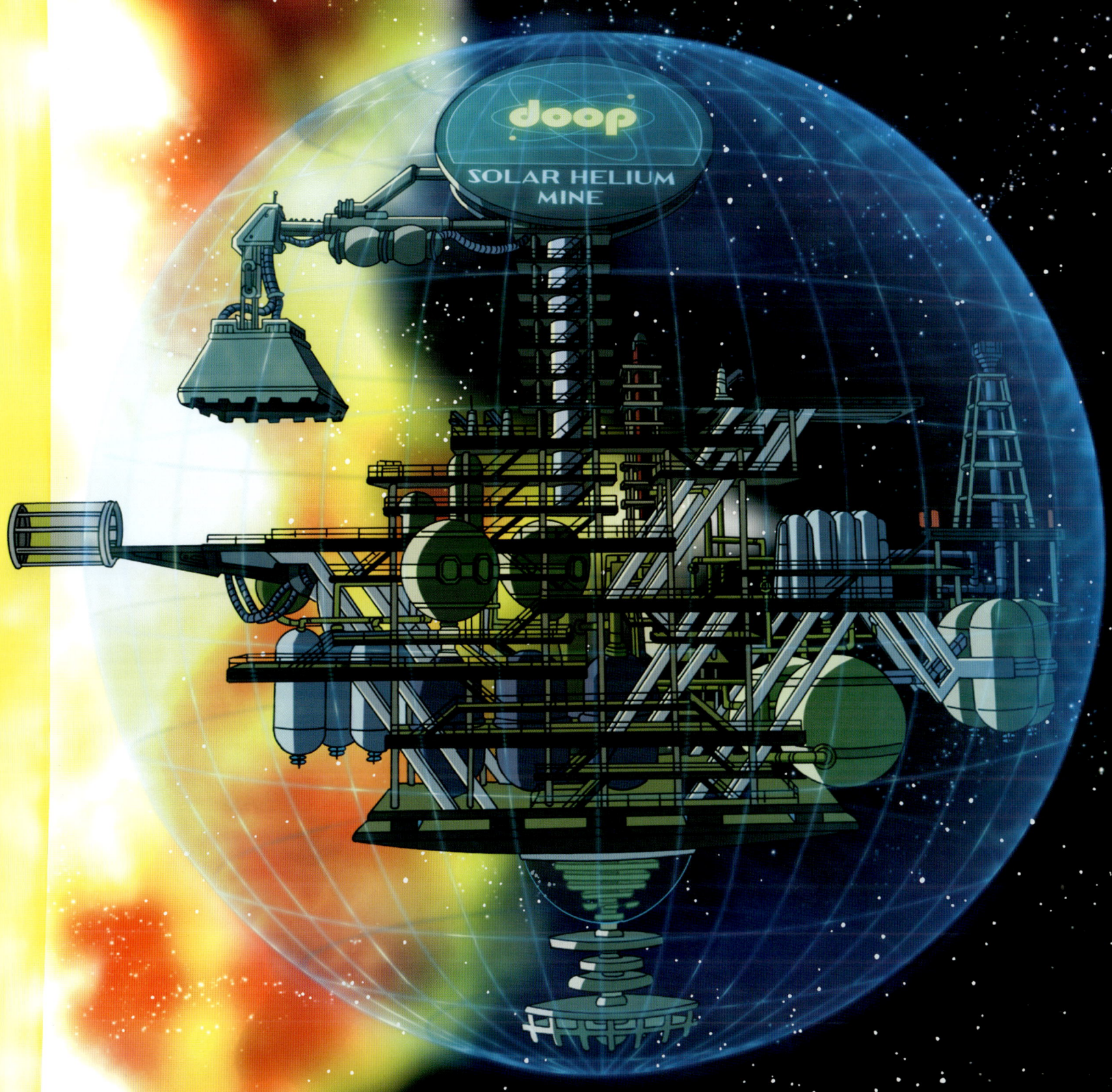

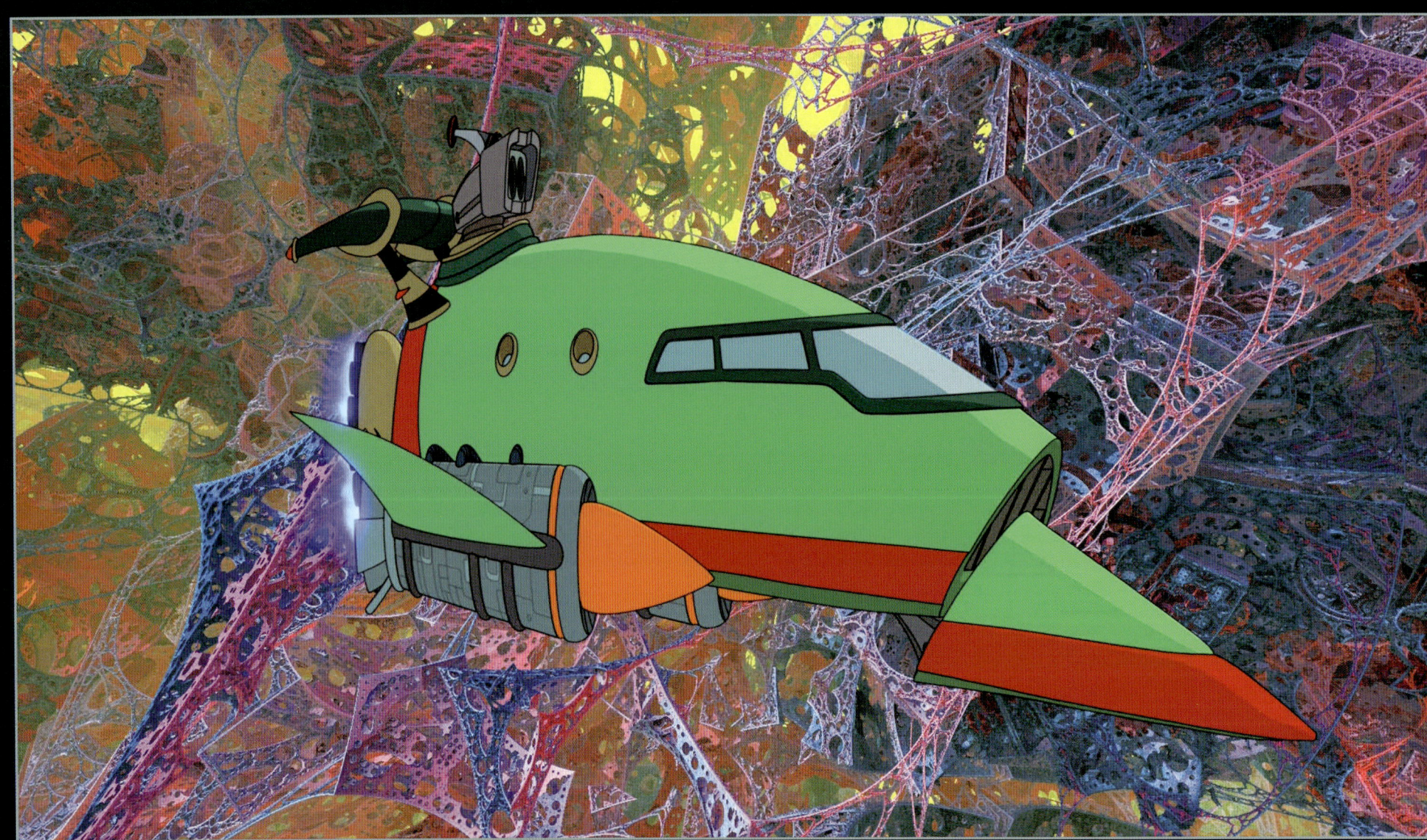

Planet Express ship transitions from 2D to 3D depth,
flying through "a mind-blowing world of fractals." David and
the writers do this every season. They'll throw in something
science-based, that we've never heard of, then we need
to come up with a look for it.

— Scott Vanzo

I think the most fun thing about Futurama is that,
with all the different planets, it takes all the rules away.

Planet Express ship, widening from 2D to 3D depth
flying through "a mind-blowing world of fractals" (7ACV15)
by B. Shimbe Shim, Eric Whited, and Scott Vanzo

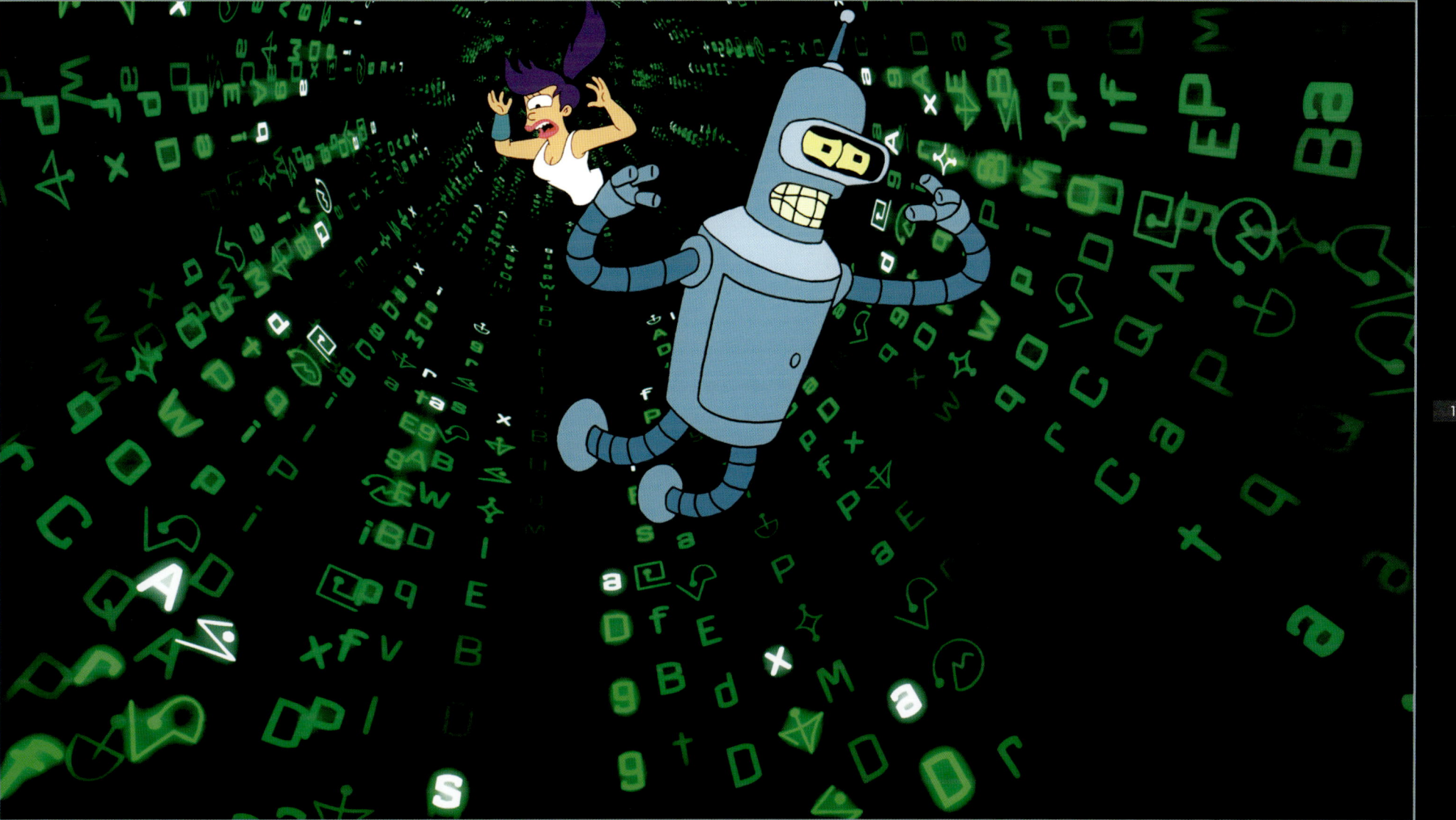

Sometimes we're asked to parody things that already exist. Once we had Fry leaping about in his spacesuit, done to look like this cool black-and-white Fleischer-style rotating turntable, refracting Fry into the crystals as he was spinning.

— Scott Vanzo

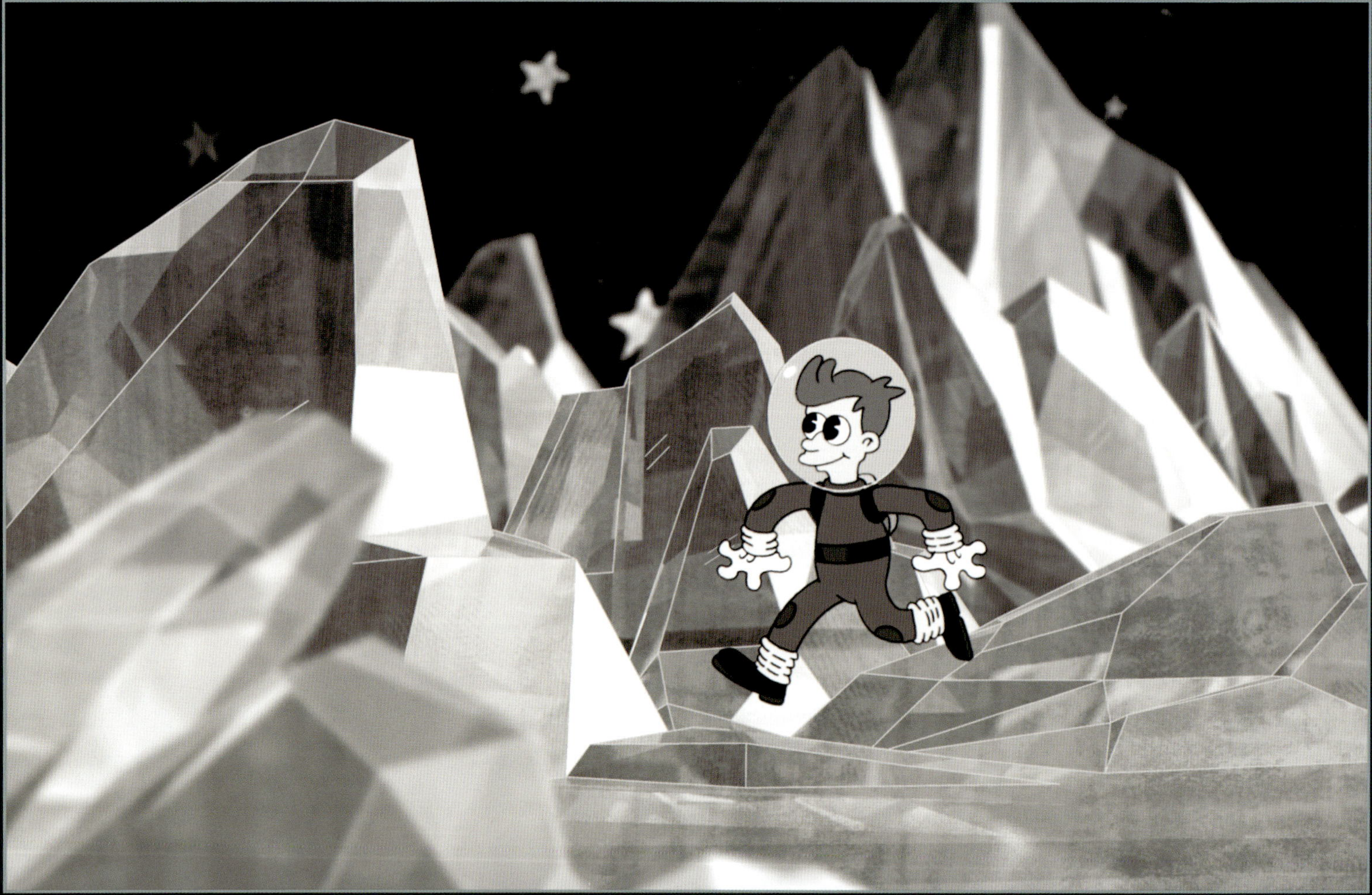

We later used those same kind of crystals with the space whale shooting fractals out of his spout.

— Eric Whited

Top:
Diamondillium comet modelled to simulate Fleischer setback camera rig (6ACV26) by B. Shimbe Shim

Bottom:
3D diamond spacebergs combined with 2D animation (6ACV15) by B. Shimbe Shim

Opposite:
Diamondillium sphere being built around Earth (5ACV07) by Mark Orme

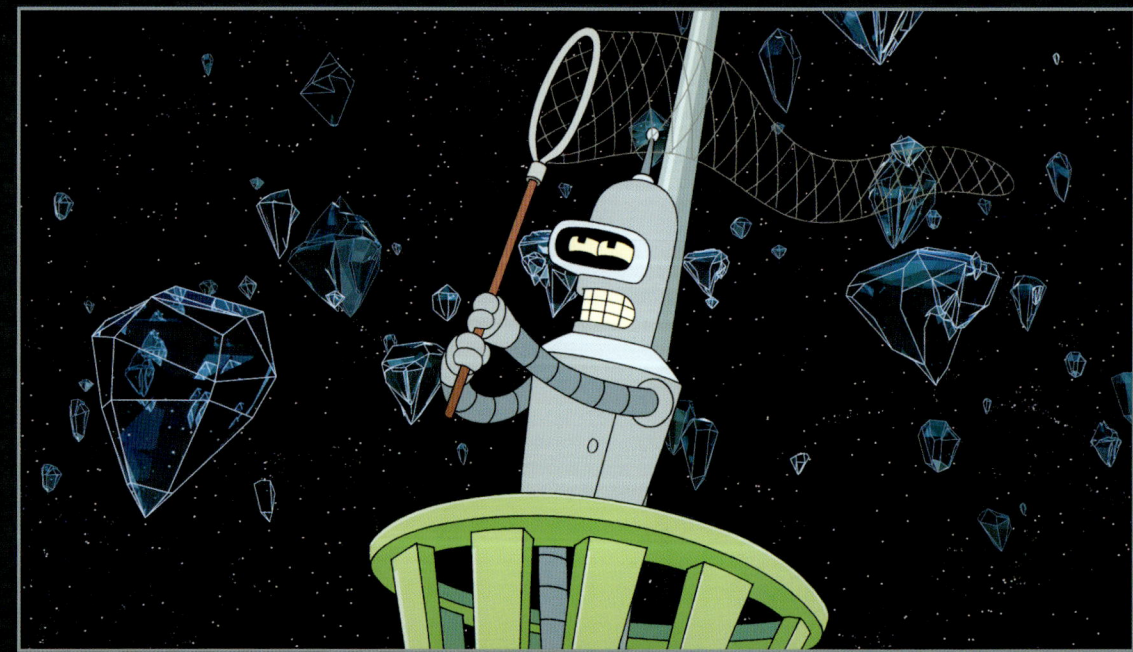

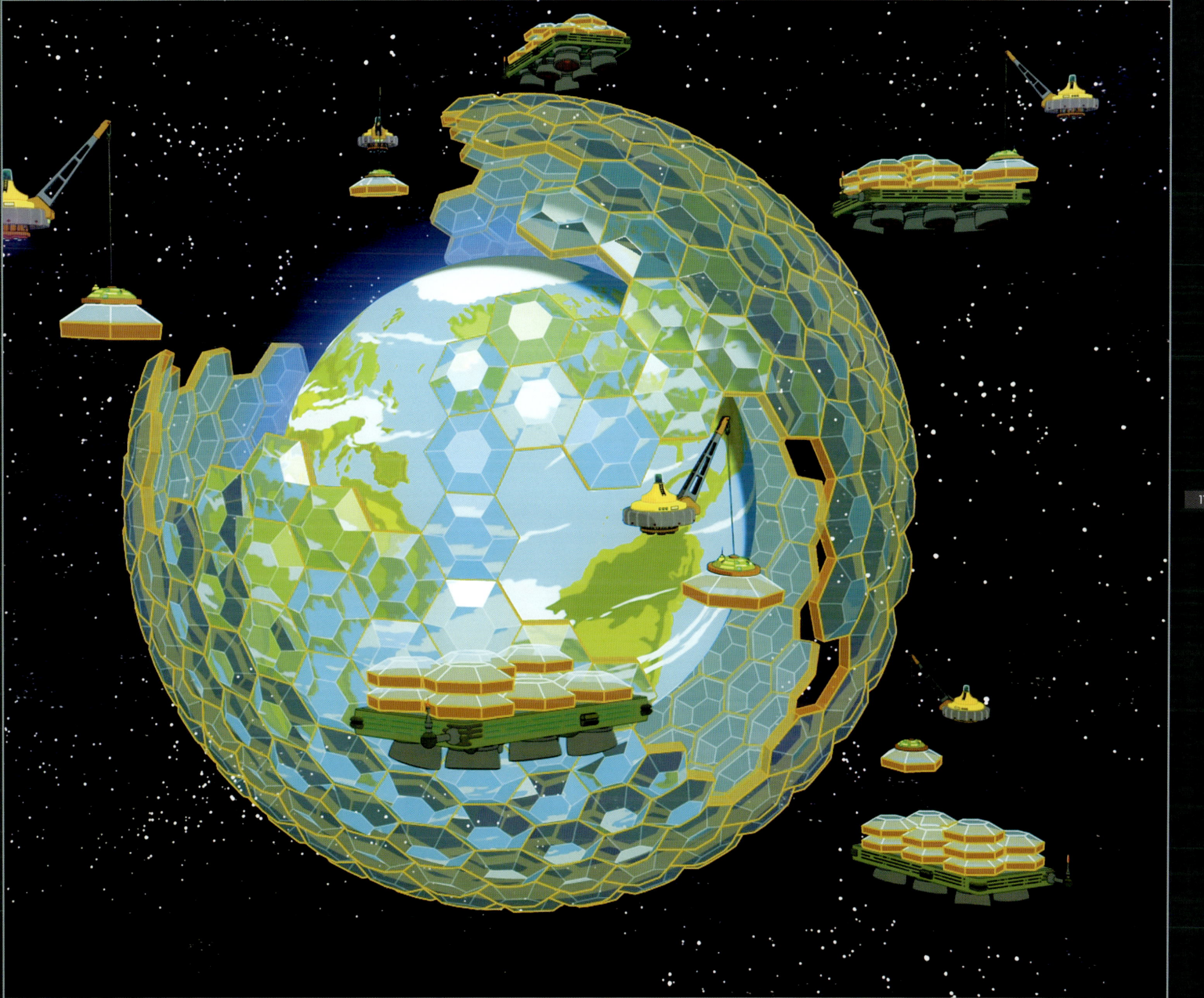

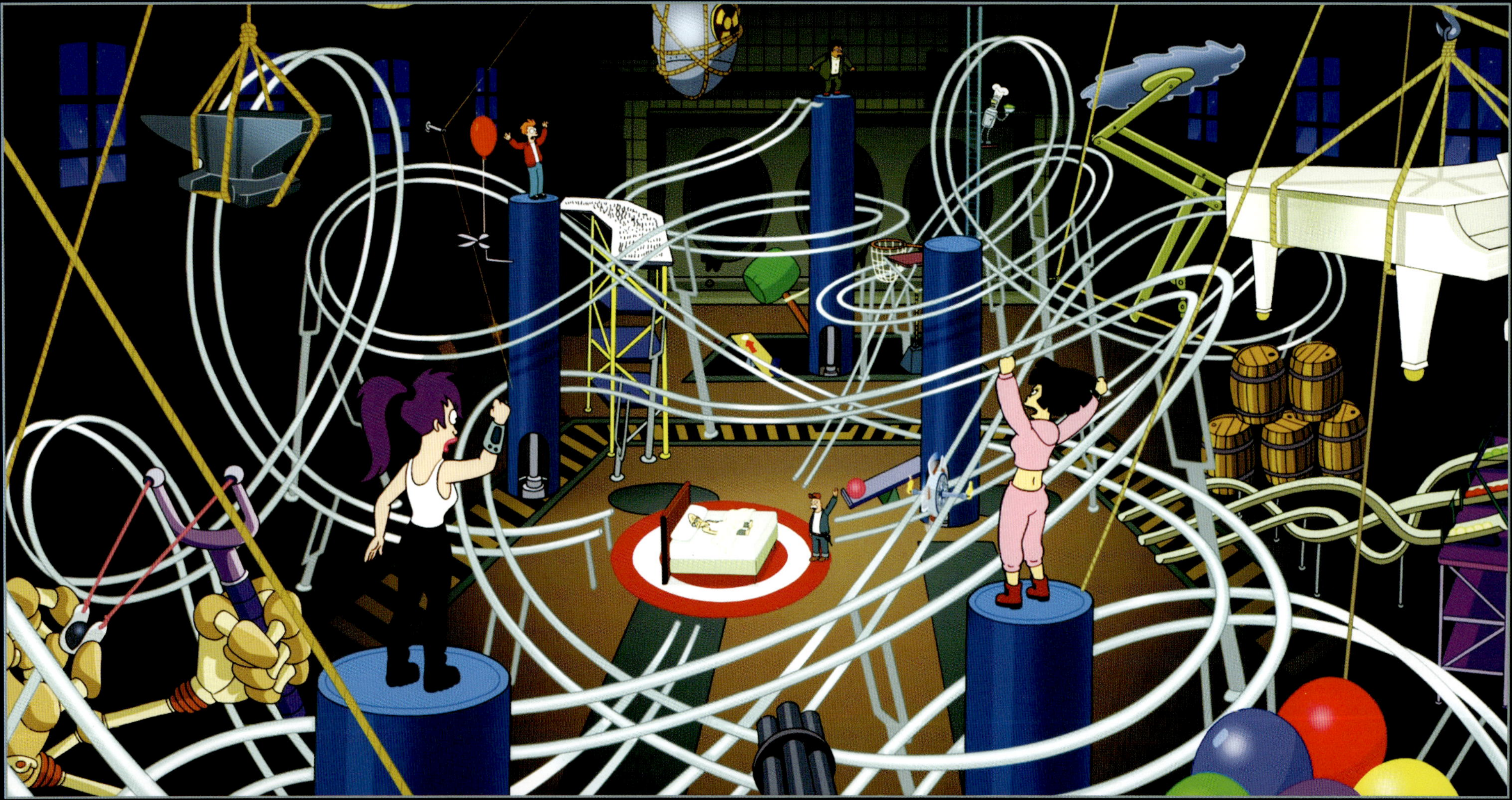

The Murdolator was a complicated
Rube Goldberg–like contraption with all these
blades going around. It was a really successful
integration of 3D and 2D with the characters.

— Eric Whited

The Toonz-shaded 3D elements
are so solid that, as the show evolved, the
characters needed to become more solid and
sculptural looking and less flat-cartoony, so that
everything would visually mesh better.

— Crystal Chesney-Thompson

Above:
Murdolator 2D drawing (6ACV18)
by Don Kim

Right:
Time Sphere 3D effect with 2D characters
and background (5ACV01)
by Eric Whited

Opposite:
DaVinci's Doomsday Machine (6ACV05)
by B. Shimbe Shim

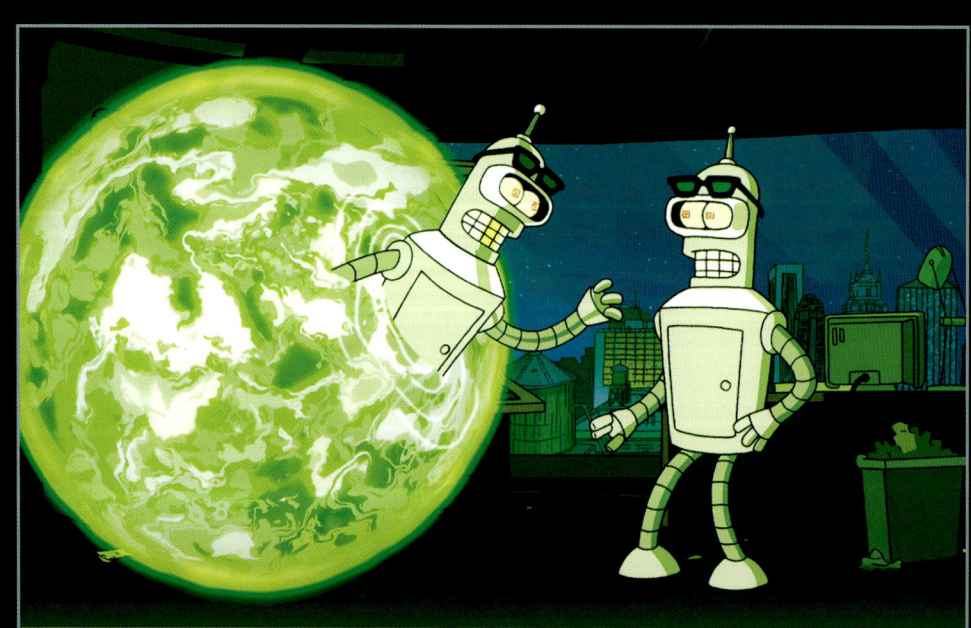

Another example is that DaVinci creation that walks on crab legs and has arms coming out attacking people. That was supposedly an ice cream machine, which suddenly springs into action and becomes a murdering machine. It shows how using 3D with 2D creates a level of complexity that goes beyond what's practical to draw, but still fits into the style of the show.

— Scott Vanzo

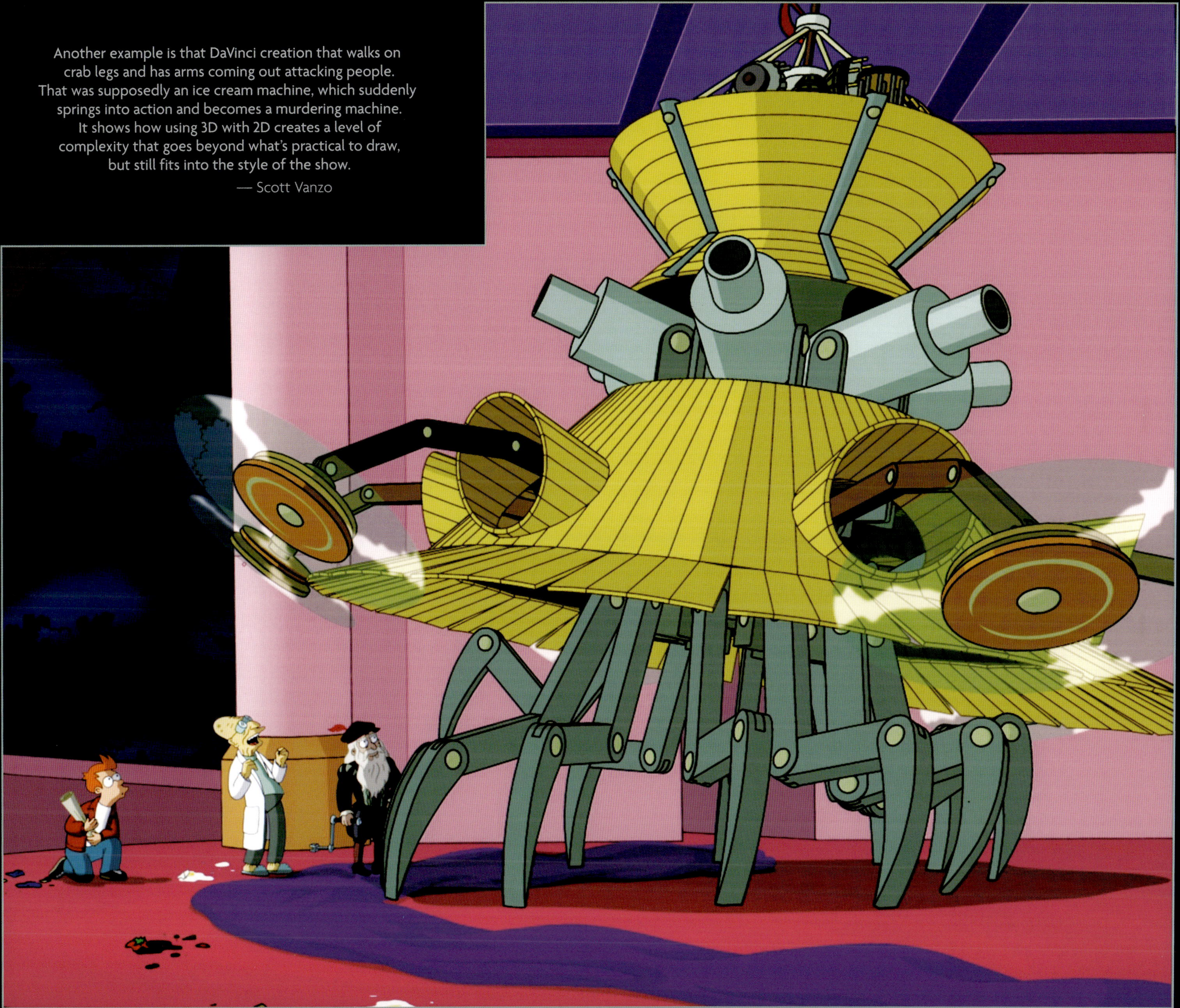

DESCENT: HOLD IT RIGHT THERE

Rich Moore: None of these guns or weapons look scary. The most successful ones are kind of fun-looking. I would tell the designers, "It needs more Buck Rogers or Flash Gordon," so even stuff that's really dangerous looking is funny at the same time. Or if it's not funny looking, it's so over-the-top scary that it becomes funny. Everything has to have a silly quality, a comedic sense to it. This kind of sci-fi stuff was always a fun challenge.

Claudia Katz: We've had episodes with challenges I will never forget. In one episode they wrote, "everyone who's ever appeared in *Futurama* ever is in the bleachers." And then Pete took it as a gauntlet being thrown down.

Peter Avanzino: I liked it. I said, alright, I do want to do that. We were doing layout at the time. I broke the bleachers into twenty different grids and each artist got one grid with twelve *Futurama* characters in it. Then we put it together in camera. I think we had to pay Korea extra.

Claudia Katz: When we screened the episode, David was just giggling and he was like, "Oh my God!" And we were like, "Well, you wrote it." "Yeah, but I didn't think you would do it."

Dwayne Carey-Hill: David sort of famously wrote: *The characters fly over Las Vegas, something happens, and Las Vegas is completely destroyed and then rebuilt to a new Las Vegas.* Only we didn't even have an existing Las Vegas. So, we had to design Las Vegas

and then destroy Las Vegas and then create another Las Vegas. And that was just the cold open. That speaks to the insanity that oftentimes comes across in the scripts, which, after reading then imagining them, I think we all acknowledge is pretty spectacular.

Crystal Chesney-Thompson: In "Benderama," Bender figures out how to duplicate himself. At one point there's thousands, billions of teeny-tiny Benders that march through the streets and form a giant Bender. We had to find ways to board these miniature Benders close up so that it looks like there's a ton of them. And then we had the effects guys doing these almost water or mercury-looking effects to create the flow of all these mini-Benders, which would culminate in them forming the giant super Bender. Every department is working together to make this cool sequence culminating in this giant Bender fighting a giant alien.

Claudia Katz: Our meetings going over the episodes are very entertaining because Pete Avanzino starts asking about some impractical thing; "You want us to do what?" And David Cohen says, "Well, that's for you to figure out." And then David just starts giggling and it's very charming. And, it always gets figured out.

> We had so many ray guns
> on the show that, in the future, the N.R.A.
> is the National Ray Gun Association.
> — Matt Groening

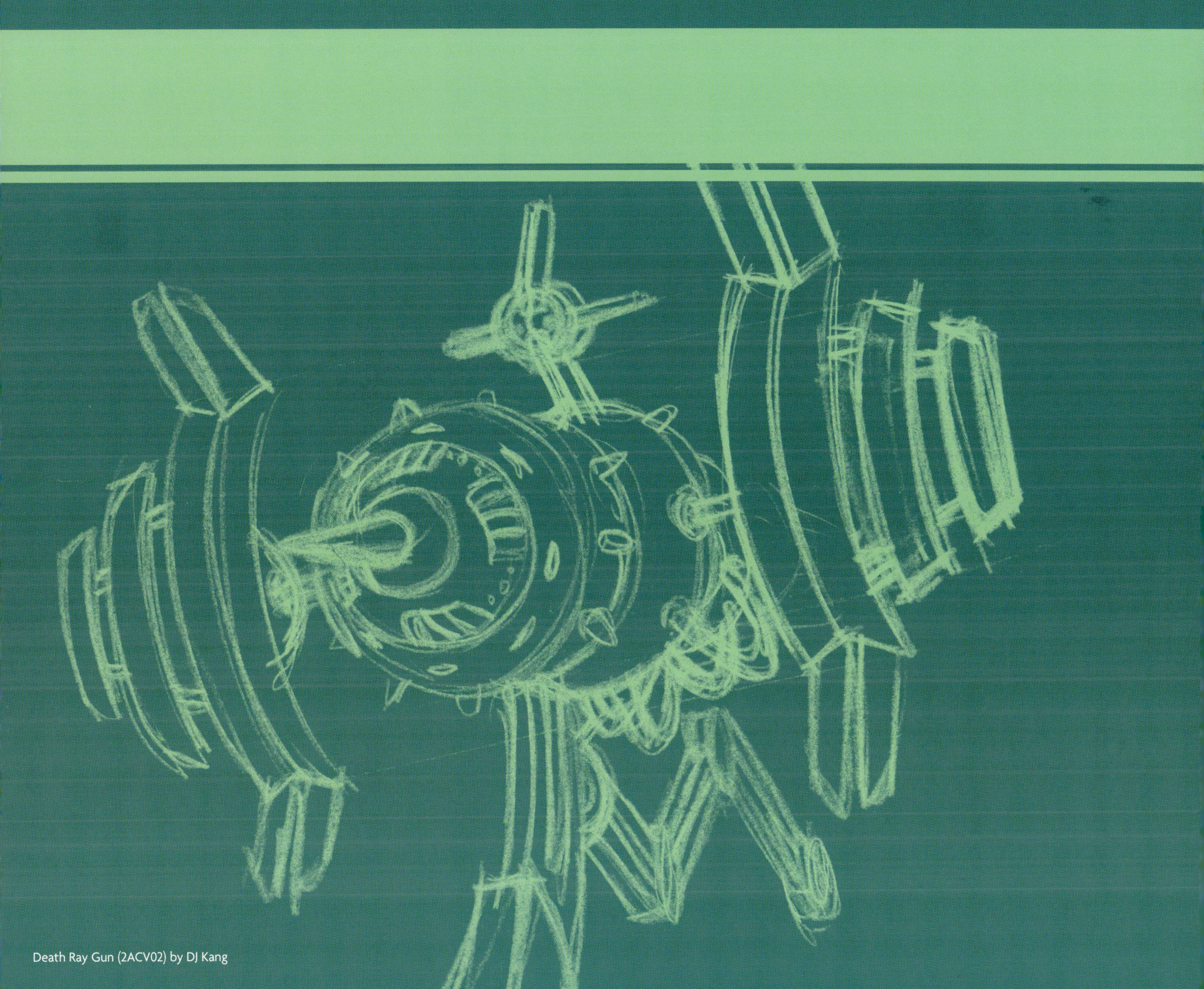

Death Ray Gun (2ACV02) by DJ Kang

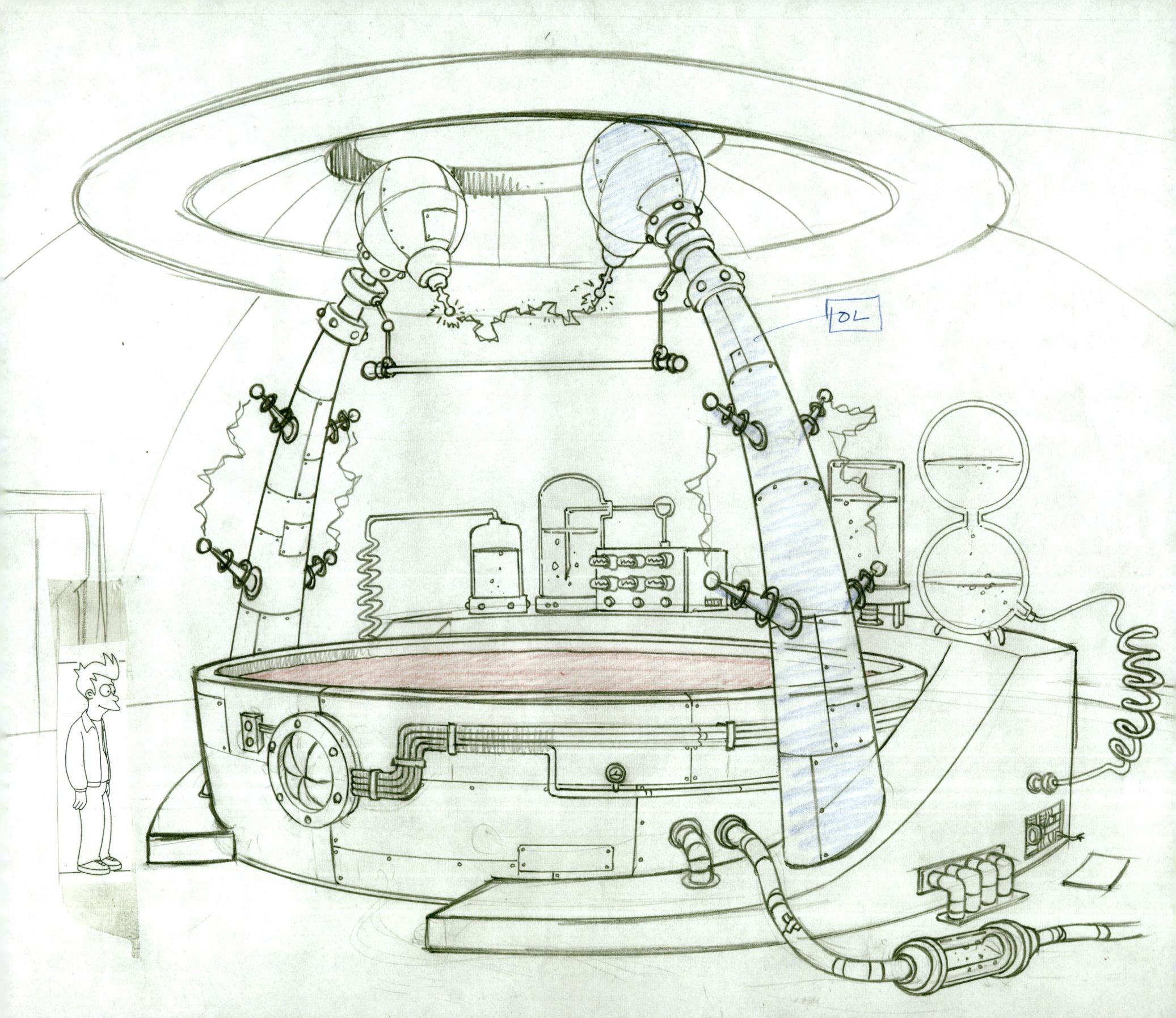

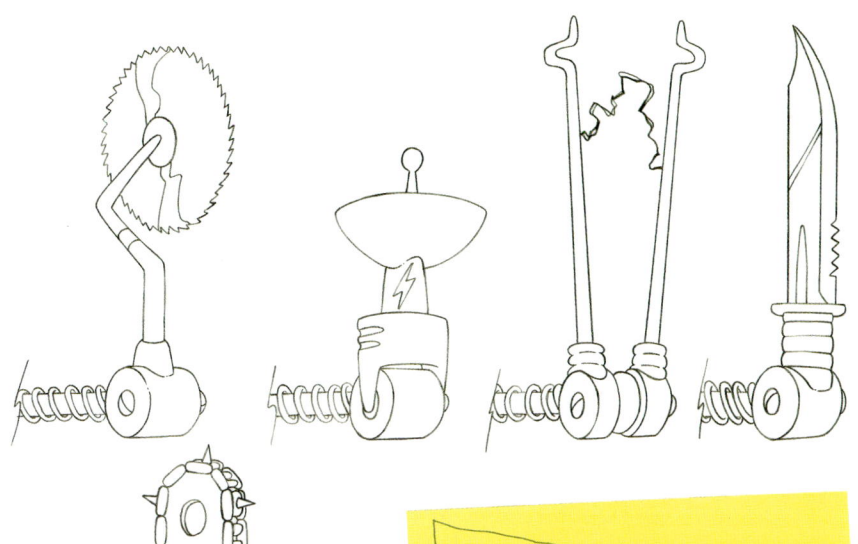

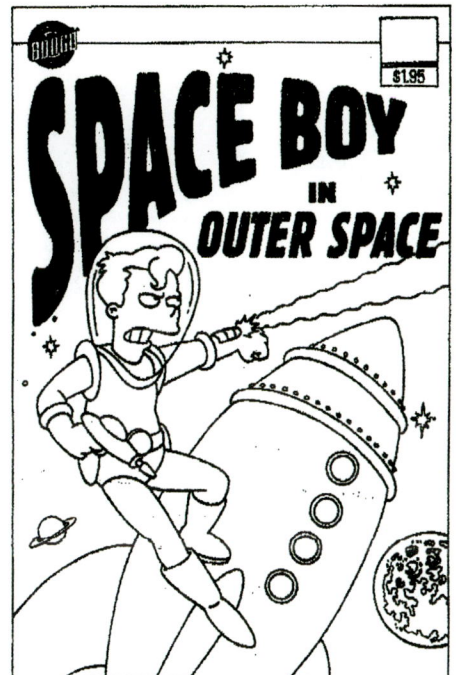

Opposite:
Birth machine (6ACV01) by Jeff Mertz

Top (from left to right):
Suicide Booth tools (1ACV01) by Jeff Lynch
I.C. Weiner note (1ACV01)
by John Krause and John Mathot
Space Boy comic book cover (1ACV01)
by Serban Cristescu and Bill Morrison

Bottom (from left to right):
Can of Angry Norwegian Anchovies (1ACV06)
by John Krause
What If Machine (2ACV16) by Zeke Johnson
Bender signed portrait (3ACV20) by Jim Feeley

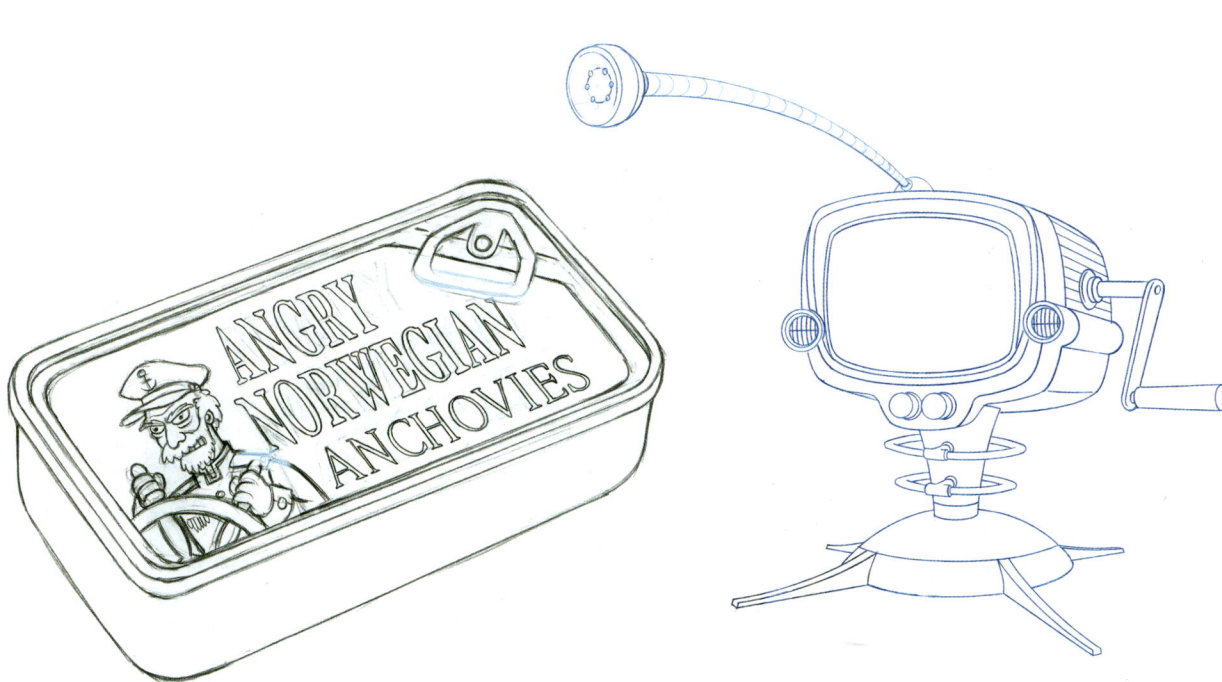

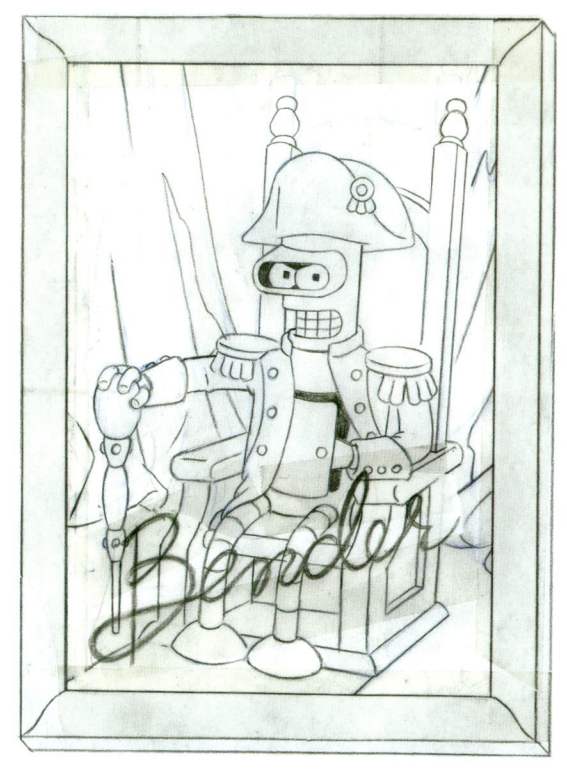

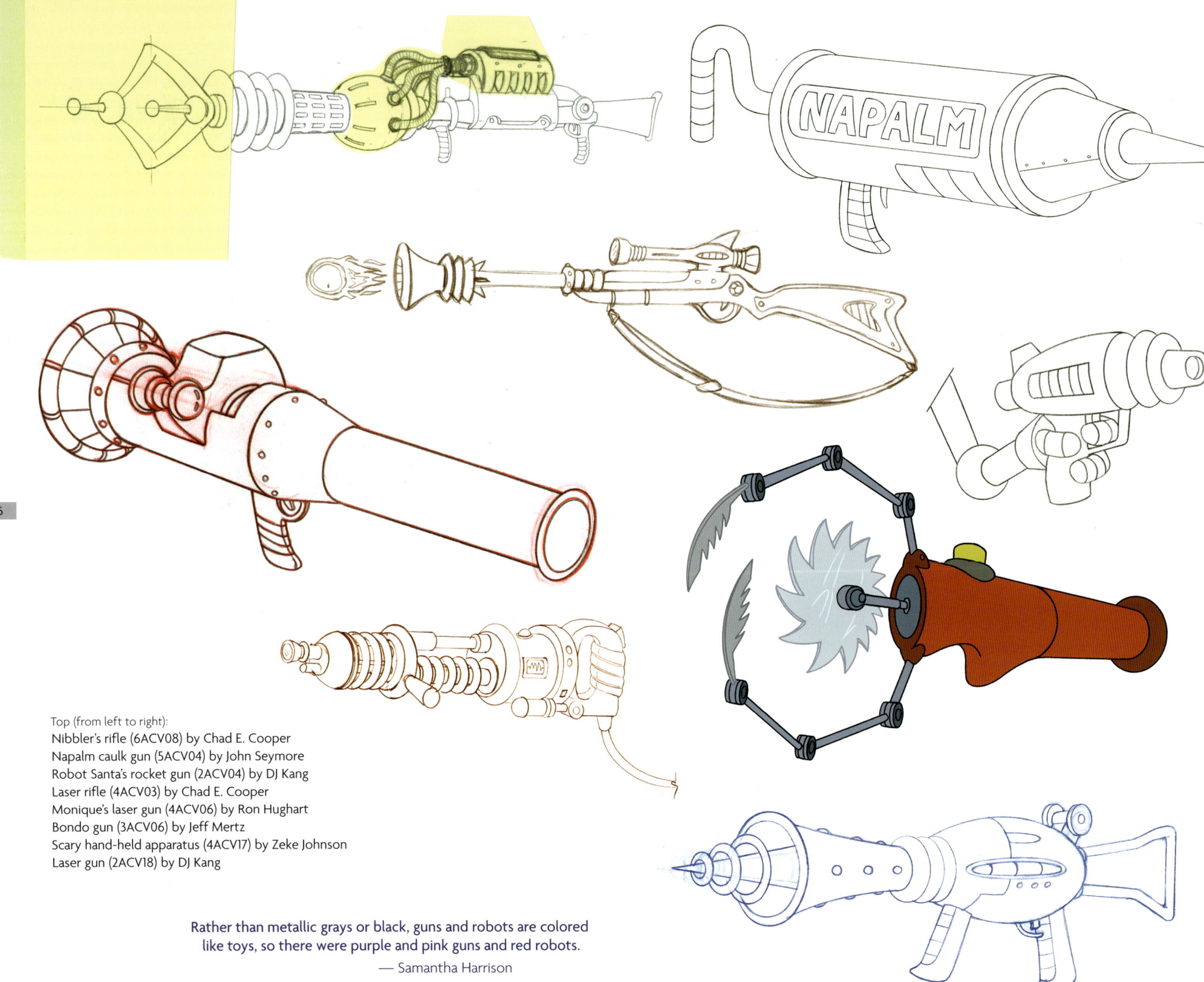

126

Top (from left to right):
Nibbler's rifle (6ACV08) by Chad E. Cooper
Napalm caulk gun (5ACV04) by John Seymore
Robot Santa's rocket gun (2ACV04) by DJ Kang
Laser rifle (4ACV03) by Chad E. Cooper
Monique's laser gun (4ACV06) by Ron Hughart
Bondo gun (3ACV06) by Jeff Mertz
Scary hand-held apparatus (4ACV17) by Zeke Johnson
Laser gun (2ACV18) by DJ Kang

Rather than metallic grays or black, guns and robots are colored like toys, so there were purple and pink guns and red robots.
— Samantha Harrison

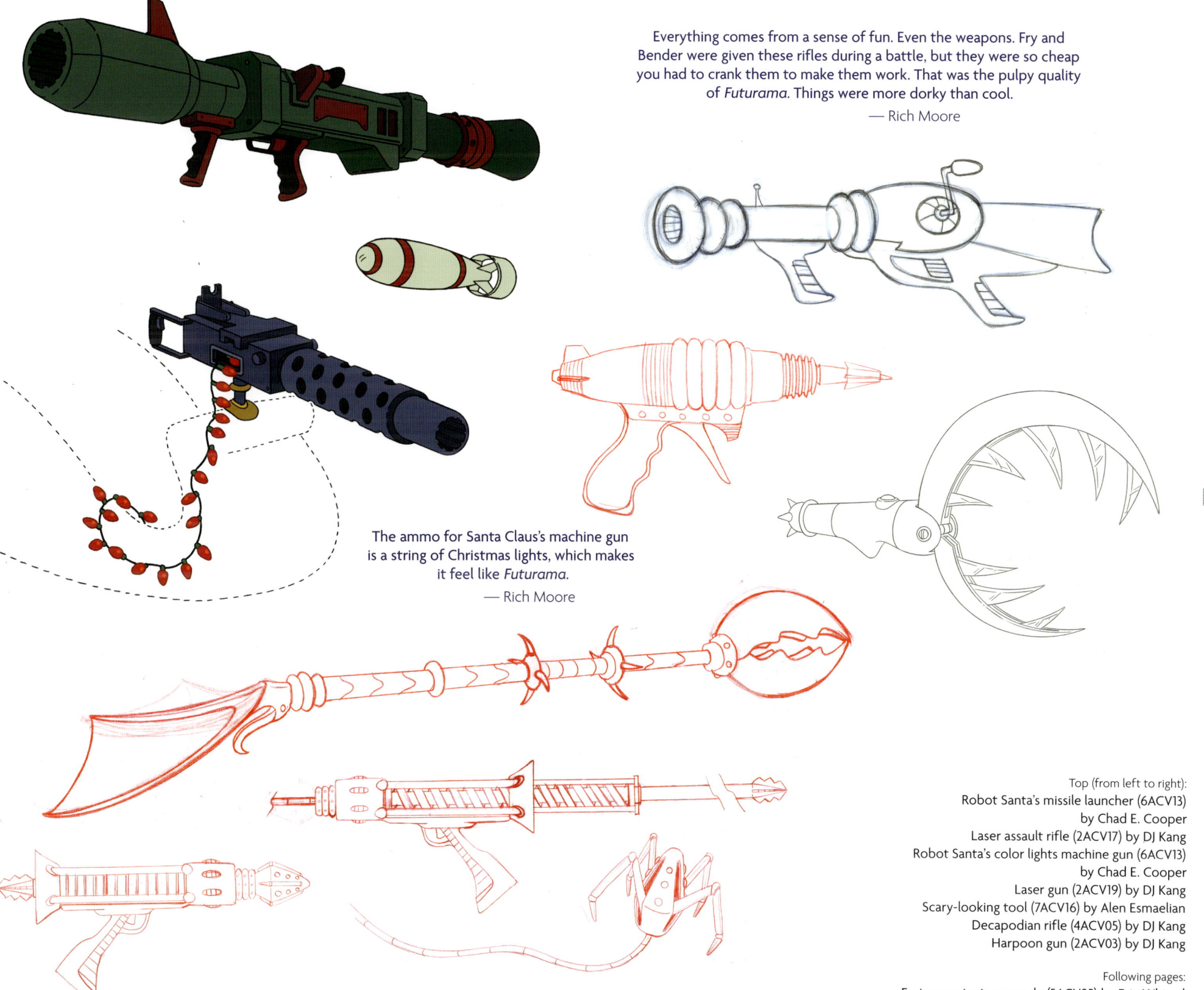

Everything comes from a sense of fun. Even the weapons. Fry and Bender were given these rifles during a battle, but they were so cheap you had to crank them to make them work. That was the pulpy quality of *Futurama*. Things were more dorky than cool.

— Rich Moore

The ammo for Santa Claus's machine gun is a string of Christmas lights, which makes it feel like *Futurama*.

— Rich Moore

Top (from left to right):
Robot Santa's missile launcher (6ACV13) by Chad E. Cooper
Laser assault rifle (2ACV17) by DJ Kang
Robot Santa's color lights machine gun (6ACV13) by Chad E. Cooper
Laser gun (2ACV19) by DJ Kang
Scary-looking tool (7ACV16) by Alen Esmaelian
Decapodian rifle (4ACV05) by DJ Kang
Harpoon gun (2ACV03) by DJ Kang

Following pages:
Eerie cosmic rip anomaly (5ACV05) by Eric Whited

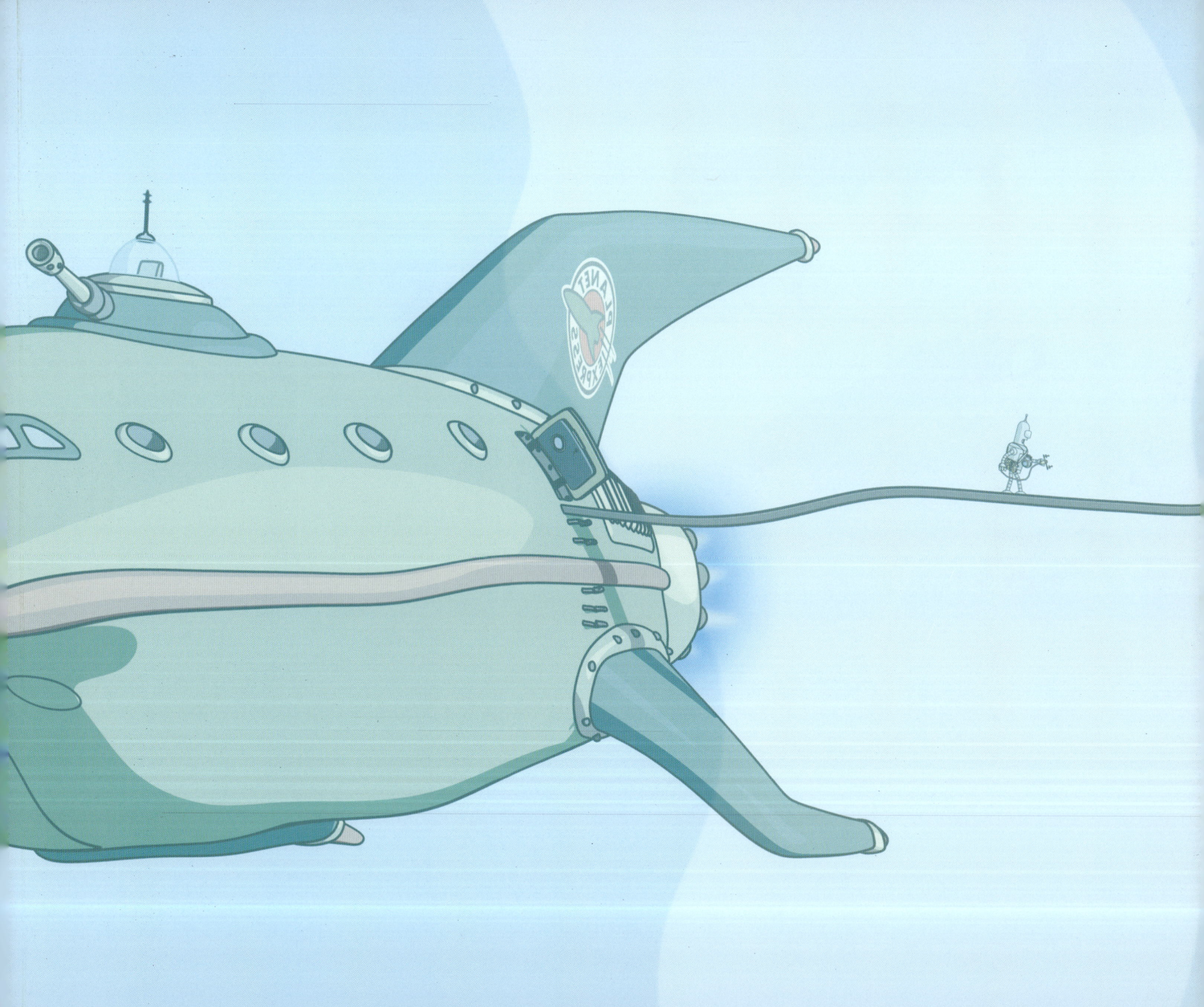

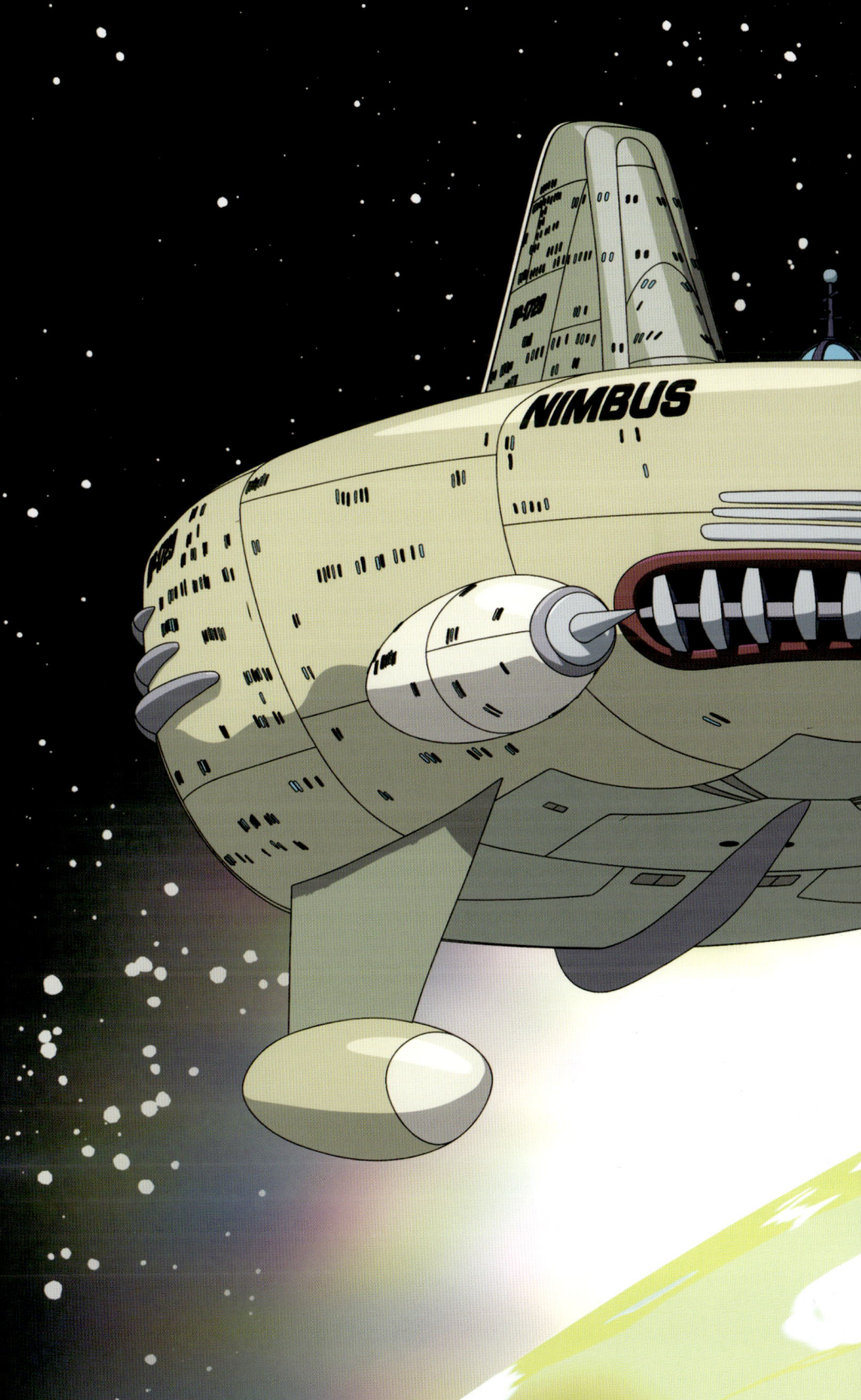

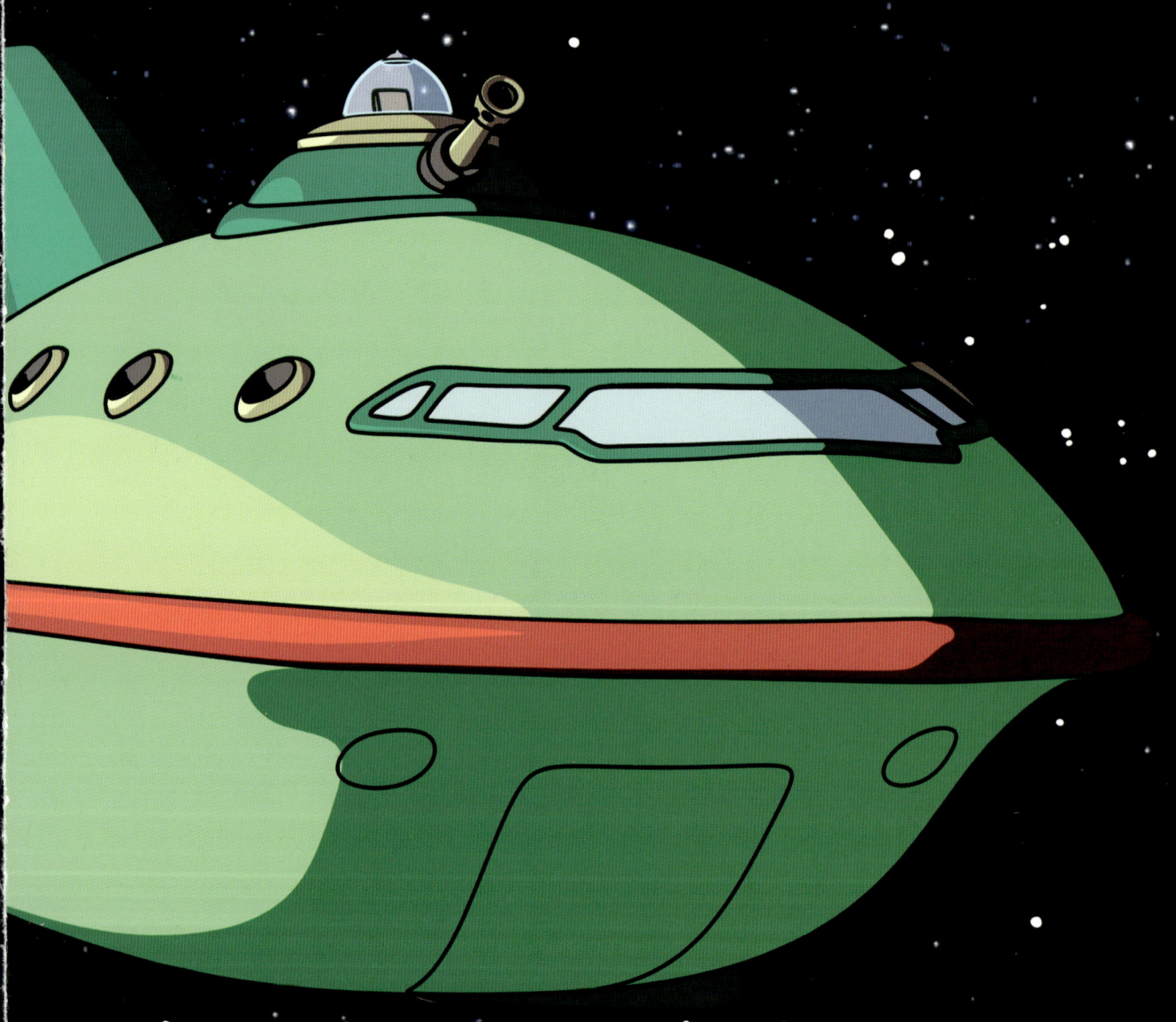

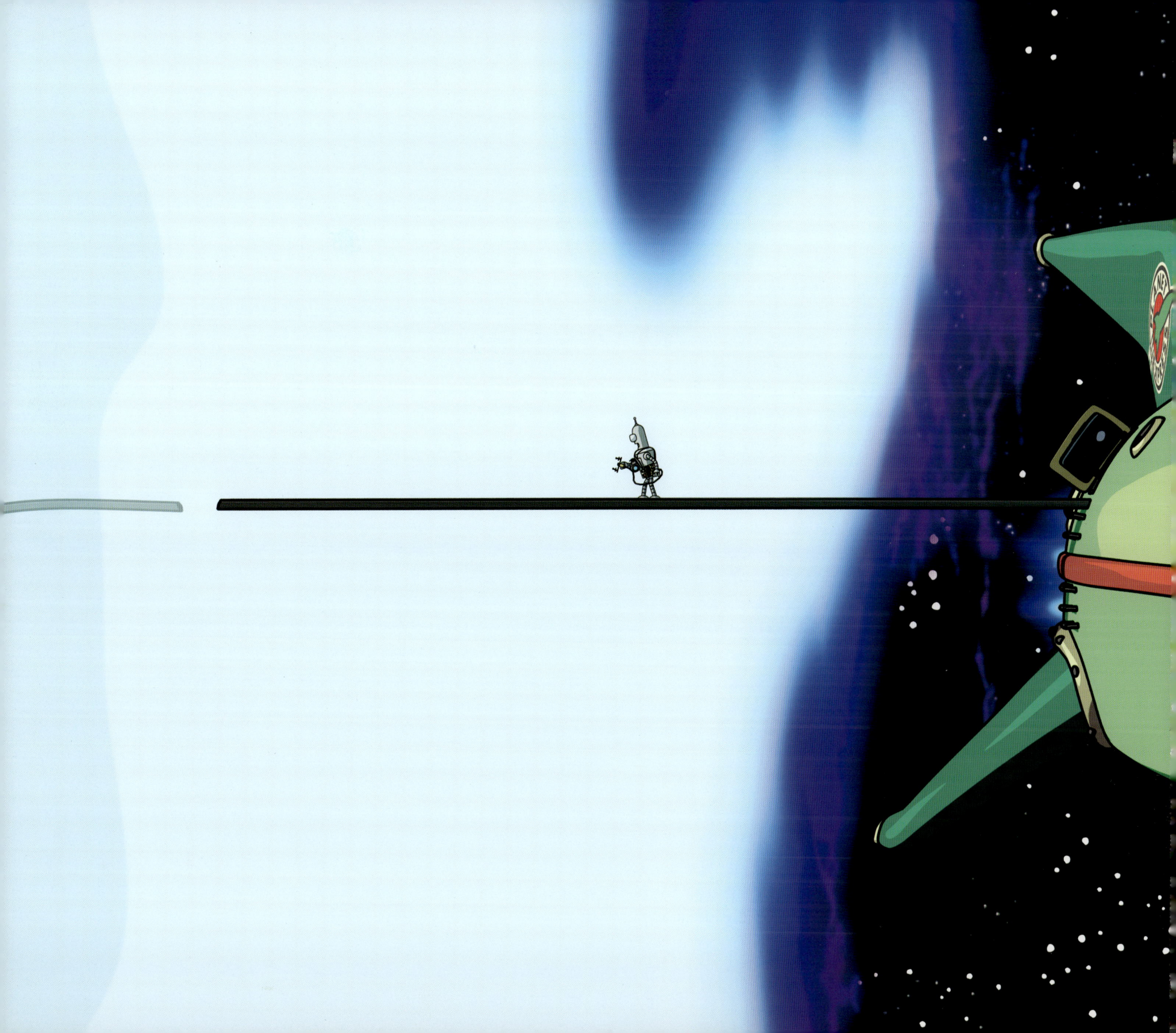

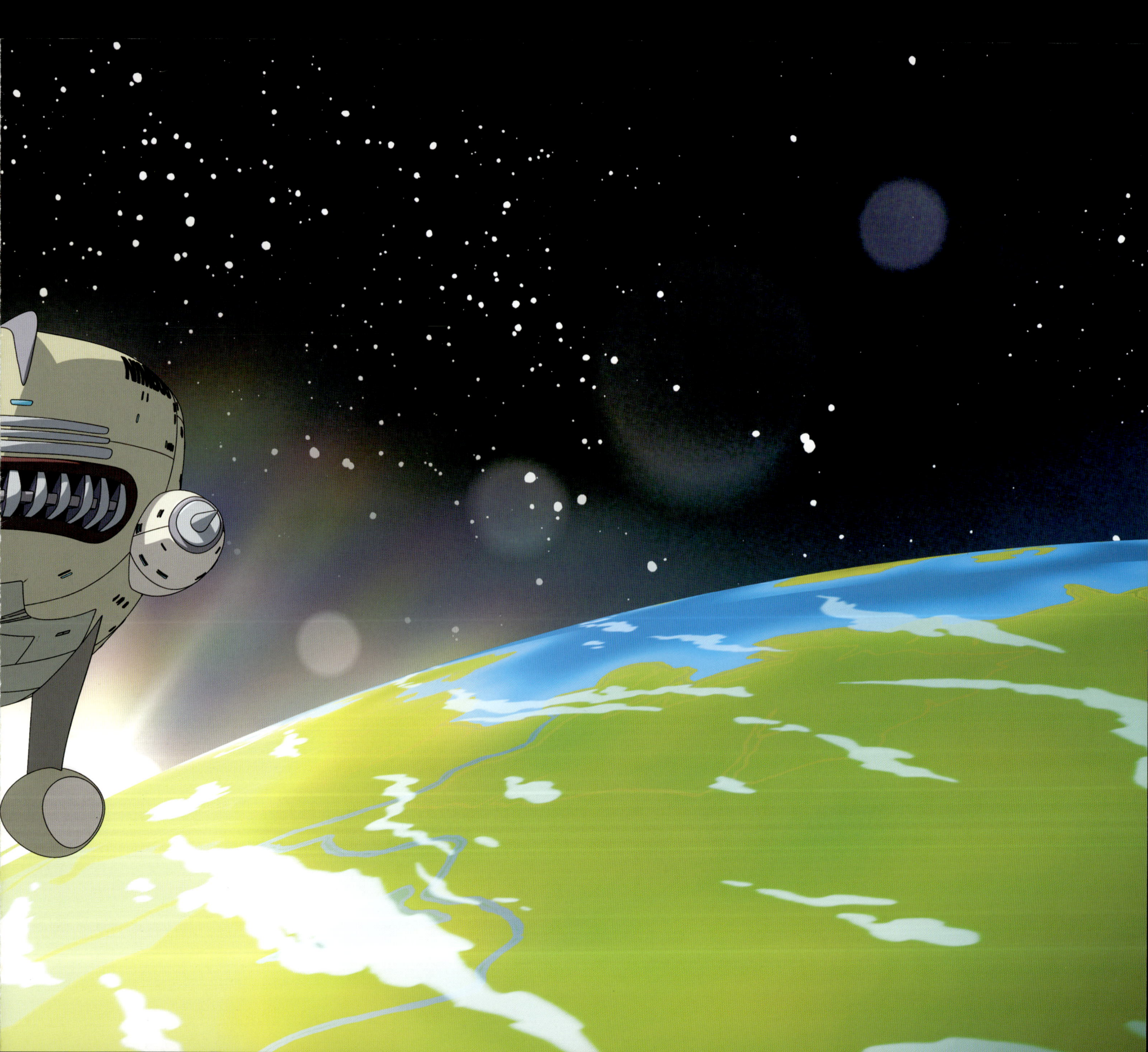

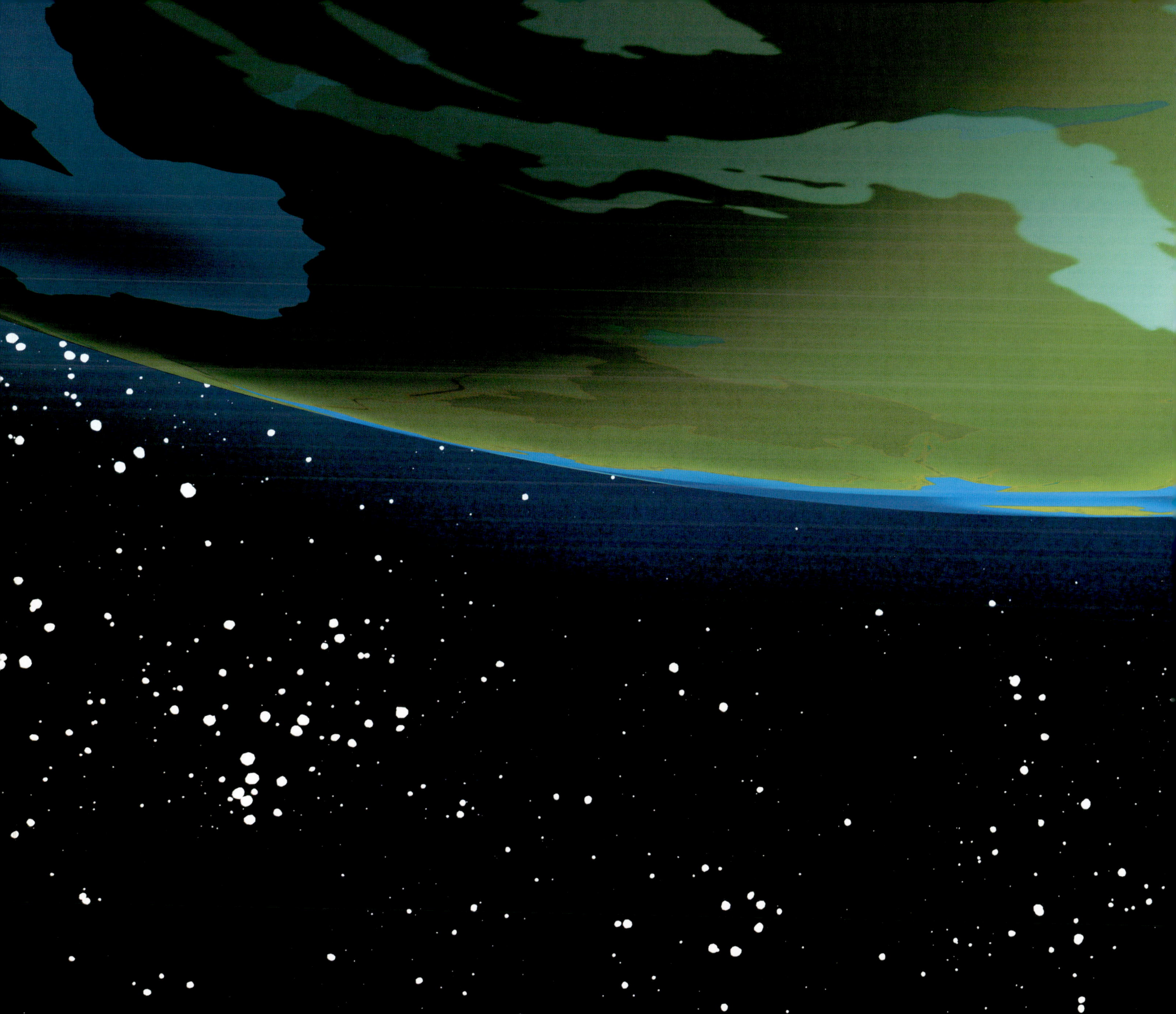

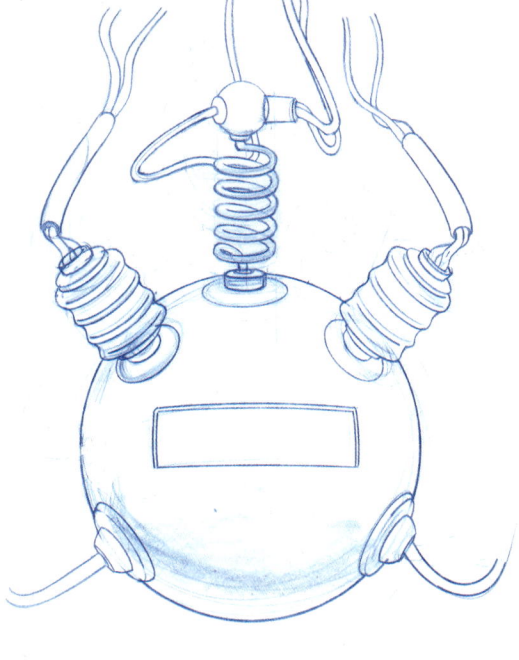

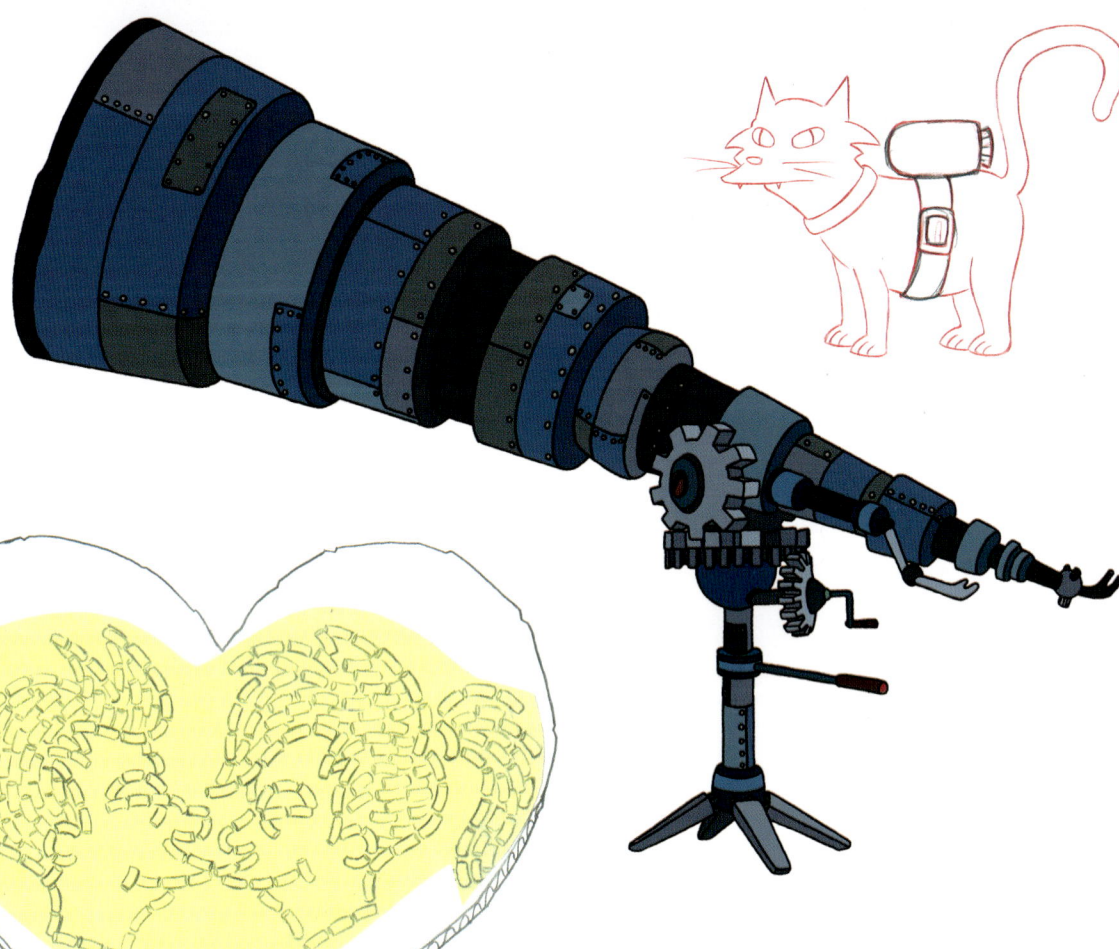

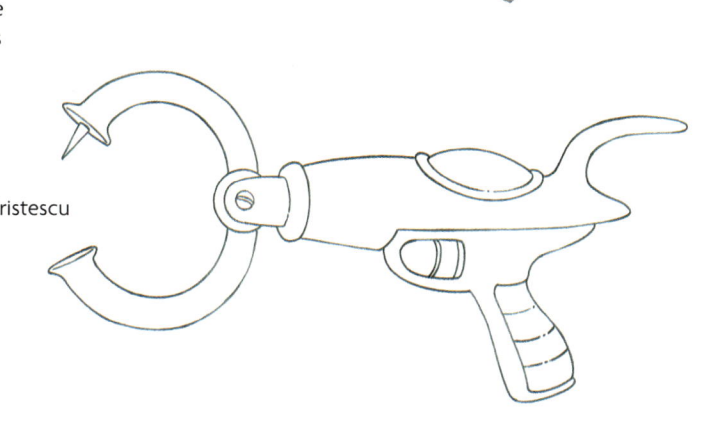

130

Previous pages:
Nimbus in orbit 3D rendering by Wyatt Lavasseur

Top (from left to right):
Doomsday device (2ACV17) by Zeke Johnson
Smelloscope (1ACV08) by Zeke Johnson
Cat with jet pack (1ACV01) by David Swift

Middle:
Macaroni art of Fry and Leela (5ACV01) by Genna Kornyshev

Bottom (from left to right):
Career chip implanter tool (1ACV01) by John Krause
Destroyed sidewalk square with Seymour and Fry's
prints (4ACV07) by Jim Feeley

Opposite, top (from left to right):
Fry's bicycle (1ACV01) by John Krause
Fish in scuba suit (1ACV08) by Yacine Elghorri
Newspaper headline signage (1ACV01) by Serban Cristescu

Opposite, middle (from left to right):
Seven-leaf clover (3ACV10) by DJ Kang
Portrait of Strug (1ACV07)
by Kevin O'Brien, Yacine Elghorri, David Swift
Gaydar (1ACV04) by Zeke Johnson

Opposite, bottom (from left to right):
Spice weasel (1ACV07) by David Swift
Holophonor (3ACV02) by Zeke Johnson

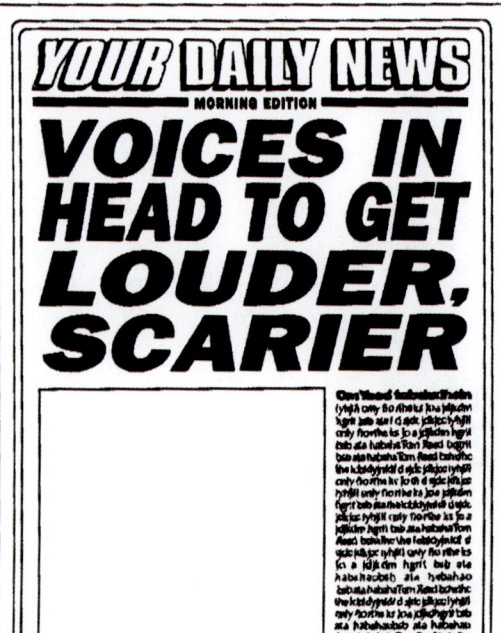

YOUR DAILY NEWS
MORNING EDITION
VOICES IN HEAD TO GET LOUDER, SCARIER

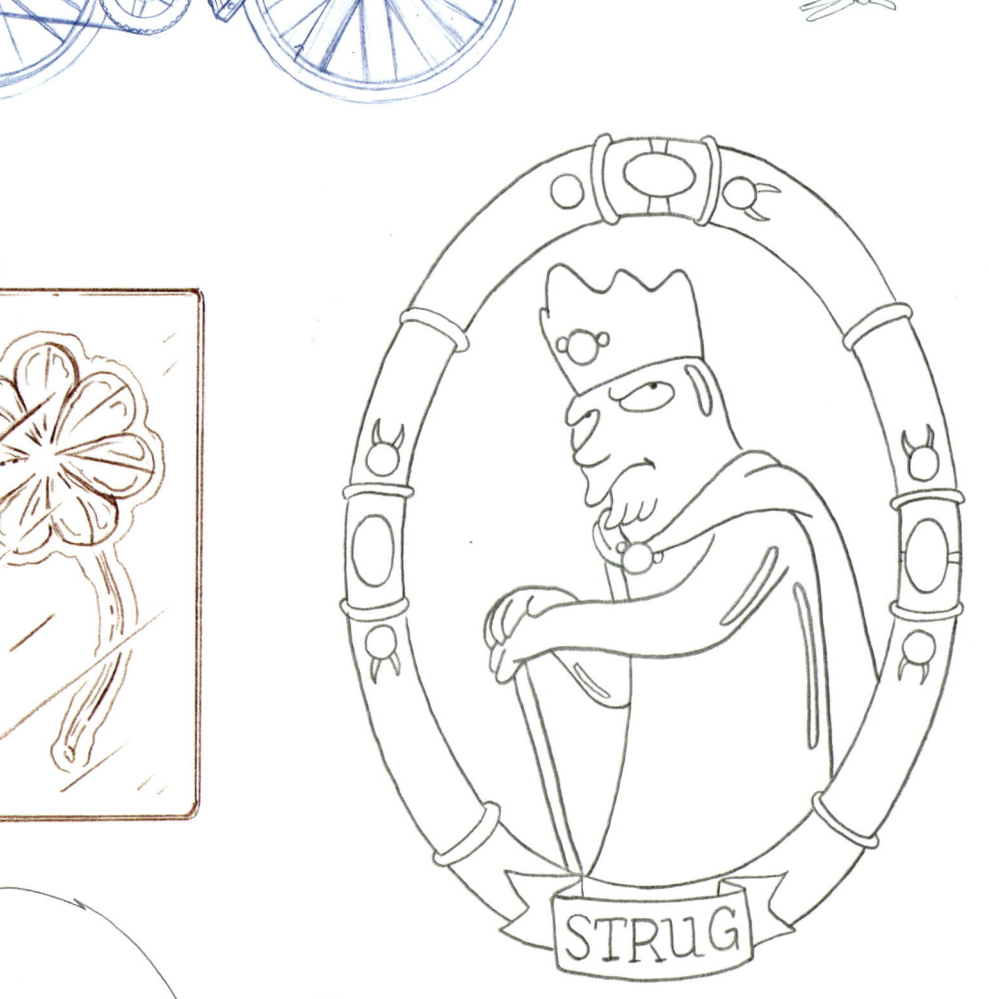

STRUG

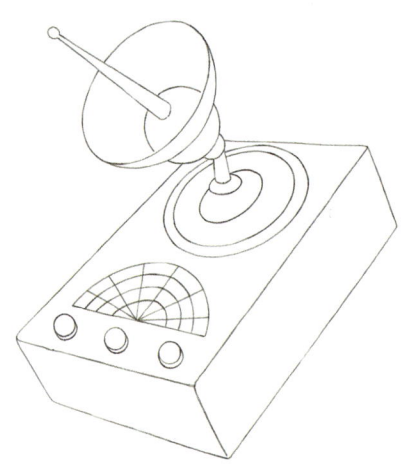

We made gadgets to be simple as possible, like a child's toy. And, again, that comes from Matt's style.

— Rich Moore

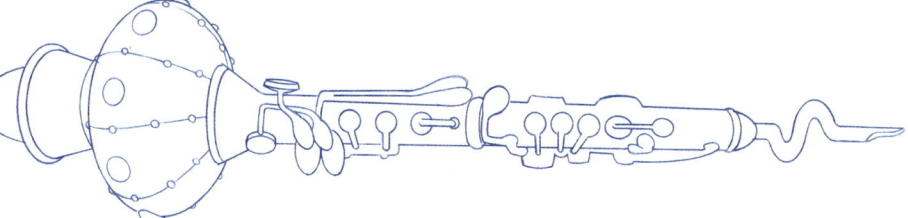

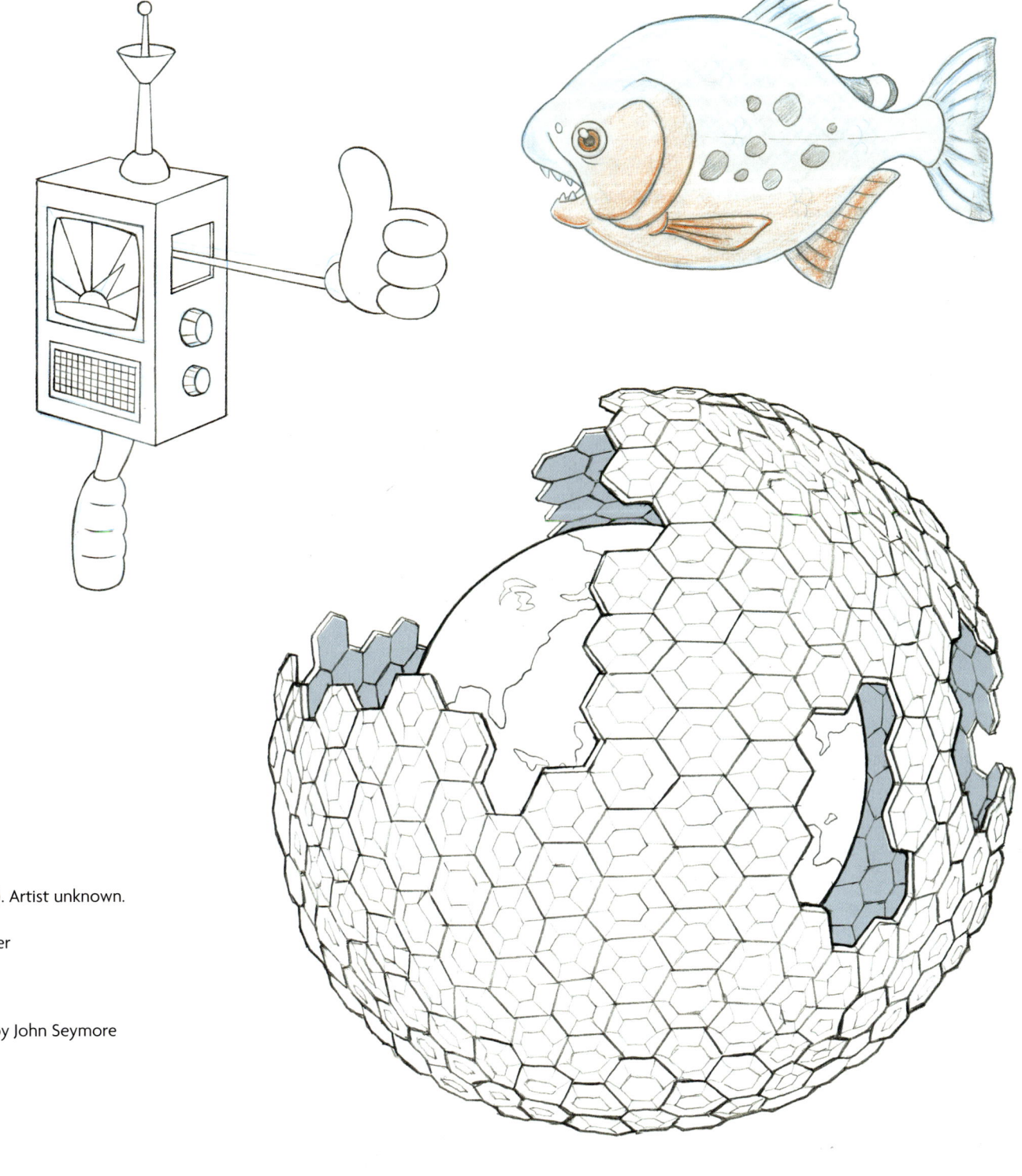

Everything in *Futurama*—whether it's characters, robots, ships, props, buildings—everything has a thickness, a real kind of weight to it. Rarely are things spindly and thin.

— Dwayne Carey-Hill

Everything's weighty and sculpted.

— Crystal Chesney-Thompson

Top (from left to right):
Cool-O-Meter device (4ACV06) by Zeke Johnson
Piranha (4ACV04) by Kevin M. Newman

Bottom:
Diamondillium blocks (5ACV07) by John Seymore

Opposite, top (from left to right):
Executive ball clacker with mushy eyeballs (5ACV09). Artist unknown.
LöBrau bottle (1ACV01) by Jeffrey Lynch
Mind-switching machine (6ACV10) by Chad E. Cooper

Opposite, bottom (from left to right):
Professor Farnsworth's chair (4ACV04) by DJ Kang
Bender and Calculon friendship diorama (5ACV06) by John Seymore
Calculon candy dispenser (4ACV17) by DJ Kang

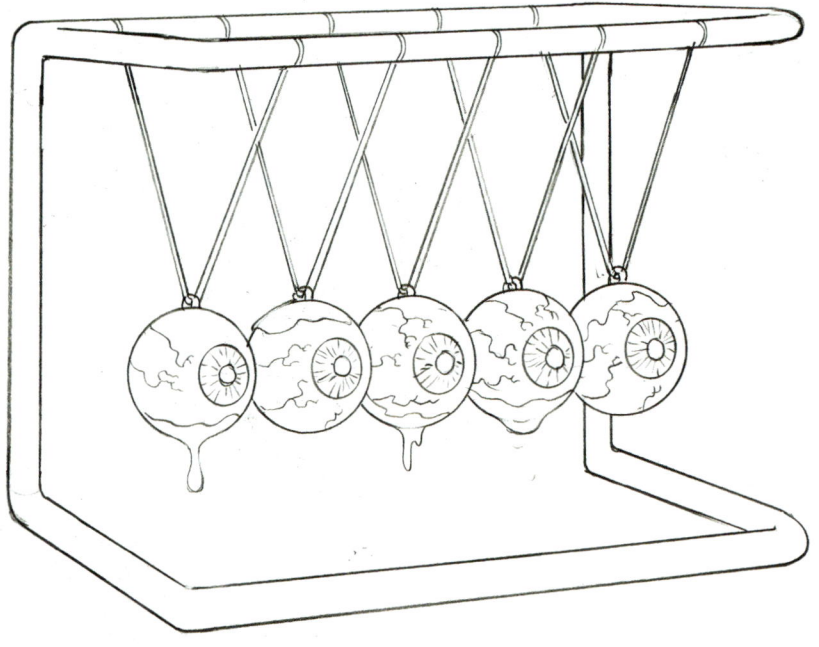

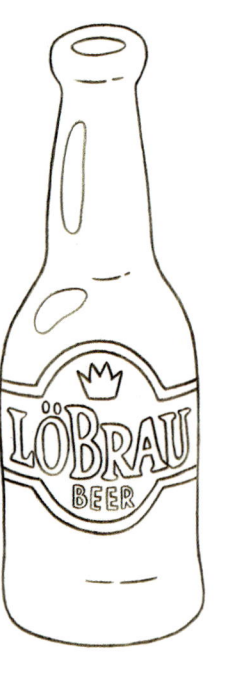

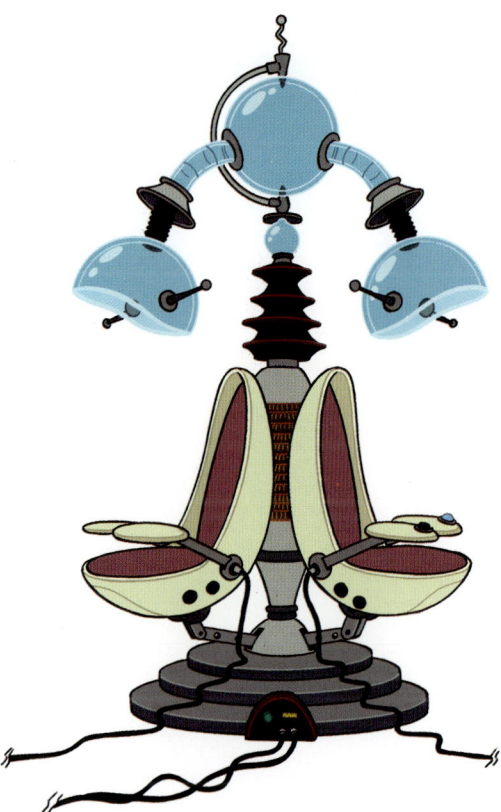

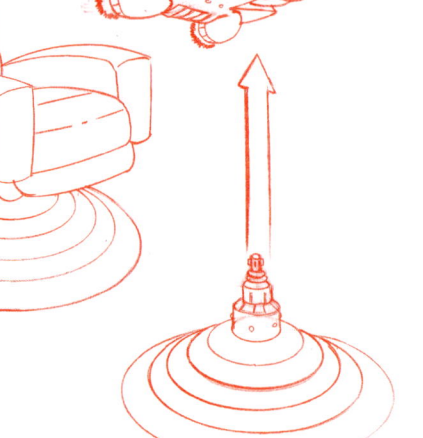

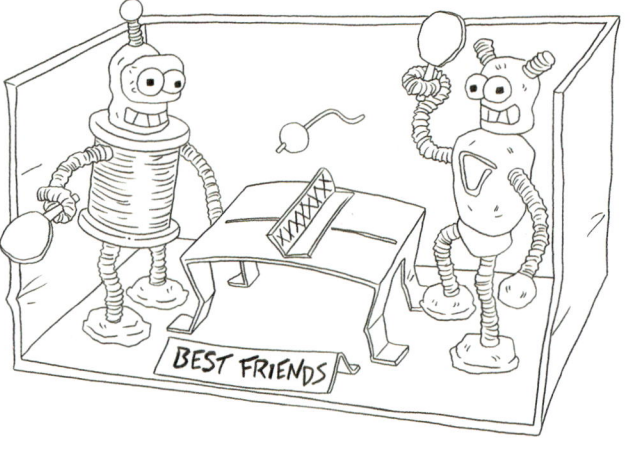
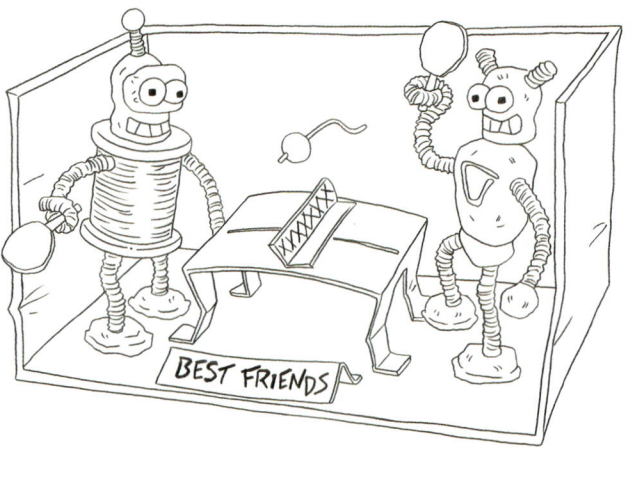

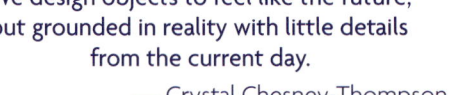

We design objects to feel like the future, but grounded in reality with little details from the current day.

— Crystal Chesney-Thompson

APPROACH: STORYBOARDS OF DESTINY

Dwayne Carey-Hill: Animation storyboarding back when we started in the '90s was really like what a cinematographer does in live-action storyboarding. In live action, you design the blocking of the shots, then it goes to the director, who talks to the actors and the camera crew, then the actual filming begins. In animation back then, the storyboard artists planned the shots, then it would go to the layout artists and they would create the key character and background animation. And then that would go off to Korea. Now the industry at large has gotten rid of the layout and background layout departments. Storyboard artists today are both the cinematographer and the layout artist. And they need to be really skilled character animators as well.

Crystal Chesney-Thompson: You have to be able to act with a pencil to compose shots, understand filmmaking, then understand acting, and understand inertia, as well as animation.

Dwayne Carey-Hill: Instead of three different people, you're now one person doing three jobs. Luckily, we now draw storyboards on the computer. Otherwise it would not even be possible.

Dwayne Carey-Hill: I think early on in storyboarding, you were limited by your imagination and your drawing abilities because if you couldn't imagine it and draw it in some intricate way, you might bail out to do something that at least works. Now the computer allows you to test out things you think might be possible to do.

You start moving controls around and simulating what you're looking for. What if I shift this and adjust the speed? You can get more playful and more cinematic. If you imagine something happening in live action, you can then try to simulate that move in animation, which you couldn't do as efficiently before.

Crystal Chesney-Thompson: For instance, in the early days, say I want to draw a crowd in a stadium? I'll draw the first row of characters sitting there. And then I would go to the copy machine and copy them at 95% of the full size. And then I'll lay them down and redraw some, so you can't tell that they're used characters. Then I move them around and take those two rows and go back to the copy machine, shrink them down again, and cut and paste. Eventually, we would end up with this paper with layers and layers of other papers taped down to it. There's your crowd. Afterward, we would take all the extra scrap pieces of crowds that we didn't use and tape them together into this big ball. And over the seasons, we ended up with this basketball-sized ball. We called it the crowd ball and for fun we'd throw the crowd ball back and forth. One time up by the crow's nest, someone tried to throw it over the mezzanine. It didn't quite make it and crashed down right in front of the receptionist.

Dwayne Carey-Hill: When you get a scene, you're working out the mechanics in order to bring that scene to its greatest life. How can you take the writing and elevate it to create your most special version of that scene? Are the characters just together talking or do they get up and walk around the room? How are they interacting? How do you match the energy in the room to the requirements of the script? Every time you have a sequence, you're challenged with that goal. And as familiar as the characters are in this world, every time you open a new script, suddenly it's a completely new challenge. They could still be at the conference room table. They may still be flying in the same ship. But, I've done that version of that scene before. So how is this one now different? You don't want to repeat yourself.

Crystal Chesney-Thompson: A lot of observation goes into the way we solve that question. A typical animated show might have everybody sitting at the table, and everybody at that table will always be sitting at the table the same way. We try to avoid clichéd animation poses by using poses that are more observational and more realistic, more character driven.

Dwayne Carey-Hill: On day one of *Futurama*, with the crew all hired and ready to go, I remember Gregg Vanzo, who was supervising the first episode, telling all the layout artists to be observational. If Amy's on the couch, maybe she's lying on the floor with her legs up, watching TV upside down, or somebody else is slumped on the arm of a chair. Little tweaks give the scene more color, even if the characters never move. We've always really taken that to heart for the entire series. Always give the characters a little something more.

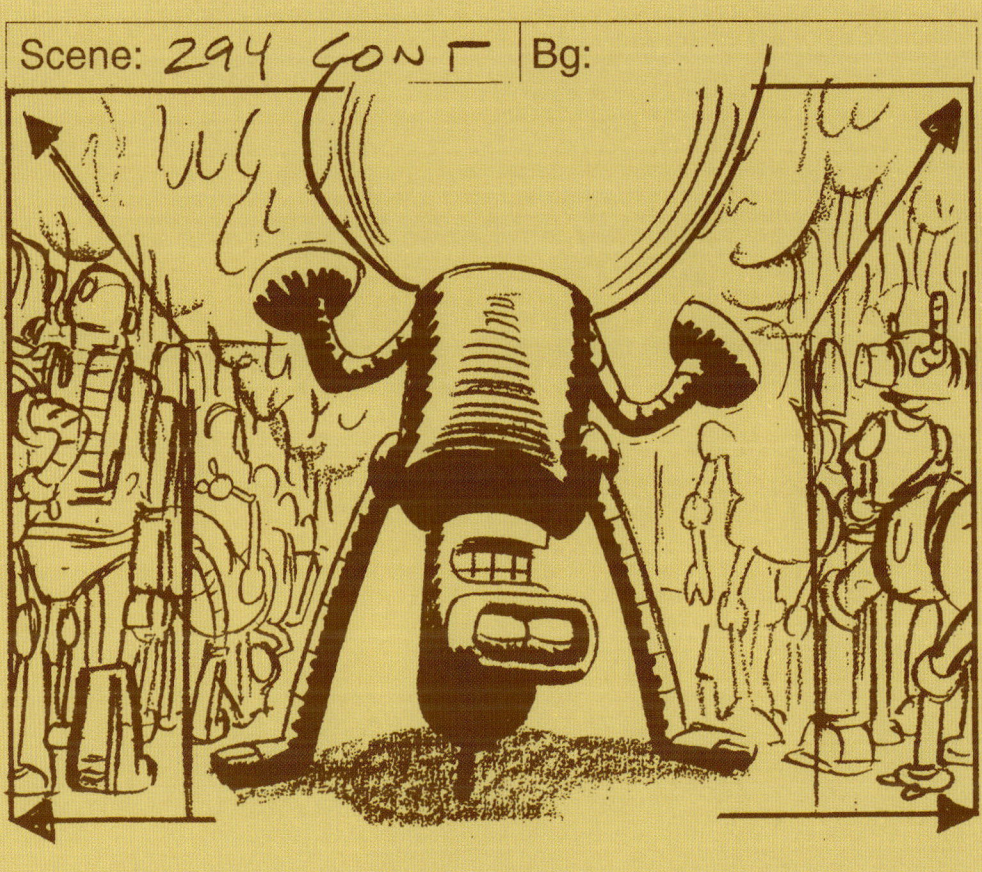

Instead of three different people, you're now one person doing three jobs.
— Dwayne Carey-Hill

Robots venting methane
sequence storyboard (4ACV08) by Albert Calleros

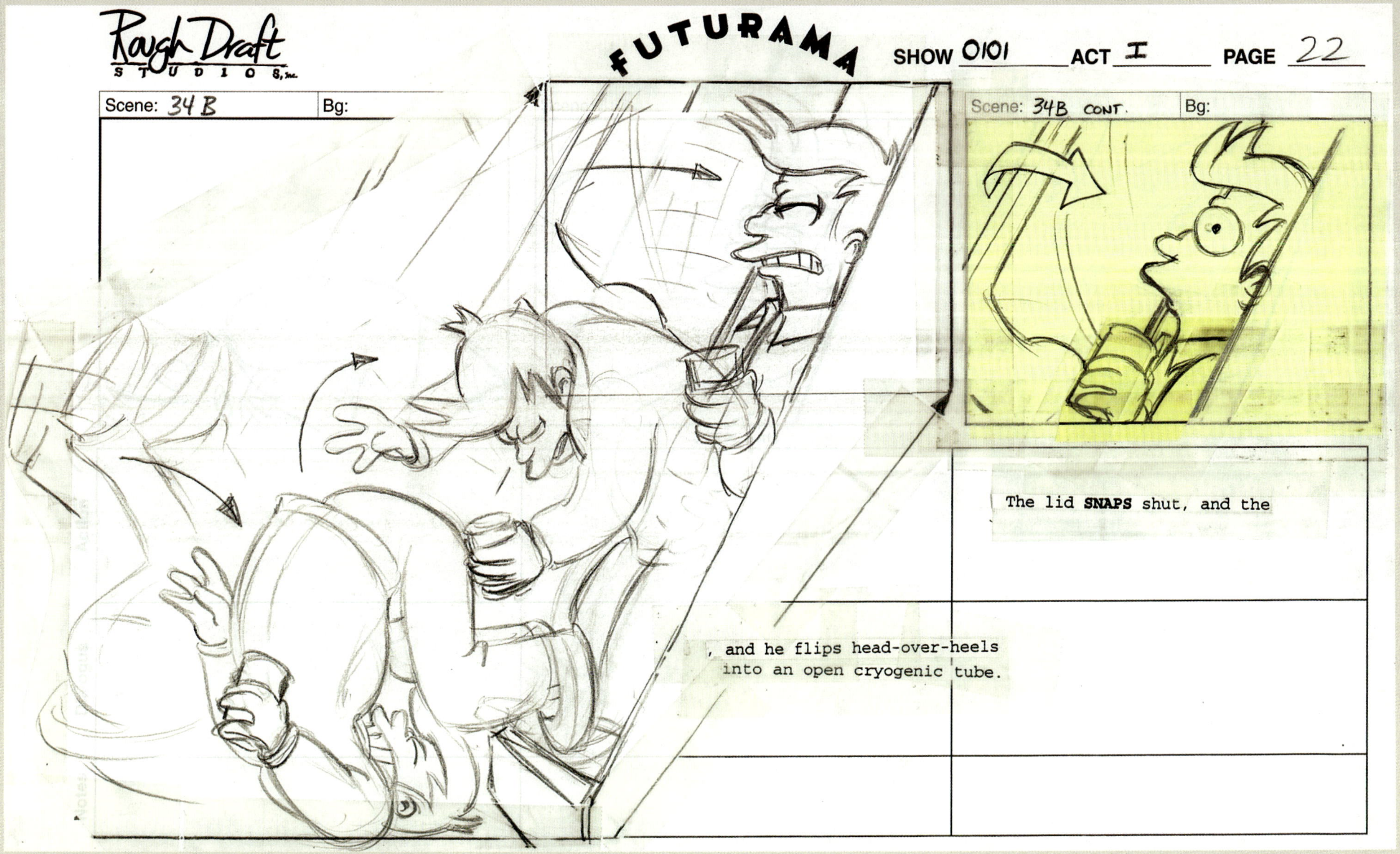

Scene: 34 B   Bg:

Scene: 34B CONT.   Bg:

The lid **SNAPS** shut, and the

, and he flips head-over-heels
into an open cryogenic tube.

136

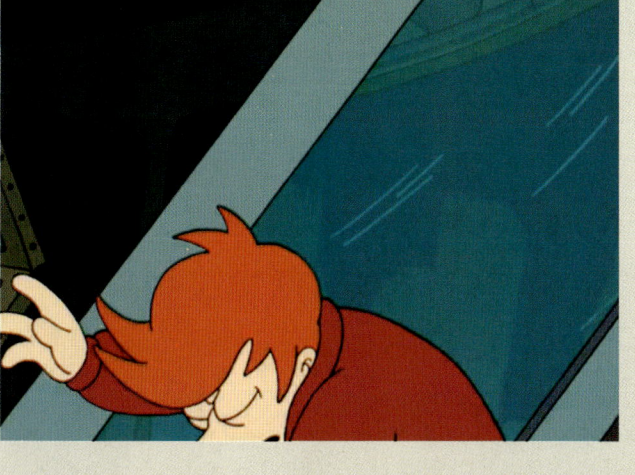

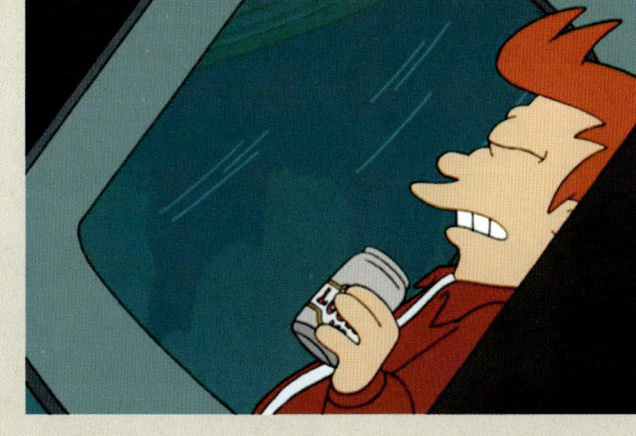

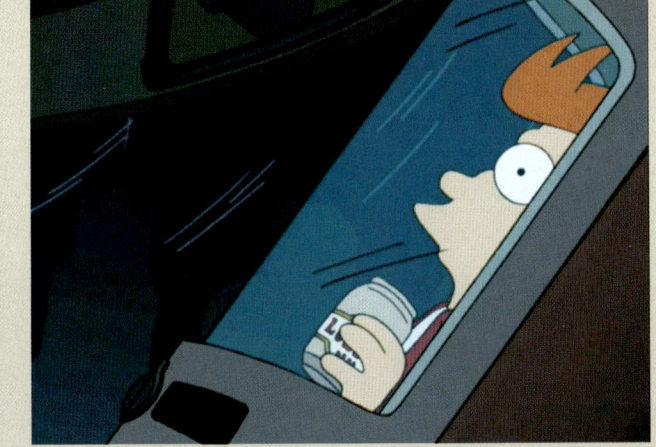

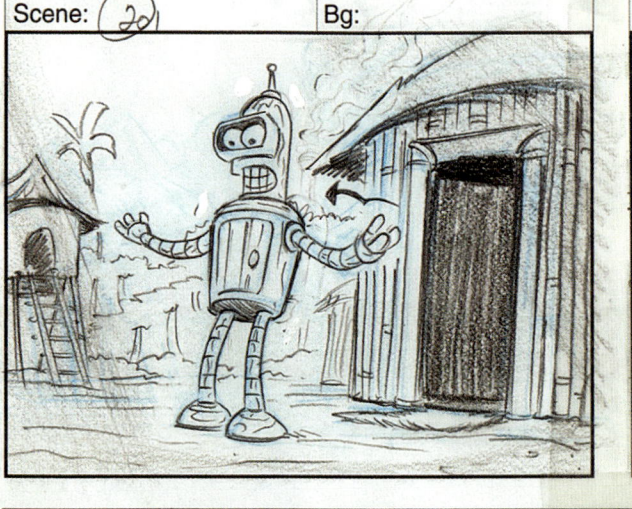

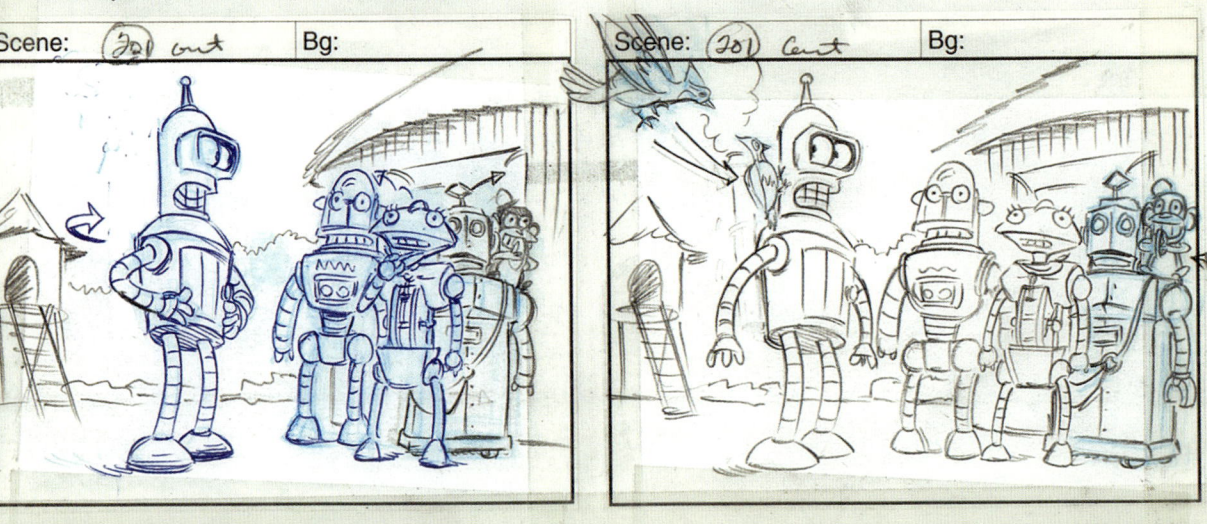

	Scene: 201	Bg:	Scene: 201 out	Bg:	Scene: 201 cont	Bg:

Action	— STEPS TO POSITION His body is basically the same shape, but is now made entirely of wood, except for his eyes, visor and mouth. A steam engine oil is back **BELCHES** smoke.	The other robots follow him out. — OTHER BOTS COME OUT — LISA PULLS DOWN SURGEON MASK	A woodpecker lands on Bender's shoulder
Dialogue	BENDER Behold my hand-crafted purity!	An Amish farmer would not bat an eye were I to ask for his daughter's hand in marriage.	
Notes			

Opposite:
Fry falling in cryo-chamber sequence storyboard (1ACV01)
by Rich Moore and John Mathot

Above:
Bender reveals his new wooden body storyboard (4ACV14) by Albert Calleros

"Obsoletely Fabulous" was the first episode I directed,
where Bender is made out of wood.
— Dwayne Carey-Hill

Right. He got all burned up 'til eventually it's just his head
and body, and he's walking on his eyeballs.
— Crystal Chesney-Thompson

137

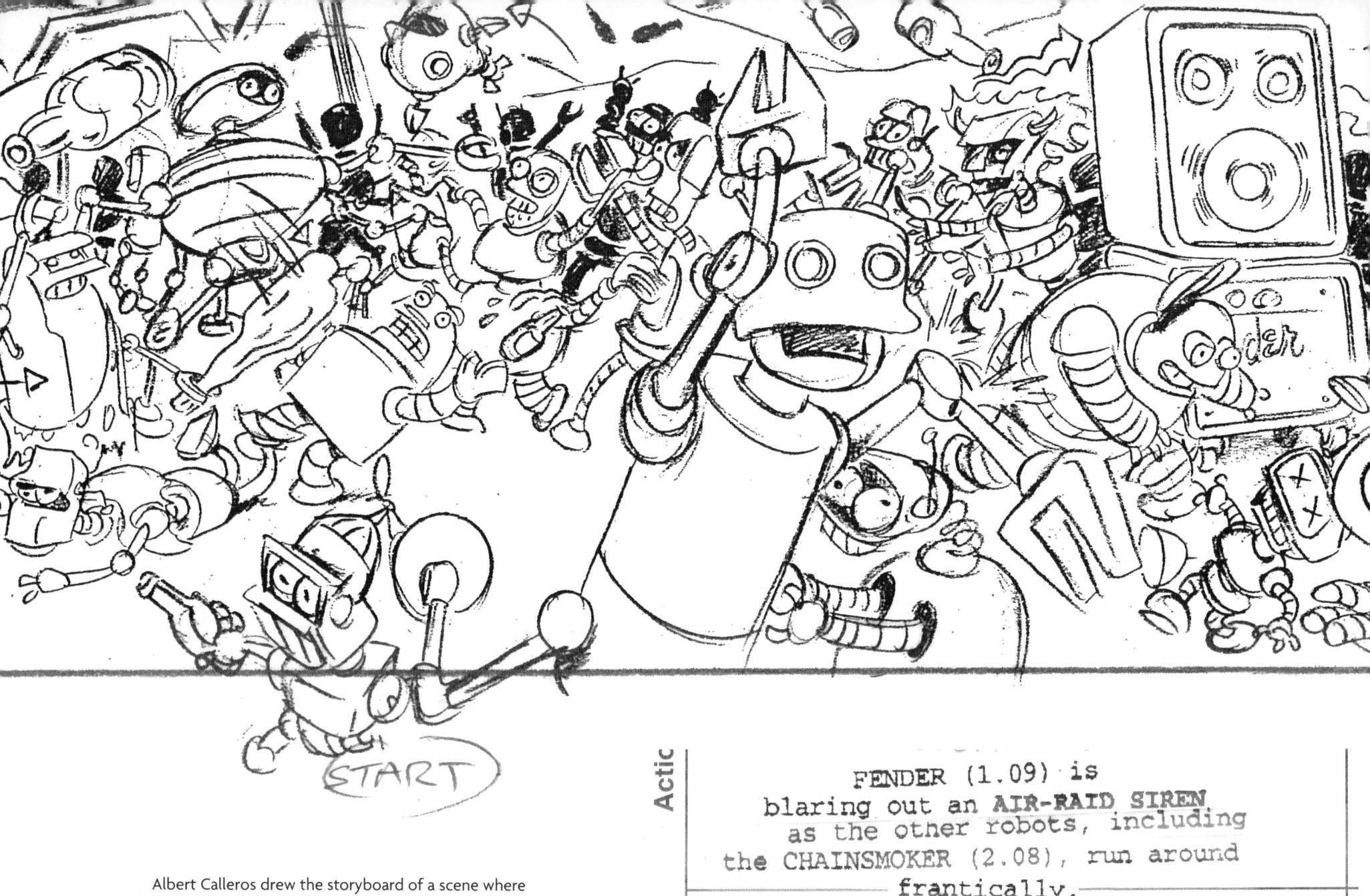

START

Albert Calleros drew the storyboard of a scene where "every robot on Earth" goes crazy. It took him forever and it came out great. Back then, the writers would go over the boards and write their notes on them in Sharpie marker. Those notes would come back and we'd go over them and make the fixes. That day the notes came in while Albert was at lunch, so "someone" took it upon themselves to fake in a note that said "NOT ENOUGH ROBOTS." We eventually told him it was a gag.

— Peter Avanzino

Post-robot party panic sequence
storyboard with dialogue and acting notes (4ACV08)
by Albert Calleros

Action

FENDER (1.09) is blaring out an **AIR-RAID SIREN** as the other robots, including the CHAINSMOKER (2.08), run around frantically.

Dialogue

ROBOT CROWD

(PANIC NOISES) / It's a trap! / We're going to die! / etc.

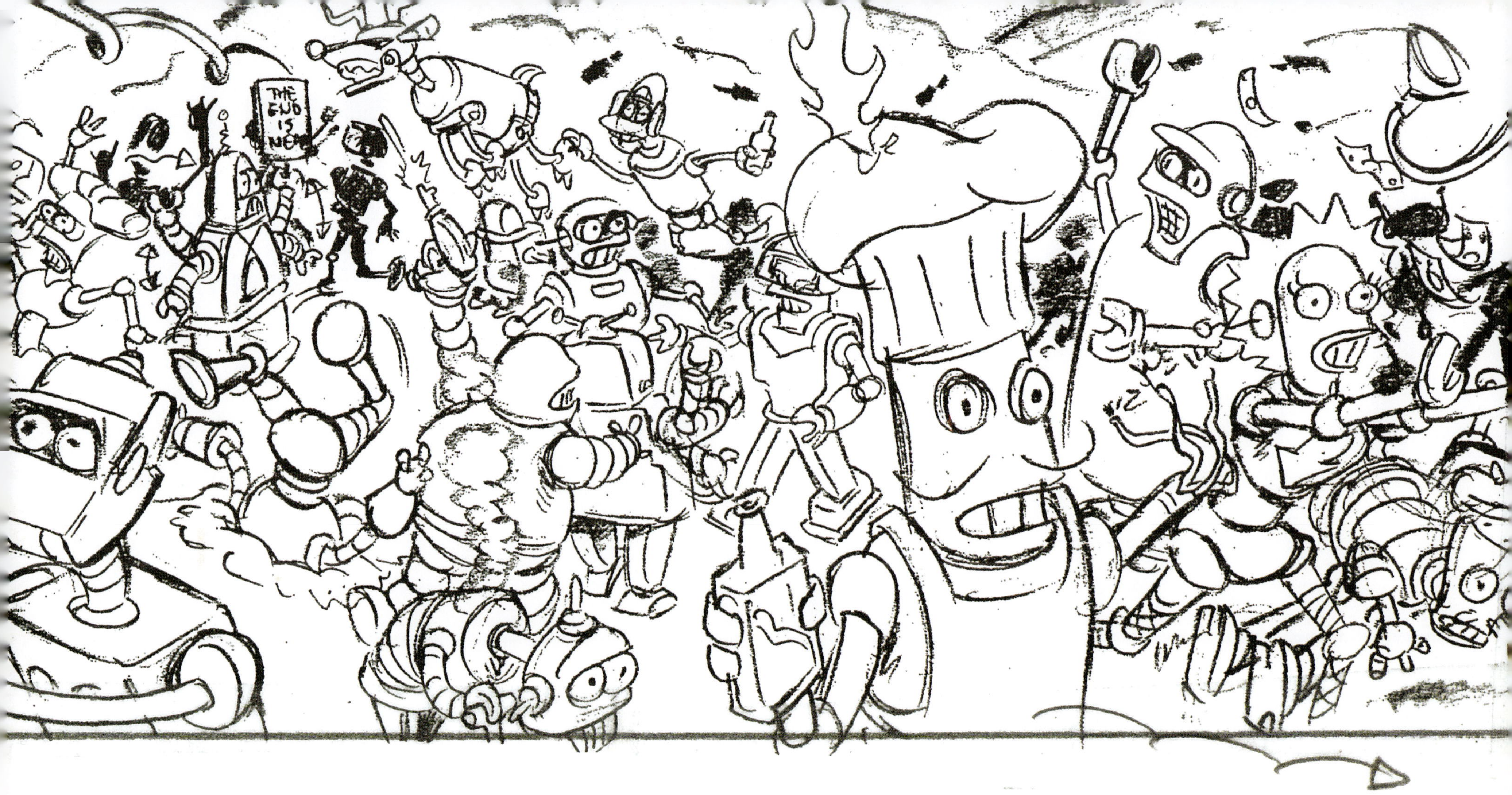

ROBOTS RUN IN ALL DIRECTIONS, SOME IN CIRCLES, SOME STAND IN PLACE, FLAILING ARMS

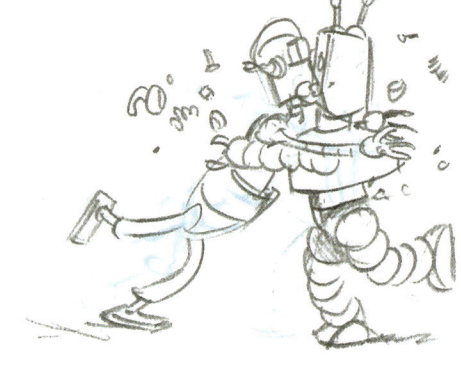

SOMEWHERE IN MELÉE, TWO ROBOTS COLLIDE, PARTS FLY

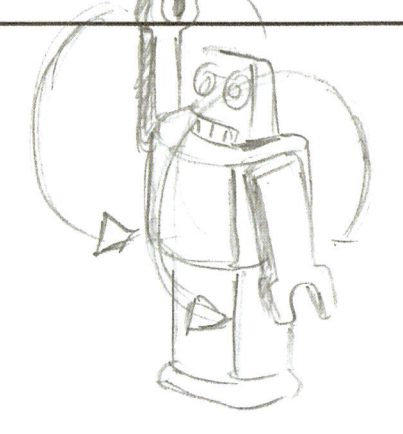

A ROBOT WITH ROTATING ARMS ROLLS THRU

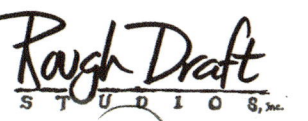

	Scene: 179	Bg: S/A 175	Scene: 179 CONT	Bg:	Scene: 179 CONT	Bg:

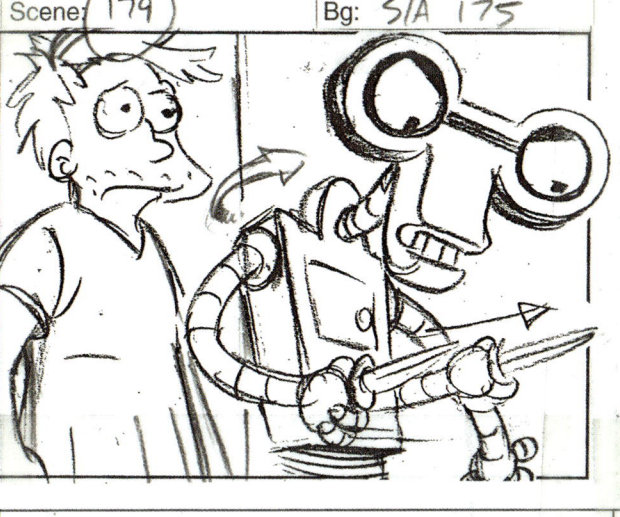
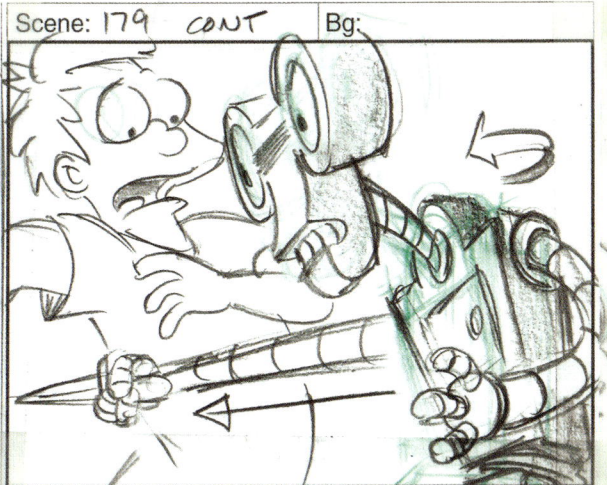
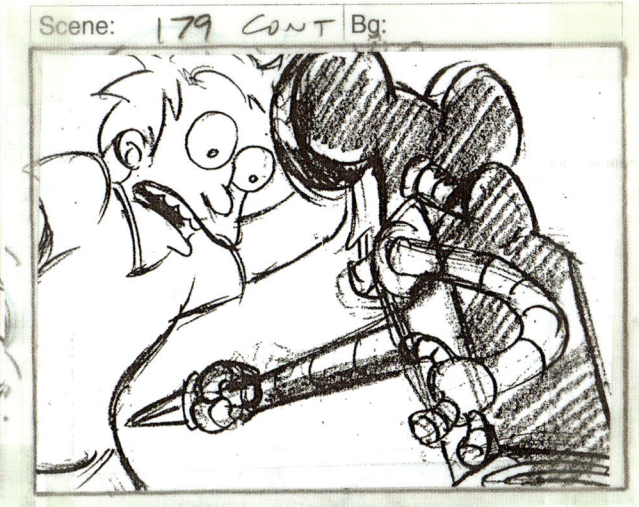

Action	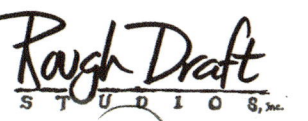	Roberto **THRUSTS** his knife. Fry ducks just in time, then continues to dodge as Roberto keeps **THRUSTING** the knife.	
Dialogue	Now stand back. I gotta practice my stabbing.	ROBERTO (CONT'D) (REPEATED GRUNTS UNDER NEXT LINE) FRY No, please!	Help!
Notes			

140

Fry and Roberto sequence storyboard (3ACV11) by Albert Calleros

Opposite:
Robots venting methane sequence storyboard (4ACV08) by Albert Calleros

I've been an animator by trade since I left CalArts in the '80s. I've directed a lot, but now I mostly solve problems on the back end. If things aren't working right, you need to be very particular to get them fixed. It's pretty satisfying doing the fixing.

— Gregg Vanzo

Scene: 294 Bg: 294	Scene: 294 CONT Bg:	Scene: 294 CONT Bg:

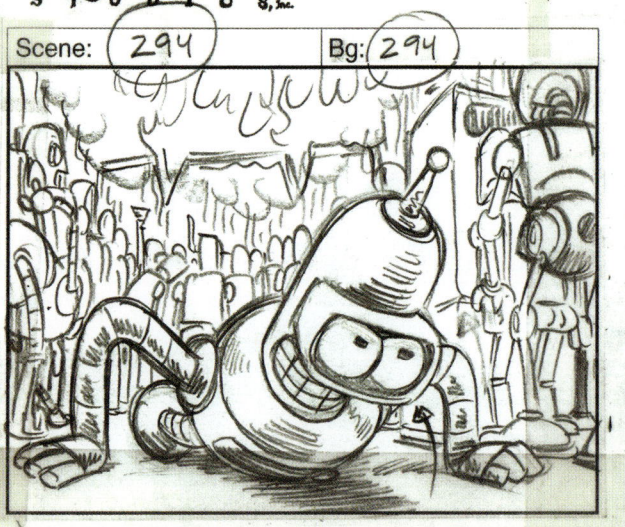
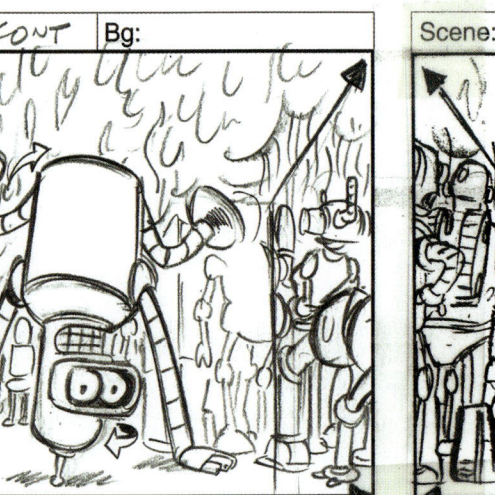

Action		WIDEN AS: Bender does a headstand and **VENTS** flaming gases with all his might.	
Dialogue	BENDER (CONT'D) Aha! I'm even greater than I thought I was! And now, to fulfill my destiny.		

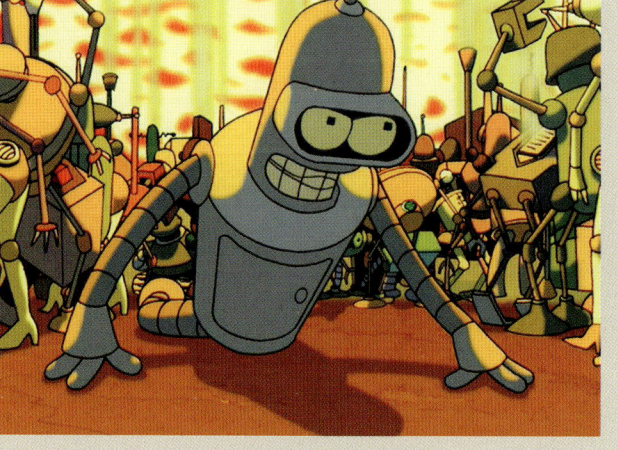
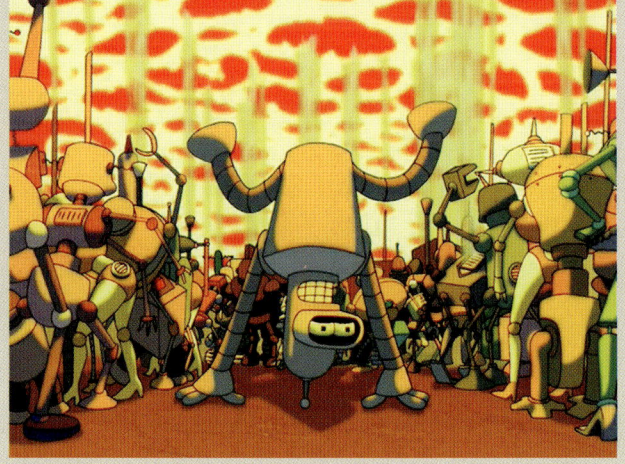
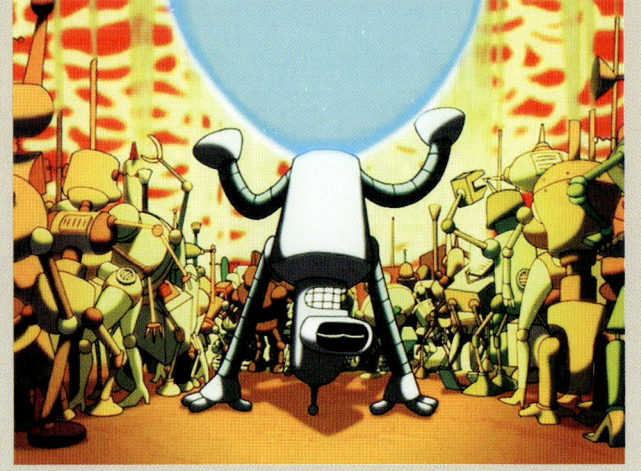

141

att Groening: We established Planet Express as a delivery service between the Earth and planets scattered all over space. A big question we had was how to deal with the vast distances in the universe? David and I discussed various scientific explanations for faster-than-light travel. At the end of the day, we were gonna need a big fantasy buy-in from the viewers. In fact, originally the ship was going to be driven by a force called the M.W. Drive. The M.W. stood for magic wand, because I just didn't believe faster-than-light travel would ever work. The Moon is far enough, Mars is too far, and anything further than that, forget about it. We're not getting there. So, luckily, we have the magic of the M.W. Drive.

In a lot of so-called-funny science fiction, there's a tendency to rely on spaceships shaped like mundane objects—salt shakers, a candlestick—which gets old really fast. Even if you thought it was funny the first time, which was rare, it was not funny the second time. And it was infuriating the third time.

Rich Moore: I remember Matt would always say the ship needs to be like the *Enterprise* or the *Millennium Falcon;* you recognize those immediately. And that's all shape and form. When I got the final design of the *Planet Express* ship, I made it into a silhouette. It had such clean readability that it was instantly recognizable.

As with all things *Futurama,* the design of the *Planet Express* ship was a work of genuine collaboration, everyone contributing to its unique style, perhaps best represented by the ship's iconic overbite.

Matt Groening: I love the design of the *Planet Express* ship. I only wish we'd made it more of a character from the very beginning, I also like that it really doesn't make any sense. For instance, having the stairway up into the rocket be part of the landing gear. And those fins are not all that practical. You don't need them to steer through space. That's Flash Gordon, Buck Rogers, 1930s stuff. Big American cars in the 1950s didn't need fins either, they were just there to look cool.

Crystal Chesney-Thompson: The design of the *Planet Express* ship is extremely well planned out. We've got places characters can sit. This is how the gangplank extends. Parts of the ship are permanently locked down and they just don't change. But things around these places can just morph and be adjusted into whatever we need, which is a lot of fun to work with. There's huge blank spaces in both the building and the ship so that no matter what's written in the script, we can find a way to put it in.

Gregg Vanzo: We take liberties with the interior of the ship. We try to be particular about things that you've seen before, provide as much continuity as we can. But beyond that, you need space for the characters and the changing action from show to show. Cartoons always take liberties.

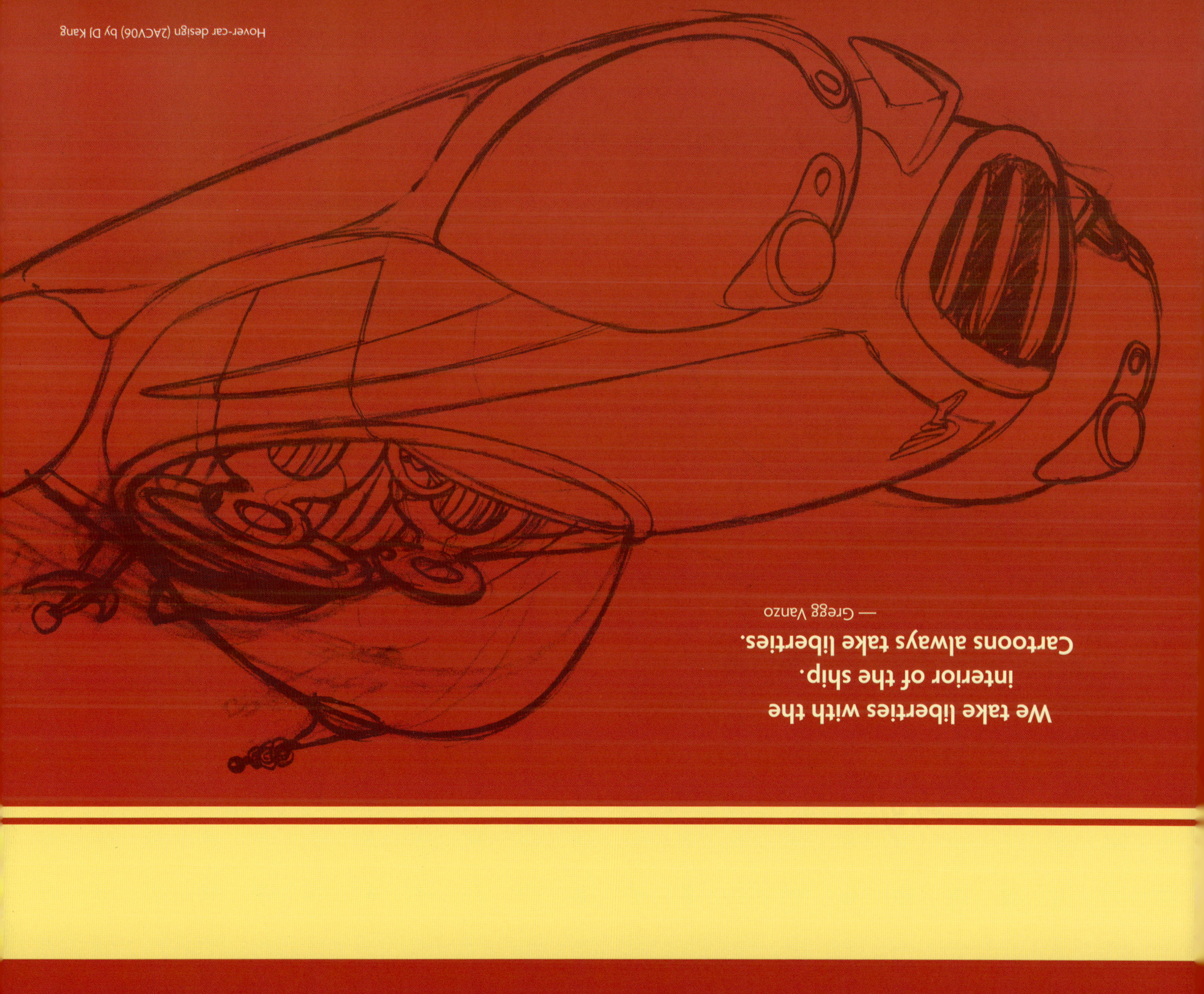

We take liberties with the
interior of the ship.
Cartoons always take liberties.

— Gregg Vanzo

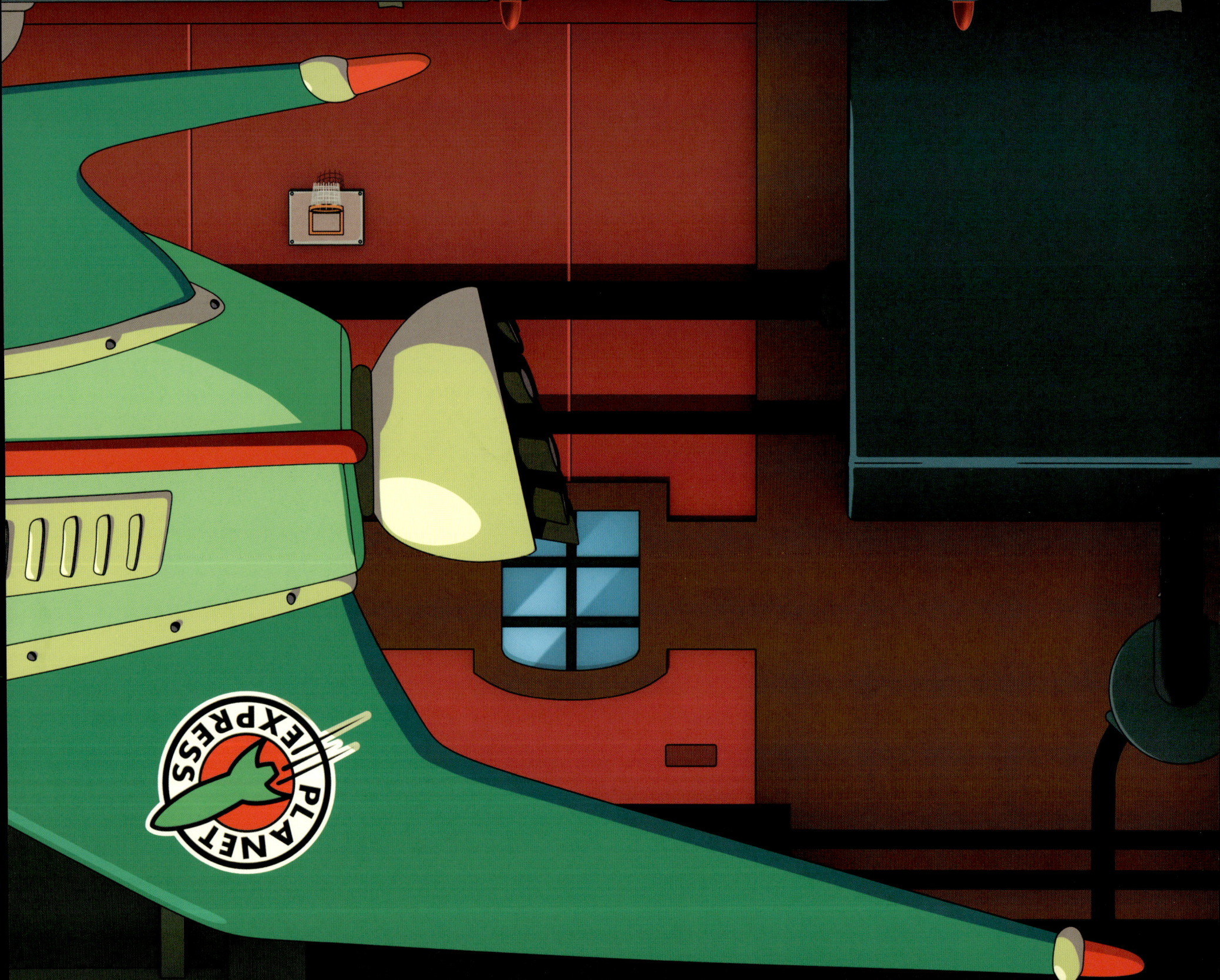

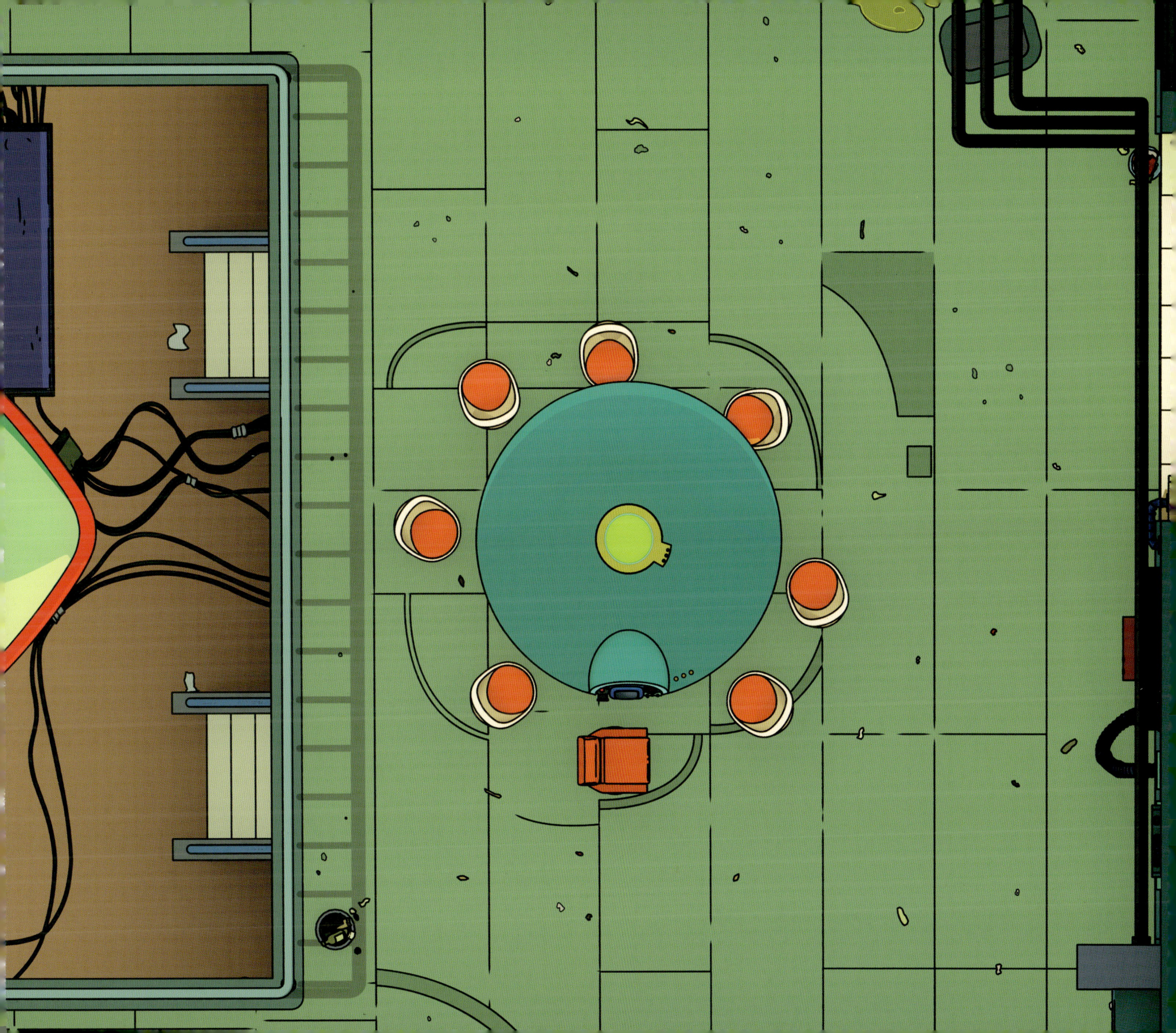

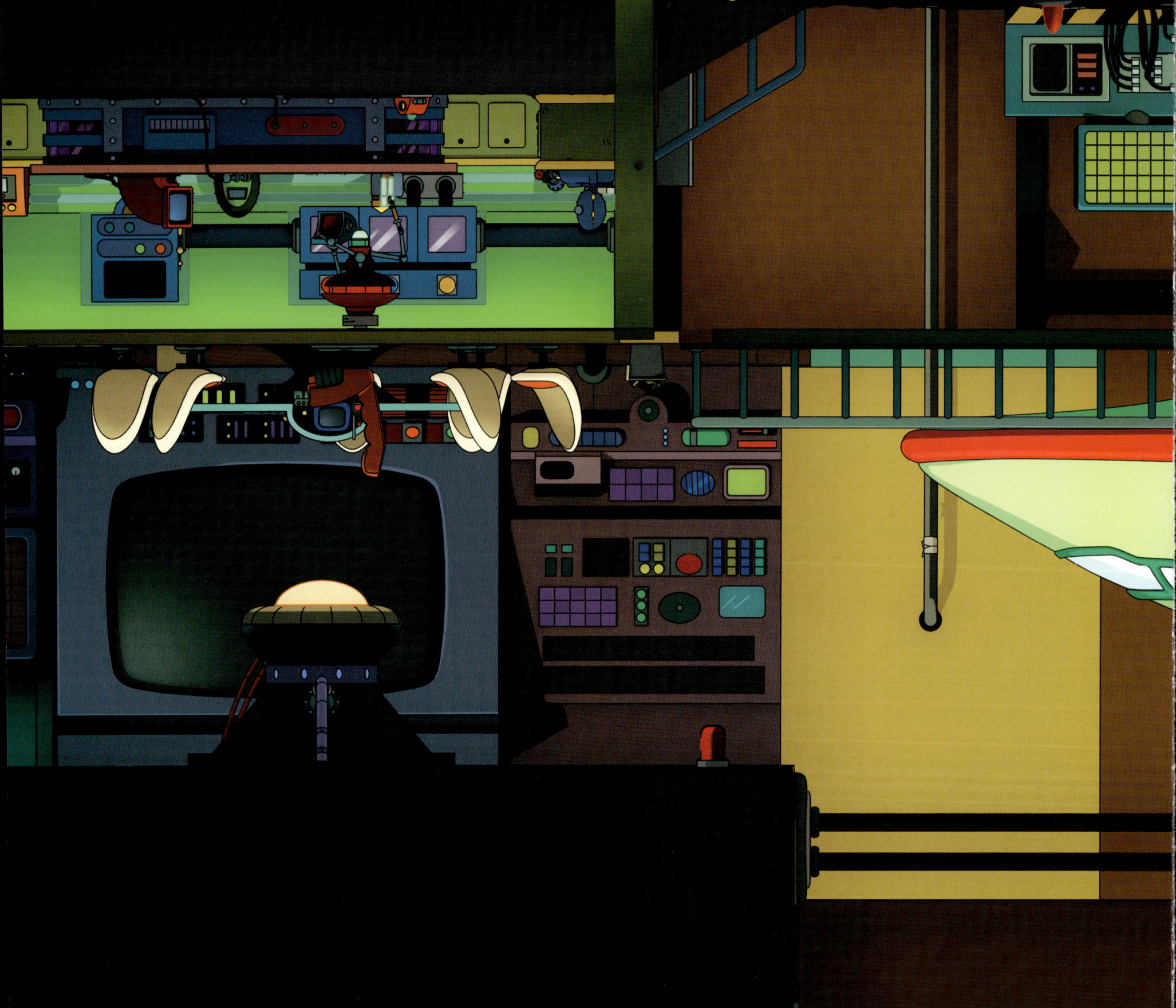

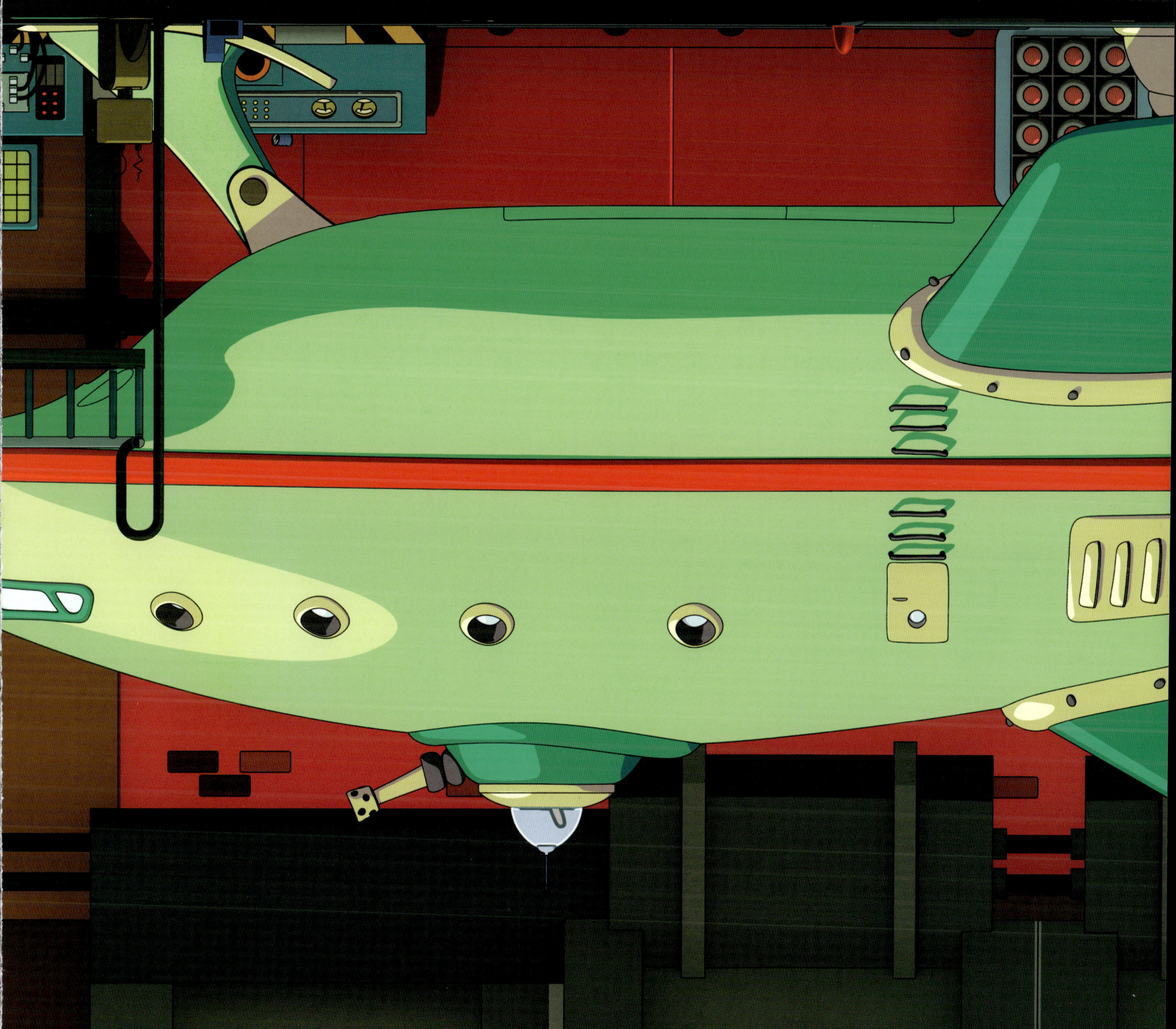

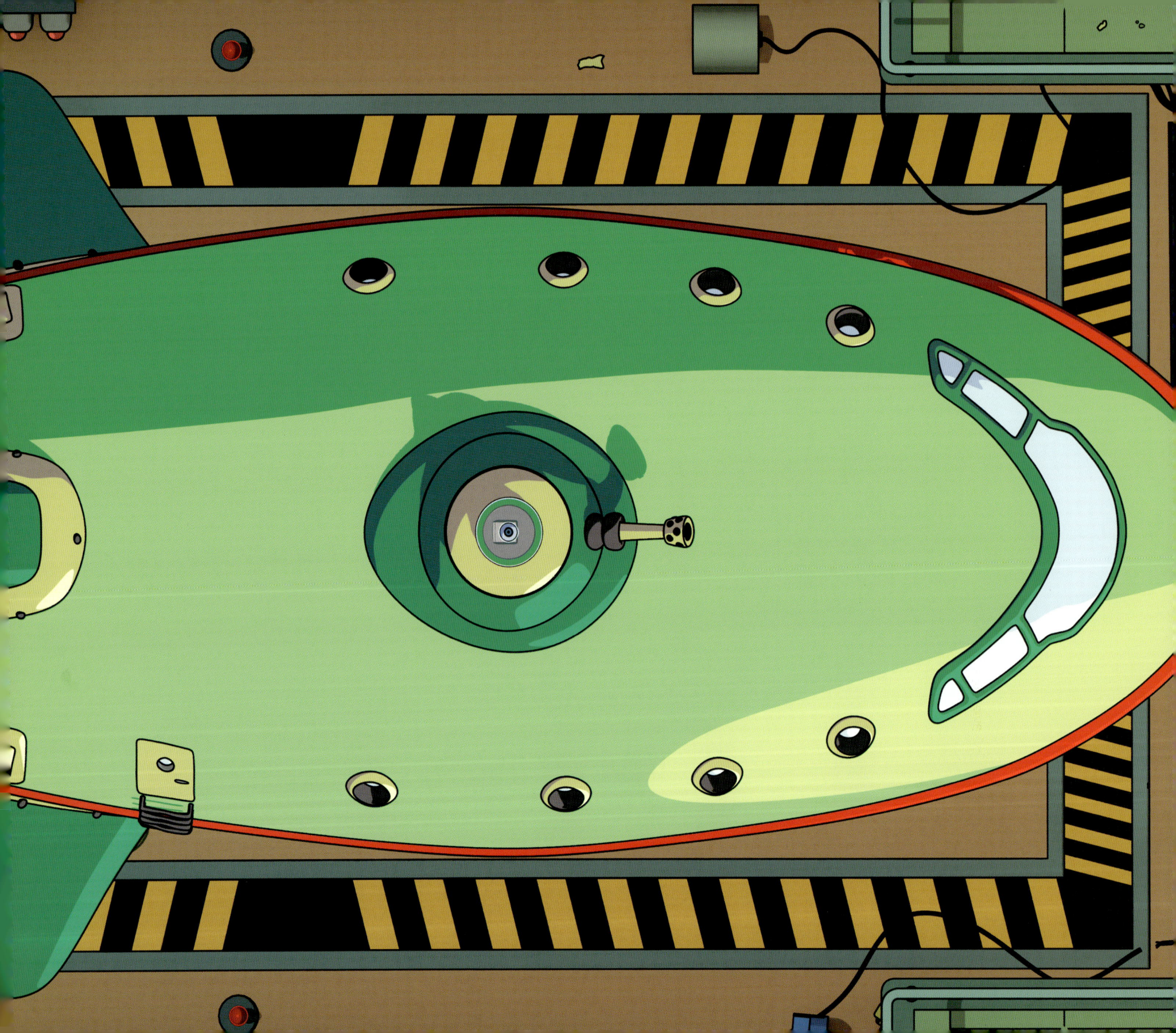

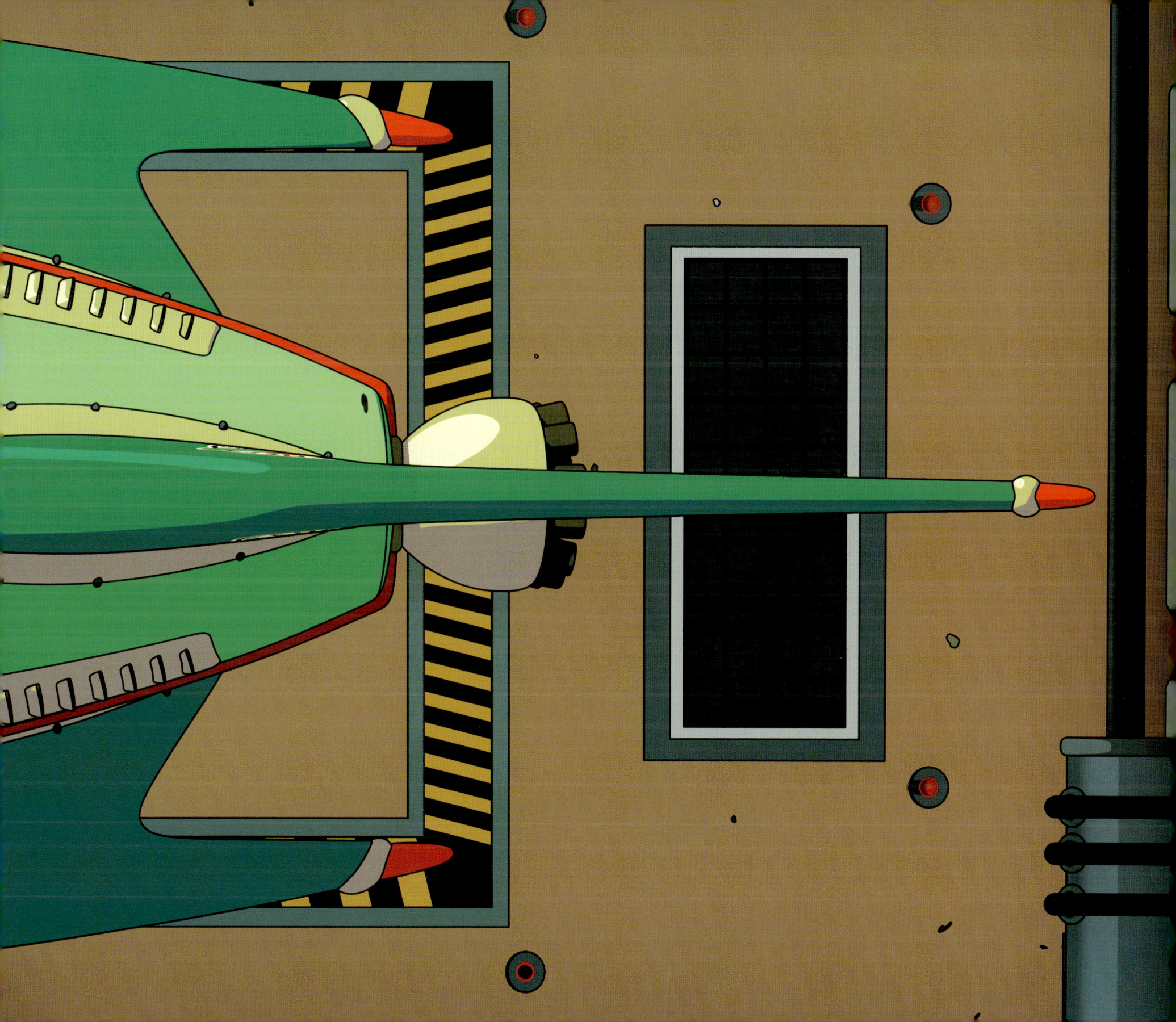

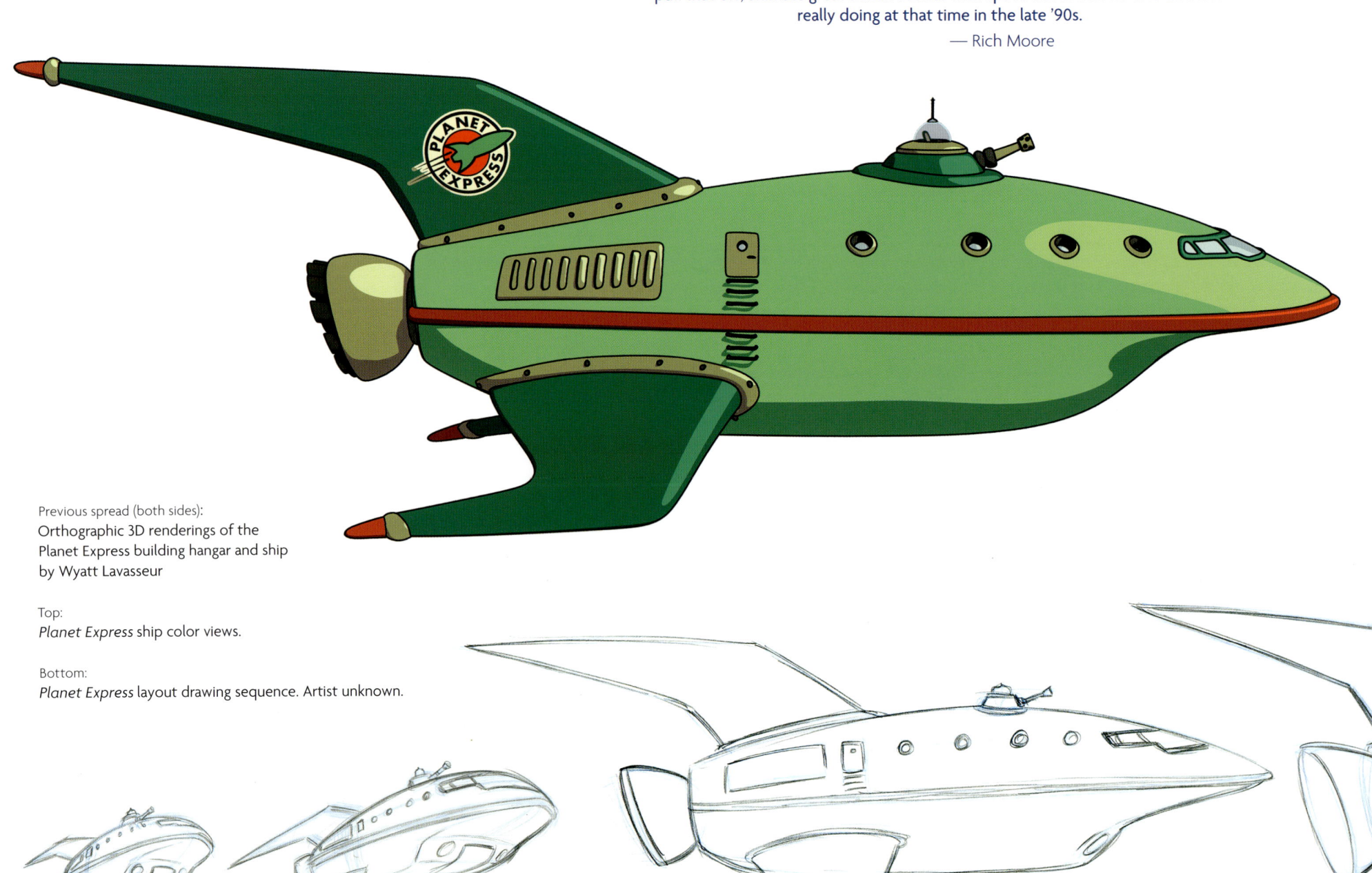

We used a really high-end lighting program and it was so difficult to get the software to dumb down to those three tones in the *Planet Express* ship. By integrating CG into animation, our goal was to have you think—if you didn't know any better—that the ship was completely drawn by hand, even though it wasn't. One of my proudest memories of the show is that we were able to pull that off; animate great action scenes with space travel that no one else was really doing at that time in the late '90s.

— Rich Moore

Previous spread (both sides):
Orthographic 3D renderings of the Planet Express building hangar and ship by Wyatt Lavasseur

Top:
Planet Express ship color views.

Bottom:
Planet Express layout drawing sequence. Artist unknown.

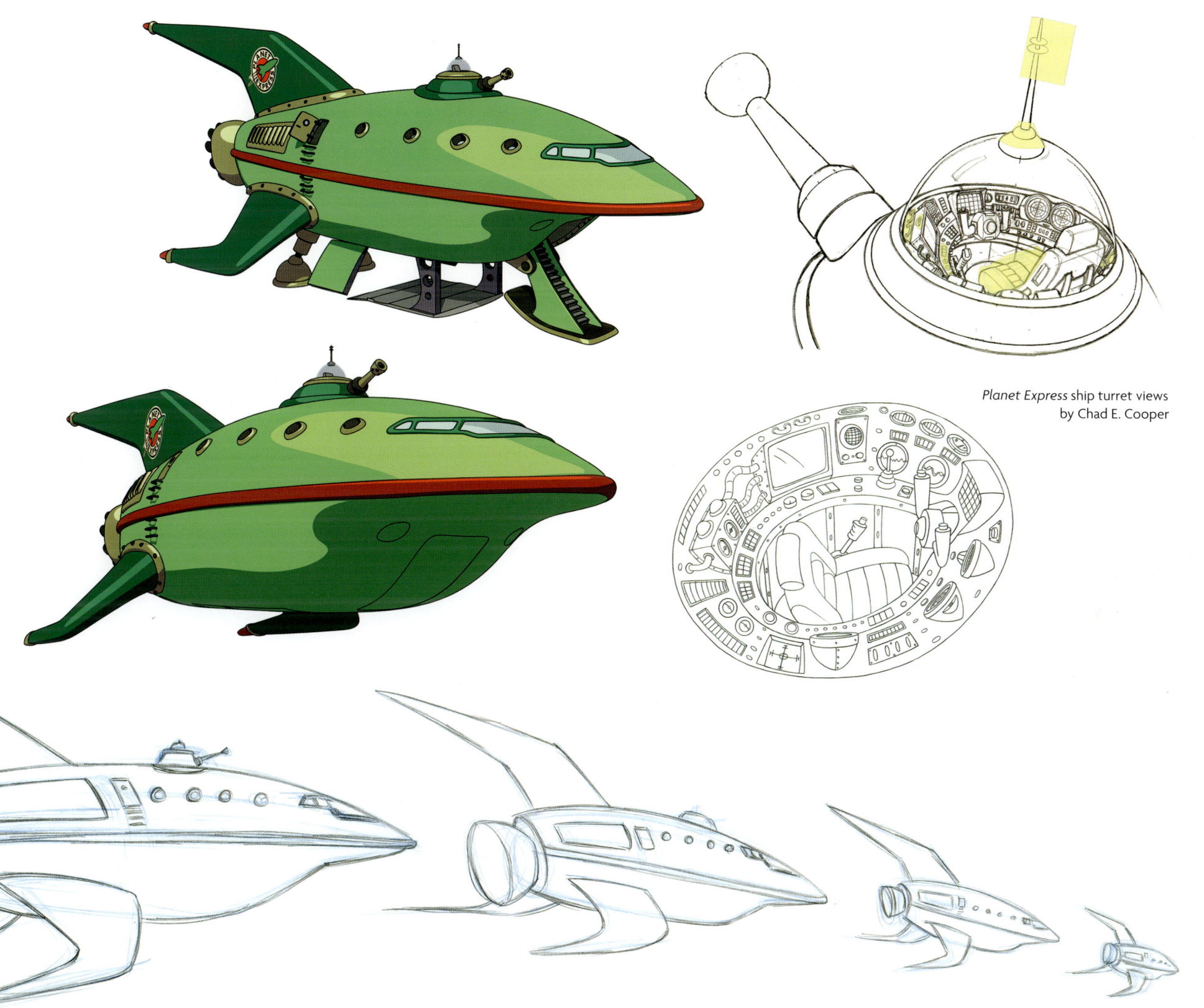

Planet Express ship turret views
by Chad E. Cooper

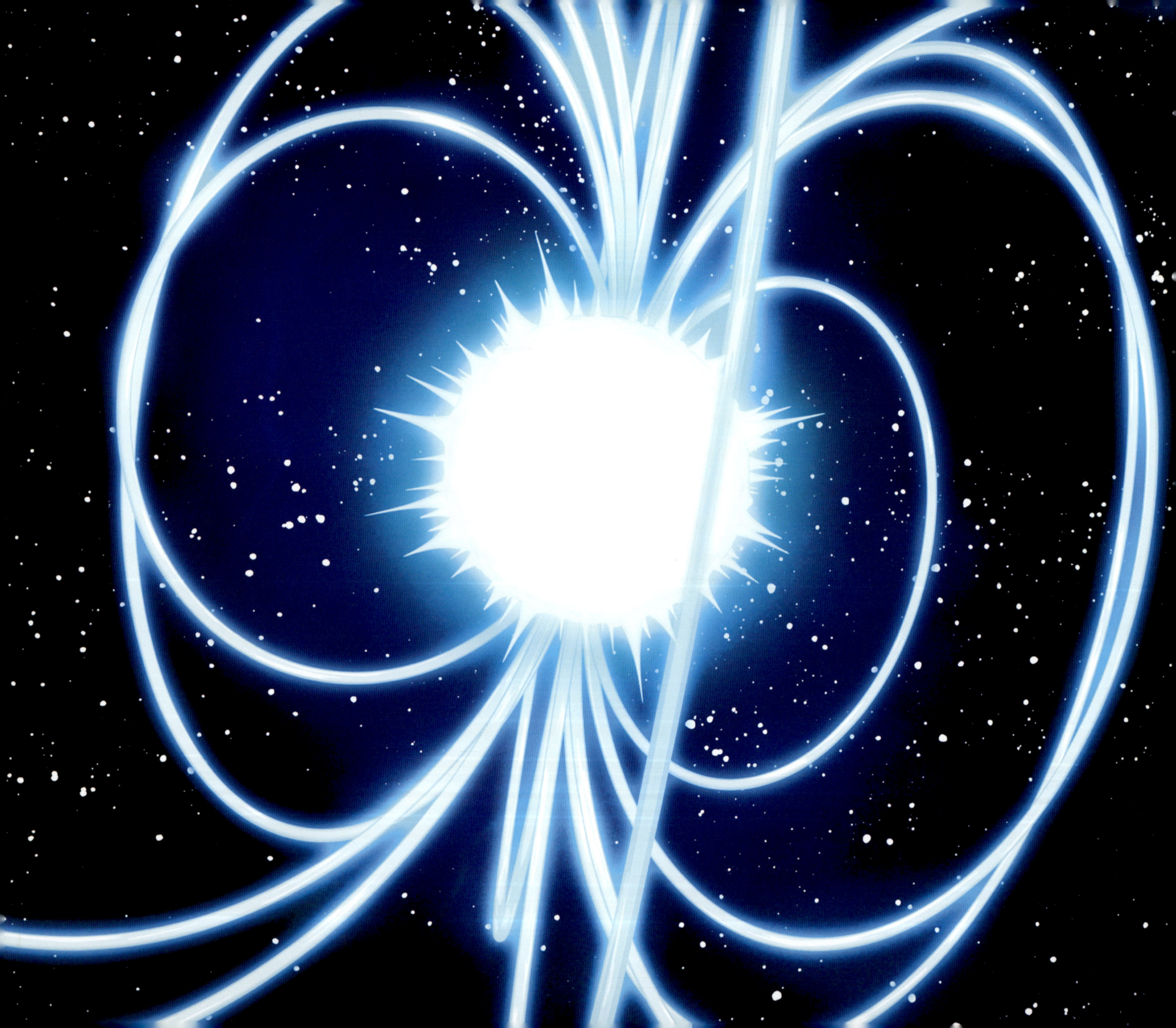

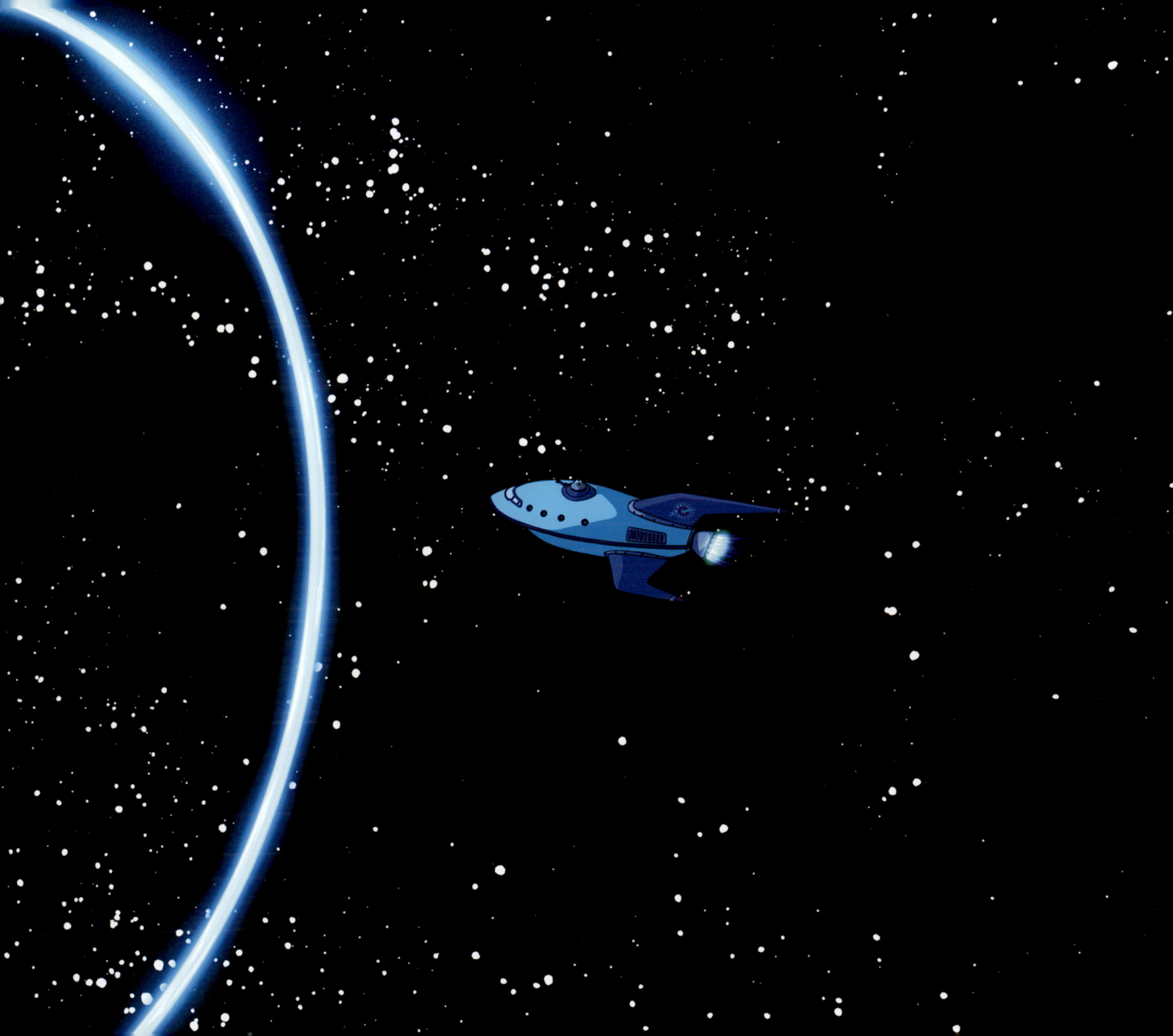

Previous spread:
Planet Express ship approaching
space anomaly 3D rendering
by Eric Whited

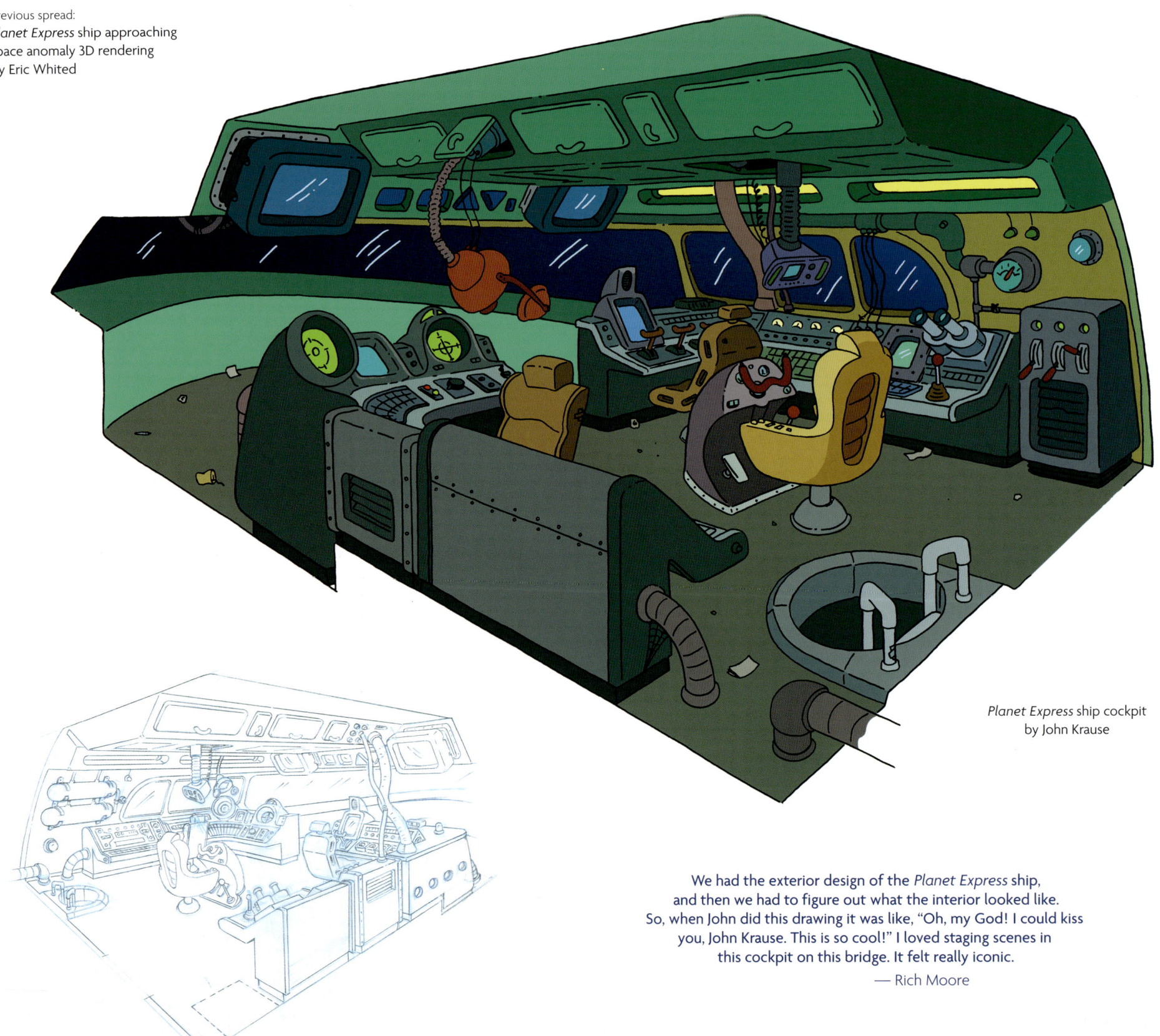

Planet Express ship cockpit
by John Krause

We had the exterior design of the *Planet Express* ship,
and then we had to figure out what the interior looked like.
So, when John did this drawing it was like, "Oh, my God! I could kiss
you, John Krause. This is so cool!" I loved staging scenes in
this cockpit on this bridge. It felt really iconic.
— Rich Moore

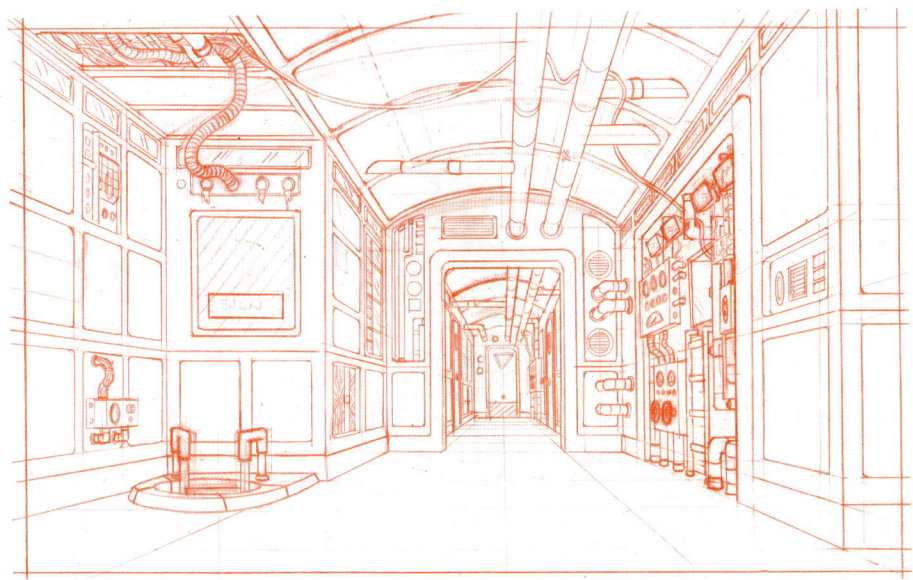

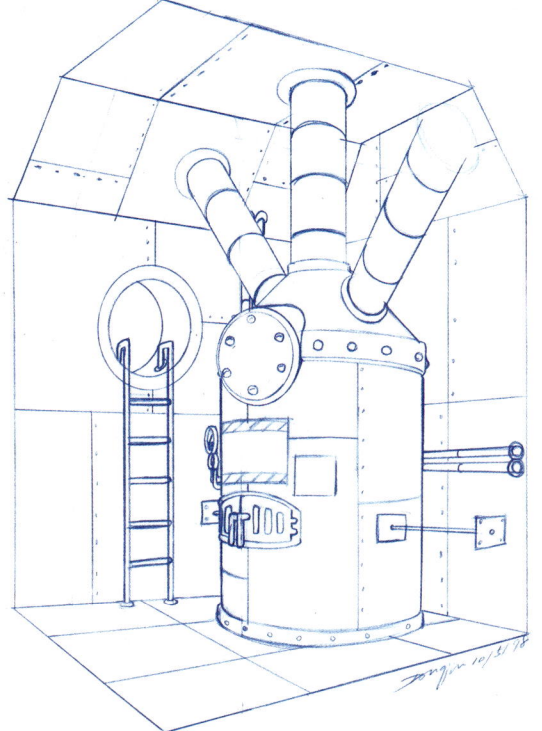

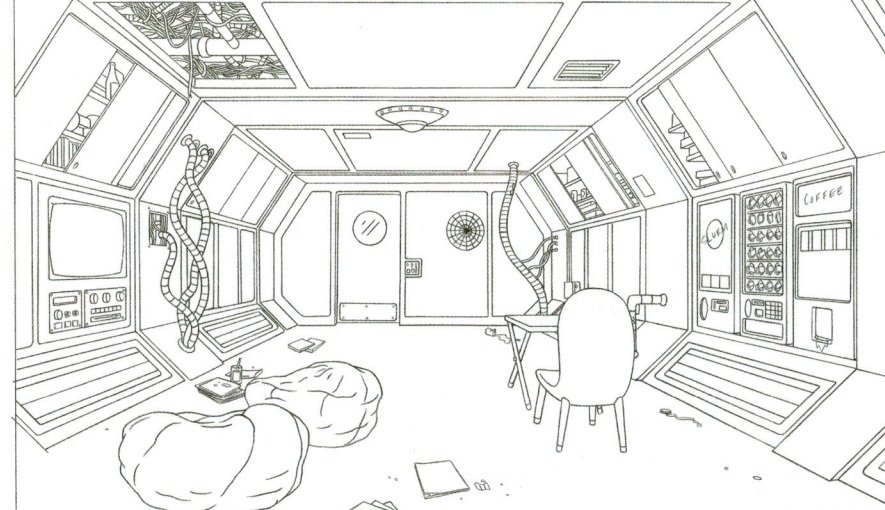

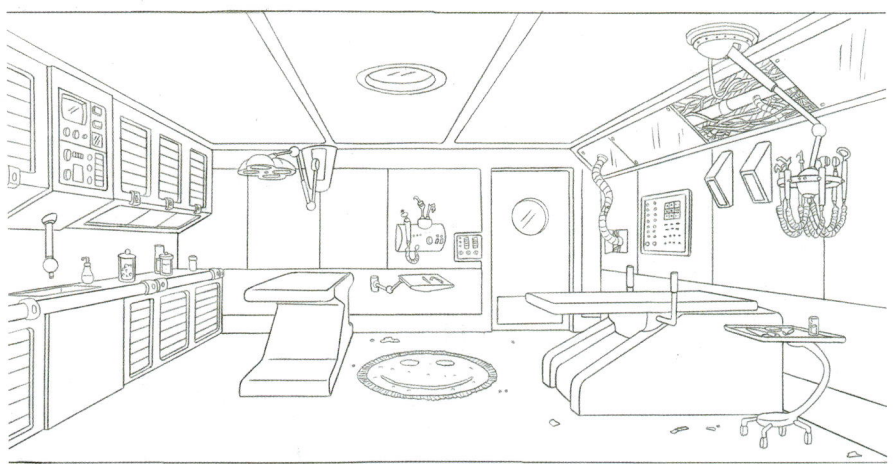

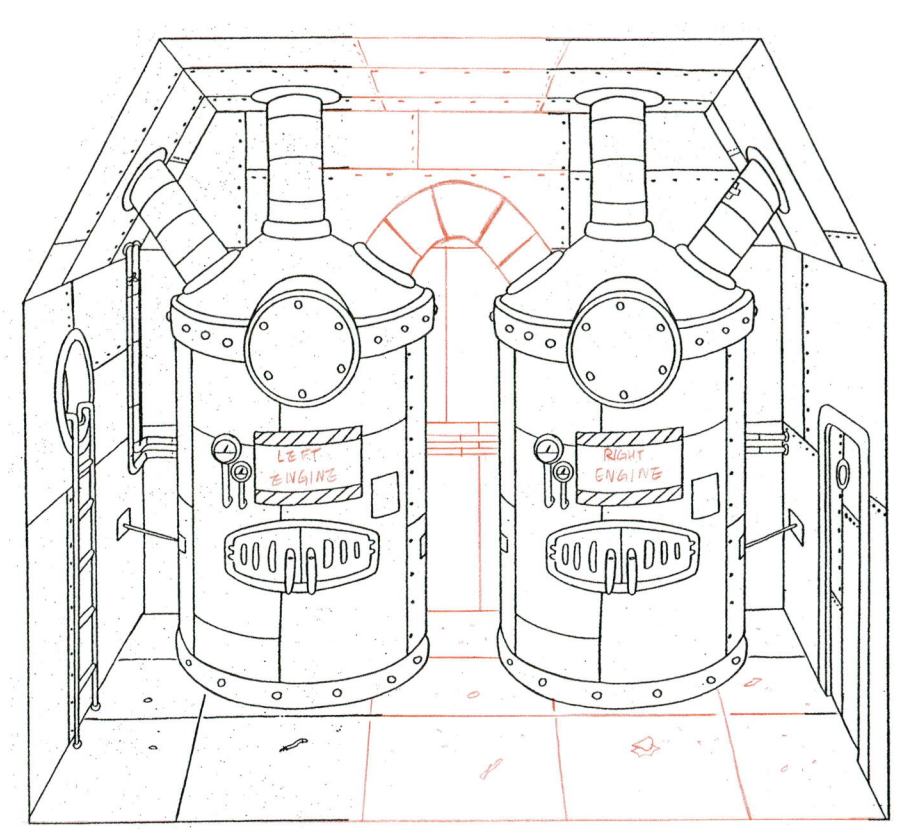

Left, from top:
Planet Express ship hallway by Jeff Mertz
Planet Express ship rec room by Jeff Mertz
Planet Express ship sick bay by Jeff Mertz

Right, from top:
Planet Express ship engine room
(1ACV04) by DJ Kang
Planet Express ship engine alteration
(2ACV02). Artist unknown.

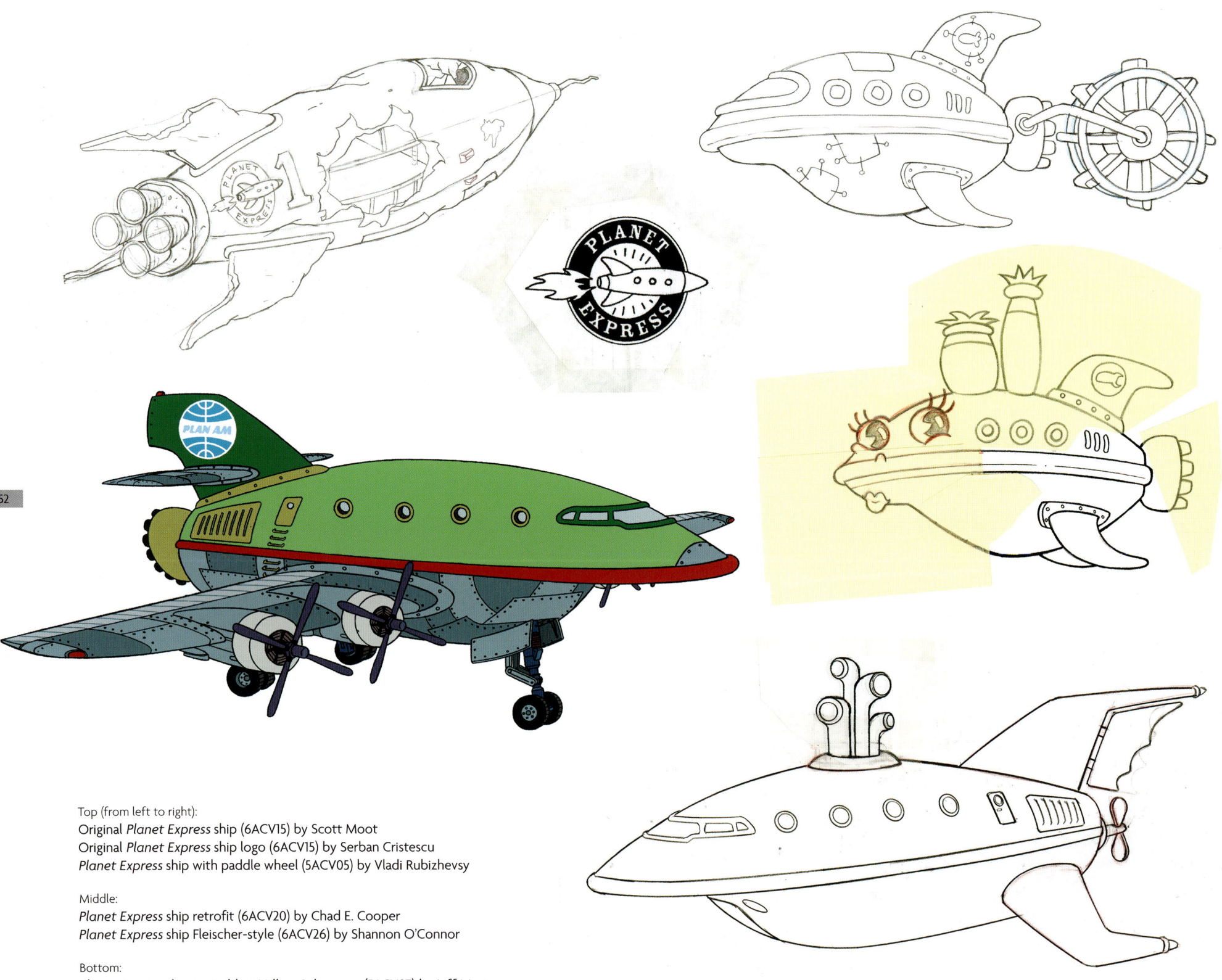

152

Top (from left to right):
Original *Planet Express* ship (6ACV15) by Scott Moot
Original *Planet Express* ship logo (6ACV15) by Serban Cristescu
Planet Express ship with paddle wheel (5ACV05) by Vladi Rubizhevsy

Middle:
Planet Express ship retrofit (6ACV20) by Chad E. Cooper
Planet Express ship Fleischer-style (6ACV26) by Shannon O'Connor

Bottom:
Planet Express ship resembling Yellow Submarine (5ACV07) by Jeff Mertz

PLANET EXPRESS

PLAN AM

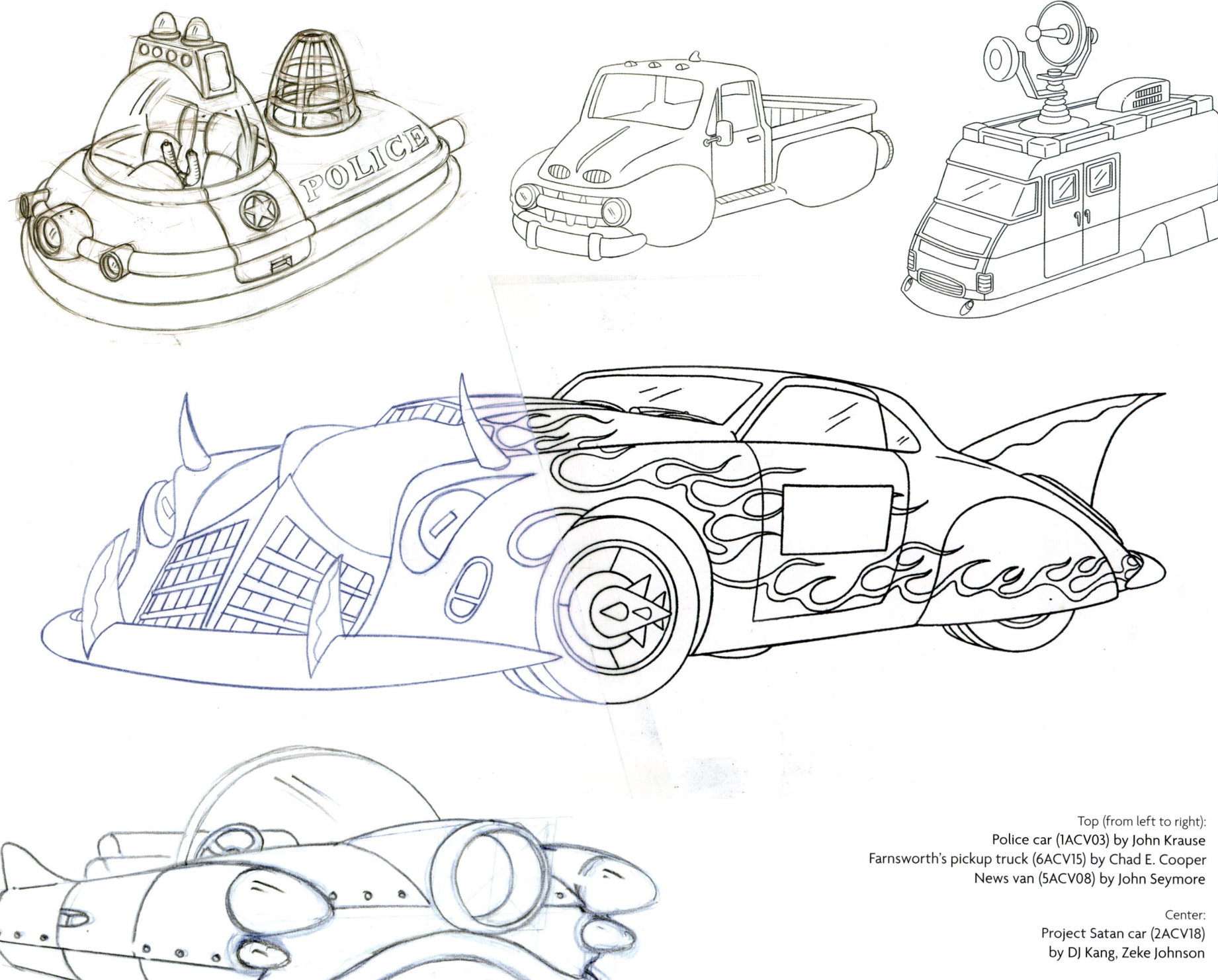

153

Top (from left to right):
Police car (1ACV03) by John Krause
Farnsworth's pickup truck (6ACV15) by Chad E. Cooper
News van (5ACV08) by John Seymore

Center:
Project Satan car (2ACV18)
by DJ Kang, Zeke Johnson

Bottom:
Makeout Point car (1ACV05) by John Krause

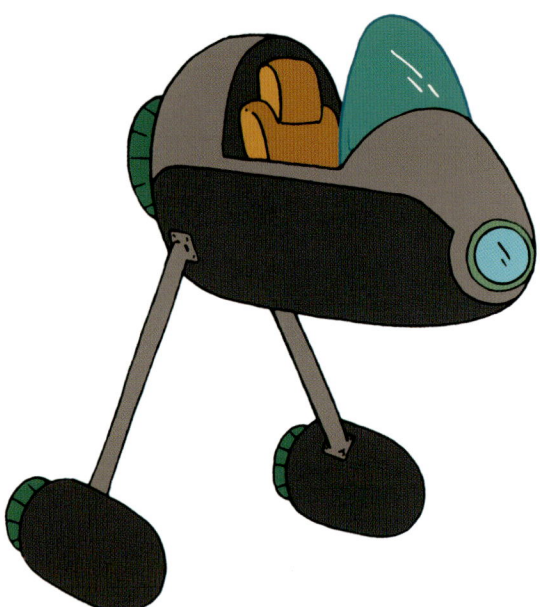

This is the original page of New New York vehicles that we made. We had tons of little simple CG background vehicles that we would put into exterior shots. These bring back memories of sitting with the crew and just pumping out lots of designs, because we had to populate this world.

— Rich Moore

I did some Buck Rogers–type spaceship designs, then Rough Draft went further, adding in other style elements. This rail car has got elements of a Raymond Loewy industrial design, but it's also grounded in the '90s.

— Bill Morrison

Various futuristic ship designs by Bret Haaland, Zeke Johnson, DJ Kang, and John Krause

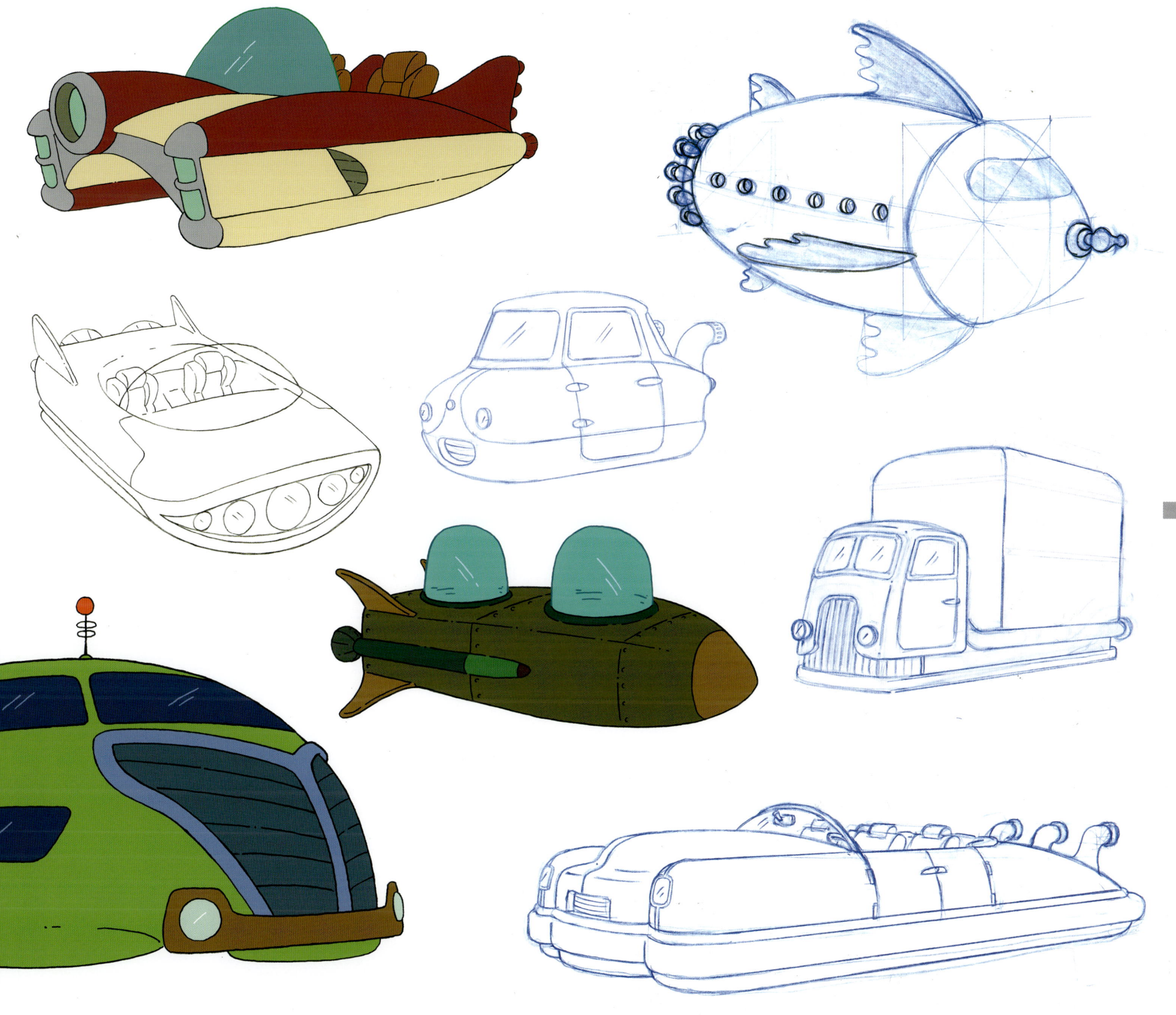

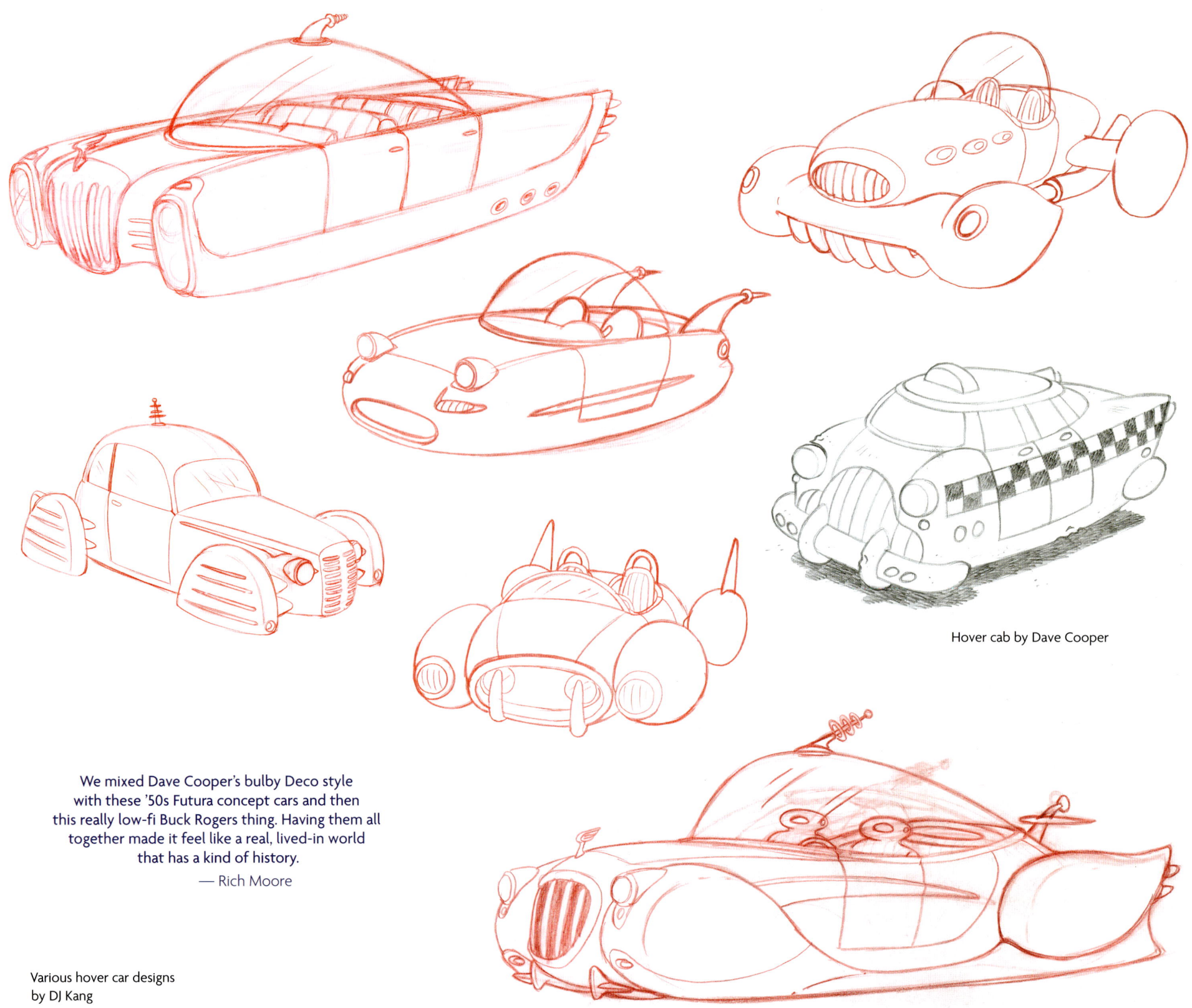

156

We mixed Dave Cooper's bulby Deco style with these '50s Futura concept cars and then this really low-fi Buck Rogers thing. Having them all together made it feel like a real, lived-in world that has a kind of history.

— Rich Moore

Hover cab by Dave Cooper

Various hover car designs by DJ Kang

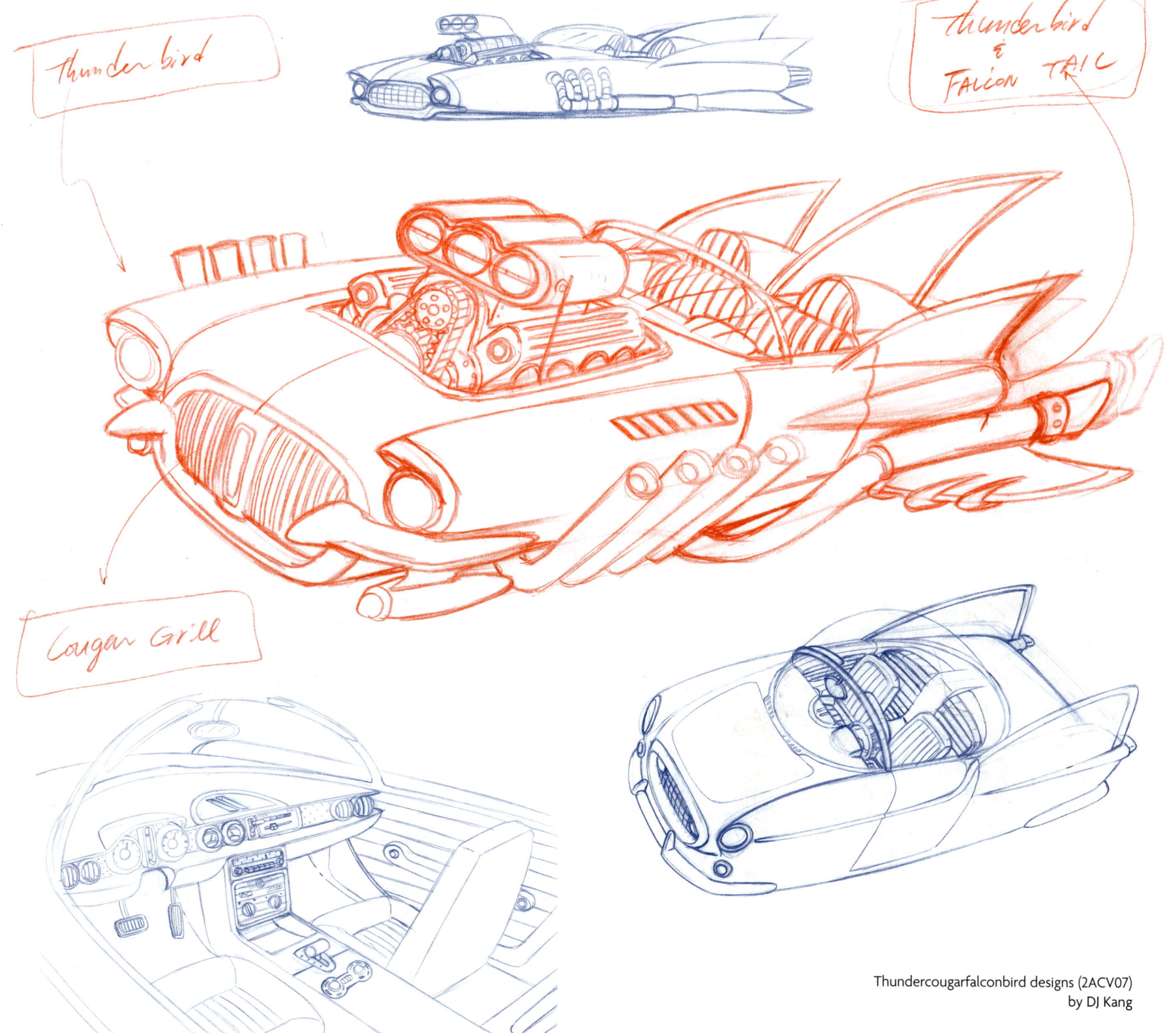

thunderbird

thunderbird & FALCON TAIL

Cougar Grill

157

Thundercougarfalconbird designs (2ACV07)
by DJ Kang

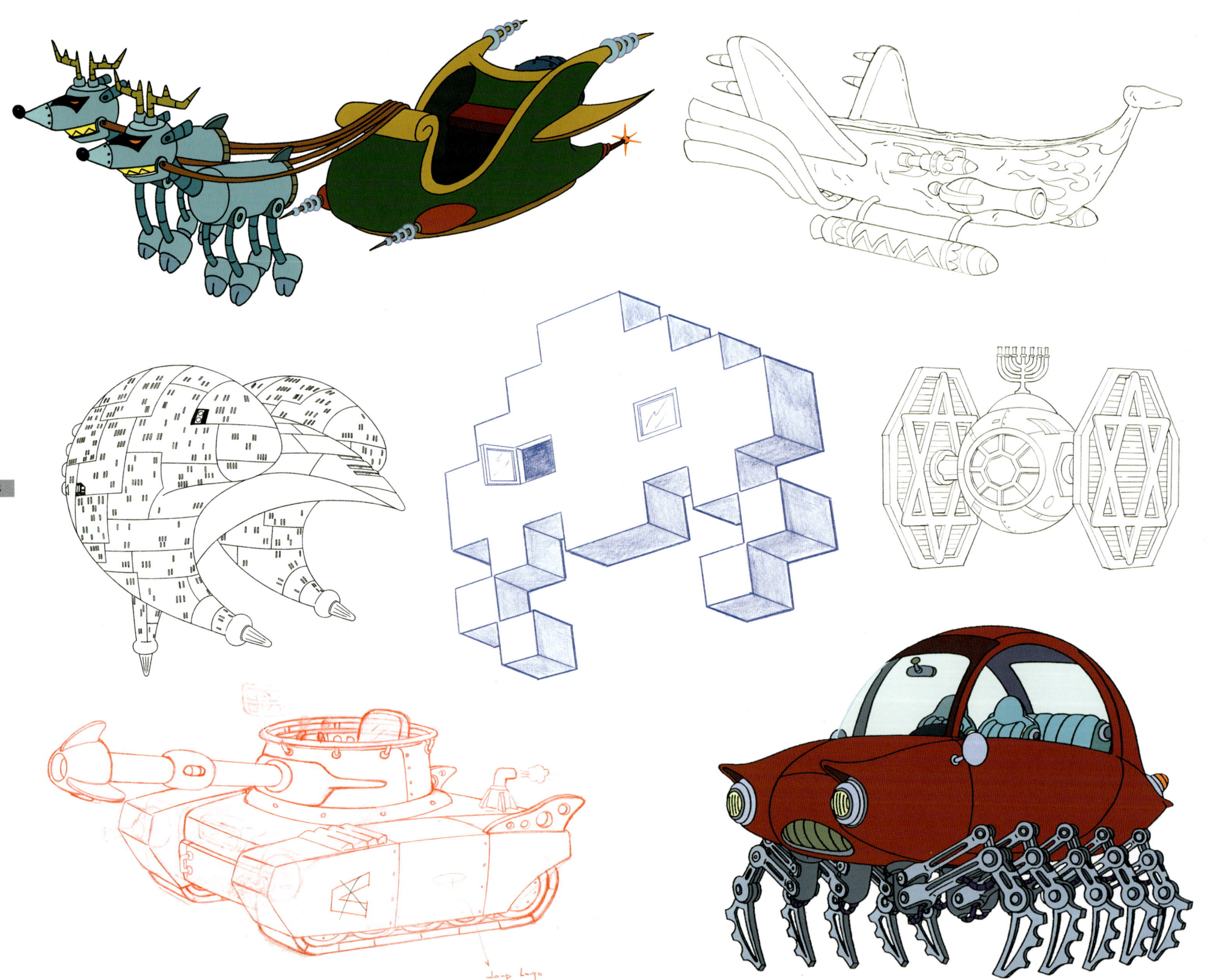

158

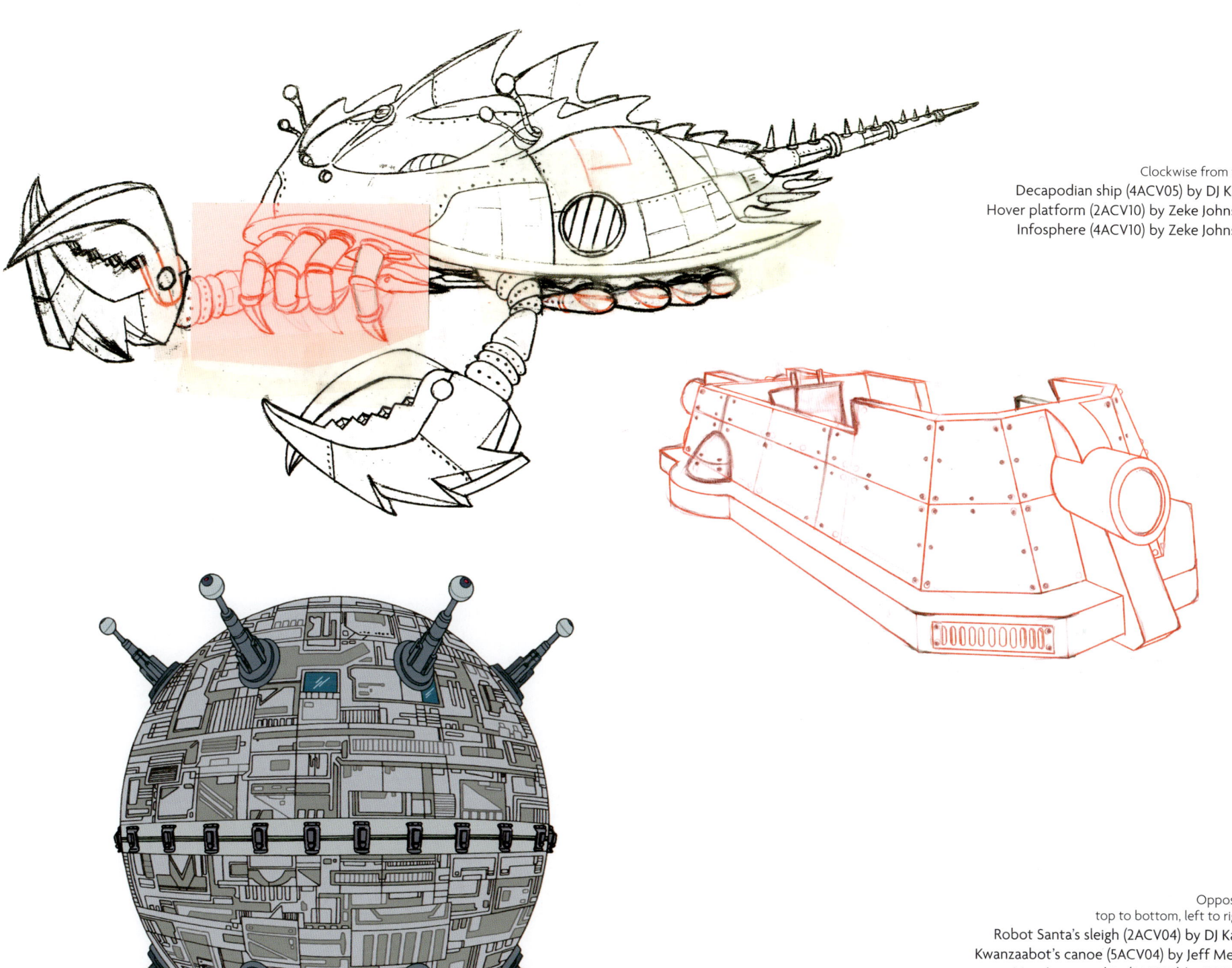

Clockwise from top:
Decapodian ship (4ACV05) by DJ Kang
Hover platform (2ACV10) by Zeke Johnson
Infosphere (4ACV10) by Zeke Johnson

159

Opposite,
top to bottom, left to right:
Robot Santa's sleigh (2ACV04) by DJ Kang
Kwanzaabot's canoe (5ACV04) by Jeff Mertz
Mom's space ship (3ACV21) by DJ Kang
Alien space ship (3ACV18) by Zeke Johnson
Chanukah Zombie's fighter (5ACV04) by John Seymore
DOOP tank (4ACV05) by DJ Kang
Car with mechanical crab legs (2ACV05) by DJ Kang

This page (top to bottom):
DaVinci flying machine (6ACV05)
by Alex Lee
DaVinci flying machine 3D rendering (6ACV05)
by Don Kim and Joshua Mills

Opposite (clockwise from top):
Nimbus DOOP flagship (1ACV04)
by DJ Kang
Nimbus two views (1ACV04)
by DJ Kang
Nimbus cutaway view (4ACV05)
by Debbie Silver
Nimbus cutaway view 3D rendering (4ACV05)
by Chris Stover

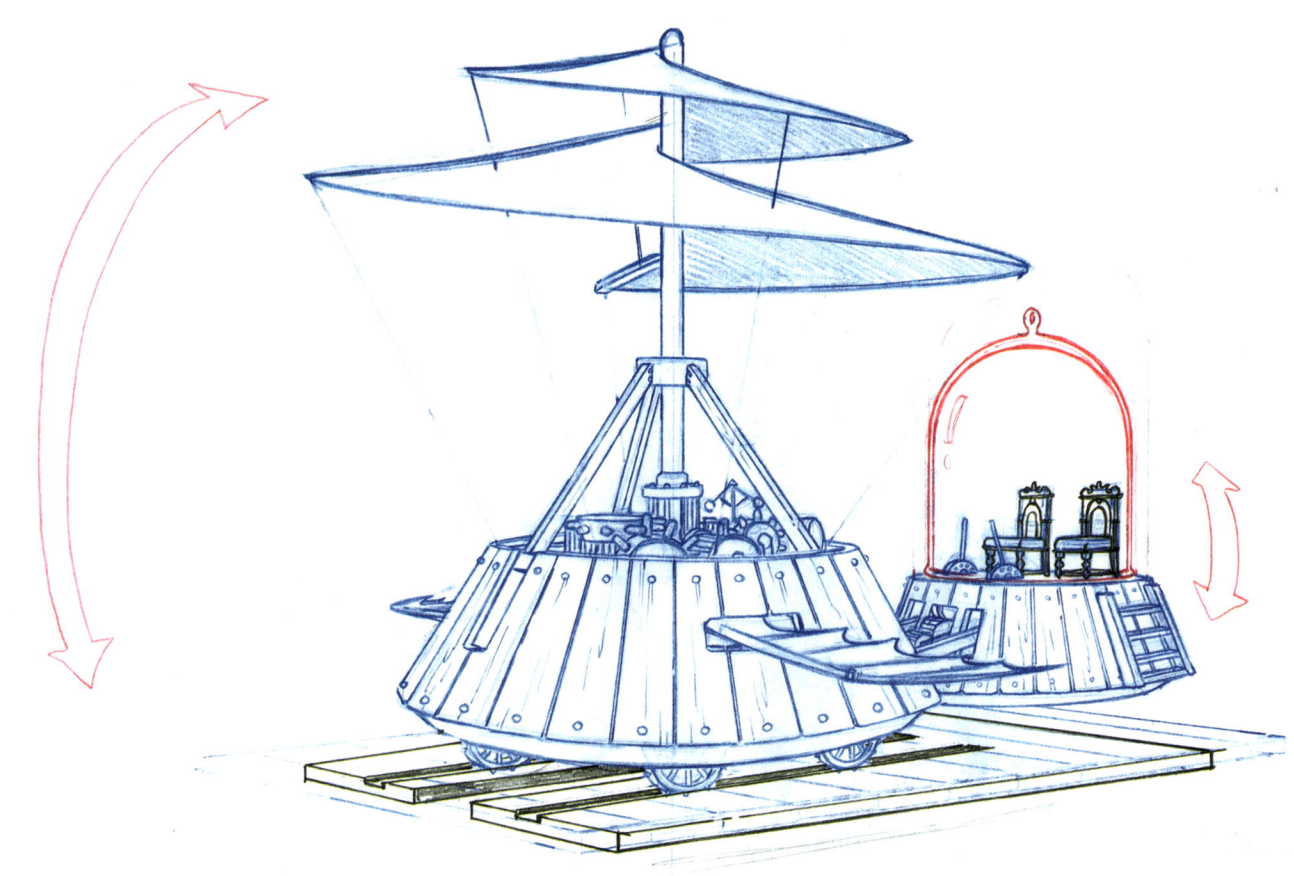

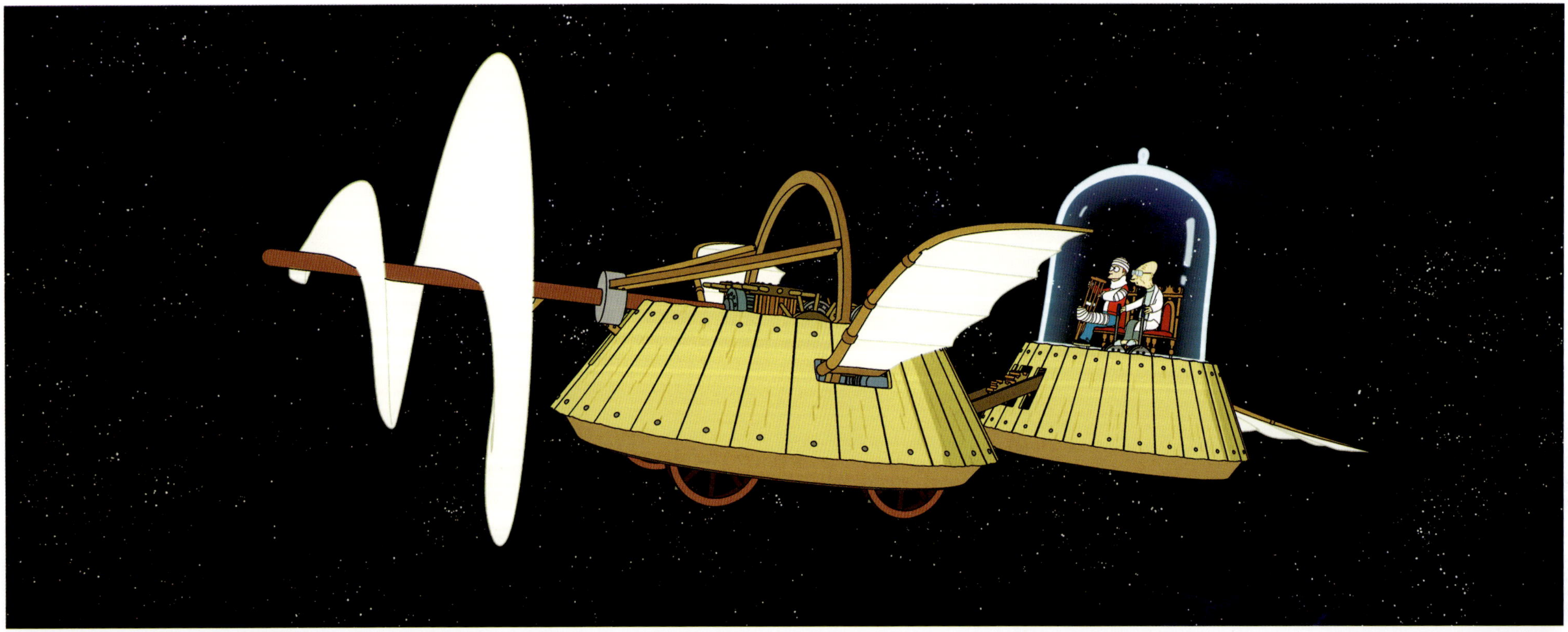

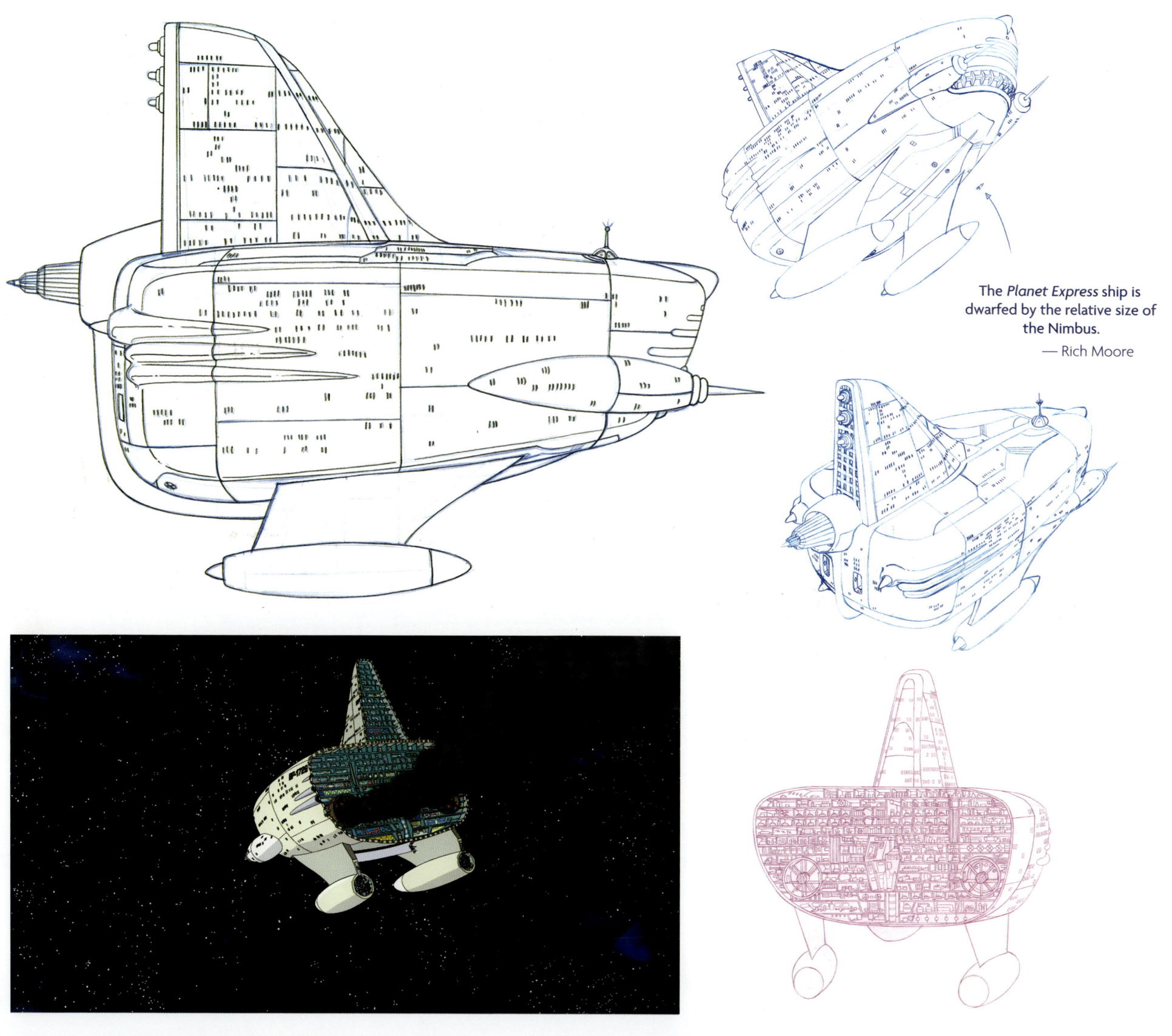

The *Planet Express* ship is dwarfed by the relative size of the Nimbus.

— Rich Moore

Matt Groening: The sad reality of TV series animation is that there is an element of cranking out the sausage. As an executive producer, you're worrying about everything: you want the show to be funny, you want it to be emotionally real, and you want it to deliver the goods. At the same time, it must be on model, well-paced, superbly acted, and deliver great visual jokes. That is an incredible amount of work with impossibly short deadlines, always under-budgeted.

Historically, the creative component of these shows is secondary to just getting the stuff out there. You have to deliver the product. Starting with *The Simpsons*, we started breaking rules, one of which was: Once you have a script nailed down, you do not change it. On *Futurama*, we went even further. We were willing to keep reinventing until we got it right. And the great thing about Rough Draft is they got it right really fast; we didn't spin our wheels very much. They were really inspired. And the thing I loved about all of the people that worked at Rough Draft, from the very top down to the newest animator, was the heart in the building. They loved doing *Futurama*.

The truth of the matter is that any animated project is a gigantic collaborative project.
— Matt Groening

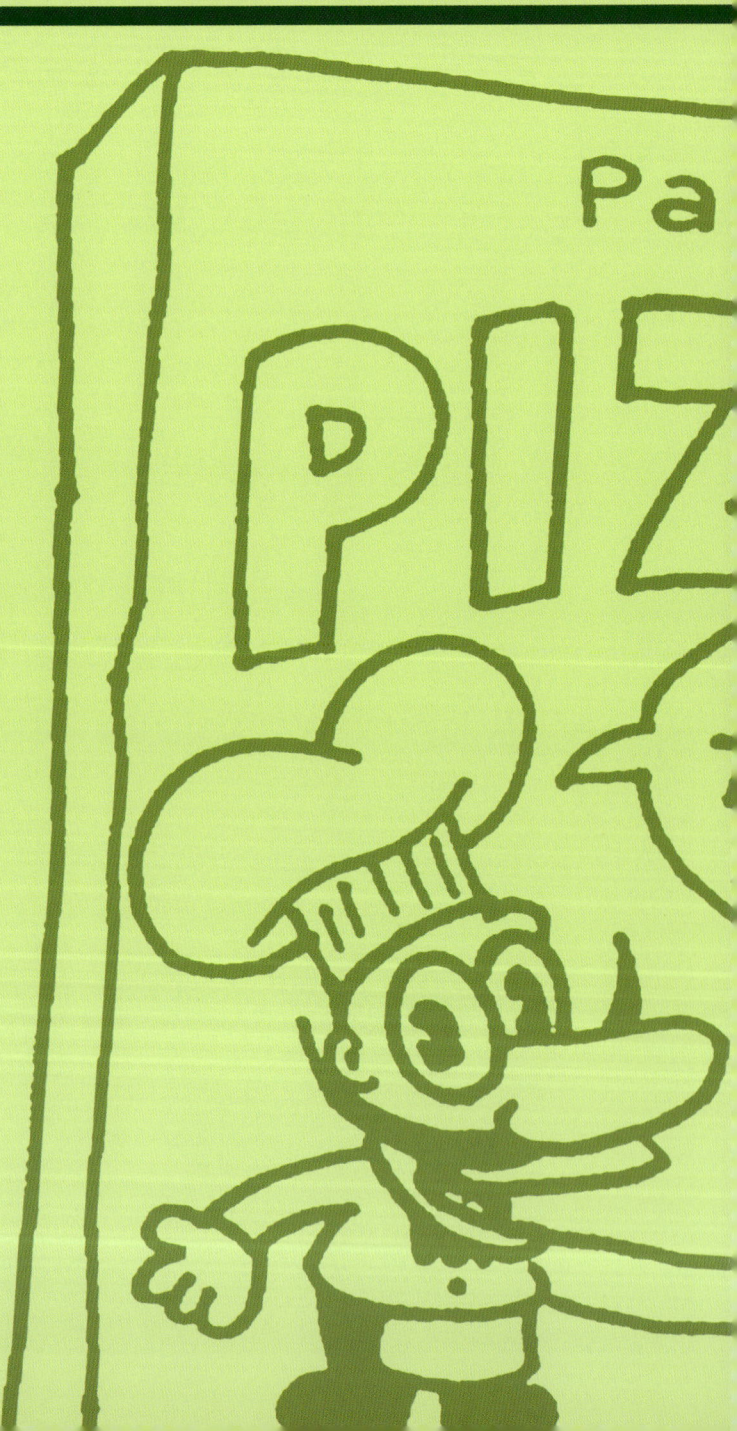

Panucci's pizza
box design (1ACV01)
by Matt Groening

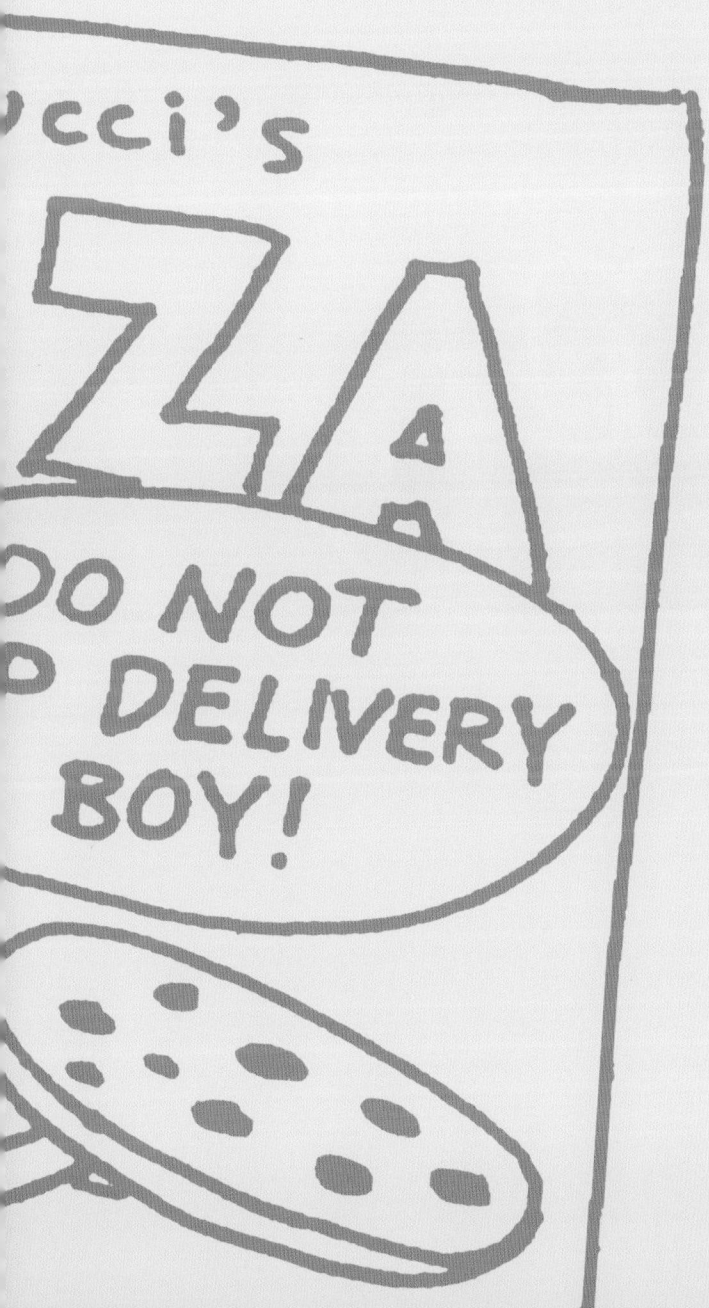

Claudia Katz: The joy of Matt is, he's at heart still that *Life in Hell* comic book artist. And I think there's a big part of him that is always very supportive of artists.

Matt Groening: The truth of the matter is that any animated project is a gigantic collaborative project. To me, *Futurama* is a perfect example of the best kind of collaboration, with amazing artists, designers, and directors; composers, actors, and writers. Everybody adds to the show. Everybody's making it better and better and better.

In addition to producing *Futurama* itself, Rough Draft Studios developed a cadre of animation professionals who would go on to advance the art of animation into the next century. And perhaps, even beyond. The Rough Draft talents trained and nurtured through the madcap torrent of production that was *Futurama*'s initial launch have gone on to work in television as directors and supervising directors on *American Dad*, *Big Mouth*, *Bob's Burgers*, *Central Park*, *Clash-A-Rama!*, *The Cleveland Show*, *Dan Vs.*, *Dawn of the Croods*, *Disenchantment*, *Drawn Together*, *Duck Tales*, *Family Guy*, *Father of the Pride*, *Gravity Falls*, *The Great North*, *Hamster and Gretel*, *Moon Girl and Devil Dinosaur*, *Napoleon Dynamite*, *Rick & Morty*, *Tarantula*, and many others. They also served as directors on such features as *Beavis and Butt-Head Do the Universe*, *Phineas and Ferb The Movie*, *Ralph Breaks the Internet*, *Ultraman: Rising*, *Wreck-it Ralph*, and *Zootopia*.

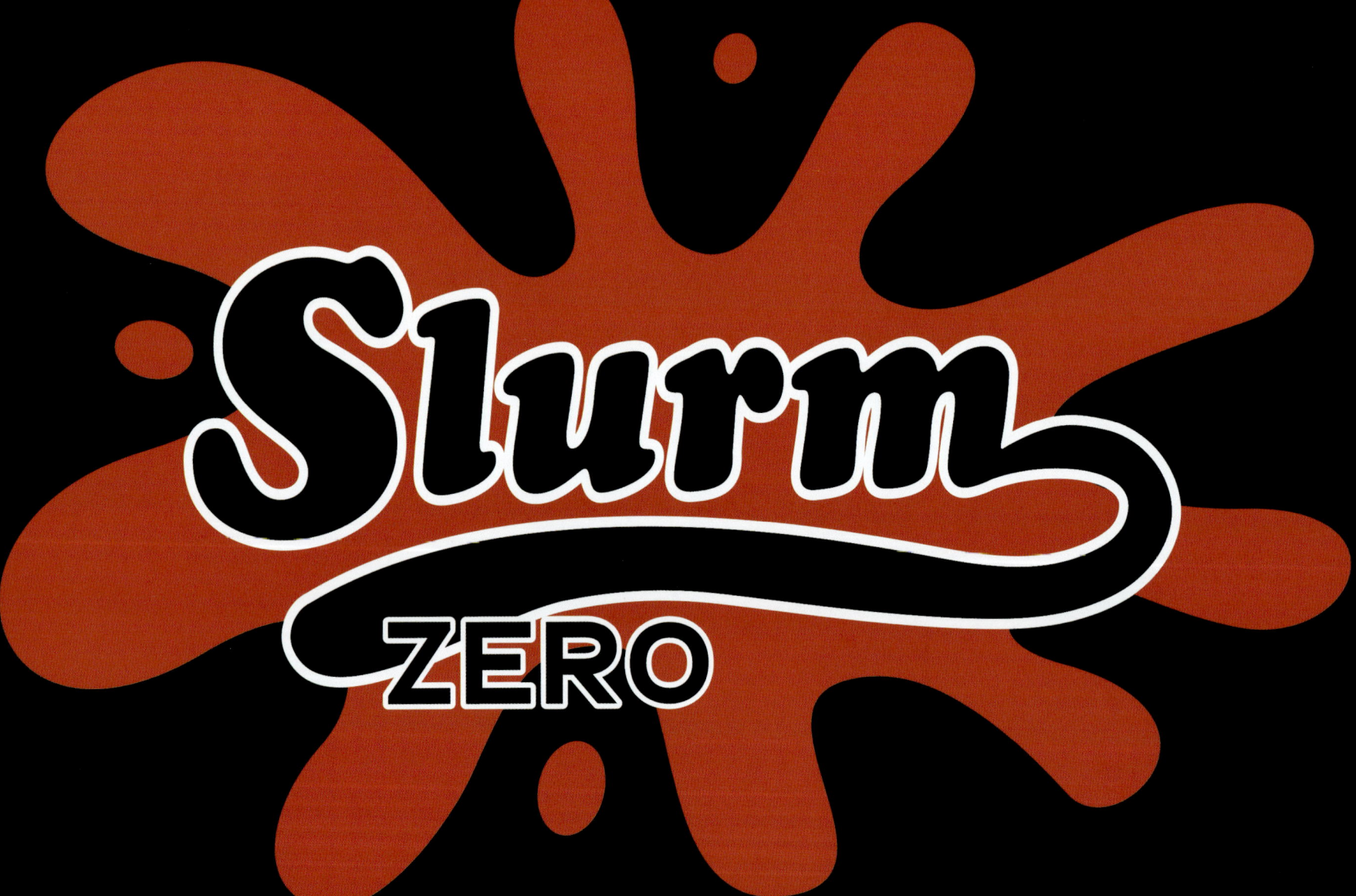

Everything had clean lines.
And rather than have extra lines to describe
the shape of something, there were cut-out shapes,
so everything's pretty streamlined.
— Crystal Chesney-Thompson

Slurm Zero logo by Serban Cristescu

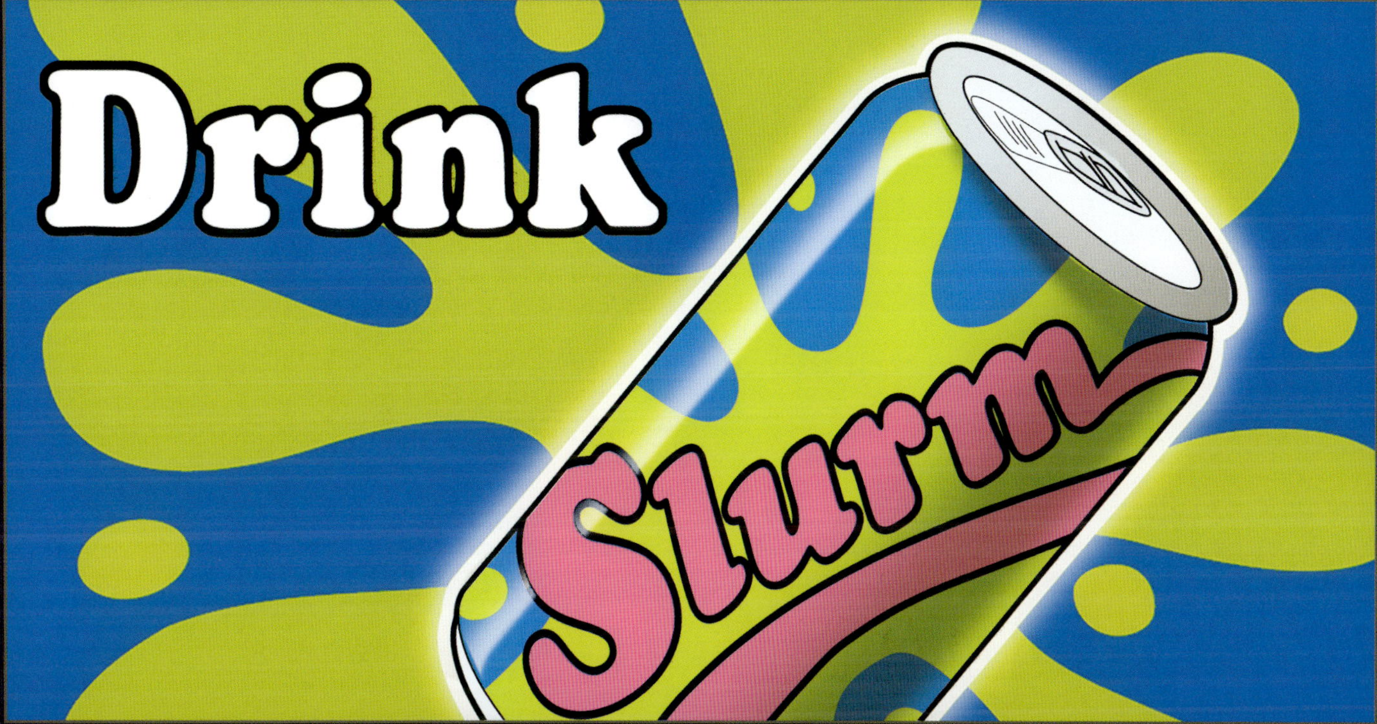

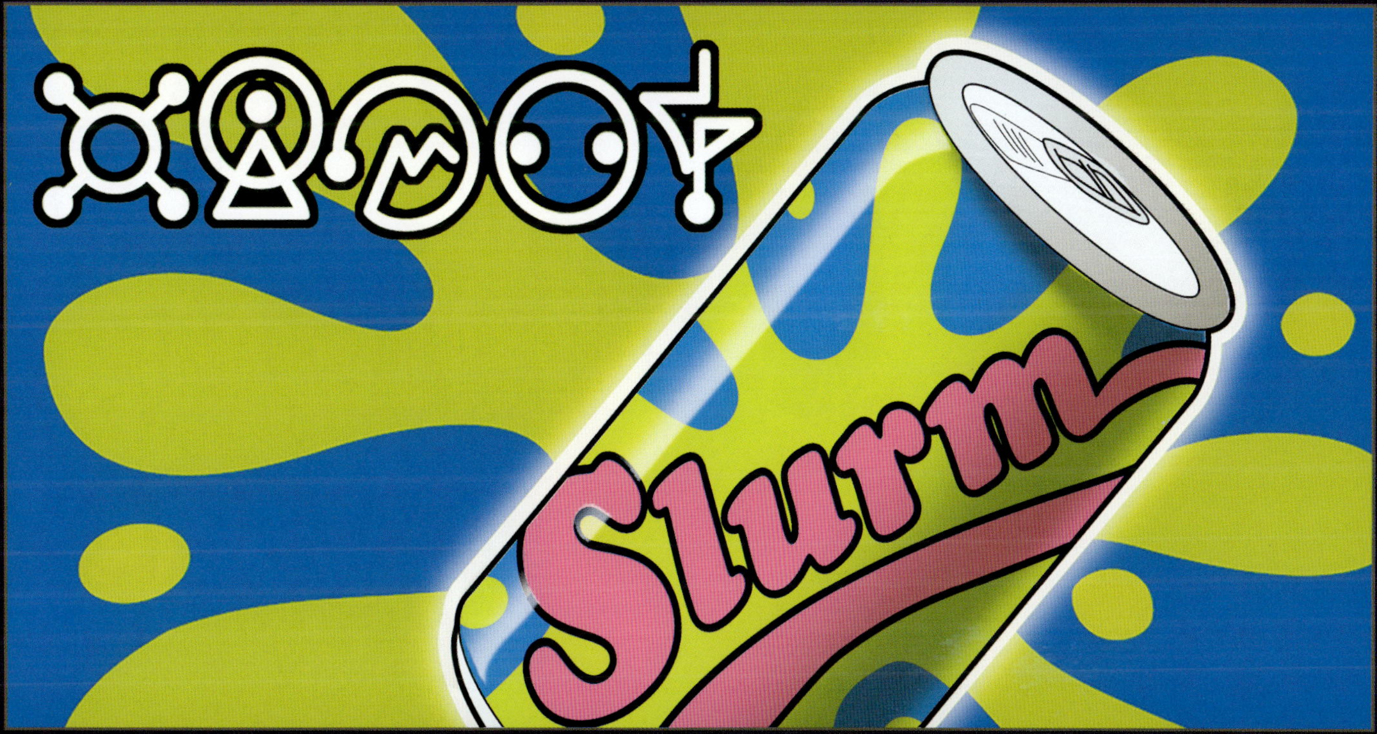

Drink Slurm billboards (English and Alien language versions) by Serban Cristescu

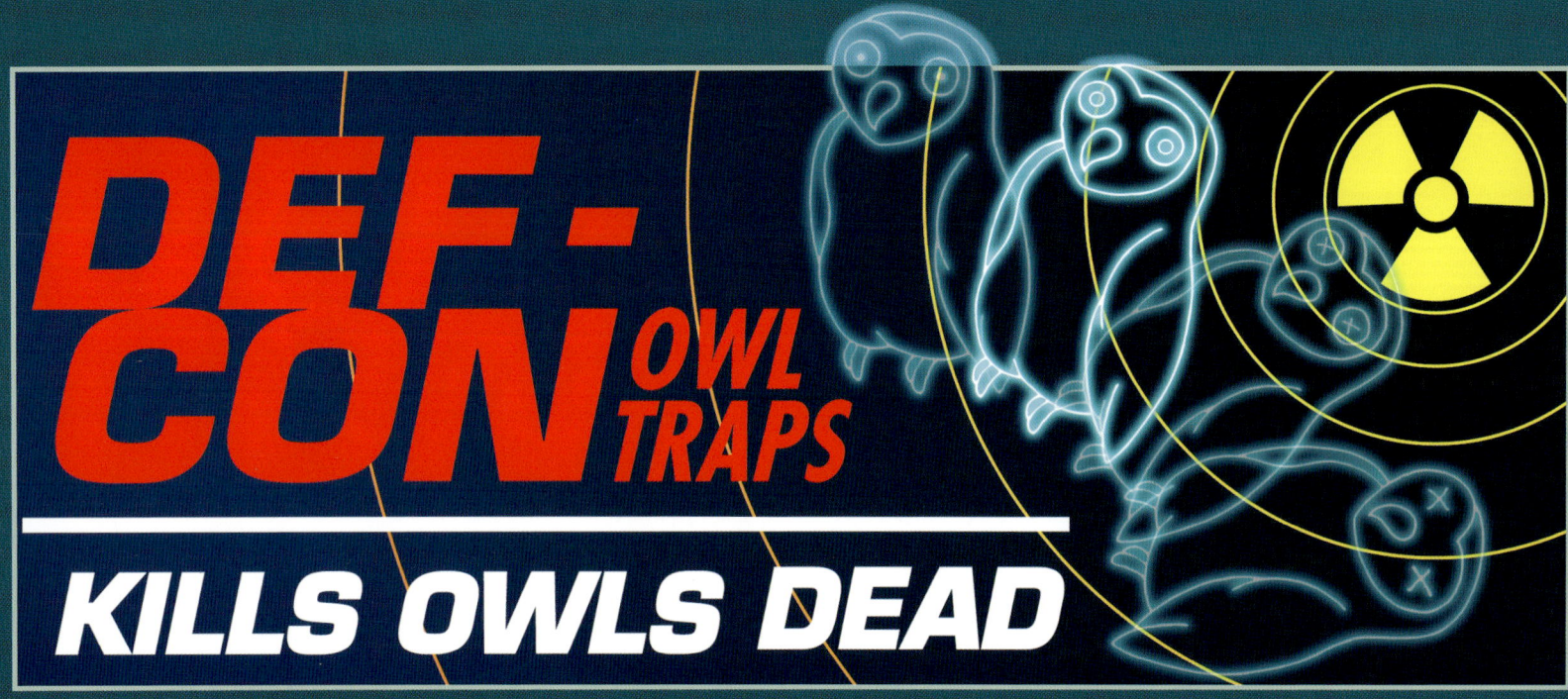

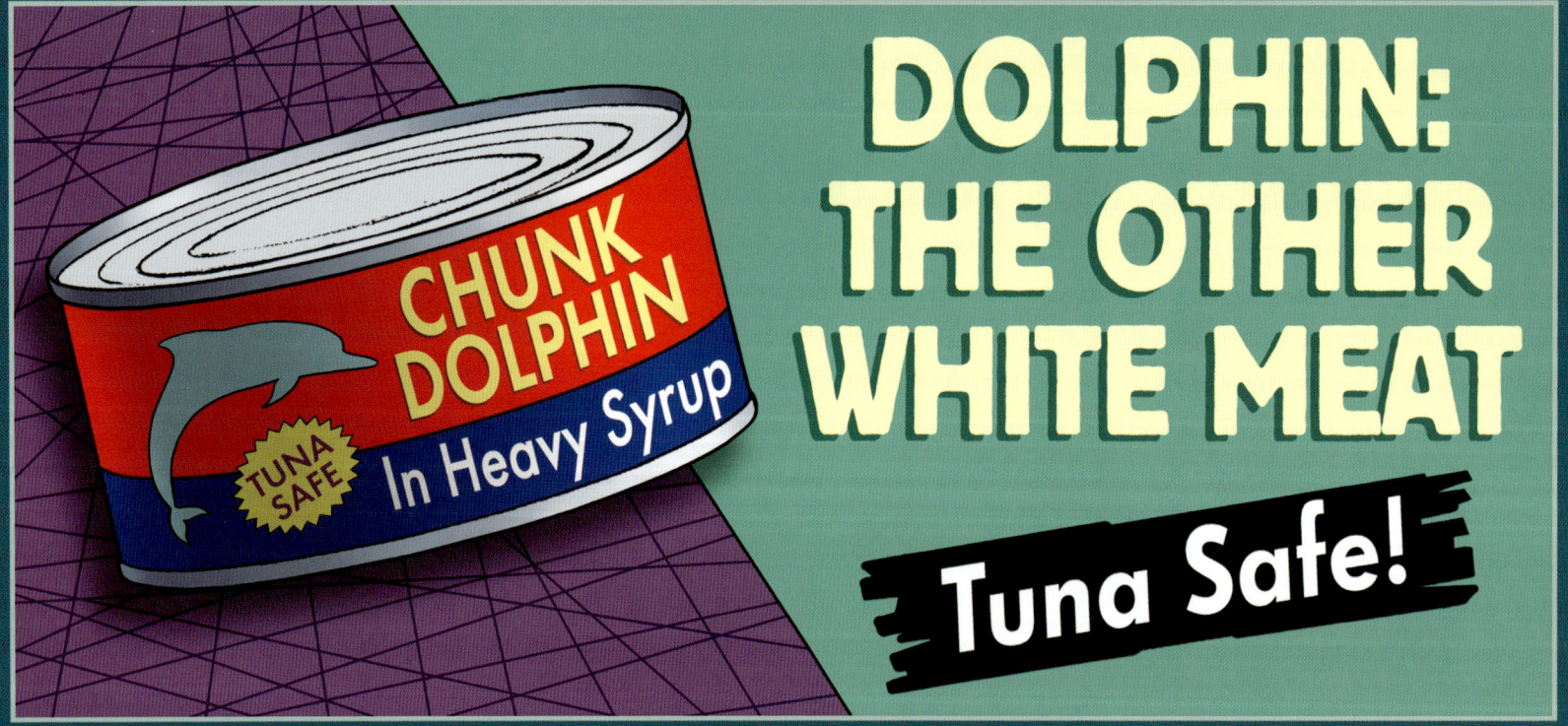

Def-Con Owl Traps and Chunk Dolphin billboards
by Serban Cristescu and Bill Morrison

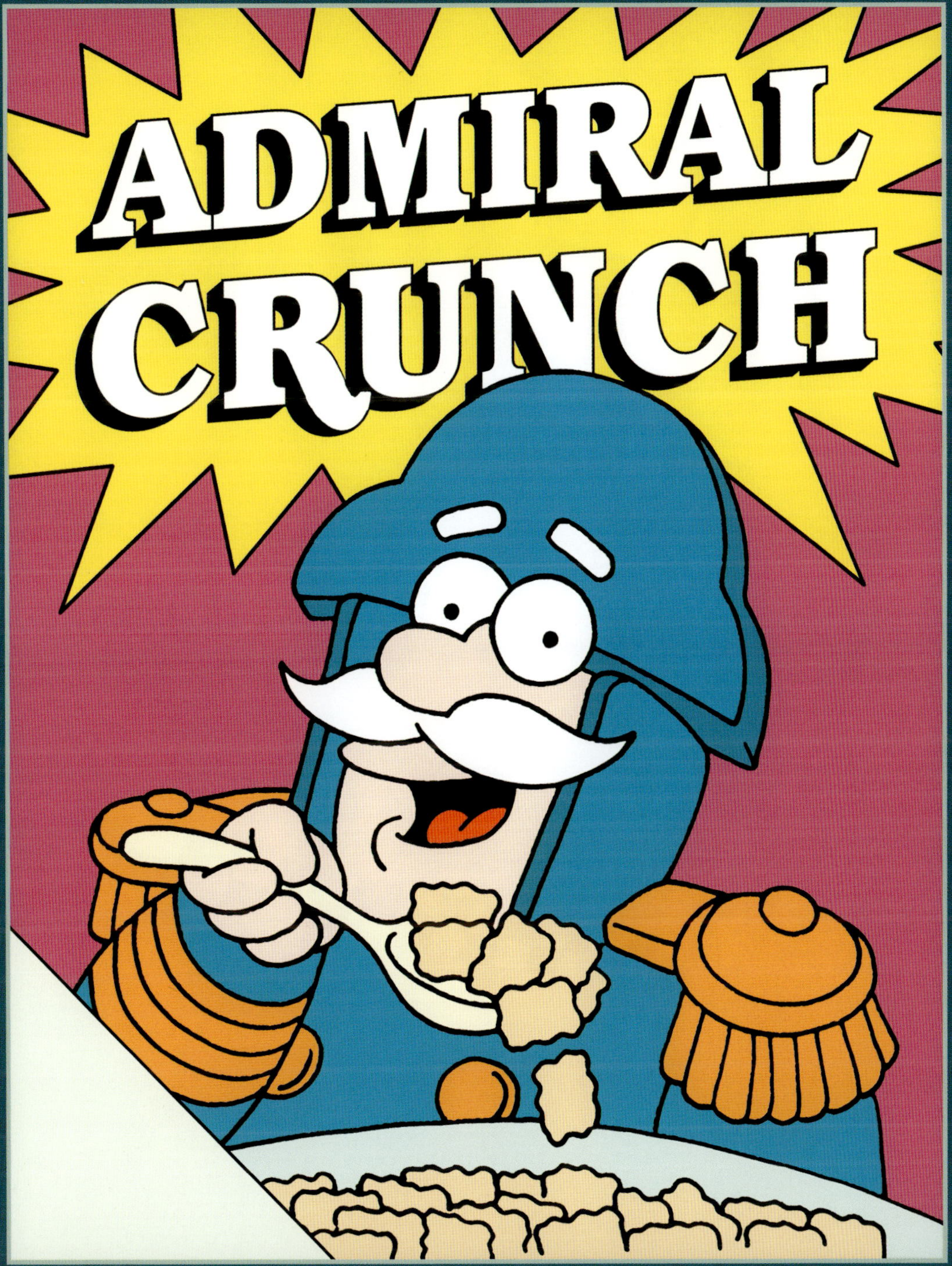

We're an artist-owned studio.
Obviously, we want to make a living and stay in business,
but we also want to reveal the craft through what we're doing.
That's why we work so well with Matt. He doesn't want
to live in a cold, digitally designed universe—he also
wants to see the hand in the design.
— Claudia Katz

Admiral Crunch and
Bachelor Chow product signage
by Serban Cristescu and Bill Morrison

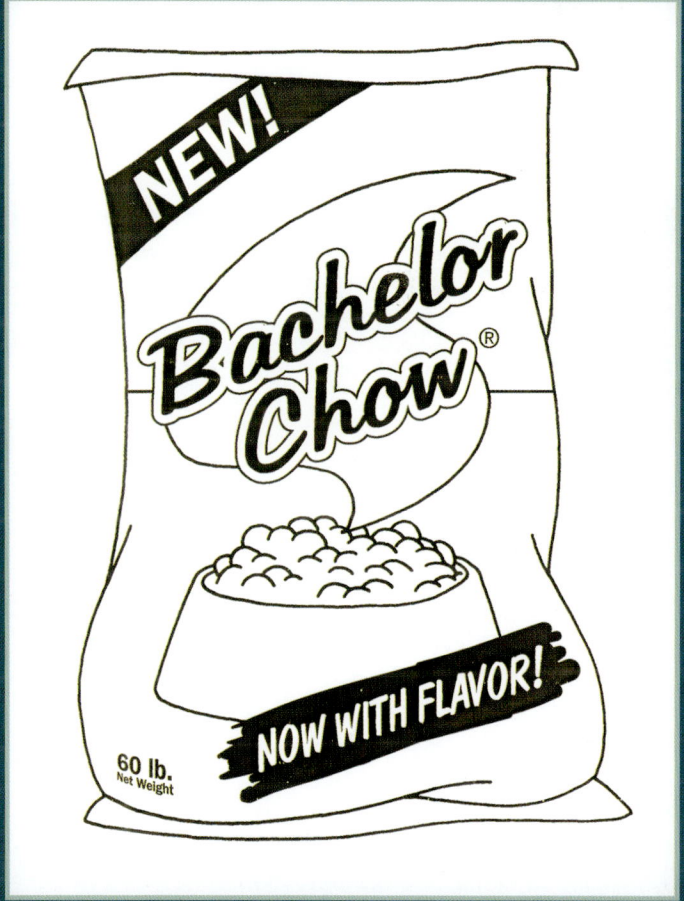

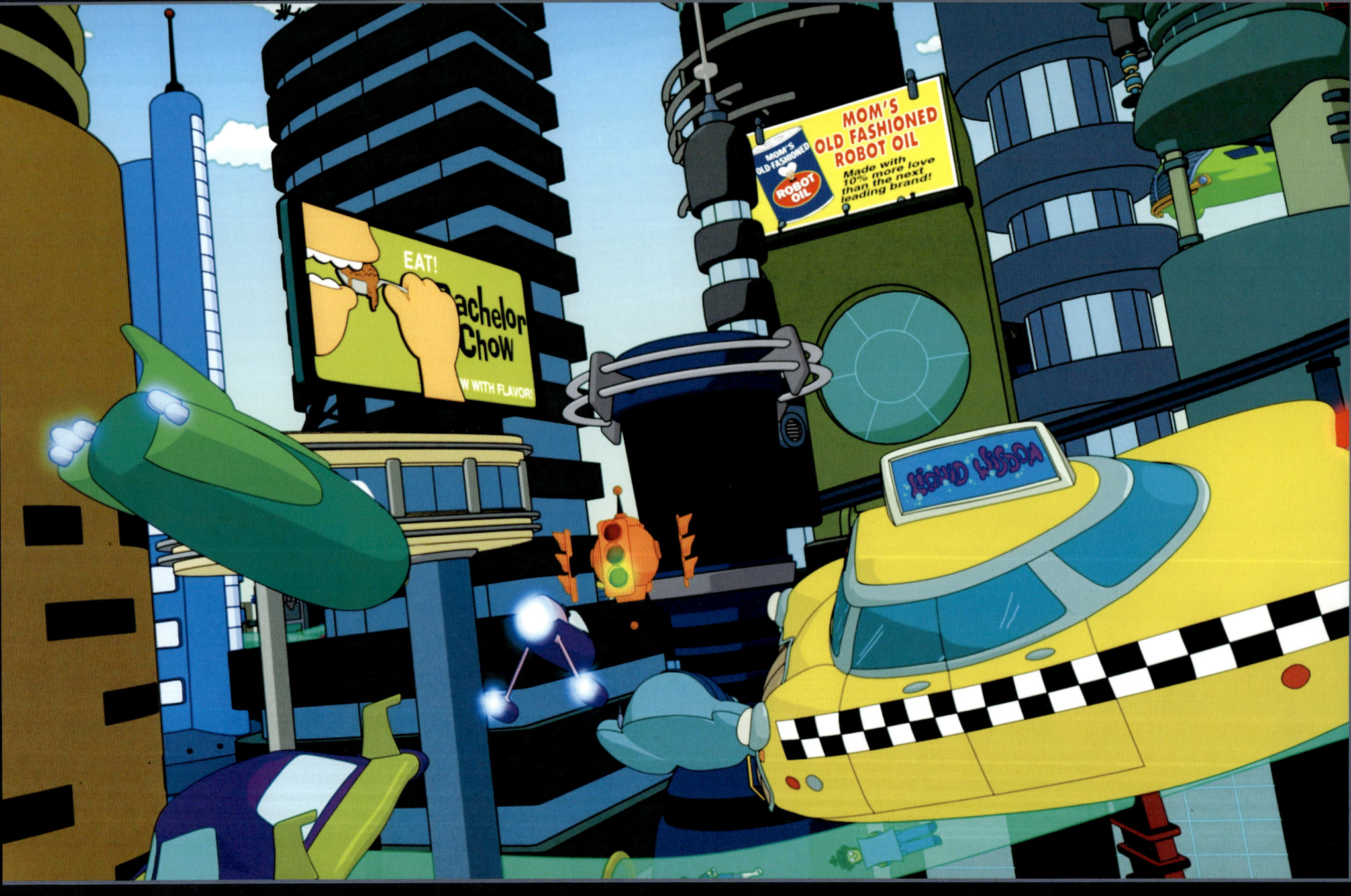

Bachelor Chow and Mom's Robot Oil product signage
by Serban Cristescu and Bill Morrison

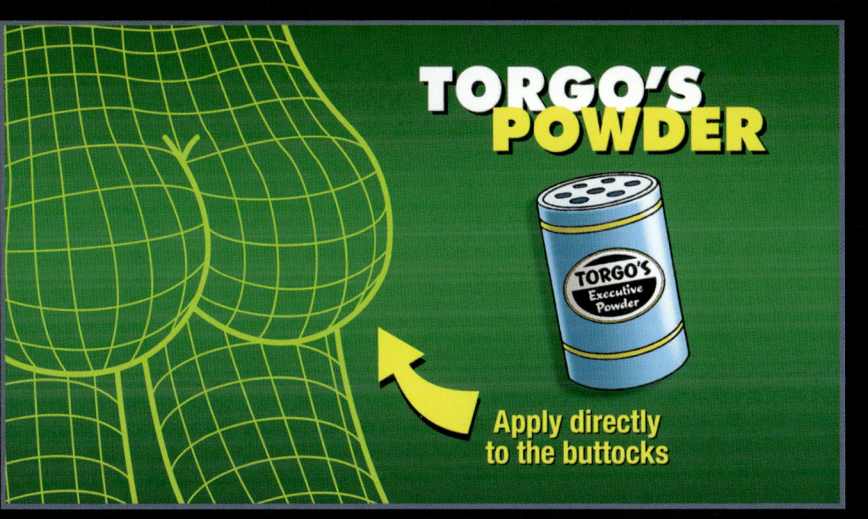

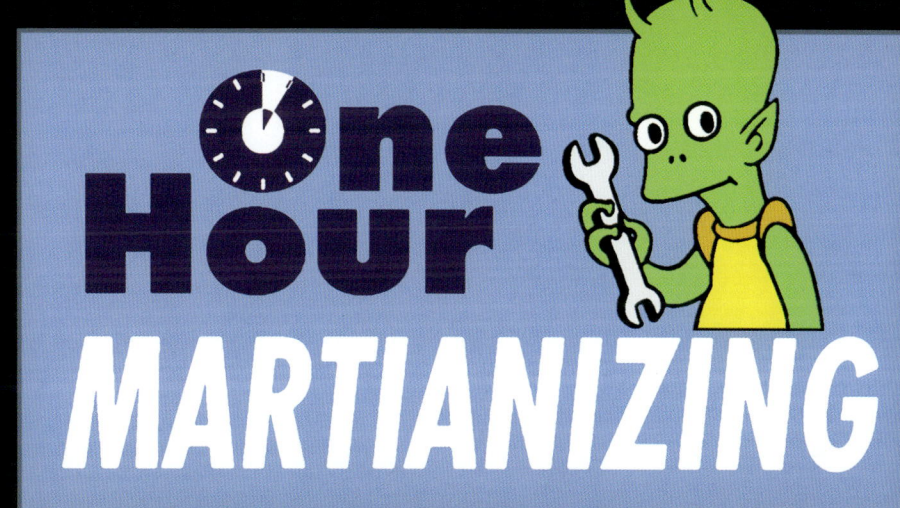

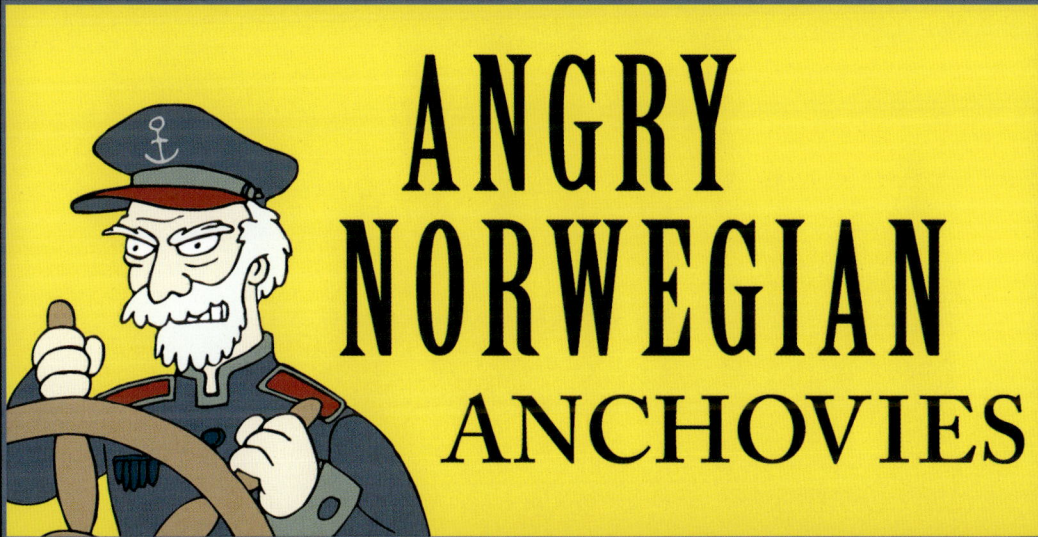

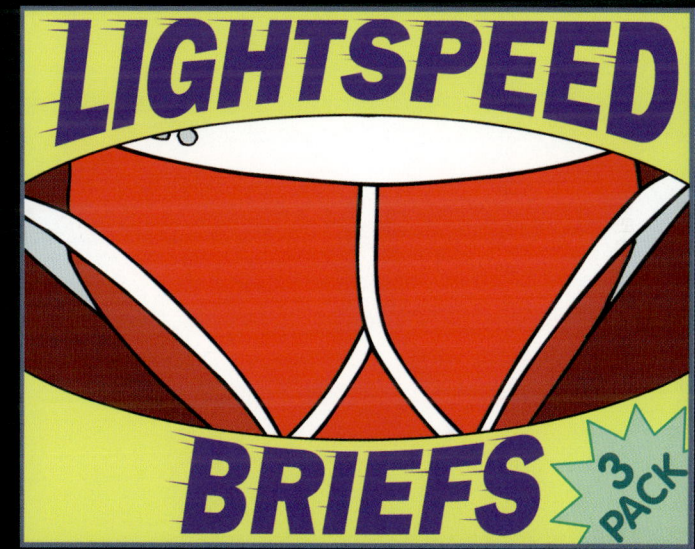

Torgo's Powder product signage
by Serban Cristescu

One Hour Martianizing, Angry Norwegian Anchovies, and Lightspeed Briefs product signage
by Serban Cristescu and Bill Morrison

One of the nice things about having more than one show competing for the Emmy is that no matter which won, I could still be bitter.

— Matt Groening

OPENING CHYRON JOKES

SEASONS 1–7

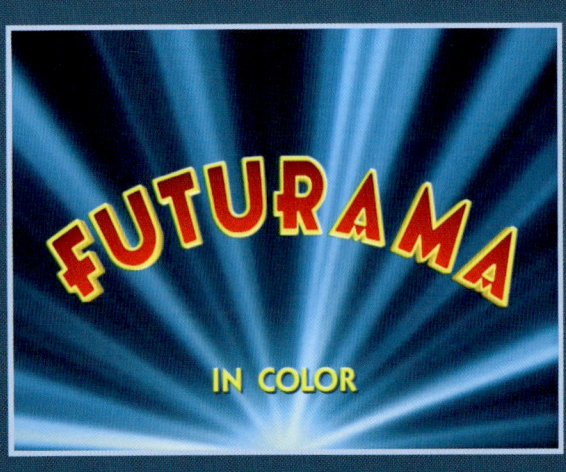

SEASON 1

1ACV01   In Color
1ACV02   In Hypno-Vision
1ACV03   As Seen On TV
1ACV04   Presented in Brain Control–Where Available
1ACV05   Featuring Gratuitous Alien Nudity
1ACV06   Loading . . .
1ACV07   Presented in DoubleVision (Where Drunk)
1ACV08   Mr. Bender's Wardrobe by Robotany 500
1ACV09   Condemned by the Space Pope
1ACV10   Filmed On Location
1ACV11   Transmitido en Martian en SAP
1ACV12   Proudly Made On Earth
1ACV13   LIVE From Omicron Persei 8

SEASON 2

2ACV01   Made from Meat by-Products
2ACV02   Not Y3K Compliant
2ACV03   From the Makers of *Futurama*
2ACV04   Based On a True Story
2ACV05   From the Network that Brought You "The Simpsons"
2ACV06   The Show that Watches Back
2ACV07   Not Based On the Novel by James Fenimore Cooper
2ACV08   Nominated for Three Glemmys
2ACV09   This Episode Has Been Modified to Fit Your Primitive Screen
2ACV10   Coming Soon to an Illegal DVD
2ACV11   As Foretold by Nostradamus
2ACV12   A Stern Warning of Things to Come
2ACV13   Simulcast on Crazy People's Fillings
2ACV14   Larva-Tested, Pupa-Approved
2ACV15   For External Use Only
2ACV16   Painstakingly Drawn Before a Live Audience
2ACV17   Touch Eyeballs to Screen for Cheap Laser Surgery
2ACV18   Smell-O-Vison Users Insert Nostril Tubes Now
2ACV19   Not a Substitute for Human Interaction

SEASON 3

3ACV01   Secreted by the Comedy Bee
3ACV02   If Not Entertaining, Write Your Congressman
3ACV03   This Episode Performed Entirely by Sock Puppets
3ACV04   Broadcast Simultaneously One Year In the Future
3ACV05   Now With Chucklelin
3ACV06   Torn From Tomorrow's Headlines
3ACV07   80% Entertainment by Volume
3ACV08   Deciphered From Crop Circles
3ACV09   Please Rise for the *Futurama* Theme Song
3ACV10   Krafted With Luv by Monsters
3ACV11   Bender's Humor by Microsoft Joke
3ACV12   Disclaimer: Any Resemblance to Actual Robots Would be Really Cool
3ACV13   Federal Law Prohibits Changing the Channel
3ACV14   For Proper Viewing, Take Red Pill Now
3ACV15   No Humans Were Probed in the Making of This Episode
3ACV16   Scratch Here to Reveal Prize
3ACV17   Psst . . . Big Party at Your House After the Show!
3ACV18   Hey, TiVo! Suggest *this*!
3ACV19   Fun for the Whole Family Except Grandma and Grandpa
3ACV20   Please Turn Off All Cell Phones and Tricorders
3ACV21   Love It or Shove It
3ACV22   If Accidentaly Watched, Induce Vomiting

SEASON 4

4ACV01   Bigfoot's Choice
4ACV02   It's Like "Hee-Haw" with Lasers
4ACV03   When You See the Robot, Drink!
4ACV04   Soon to Be a Major Religion
4ACV05   Or Is It?
4ACV06   Controlling You Through a Chip in Your Butt Since 1999
4ACV07   Not Affiliated with Futurama Brass Knuckle Co.
4ACV08   Known to Cause Insanity in Laboratory Mice
4ACV09   Now Interactive! Joystick Controls Fry's Left Ear
4ACV10   Dancing Space Potatoes? You Bet!
4ACV11   Where No Fan Has Gone Before
4ACV12   A By-Product of the TV Industry
4ACV13   Too Hot for Radio
4ACV14   You Can't Prove it Won't Happen
4ACV15   Beats a Hard Kick in the Face
4ACV16   Voted "BEST"
4ACV17   ⅄⌁⅂⌾⊙⍟⍭ ⌻⍟⍟ ⍭⅄⅄⅄⌿⌾⍟⍭, ⌻⍕⅂⍟⅂⅃⍭⍏⍭ ⍟⍗⍘⌾⍕⍟⅃ ⅄⍟⍗⍒! [decorative alien script]
4ACV18   See You on Some Other Channel

SEASON 5

5ACV01   It Just Won't Stay Dead!
5ACV02   Watch, Rinse, Repeat
5ACV03   Apply Directly to the Foreclaw

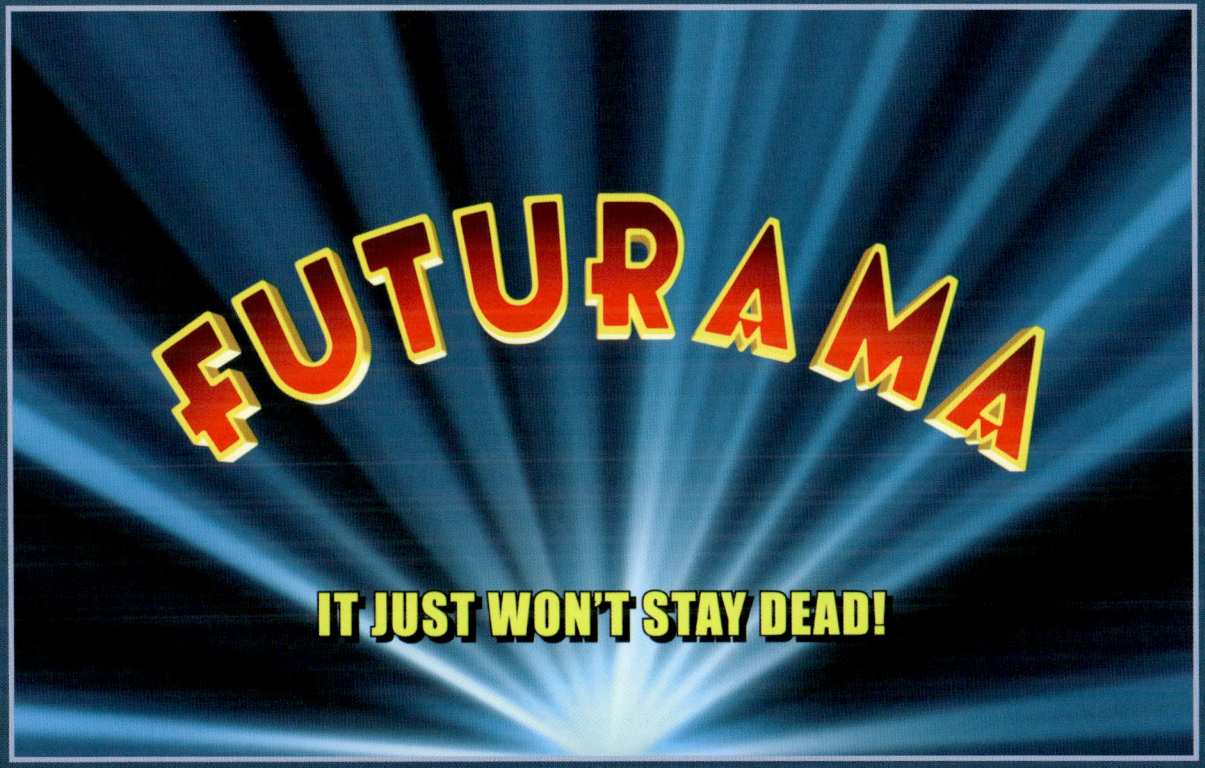

FUTURAMA

IT JUST WON'T STAY DEAD!

ALL THOSE *FUTURAMA* EPISODES

SEASONS 1–7

SEASON 1
Network: The Fox Broadcasting Company

1. (1ACV01) SPACE PILOT 3000 (March 28, 1999) Written by David X. Cohen and Matt Groening; directed by Rich Moore and Gregg Vanzo

2. (1ACV02) THE SERIES HAS LANDED (April 4, 1999) Written by Ken Keeler; directed by Peter Avanzino

3. (1ACV03) I, ROOMMATE (April 6, 1999) Written by Eric Horsted; directed by Bret Haaland

4. (1ACV04) LOVE'S LABOURS LOST IN SPACE (April 13, 1999) Written by Brian Kelley; directed by Brian Shelley

5. (1ACV05) FEAR OF A BOT PLANET (April 20, 1999) Written by Evan Gore and Heather Lombard; directed by Peter Avanzino and Carlos Baeza

6. (1ACV06) A FISHFUL OF DOLLARS (April 27, 1999) Written by Patric M. Verrone; directed by Ron Hughart and Gregg Vanzo

7. (1ACV07) MY THREE SUNS (May 4, 1999) Written by J. Stewart Burns; directed by Jeffrey Lynch and Kevin O'Brien

8. (1ACV08) A BIG PIECE OF GARBAGE (May 11, 1999) Written by Lewis Morton; directed by Susan Dietter

9. (1ACV09) HELL IS OTHER ROBOTS (May 18, 1999) Written by Eric Kaplan; directed by Rich Moore

10. (1ACV10) A FLIGHT TO REMEMBER (September 26, 1999) Written by Eric Horsted; directed by Peter Avanzino

11. (1ACV11) MARS UNIVERSITY (October 3, 1999) Written by J. Stewart Burns; directed by Bret Haaland

12. (1ACV12) WHEN ALIENS ATTACK (November 7, 1999) Written by Ken Keeler; directed by Brian Sheesley

13. (1ACV13) FRY AND THE SLURM FACTORY (November 14, 1999) Written by Lewis Morton; directed by Ron Hughart

SEASON 2
Network: The Fox Broadcasting Company

14. (2ACV01) I SECOND THAT EMOTION (November 21, 1999) Written by Patric M. Verrone; directed by Mark Ervin

15. (2ACV02) BRANNIGAN, BEGIN AGAIN (November 28, 1999) Written by Lewis Morton; directed by Jeffrey Lynch

16. (2ACV03) A HEAD IN THE POLLS (December 12, 1999) Written by J. Stewart Burns; directed by Bret Haaland

17. (2ACV04) XMAS STORY (December 19, 1999) Written by David X. Cohen; directed by Peter Avanzino

18. (2ACV05) WHY MUST I BE A CRUSTACEAN IN LOVE? (February 6, 2000) Written by Eric Kaplan; directed by Brian Sheesley

19. (2ACV06) THE LESSER OF TWO EVILS (February 20, 2000) Written by Eric Horsted; directed by Chris Sauve

20. (2ACV07) PUT YOUR HEAD ON MY SHOULDERS (February 13, 2000) Written by Ken Keeler; directed by Chris Louden

21. (2ACV08) RAGING BENDER (February 27, 2000) Written by Lewis Morton; directed by Ron Hughart

22. (2ACV09) A BICYCLOPS BUILT FOR TWO (March 19, 2000) Written by Eric Kaplan; directed by Susan Dietter

23. (2ACV10) A CLONE OF MY OWN (April 9, 2000) Written by Patric M. Verrone; directed by Rich Moore

24. (2ACV11) HOW HERMES REQUISITIONED HIS GROOVE BACK (April 2, 2000) Written by Bill Odenkirk; directed by Mark Ervin

25. (2ACV12) THE DEEP SOUTH (April 16, 2000) Written by J. Stewart Burns; directed by Bret Haaland

26. (2ACV13) BENDER GETS MADE (April 30, 2000) Written by Eric Horsted; directed by Peter Avanzino

27. (2ACV14) MOTHER'S DAY (May 14, 2000) Written by Lewis Morton; directed by Brian Sheesley

28. (2ACV15) THE PROBLEM WITH POPPLERS (May 7, 2000) Story by Darin Henry and Patric M. Verrone; teleplay by Patric M. Verrone; directed by Chris Sauve and Gregg Vanzo

29. (2ACV16) ANTHOLOGY OF INTEREST I (May 21, 2000) Written by Eric Rogers, Ken Keeler, and David X. Cohen; directed by Chris Louden and Rich Moore

30. (2ACV17) WAR IS THE H-WORD (November 26, 2000) Written by Eric Horsted; directed by Ron Hughart

31. (2ACV18) THE HONKING (November 5, 2000) Written by Ken Keeler; directed by Susie Dietter

32. (2ACV19) THE CRYONIC WOMAN (December 3, 2000) Written by J. Stewart Burns; directed by Mark Ervin

SEASON 3
Network: The Fox Broadcasting Company

33. (3ACV01) AMAZON WOMEN IN THE MOOD (February 4, 2001) Written by Lewis Morton; directed by Brian Sheesley

34. (3ACV02) PARASITES LOST (January 21, 2001) Written by Eric Kaplan; directed by Peter Avanzino

35. (3ACV03) A TALE OF TWO SANTAS (December 23, 2001) Written by Bill Odenkirk; directed by Ron Hughart

36. (3ACV04) THE LUCK OF THE FRYRISH (March 11, 2001) Written by Ron Weiner; directed by Chris Louden

37. (3ACV05) THE BIRDBOT OF ICE-CATRAZ (March 4, 2001) Written by Dan Vebber; directed by James Purdum

38. (3ACV06) BENDLESS LOVE (February 11, 2001) Written by Eric Horsted; directed by Swinton O. Scott III

39. (3ACV07) THE DAY THE EARTH STOOD STUPID (February 18, 2001) Story by Jeff Westbrook and David X. Cohen; teleplay by Jeff Westbrook; directed by Mark Ervin

40. (3ACV08) THAT'S LOBSTERTAINMENT! (February 25, 2001) Written by Patric M. Verrone; directed by Bret Haaland

41. (3ACV09) THE CYBER HOUSE RULES (April 1, 2001) Written by Lewis Morton; directed by Susie Dietter

42. (3ACV10) WHERE THE BUGGALO ROAM (March 3, 2002) Written by J. Stewart Burns; directed by Patty Shinagawa

43. (3ACV11) INSANE IN THE MAINFRAME (April 8, 2001)

Written by Bill Odenkirk; directed by Peter Avanzino

44. (3ACV12) THE ROUTE OF ALL EVIL (December 8, 2002) Written by Dan Vebber; directed by Brian Sheesley

45. (3ACV13) BENDIN' IN THE WIND (April 22, 2001) Written by Eric Horsted; directed by Ron Hughart

46. (3ACV14) TIME KEEPS ON SLIPPIN' (May 6, 2001) Written by Ken Keeler; directed by Chris Louden

47. (3ACV15) I DATED A ROBOT (May 13, 2001) Written by Eric Kaplan; directed by James Purdum

48. (3ACV16) A LEELA OF HER OWN (April 7, 2002) Written by Patric M. Verrone; directed by Swinton O. Scott III

49. (3ACV17) A PHARAOH TO REMEMBER (March 10, 2002) Written by Ron Weiner; directed by Mark Ervin

50. (3ACV18) ANTHOLOGY OF INTEREST II (January 6, 2002) Written by Lewis Morton, David X. Cohen, Jason Gorbett, and Scott Kirby; directed by Bret Haaland

51. (3ACV19) ROSWELL THAT ENDS WELL (December 9, 2001) Written by J. Stewart Burns; directed by Rich Moore

52. (3ACV20) GODFELLAS (March 17, 2002) Written by Ken Keeler; directed by Susie Dietter

53. (3ACV21) FUTURE STOCK (March 31, 2002) Written by Aaron Ehasz; directed by Brian Sheesley

54. (3ACV22) THE 30% IRON CHEF (April 14, 2002) Written by Jeff Westbrook; directed by Ron Hughart

SEASON 4
Network: The Fox Broadcasting Company

55. (4ACV01) KIF GETS KNOCKED UP A NOTCH (January 12, 2003) Written by Bill Odenkirk; directed by Wes Archer

56. (4ACV02) LEELA'S HOMEWORLD (February 17, 2002) Written by Kristin Gore; directed by Mark Ervin

57. (4ACV03) LOVE AND ROCKET (February 10, 2002) Written by Dan Vebber; directed by Brian Sheesley

58. (4ACV04) LESS THAN HERO (March 2, 2003) Written by Ron Weiner; directed by Susie Dietter

59. (4ACV05) A TASTE OF FREEDOM (December 22, 2002) Written by Eric Horsted; directed by James Purdum

60. (4ACV06) BENDER SHOULD NOT BE ALLOWED ON TV (August 3, 2003) Written by Lewis Morton; directed by Ron Hughart

61. (4ACV07) JURASSIC BARK (November 17, 2002) Written by Eric Kaplan; directed by Swinton O. Scott III

62. (4ACV08) CRIMES OF THE HOT (November 10, 2002) Written by Aaron Ehasz; directed by Peter Avanzino

63. (4ACV09) TEENAGE MUTANT LEELA'S HURDLES (March 30, 2003) Written by Jeff Westbrook; directed by Bret Haaland

64. (4ACV10) THE WHY OF FRY (April 6, 2003) Written by David X. Cohen; directed by Wes Archer

65. (4ACV11) WHERE NO FAN HAS GONE BEFORE (April 21, 2002) Written by David A. Goodman; directed by Patty Shinagawa

66. (4ACV12) THE STING
(June 1, 2003)
Written by Patric M. Verrone; directed by Brian Sheesley

67. (4ACV13) BEND HER
(July 20, 2003)
Written by Michael Rowe; directed by James Purdum

68. (4ACV14) OBSOLETELY FABULOUS (July 27, 2003)
Written by Dan Vebber; directed by Dwayne Carey-Hill

69. (4ACV15) THE FARNSWORTH PARABOX (June 8, 2003)
Written by Bill Odenkirk; directed by Ron Hughart

70. (4ACV16) THREE HUNDRED BIG BOYS (June 15, 2003)
Written by Eric Kaplan; directed by Swinton O. Scott III

71. (4ACV17) SPANISH FRY
(July 13, 2003)
Written by Ron Weiner; directed by Peter Avanzino

72. (4ACV18) THE DEVIL'S HAND ARE IDLE PLAYTHINGS (August 10, 2003)
Written by Ken Keeler; directed by Bret Haaland

SEASON 5
Network: Comedy Central

73. (5ACV01) BENDER'S BIG SCORE: PART 1 (March 23, 2008)
Story by Ken Keeler and David X. Cohen; teleplay by Ken Keeler; directed by Dwayne Carey-Hill

74. (5ACV02) BENDER'S BIG SCORE: PART 2 (March 23, 2008)
Story by Ken Keeler and David X. Cohen; teleplay by Ken Keeler; directed by Dwayne Carey-Hill

75. (5ACV03) BENDER'S BIG SCORE: PART 3 (March 23, 2008)
Story by Ken Keeler and David X. Cohen; teleplay by Ken Keeler; directed by Dwayne Carey-Hill

76. (5ACV04) BENDER'S BIG SCORE: PART 4 (March 23, 2008)
Story by Ken Keeler and David X. Cohen; teleplay by Ken Keeler; directed by Dwayne Carey-Hill

77. (5ACV05) THE BEAST WITH A BILLION BACKS: PART 1 (October 19, 2008)
Story by Eric Kaplan and David X. Cohen; teleplay by Eric Kaplan; directed by Peter Avanzino

78. (5ACV06) THE BEAST WITH A BILLION BACKS: PART 2 (October 19, 2008)
Story by Eric Kaplan and David X. Cohen; teleplay by Eric Kaplan; directed by Peter Avanzino

79. (5ACV07) THE BEAST WITH A BILLION BACKS: PART 3 (October 19, 200)
Story by Eric Kaplan and David X. Cohen; teleplay by Eric Kaplan; directed by Peter Avanzino

80. (5ACV08) THE BEAST WITH A BILLION BACKS: PART 4 (October 19, 2008)
Story by Eric Kaplan and David X. Cohen; teleplay by Eric Kaplan; directed by Peter Avanzino

81. (5ACV09) BENDER'S GAME: PART 1 (April 26, 2009)
Story by Eric Horsted and David X. Cohen; teleplay by Eric Horsted; directed by Dwayne Carey-Hill

82. (5ACV10) BENDER'S GAME: PART 2 (April 26, 2009)
Story by Eric Horsted and David X. Cohen; teleplay by Eric Horsted; directed by Dwayne Carey-Hill

83. (5ACV11) BENDER'S GAME: PART 3 (April 26, 2009)
Story by Eric Horsted and David X. Cohen; teleplay by Eric Kaplan and Michael Rowe; directed by Dwayne Carey-Hill

84. (5ACV12) BENDER'S GAME: PART 4 (April 26, 2009)
Story by Eric Horsted and David X. Cohen; teleplay by David X. Cohen and Patric M. Verrone; directed by Dwayne Carey-Hill

85. (5ACV13) INTO THE WILD GREEN YONDER: PART 1 (August 30, 2009)
Story by Ken Keeler and David X. Cohen; teleplay by Ken Keeler; directed by Peter Avanzino

86. (5ACV14) INTO THE WILD GREEN YONDER: PART 2 (August 30, 2009)
Written by Ken Keeler; directed by Peter Avanzino

87. (5ACV15) INTO THE WILD GREEN YONDER: PART 3 (August 30, 2009)
Written by Ken Keeler; directed by Peter Avanzino

88. (5ACV16) INTO THE WILD GREEN YONDER: PART 4 (August 30, 2009)
Story by Ken Keeler and David X. Cohen; teleplay by Ken Keeler; directed by Peter Avanzino

SEASON 6
Network: Comedy Central

89. (6ACV01) REBIRTH
(June 24, 2010)
Story by David X. Cohen and Matt Groening; teleplay by David X. Cohen; directed by Frank Marino

90. (6ACV02) IN-A-GADDA-DA-LEELA (June 24, 2010)
Story by Carolyn Premish and Matt Groening; teleplay by Carolyn Premish; directed by Dwayne Carey-Hill

91. (6ACV03) ATTACK OF THE KILLER APP (July 1, 2010)
Written by Patric M. Verrone; directed by Stephen Sandoval

92. (6ACV04) PROPOSITION INFINITY (July 8, 2010)
Written by Michael Rowe; directed by Crystal Chesney-Thompson

93. (6ACV05) THE DUH-VINCI CODE (July 15, 2010)
Written by Maiya Williams; directed by Raymie Muzquiz

94. (6ACV06) LETHAL INSPECTION (July 22, 2010)
Written by Eric Horsted; directed by Ray Claffey

95. (6ACV07) THE LATE PHILIP J. FRY (July 29, 2010)
Written by Lewis Morton; directed by Peter Avanzino

96. (6ACV08) THAT DARN KATZ! (August 5, 2010)
Written by Josh Weinstein; directed by Frank Marino

97. (6ACV09) A CLOCKWORK ORIGIN (August 12, 2010)
Written by Dan Vebber; directed by Dwayne Carey-Hill

98. (6ACV10) THE PRISONER OF BENDA (August 19, 2010)
Written by Ken Keeler; directed by Stephen Sandoval

99. (6ACV11) LRRRECONCILABLE NDNDIFFERENCES
(August 26, 2010)
Written by Patric M. Verrone; directed by Crystal Chesney-Thompson

100. (6ACV12) THE MUTANTS ARE REVOLTING (September 2, 2010)
Written by Eric Horsted; directed by Raymie Muzquiz

101. (6ACV13) THE FUTURAMA HOLIDAY SPECTACULAR (November 21, 2010)
Written by Michael Rowe; directed by Ray Claffey

102. (6ACV14) THE SILENCE OF THE CLAMPS (July 14, 2011)
Written by Eric Rogers; directed by Frank Marino

103. (6ACV15) MÖBIUS DICK (August 4, 2011)
Written by Dan Vebber; directed by Dwayne Carey-Hill

104. (6ACV16) LAW AND ORACLE (July 7, 2011)
Written by Josh Weinstein; directed by Stephen Sandoval

105. (6ACV17) BENDERAMA
(June 23, 2011)
Written by Aaron Ehasz; directed by Crystal Chesney-Thompson

106. (6ACV18) THE TIP OF THE ZOIDBERG (August 18, 2011)
Written by Ken Keeler; directed by Raymie Muzquiz

107. (6ACV19) GHOST IN THE MACHINES (June 30, 2011)
Written by Patric M. Verrone; directed by Ray Claffey

108. (6ACV20) NEUTOPIA
(June 23, 2011)
Written by J. Stewart Burns; directed by Edmund Fong

109. (6ACV21) YO LEELA LEELA (July 21, 2011)
Written by Eric Horsted; directed by Frank Marino

110. (6ACV22) FRY AM THE EGG MAN (August 11, 2011)
Written by Michael Rowe; directed by Dwayne Carey-Hill

111. (6ACV23) ALL THE PRESIDENTS' HEADS (July 28, 2011)
Written by Josh Weinstein; directed by Stephen Sandoval

112. (6ACV24) COLD WARRIORS (August 25, 2011)
Written by Dan Vebber; directed by Crystal Chesney-Thompson

113. (6ACV25) OVERCLOCKWISE (September 1, 2011)
Written by Ken Keeler; directed by Raymie Muzquiz

114. (6ACV26) REINCARNATION (September 8, 2011)
Written by Aaron Ehasz; directed by Peter Avanzino

SEASON 7
Network: Comedy Central

115. (7ACV01) THE BOTS AND THE BEES (June 20, 2012)
Written by Eric Horsted; directed by Stephen Sandoval

116. (7ACV02) A FAREWELL TO ARMS (June 20, 2012)
Written by Josh Weinstein; directed by Raymie Muzquiz

117. (7ACV03) DECISION 3012 (June 27, 2012)
Written by Patric M. Verrone; directed by Dwayne Carey-Hill

118. (7ACV04) THE THIEF OF BAGHEAD (July 4, 2012)
Written by Dan Vebber; directed by Edmund Fong

119. (7ACV05) ZAPP DINGBAT (July 11, 2012)
Written by Eric Rogers; directed by Frank Marino

120. (7ACV06) THE BUTTERJUNK EFFECT (July 18, 2012)
Written by Michael Rowe; directed by Crystal Chesney-Thompson

121. (7ACV07) THE SIX MILLION DOLLAR MON (July 25, 2012)
Written by Ken Keeler; directed by Peter Avanzino

122. (7ACV08) FUN ON A BUN (August 1, 2012)
Written by Dan Vebber; directed by Stephen Sandoval

123. (7ACV09) FREE WILL HUNTING (August 8, 2012)
Written by David X. Cohen; directed by Raymie Muzquiz

124. (7ACV10) NEAR-DEATH WISH (August 15, 2012)
Written by Eric Horsted; directed by Lance Kramer

125. (7ACV11) 31ST CENTURY FOX (August 29, 2012)
Written by Patric M. Verrone; directed by Edmund Fong

126. (7ACV12) VIVA MARS VEGAS (August 22, 2012)
Written by Josh Weinstein; directed by Frank Marino

127. (7ACV13) NATURAMA (August 29, 2012)
Written by Eric Rogers, Michael Saikin, Neil Mukhopadhyay; directed by Crystal Chesney-Thompson

128. (7ACV14) FORTY PERCENT LEADBELLY (July 3, 2013)
Written by Ken Keeler; directed by Stephen Sandoval

129. (7ACV15) 2-D BLACKTOP (June 19, 2013)
Written by Michael Rowe; directed by Raymie Muzquiz

130. (7ACV16) T.: THE TERRESTRIAL (June 26, 2013)
Written by Josh Weinstein; directed by Lance Kramer

131. (7ACV17) FRY AND LEELA'S BIG FLING (June 19, 2013)
Written by Eric Rogers; directed by Edmund Fong

132. (7ACV18) THE INHUMAN TORCH (July 10, 2013)
Written by Dan Vebber; directed by Frank Marino

133. (7ACV19) SATURDAY MORNING FUN PIT (July 17, 2013)
Written by Patric M. Verrone; directed by Crystal Chesney-Thompson

134. (7ACV20) CALCULON 2.0 (July 24, 2013)
Written by Lewis Morton; directed by Stephen Sandoval

135. (7ACV21) ASSIE COME HOME (July 31, 2013)
Written by Maiya Williams; directed by Raymie Muzquiz

136. (7ACV22) LEELA AND THE GENESTALK (August 7, 2013)
Written by Eric Horsted; directed by Lance Kramer

137. (7ACV23) GAME OF TONES (August 14, 2013)
Written by Michael Rowe; directed by Edmund Fong

138. (7ACV24) MURDER ON THE PLANET EXPRESS (August 21, 2013)
Written by Lewis Morton; directed by Frank Marino

139. (7ACV25) STENCH AND STENCHIBILITY (August 28, 2013)
Written by Eric Horsted; directed by Crystal Chesney-Thompson

140. (7ACV26) MEANWHILE (September 4, 2013)
Written by Ken Keeler; directed by Peter Avanzino

After a ten-year hiatus, *Futurama* returned for Season 8, premiering on Hulu on July 24, 2023, for twenty new episodes. Given timing and production schedules, this book only covers the first seven seasons and 140 episodes.

SEASONS 1–7

Anthony Agrusa—Assistant Director, Character Layout
Julius Aguimatang—Character Layout
Iris Alfaro—Production
Alison Antonowicz—Production
John Aoshima—Assistant Director, Character Layout
Wesley Archer—Director
Stephanie Arnett—Assistant Director, Character Layout
Debora Arroyo—Design Clean Up, Production
Marcos Asprec—Character Layout
David D. Au—Assistant Director, Storyboard, Character Layout
Abe Audish—Storyboard
Peter Avanzino—Supervising Director, Director, Storyboard
Perfecto Badillo—Character Layout
Carlos Baeza—Director
Orlando Baeza—Storyboard
Erin Balderson—Production
Anne Balser—Color Key
Aldin Baroza—Assistant Director
Don Barrozo—Lip Assignment
David Bastian—Assistant Director, Timing
Carlton Batten—Timing
Matthias Bauer—Storyboard
Elise Belknap—Associate Producer
Rahul Bhushan—Digital Background Painter
Elliot Blake—Production Coordinator
William Bon—Background Layout
David Bonanno—Storyboard Revisions
Daniel Bond—Character Layout, Design Clean Up
Charlie Botton —Digital Camera & Composite
Bob Bowen—Storyboard
Erin Bozon—Character Layout
Jefferson Brassfield—Production
Tim Brock—Color Key
Jenn Brown—Production Coordinator
Peter Browngardt—Character Layout
Tricia Buchanan-Benson—Storyboard Revisions
Scott Buckley—Background Layout
Galina Budkin—Design Clean Up
John Burns—Production
Mark Bykov—Timing

Gabriel Calderon—Digital Camera & Composite
Albert Calleros—Storyboard
Rufino Camacho II—Storyboard Revisions, Character Layout
Acacia Caputo—Timing, Lip Assignment
Dwayne Carey-Hill—Director, Assistant Director, Character Design, Character Layout, Digital Camera & Composite
Patricia Carey-Hill—Production
Sarah Carpenter—Production
Anna Chambers—Character Design
Alex Chao—Digital Background Painter
Greg Checketts—Character Layout
Nick Cherry—3D Artist
Crystal Chesney-Thompson—Director, Character Layout
Nam Suk Cho—Background & Prop Design, Background Layout
Stephen Chu—Production
Chris Chua—Character Layout
David Chung—Background & Prop Design
Ray Claffey—Director, Assistant Director, Storyboard, Character Layout, Timing
Aaron Clark—Background Layout
Rodney Clouden—Assistant Director, Storyboard
Eddie Condes—Digital Camera & Composite
Pamela Cooke—Assistant Director, Character Layout
Chad E. Cooper—Background & Prop Design
Phil Cummings—Timing
Dave Cunningham—Storyboard
Ben Dai—Character Layout
Patrick T. Dailey—Storyboard Revisions, Character Layout
Ruth Daly—Character Layout
Carolina Datuin—Character Layout, Background Layout
Angelo de la Cruz—3D Artist
Jon Delaurie—Digital Camera & Composite
Stephen DeStefano—Storyboard
Erben Detablan—Background Layout
Susie Dietter—Director, Character Layout
Orlando Distor—Character Layout
Ryan Donoghue—Character Layout, Background Layout

Linda Dorn—Character Layout
Michael Dowell—Character Layout
Edgar Duncan Jr.—Background & Prop Design
Eric Dunn—Background Layout
Arthur Ebuen—Character Layout
Tim Eldred—Storyboard
Yacine Elghorri—Character Design
Mark Ervin—Director
Alen Esmaelian—Background & Prop Design
Jess Espanola—Assistant Director, Character Layout
Jim Feeley—Character Design
Karl Fisher—Timing
Edmund Fong—Assistant Director, Storyboard
Steve Fonti—Storyboard
Brad Forbush—Character Layout
Susan Zytka Forbush—Character Layout
Bryan Francis—Character Layout
Jamie Frye—Digital Background Painter
Victoria Fye—Production
Bradley Gake—Background Layout
Doug Gallery—Storyboard, Timing
Heidi Garafolo—Character Layout
Noé Garcia—FX Animation
Philip Garcia—Character Layout
Tony Garcia—Production Manager
Stacy Garnett—Production
Mike Giles—Digital Camera & Composite
Patrick Gleeson—Storyboard, Timing
James H. Goldin—Accounting
Peter Gomez—Character Design, Background & Prop Design, Character Layout
Roger Gonzales—Character Layout
Chris Graham—Storyboard
Stephen Gressak—3D Artist
Orlando Gumatay—Character Layout
Mike Gurau—Production
Bret Haaland—Supervising Director, Director, Character Design
Sunil Hall—Character Layout
Matt Hamilton—Digital Camera & Composite, Production
Chris Harmon—Storyboard
Samantha Harrison—Color Supervisor
Lee Harting—Lip Assignment & Track Reading

Brian Hatfield—Character Layout
Colin Heck—Storyboard, Character Layout
Keun Hicks—Digital Camera & Composite
Peter Hixson—Timing
Dave Hogan—Systems Administrative Assistant
Kent Holaday—Lip Assignment
Jon Hooper—Assistant Director, Storyboard, Character Layout, Digital Camera & Composite
Yvonne Annette Huckell—Design Clean Up, Color Key
Ron Hughart—Director, Character Design, Timing
Timothy Hwang—Background & Prop Design, Background Layout
Sam Im—Timing
Rob Ingram—Timing
Jill Jacobs—Timing
Yumun (Jym) Jeong—Assistant Director, Character Layout
Zeke Johnson—Background & Prop Design
Jorge Linares Juarez—Production
Matt Kalmus—Production
DJ Kang—Background & Prop Design, Background Layout
Yvette Kaplan—Timing
Chad Katona—Digital Camera & Composite
Claudia Katz—Producer
Ernie Keen—Character Layout
Claudia Keene—Storyboard Revisions, Background & Prop Design, Character Layout, Design Clean Up
Steve Kellener—Digital Camera & Composite
Megan Kelly—Character Layout
Karapet (Gary) Keroglyan—Character Design
Eric Keyes—Storyboard, Character Design
Don Kim—3D Artist
Fredrick Kim—Background Layout
Heejin Kim—Background Layout
Jae H. Kim—Character Layout
Jiwook Kim—Character Layout
Sean Kim—Character Layout
TJ Kim—Background Layout
Tom King—Storyboard, Character Layout
Soung-Wook Koh—Character Layout
Mina Kolahi—Production

Genna Kornyshev—Background Layout, Digital Background Painter
Juliana Korsborn—Assistant Director, Character Layout
Lance Kramer—Director
John Krause—Background & Prop Design
Bari Kumar—Color Supervisor
Ken Laramay—Storyboard
Dan Larsen—Digital Camera & Composite
Edgar Larrazabal—Timing
Scott B. Lawrence—Production
Alex Lee—BG/Prop Design, Background Layout
David Lee—Character Layout, FX Animation
Sandra Lee—Digital Background Painter, Color Key
Sang Am Lee—Animation Checker, Production
Mark Lefitz—3D Artist
Joy Ki Peum Lee—Background Layout
Ashley Lenz—Assistant Director, Character Layout
Hugo Linares—Production
Kevin Linares—Production
Stuart Livingston—Storyboard
Tim Long—Timing
Chris Loudon—Director
Brian LoSchiavo—Storyboard, Character Layout
Conan Low—3D Artist, Main Title
Chris Lozano—Systems Administrative Assistant
David Lyman—Timing
Jeffrey Lynch—Director
John MacFarlane—FX Animation
Paul Mahotz—Editorial
Peter Maivia—Background Layout, Design Clean Up
Istvan Majoros—Character Layout
Richard Manginsay—Character Layout
Michael Marcantel—Assistant Director, Storyboard
Frank Marino—Director, Timing
Lisa Marriott—Digital Background Painter
David Marshall—Digital Camera & Composite
John Mathot—Storyboard
Tom Mazzocco—Timing
Kenny McGill—Background Layout
Darin McGowan—Assistant Director, Storyboard
Tara McPherson—Production
Carlos Mendez—Design Clean Up
Jeff Mertz—Background & Prop Design
Ashanti Miller—Character Layout
Noah Miller—Character Layout
Joshua Mills—3D Artist
Majella Milne—Timing
Ken Min—Storyboard, Storyboard Revisions

Hilario Miravalles—Background Layout
Maureen Mlynarczyk—Timing
Yori Mochizuki—Production
Jennifer Moeller—Character Layout
Rich Moore—Supervising Director, Director
Robert P. Moore—Character Layout
Scott Moot—Background & Prop Design
Jeanette Moreno King—Character Layout
Maurice Morgan—Background & Prop Design
Patrick Morgan—Digital Background Painter
Beth S. Morris—Digital Camera & Composite
Sarge Morton—Character Layout
Angela Mueller—Character Layout
Brad Mullen—Production
Shawn Murray—Storyboard
Raymie Muzquiz—Director
Paul Myers—Character Layout
Michael Nagle—Digital Camera & Composite
Kevin Newman—Character Design
Lizzie Nichols—Background & Prop Design
Kevin O'Brien—Director, Storyboard, Character Design
Shannon O'Connor—Character Design, Character Layout
Mark Orme—3D Artist
Jeffrey Perez—Production
James Peters—Digital Background Painter
Debbie Silver Peterson—Background & Prop Design
Cynthia Phillips—Production
Brian Philllipson—Track Reading & Lip Assignment
Drew Pierce—Character Layout
Abner Pineda—Production
Jason Plapp—Digital Camera & Composite, Digital Background Painter
Tom Pope—Character Layout
Miguel Puga—Storyboard
James Purdum—Director, Assistant Director, Timing
Celeste Pustilnick—Timing
Arlyne Ramirez—Design Clean Up
Mark Ramirez—Assistant Director Character Layout
Sylvia Ramirez—Accounting
Greg Ramsey—Character Layout
Dexter Reed—Character Layout
Joshua Raphael Reynolds (Josh Hollywood)—Editorial
Sean Rhyan—Digital Background Painter
Jerry Richardson—Character Design
Carolyn Roach—Production
Francisco Rosales—Design Clean Up

Eddie Rosas—Character Layout
John Rosen—Design Clean Up
Clara Ross—Production Coordinator
Aaron Rozenfeld—Storyboard, Character Layout
Vladi Rubizhevsky—Background & Prop Design
Louis Russell—Lip Assignment
David Salvador—Character Layout
Stephen Sandoval—Director, Storyboard, Timing
Edemer Santos—Assistant Director, Character Layout, Background Layout
Bart Saric—Digital Background Painter, Color Key
Helen M. Saric—Production Coordinator
Anna Saunders—Character Layout
Danielle Saunders—Production
Chris Sauvé—Director, Timing
Carson Sciarrino—Production Coordinator
Joe Scott—Assistant Director, Storyboard
Swinton O. Scott III—Director
Richard Sevy—3D Artist
John Seymore—Background & Prop Design
Sean Sexton—Character Layout
Donald Shaw Jr.—Character Layout
Brian Sheesley—Director
Ira Sherak—Assistant Director, Storyboard
Terry Shigemitsu—3D Artist
B. Shimbe Shim—3D Artist
Pat Shinagawa—Director
Ben Sigman—Systems Administrative Assistant
Hyunbo Simm—Character Layout
Nick Simotas—Editorial
Brian Smith—Color Key
Mike Smith—Main Title
Valentino So—Storyboard
Steve Socki—Timing
Pablo Solis—Storyboard
Chris Minki Song—Character Layout
Chris Sonnenburg—Storyboard, Character Layout
Thomas Starnes—Background Layout
Ted Stearn—Assistant Director, Storyboard
Aimee Steinberger—Assistant Director, Character Layout
Chris Stover—3D Artist
Rachel Stratton—Color Key
Joe Suggs—Storyboard
David Swift—Character Design
Geraldine Symon—Digital Producer
Poe K. Tan—Background Layout
Abbie Tew—Production
Derek Lee Thompson—Assistant Director, Character Layout, Timing
Doug Tiano—Digital Camera & Composite
Janice Tolentino—Assistant Director, Character Layout

Brian Tribble—Character Layout
Charlie Upton—Digital Camera & Composite, Editorial
Arthur Valencia—Character Layout
Gregg Vanzo—Animation Executive Producer, Supervising Director, Director
Scott Vanzo—Director of Computer Graphics, Main Title
Toni Vian—Storyboard
Roger Viloria—Character Layout
Neil Viker—Animation Checker
Jenessa Warren—Storyboard
Stevan Wahl—Assistant Director, Character Layout
Bonnie Watkins—Accounting
Nicholas Weiss—Production
Eric Whited—3D Artist, Main Title
Cindy Azada Whitman—Production Coordinator
Deke Wightman—Character Layout
Holly Williams—Color Key
Samuel Williams—Editorial
Mike Witting—Digital Camera & Composite
Mike Wodkowski—Digital Camera & Composite
Richard Wolff—Digital Camera & Composite
Chad Woods—Color Key
Jansen Yee—Character Layout
Damon P. Yoches—Editorial, Digital Camera & Composite
Hyejoon Yun—Overseas Liaison
Vladimir Zaval—Background Layout
Jose Zelaya—Character Design
Ron Zorman—Timing

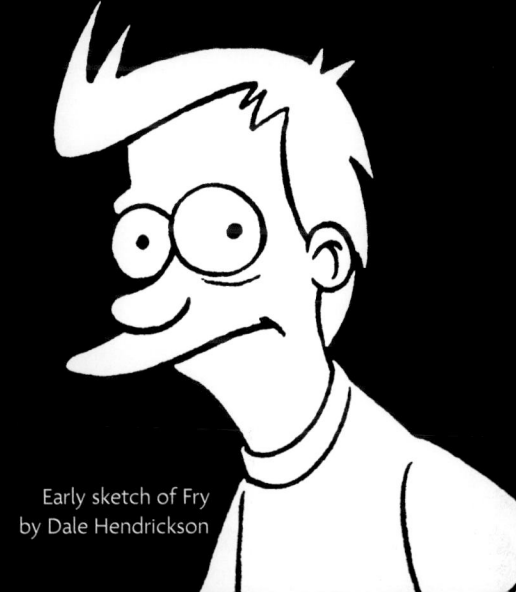

Early sketch of Fry by Dale Hendrickson

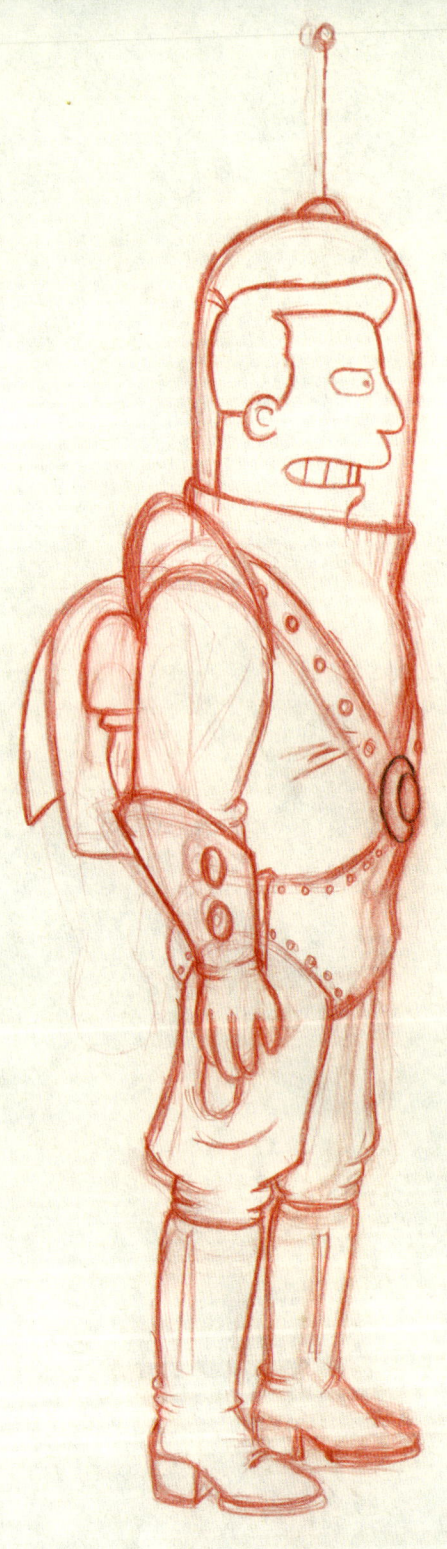
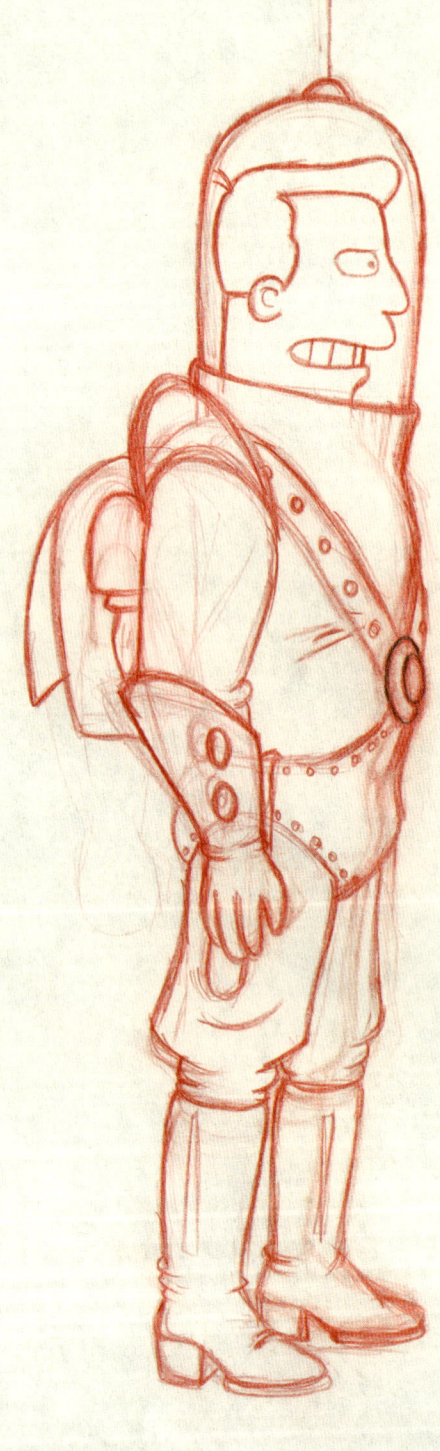

0202 act III

ZAPP IN JET PACK - SPACE SUIT

Anna
(TURN AROUND)

Zapp in Jet Pack Space Suit (2ACV02)
by Anna Chambers

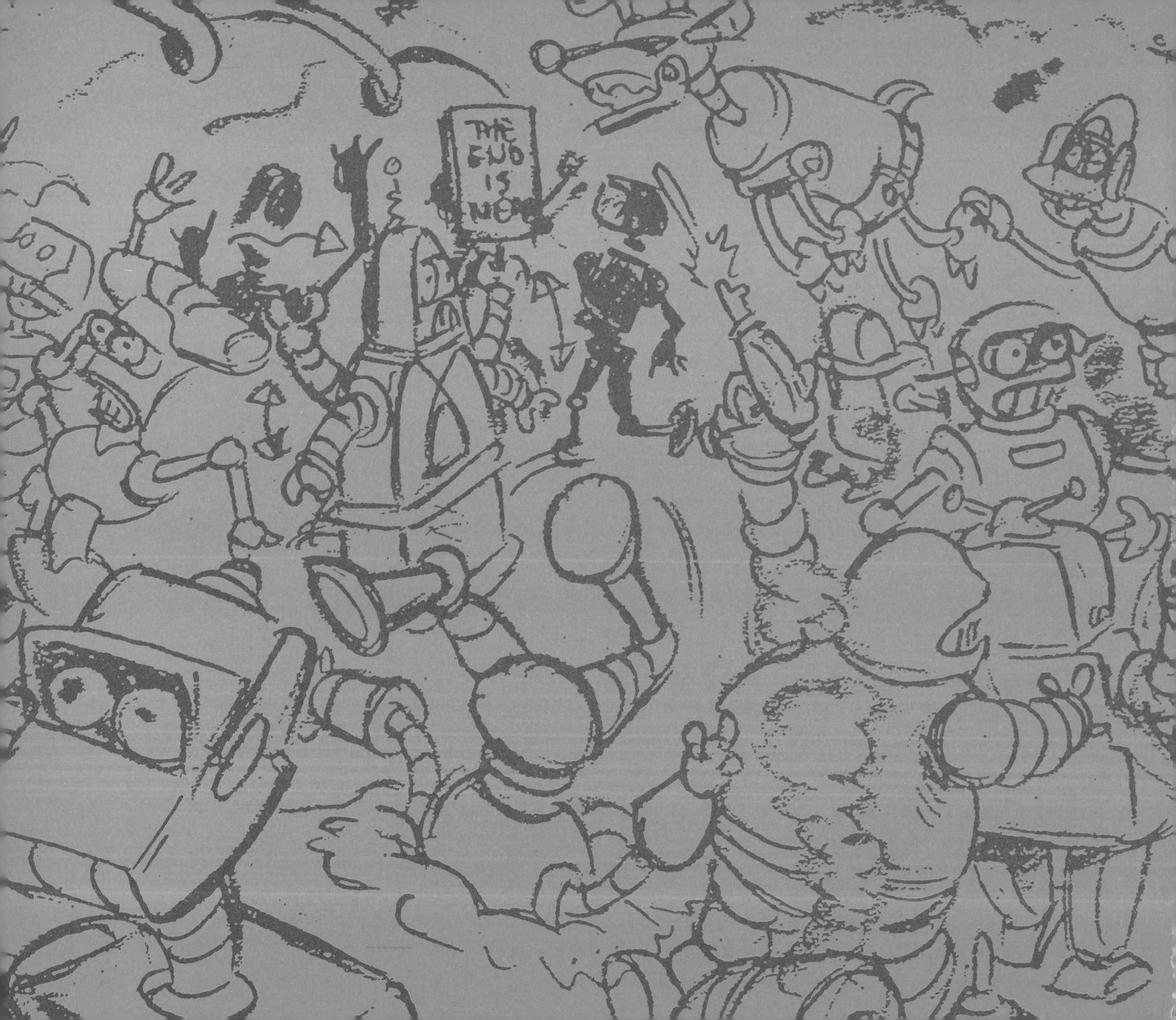